THE FACES OF TERRORISM

THE FACES OF TERRORISM
Multidisciplinary Perspectives

Edited by

David Canter

A John Wiley & Sons, Ltd., Publication

This edition first published 2009
© 2009 John Wiley & Sons Ltd.

Wiley-Blackwell is an imprint of John Wiley & Sons, formed by the merger of Wiley's global
Scientific, Technical, and Medical business with Blackwell Publishing.

Registered Office
John Wiley & Sons Ltd, The Atrium, Southern Gate, Chichester, West Sussex, PO19 8SQ, UK

Editorial Offices
The Atrium, Southern Gate, Chichester, West Sussex, PO19 8SQ, UK
9600 Garsington Road, Oxford, OX4 2DQ, UK
350 Main Street, Malden, MA 02148-5020, USA

For details of our global editorial offices, for customer services, and for information about how
to apply for permission to reuse the copyright material in this book please see our website at
www.wiley.com/wiley-blackwell.

The right of the editor to be identified as the author of the editorial material in this work has
been asserted in accordance with the Copyright, Designs and Patents Act 1988.

Library of Congress Cataloging-in-Publication Data

The faces of terrorism : multidisciplinary perspectives / edited by David Canter.
    p. cm.
  Includes index.
  ISBN 978-0-470-75380-4 (cloth) – ISBN 978-0-470-75381-1 (pbk.)   1. Terrorism–
Psychological aspects.   2. Terrorists–Psychology.   3. Terrorism–Prevention.   I. Canter,
David V.
  HV6431.F24 2009
  363.325–dc22
                                                                      2009021003

A catalogue record for this book is available from the British Library.

Set in 10 on 12 pt Minion by Toppan Best-set Premedia Limited
Printed and bound in Singapore by Fabulous Printers Pte Ltd

1   2009

Contents

List of Contributors

Kevin Borgeson, PhD is Assistant Professor in the Criminal Justice Department at Salem State College, Salem, MA, where he teaches courses in crime scene investigation, profiling, and bias crimes. Borgeson's work has appeared in the *Journal of Applied Sociology*, *Michigan Sociological Review*, and *American Behavioral Science*. He is co-editor of the book *Terrorism in America* (Jones & Bartlett Publishers, 2008).

Mary Brinson is a doctoral candidate in the department of Communication at University of California, Santa Barbara. She earned a B.A. in political science and communication from Loyola University, Chicago, as well as an M.A. in Communication from St. Louis University. Mary's research areas include media and intercultural communication. She has published in Arab Studies Quarterly and the Harvard Asian Pacific Review, as well as at several communication and Middle Eastern studies conferences. Her dissertation, "Muslims in the Media: Social Consequences for Muslims in America" focuses on how images of Muslims in the media impact their self-esteem, identity, and acculturation patterns.

Mark Burgess is a Senior Lecturer at Oxford Brookes University, UK. Mark specializes in the social psychology of defiance and has conducted laboratory experiments as well as having interviewed both violent and non-violent individuals from Europe and North America. Mark's other dominant line of research relates to interview methods.

David Canter is Professor of Psychology at The University of Huddersfield, UK, where he directs the International Research Centre for Investigative Psychology. He is internationally known for his development of Offender Profiling into an area of Applied Psychology that incorporates many aspects of research of relevance to investigations. This grew out of his earlier work in Environmental Psychology and the study of human actions in fires and other emergencies. He has published widely on many aspects of applied social psychology and given keynote presentations at many international conferences as well as being a consultant to many investigations, court cases and government enquiries. He writes for major newspapers and contributes to many documentaries.

Neil Ferguson is the Director of the Desmond Tutu Centre for War and Peace and Associate Professor of Political Psychology at Liverpool Hope University. He has been a visiting lecturer to Lock Haven University of Pennsylvania and the University of York, a Research Fellow at University of St Andrews, and previously lectured at the University of Ulster prior to joining Liverpool Hope University in 1996. His research and writings deal with moral development and a number of topics located within political psychology. Dr Ferguson is currently the chair of the *MOSAIC*, serves on the Governing Council of the *International Society of Political Psychology*, is a member of the Editorial Board for the *Journal of Moral Education* and *Irish Journal of Psychology*.

Dipak K. Gupta is the Fred J. Hansen Professor of Peace Studies and is a Distinguished Professor in Political Science, and the Director of International Security & Conflict Resolution program at San Diego State University. He is the author of eight books and over 100 articles, published in professional journals, edited volumes, and in newspapers.

Dr. John Horgan is Director of the International Center for the Study of Terrorism at the Pennsylvania State University, where he is also Associate Professor of Science, Technology and Society. He was previously Senior Research Fellow of the University of St Andrews' Centre for the Study of Terrorism and Political Violence (CSTPV) in Scotland, where he retains an honorary position. His books include The Psychology of Terrorism (2005), and The Future of Terrorism (1999, with Max Taylor), and Leaving Terrorism Behind: Individual and Collective Disengagement (2009, with Tore Bjorgo). His latest book Walking Away from Terrorism: Accounts of Disengagement from Radical and Extremist Movements was published in June 2009.

George Kassimeris is a Senior Research Fellow in Conflict and Terrorism at Wolverhampton University, and is the author of *Europe's Last Red Terrorists* the first book on the 17 November group (New York University Press) and the editor of *The Barbarisation of Warfare* (New York University Press) and *Playing Politics with Terrorism: A User's Guide* (Columbia University Press).

Fathali M. Moghaddam is Professor, Department of Psychology, and Director, Conflict Resolution Program, Department of Government, Georgetown

University, and Senior Fellow, Stanford Center for Interdisciplinary Policy, Education, and Research on Terrorism. His most recent books are *Multiculturalism and Intergroup Relations: Psychological Implications for Democracy in Global Context* (APA Press, 2008), *Global Conflict Resolution Through Positioning Analysis* (Springer, 2008, with Rom Harre and Naomi Lee), and *How Globalization Spurs Terrorism* (Praeger, 2008). His forthcoming book is 'The New Global Insecurity' (Praeger, 2010).

Sam Mullins gained an MA Hons in Psychology from the University of Glasgow before completing an MSc in Investigative Psychology, with distinction, at the University of Liverpool, UK. He is currently researching homegrown Islamist terrorism for his PhD at the Centre for Transnational Crime Prevention at the University of Wollongong, Australia. He has published material on terrorism, crime and policing.

Everard Phillips is a PhD candidate at the University of Liverpool researching extortive kidnapping behaviour. Everard specializes in profiling factors that lead to post-settlement hostage homicide, hostage victimization, and the tactical negotiation behaviour of kidnappers who ransom. Although his focus covers contemporary political motivated kidnapping as seen in Iraq and Afghanistan, his primary focus is behaviours of the differing kidnap syndicates that operate in Latin America, South East Asia and West Africa. Everard has spoken extensively on the subject to a broad spectrum of audiences that have included diplomatic, military, and various international risk and security organizations.

Jeffrey Ian Ross is an Associate Professor in the Division of Criminology, Criminal Justice and Forensic Studies, and a Fellow of the Center for International and Comparative Law at the University of Baltimore. He has researched, written, and lectured on national security, political violence, political crime, violent crime, corrections, and policing for over two decades. Ross' work has appeared in many academic journals and books, as well as popular outlets. He has also published a number of books in his areas of expertise as well as contributing to many broadcast and printed news media. He has acted as consultant to a number of government agencies and commercial organizations.

Sudhanshu Sarangi is a Senior Police Officer in India and is presently the head of the Anti-Terror Command in the Eastern State of Orissa as Inspector General of Police (Operations). He has long years of experience in dealing with Left Wing Extremism. Mr Sarangi is a former British Chevening scholar and is pursuing a PhD, supervised by Professor David Canter on the Psychological Pathways to Militant Jihad.

Michael Stohl is Professor and Chair of the Department of Communication and Professor of Political Science at the University of California, Santa Barbara (UCSB). His research focuses on political communication and international relations with special reference to political violence, terrorism, and human rights. He is the author or co-author of more than one hundred scholarly journal articles and book chapters and the author, editor or co-editor of twelve books. Currently, he is International Partner Investigator for the Australian Research Council funded Centre of Excellence for Policing and Security, a partnership of the Australian National University and Griffith University.

Amanda M. Sharp Parker is a doctoral student of Criminology at the University of South Florida in Tampa, Florida. She obtained her Bachelor and Masters degrees in Criminal Justice from East Carolina University in Greenville, North Carolina. Her areas of research interest include emerging terrorism threats (specifically cyberterrorism), the causation of terrorism and cross-national terrorism trends. Amanda has presented throughout the United States and in England, Spain, Poland and Northern Ireland on these topics.

Dr. Alex P. Schmid is Director of the Terrorism Research Initiative (TRI) and Editor of its electronic journal 'Perspectives on Terrorism'. During his career he worked at eight different universities and at the United Nations where he was Officer-in-Charge of the Terrorism Prevention Branch. Unitl May 2009 he was Director of the Centre for the Study of Terrorism and Political Violence at the University of St. Andrews. He is a Corresponding Member of the Netherlands Royal Academy of Sciences and presently resides in Austria where is completing a Handbook of Terrorism Research.

Clive Williams MG is a specialist on terrorism and politically motivated violence, with a career background in Australian military intelligence and Australian Defence's strategic policy and intelligence areas. He has worked on terrorism-related issues since 1980. In the past three years he has been a Visiting Professor at the University of California and at the George Washington University. In 2006 he was appointed an Adjunct Professor at Macquarie University's Centre for Policing Intelligence and Counter-Terrorism (PICT) in Sydney and a Visiting Professor at the Australian Defence Force Academy. He is a member of the International Association of Chiefs of Police (IACP), the International Association of Bomb Technicians and Investigators (IABTI), and the Australian Institute of Professional Intelligence Officers (AIPIO).

Robin Maria Valeri, PhD earned her BA in Psychology and Economics from Cornell University and her MA and PhD in Psychology from Syracuse University. She is currently a Professor of Psychology at St Bonaventure University. Her work has appeared in various psychology and sociology journals including the *American Behavioral Scientist, Journal of Applied Social Psychology, Journal of Applied Sociology, Michigan Sociological Review,* and *Society and Animals.*

Dr Michael Vishnevetsky is a part-time lecturer in Criminology at Salford University, UK and Co-ordinator of the Salford University Centre for Prison Studies (www.sucps.salford.ac.uk). He obtained his PhD in Criminology from Keele University, UK with a thesis entitled 'A socio-historical study into the emergence and development of terrorist networks in the post-Soviet Chechen Republic'. The chapter he has contributed to this edited collection draws from the findings of his PhD research.

Dr Vishnevetsky has lectured on a variety of criminology and politics courses, and his research interests span terrorism, political violence and radicalization, Chechnya, and prisons. He can be contacted at M.Vishnevetsky@salford.ac.uk.

Preface

The many different facets of terrorism are explored in this book, seeking to produce a rounded picture of what it means to be a terrorist and what terrorism means for present day society. By bringing together an international selection of experts who cover a wide range of issues, considered from the perspectives of a variety of disciplines, the diverse faces of terrorism are revealed. Although, inevitably, the focus is on current concerns with terrorism that has its roots in Islam, the links between organized crime and radical violence are reviewed and acts that go beyond bombing to kidnap for ransom and cyberterrorism are also examined.

By their very nature terrorist acts seek to change public opinion and influence political processes. Therefore there is a constant need to review the ways in which these acts are conceptualized by the public and by national leaders. These political interpretations may be far removed from the objectives and personal ambitions of the people who kill others in the name of a cause. Completing the cycle from terrorist to public perception thus has a significant role to play in facilitating effective responses to these acts of violence and finding ways to reduce the radicalization of those who would follow in terrorists' footsteps.

In early 2006 the word 'terrorism' elicited 7,867 items in the books category on Amazon.co.uk, in the summer of 2008 there were 11,444, and, for some reason, there were 55,692 and 80,337 items on Amazon.com. Most of these are books that have been published in the last few years. This reflects a phenomenal interest in all aspects of terrorism and a veritable industry of academic and popular writing that is growing ever more rapidly to service that interest. But this outpouring of books has, in the main, been based on historical reviews and information available in the public domain. It has therefore been dominated by consideration of the rhetoric and propaganda of terrorist groups or by geo-political considerations.

With some notable exceptions, there has been little attempt to explore the consensus that may exist across disciplines in understanding the way present-day terrorists actually see the world, independently of the mythologies their leaders try to weave. Nor has there been any concerted effort to explore the ways in which the conceptualization of terrorism in the public mind is influencing and distorting government response to what most people accept is a growing and changing menace.

Yet in the last few years a few intrepid researchers have tried to get much closer to the perspectives of the actual perpetrators of ideologically driven acts of violence. Their studies have been paralleled by serious considerations of the logic and coherence of any claims that particular ideologies or religious beliefs do indeed promulgate terrorism, or whether these broad perspectives have been hi-jacked and distorted by radical groups, as much as by their Western antagonists, for quite other personal and political aims.

The Faces of Terrorism thus offers a much needed account of the growing consensus between people from many different disciplines of the multivariate nature of terrorism. This shows that counterinsurgency activities need to embrace both the public rhetoric that castigates terrorism as well as engaging with the conceptual systems of those who start on the pathways to violent action.

I am grateful to Maria Ioannou for her assistance in organizing the conference out of which this book grew.

Professor David Canter
September 2008

1

The Multi-Faceted Nature of Terrorism: An Introduction[1]

David Canter

Synopsis: As an introduction to the present volume the wide-ranging nature of terrorist activity, over time and place, is briefly reviewed. Terrorism is multi-faceted and, as a consequence, no one explanation, theory or discipline will ever fully account for all terrorist activities. However, the psychological and social psychological processes that lead any given person to commit a terrorist act tend to have been under-represented in the terrorist literature. This is doubtless in part due to the difficulty of conducting studies that engage directly with those individuals who carry out terrorist acts. Consideration of the actions of the individuals involved makes possible the understanding of terrorism as a process that people move through. At every stage questions emerge about how and why given individuals get drawn into, or leave, terrorist groups. But because some form of terrorist activity will always be with us understanding the many faces of terrorism and the psychological processes underlying it, should help to reduce its prevalence and mitigate its impact.

The Wide-ranging Nature of Terrorism

Acts of violence with political objective have always been with us. From the fight against Roman domination of Judea by Zealots in the 1st century, through the assassins in the 13th century who were a breakaway faction of Shia Islam, to

---

[1] This chapter draws heavily on (Canter, 2006) where a fuller account of the psychology of suicide bombers is given.

The Faces of Terrorism: Multidisciplinary Perspectives Edited by David Canter
© 2009 John Wiley & Sons Ltd.

the Fenians in the 19th century, who challenged British rule in Ireland, to the anarchists at the start of the 20th century , who contributed to the start of the Great War and through their writing articulated the notion of 'the propaganda of the deed', there have always been groups who sought to have an impact on public opinion and the stability of governments through attacks on people or buildings that were seen as being of political or ideological significance.

The emergence of nation states almost inevitably gave rise to forces that tried to challenge or overthrow those states by violent means. Thus by the late 20th century well over 150 different terrorist organizations were known to exist around the world. The US State Department currently lists more than 50 such organizations as being active.

The longevity and number of terrorist groups indicates that terrorism is likely to be diverse and varied. So the present-day popular assumption that acts of political and/or ideological violence are likely to be related to Islamic belief systems is far from being valid. Indeed many books on terrorism written before 11 September 2001 made no mention of Islam or jihad at all. Even the most elementary review of terrorist activities will show that people of all religions, and none, men and women, people under occupation in tyrannies and living freely in democracies, people who have clear and those who have vague objectives, have all participated in some form of terrorist activity. The challenge therefore is to determine whether there is any core to terrorist activity or if indeed the whole concept is too amorphous to be of any academic or practical value.

A Definition

The variety of events that may be considered terrorist is so diffuse that some focus is required on how they may be identified. But as with most concepts that have had more currency in public debate than in academic discourse this is not a straightforward task. It is therefore of value to proffer one of the clearest definitions, even if only to help clarify questions that it raises. Richardson (2006) chose to define terrorism in terms of seven characteristics that any act must have in order to attract that label, as briefly listed in Table 1.1.

The central idea behind this definition is that the acts of violence are a political strategy carried out by groups that are not themselves an established state. From this perspective the strategy is very much aimed at carrying actions that have symbolic, propaganda significance. In Chapter 6 the most obvious example of this, the little known 17N group in Greece, has all the characteristics that Richardson requires to call it terrorist. Although, importantly even in a group so dedicated to a Marxist mission, the close kinship ties within the group raises the question of how significant politics is for all those involved.

Table 1.1. Seven crucial characteristics for terrorism (based on Richardson, 2006)

1. Politically inspired
2. Violent or threatens violence
3. Communicates a message
4. Act and victim symbolically significant
5. Carried out by sub-state groups
6. Victim is different from the audience
7. Deliberate targeting of civilians

Richardson's definition, however, will tend to rule out, for example, kidnap for ransom explored by Phillips in Chapter 11 because it has no obvious symbolic or overtly political objectives, even though in many cases it may link into terrorist activities. Similarly, Russell's account in Chapter 12 of the authoritarian leader of Chechnya, Ramzan Kadyrov, cannot portray him as a terrorist leader in the sense that he is a head of state and not part of a sub-state group, although he clearly emerged out of terrorist attacks on Russia and much of his leadership is rooted in his violent past. Thus, as Gupta and his colleagues make clear in Chapter 7 it is naïve to separate out the states that promote terrorism and the criminal activity that underwrites it if we are to understand its development and underlying processes.

So although Richardson's (2006) seven-point set of criteria does provide us with a clear understanding of what is at the heart of terrorist activity, we need to have a grasp of all the other faces this activity can take on if we are to have a full picture. The idea of a devoted, integrated group of people who make a strong, clear political statement through acts of violence may be the stereotypical vision of terrorism, but all the emerging information indicates that, like all stereotypes, it helps to know what we are looking for, since its existence in some pure form is exceedingly rare. The nature of the 'enemy' that terrorist groups identify may not even be as obvious as one would expect. This is brought home particularly in Borgeson and Valeri's account in Chapter 10 of how some of the fiercely Christian Aryan Nations groups in the US are willing to co-operate with radical Islamists against some perceived common foe.

Difficulties in Studying Terrorists

The many difficulties in uncovering the truth about the actual people involved in terrorism cannot be overestimated. The only people available for interview, if access can be gained to them, are those who have been detected or captured, frequently through failure to achieve their goals. These people may not be representative of the possibly more determined individuals who succeeded in carrying out their violent acts. Even if access can be gained to these people what they tell the security services is unlikely to be made public and what they tell the few researchers who have gained access (e.g. Merari, 1990; Soibelman, 2004) is likely to be distorted by their own view of their failure and the current incarceration in which they find themselves. However, as Speckhard (2006) shows from her interviews with the families and associates of Chechen suicide bombers, it is important to attempt to get some understanding of the social and psychological processes involved in these outrages even if there is inevitable bias in the information obtained.

It is also important to point out, as Horgan (2005) does in some detail, that gaining access to people involved in or associated with any form of terrorism may be dangerous, and is often a lengthy drawn out process. It is therefore understandable that most researchers are reluctant to follow this path and rely instead on secondary and tertiary sources. This is one of the reasons why public understanding of terrorists is often so misinformed, making it prey to the political distortions that Danis and Stohl explore in Chapter 13.

Statements made by terrorists, notably those by suicide bombers recorded for broadcast after their death, suffer from similar difficulties. Merari (1990) suggests that the preparation of such a statement is part of the process by which the bomber is tied into the intended act. By committing him/herself to the action in writing or on video it is much more difficult to back out at a later stage without a tremendous loss of face.

Schooling in the appropriate rhetoric for making such a statement is likely to be drawn from the writings and lectures of the leaders of terrorist movements as discussed by Sarangi and Canter in Chapter 3. A clear example of this is the widely broadcast tape of Mohammad Sidique Khan (2005), one of the 7/7 London bombers. This is clearly a paraphrasing of the writings of Osama bin Laden and his apologists. It is therefore difficult to gauge from such broadcast material how totally it captures the psychology and personal perspective of the individual making the statement. Furthermore, it would be expected that such statements would claim international significance and grand motivations for the suicidal act rather than belittling it by reference to personal frustrations or individual experiences.

We must also be careful about generalizing from what is known about the psychology of one set of terrorists to all others. Most information comes from very limited sources, typically the IRA or Palestinian terrorists. The changing world scene and evolving social processes also mean that there is unlikely to be one psychology of the bomber that is valid for all places and all times.

Despite the many difficulties in obtaining detailed information about the processes by which a person becomes a terrorist, the slowly growing series of studies can be put alongside what is known about other acts of violence and of suicide, to sketch a picture of how people find their way into these activities and what may lead them out.

Explanations of Terrorism

Is deprivation a direct cause of terrorism?

In his review of the psychological causes of terrorism Moghaddam (2005) makes clear that "material factors such as poverty and lack of education are problematic as explanations of terrorist acts" (p. 162). He quotes Coogan's (2002) account of the IRA as giving no support to the view "that they are mindless hooligans drawn from the unemployed and unemployable" (p. 162). The Singapore Ministry of Home Affairs reported in 2003 that captured al-Qaeda terrorists were not typically from impoverished backgrounds and had reasonable levels of education. Indeed accounts of the people who carried out the 7/11 attacks on New York and Washington showed that they did not come out of refugee camps, ignorant and lacking education (Bodansky, 2001). So a simple-minded analysis proposing that acts of terrorism are the first stages of a people's revolution, being the actions of a down-trodden proletariat that has no other means of bettering its lot, does not have much empirical support.

Indeed any equation of terrorism with acts of revolution as a response to a repressive state needs to be treated with great caution. The concomitant idea that if people are given at least some limited material comfort then they are unlikely to want to overthrow their regime also needs careful evaluation. This was the view expressed so amusingly by George Orwell (1933) when he wrote:

> It is quite likely that fish-and-chips, art-silk stockings, tinned salmon, cut-price chocolate (five two-ounce bars for sixpence), the movies, the radio, strong tea, and the Football Pools have between them averted revolution. *The Road to Wigan Pier*, Chapter 5.

Just as is it is a great over-simplification to propose that deprivation and oppression provoke acts of terrorism, so the proposal that no one who lives in relative comfort would be willing to take up a cause that violently challenges the status quo must also be questioned. The search for the origins of terrorism of any sort as being fundamentally in material deprivation is not likely to prove successful.

A slightly more sophisticated argument would be that although an individual has some material comfort, if they live within a repressive regime the deprivation of their liberty is the source of their terrorist zeal. This view is also difficult to support from the facts. As Youngs (2006) makes clear in his analysis of the influence of political repression on the prevalence of terrorism, there is little correlation between relative degrees of political repression and 'radicalism'. He compares various Middle Eastern countries, India and China and the source of revolution in other areas of the world to show that, if anything, repressive regimes serve to keep terrorist activity under control and that those who wish to attack civilians benefit from the freedoms associated with democracy.

To account for the greater dissatisfaction and related violence in less repressive regimes it is fruitful to consider the widely explored issue of 'relative deprivation'. Walker and Smith (2002) review over 50 years of study of how people tend to compare their own experiences with those of others that they know about, and assess their personal deprivation relative to those other experiences. This subjective relativity has been taken to explain many paradoxes such as why working women are more willing to accept disadvantageous pay differentials than would be expected (Crosby, 1982), because they compared themselves with other women rather than men; or the lack of impact of the removal of apartheid on inter-racial attitudes in South Africa (Duckitt & Mphuting, 1998), because the racial groups still made comparisons within their own groups.

Relative deprivation has also been elaborated by distinguishing between personal experiences and experience perceived to be shared by a social group (Smith & Leach, 2004). These are mainly somewhat artificial, laboratory-based experimental studies because it is so difficult to establish clearly what an individual's view of the experiences of a social group is. Nonetheless they do indicate that when a person's identity is closely associated with membership of a particular group then the belief that the group as a whole experiences certain deprivations can have a significant influence on that person's levels of dissatisfaction beyond their own personal comparisons. These complexities thus help to point towards the need to consider the individual psychological processes and how an individual makes sense of his/her experiences rather than relying on some notion of the objective, material situation the person is part of.

Mental illness and suicide bombing

The psychological explanation of suicide bombing is particularly difficult to fathom. It seems to go against all notions of self-preservation unless the person was out of contact with reality. As a consequence one common view about the psychology of suicide bombers is that they must be 'mad' in some sense of being severely mentally disturbed. However, even an elementary consideration of the July 2005 bombings in London would make clear that the perpetrators could not have been insane in the usual sense of being out of contact with reality, drugged or even highly trained fanatics. The New York aeroplane hijackers similarly indicated a determination and coolness of purpose that is not compatible with a psychosis or other extreme form of mental illness. This accords with the reviews of both Silke (2003) and Moghaddam (2005), who make clear that there is no evidence at all that suicide bombers are overtly mentally disturbed. The five failed Palestinian suicide bombers that Soibelman (2004) had interviewed showed no signs of mental illness and were able to discuss many matters with their interviewers in an apparently rational way. But then, the incidence of overt mental illness in another homicidal group that challenges our understanding of sanity, serial killers, appears to be no greater than in the population at large, such that it is very rare indeed for insanity to be used as a defence (Hickey, 2005). Neither are those possibly more bizarre acts of spree killing, in which a number of people are killed in one onslaught, as in the Columbine School shootings in 1999, or in Hungerford in 1987 or Dunblane in 1996, committed by people with any obvious psychotic illness (Canter, 1995). With hindsight their acquaintances may claim they were strange people who did not relate well to others, but people with diagnosed mental illnesses are far more likely to hurt themselves rather than anyone else.

Far from being disturbed there is some evidence that those recruiting people to commit these atrocities go to some pains to exclude people who may be mentally unstable. Merari (1990) claims that only a minority of all those who volunteer to be suicide bombers are selected to do so. This is understandable in military terms. A person who was mentally unstable could not be relied upon to focus and follow through with the desired objective and so would weaken the whole operation and put disclosure of its methods at risk.

Brainwashing?

The graphic metaphor for clearing a person of previously held beliefs, washing their brains, in order to insert some alien set of perspectives, has become a further explanation of how people could turn from reasonably well-adjusted citizens to violent terrorists. This perspective puts people such as Osama bin Laden and the Hamas leader Sheikh Yassin in roles that have only ever been demonstrated clearly in George du Maurier's fictional story of the control of the opera singer Trilby by the manipulative Svengali. Many other studies show that in real life it is difficult to demonstrate the possibility of such quasi-occult powers (cf. Heap and Kirsch, 2006 for a review of these issues).

This view of the influence of terrorist leaders also implies a very strong hierarchy, very similar indeed to what would be expected in a rigid military structure. In general, however, as with all illegal groups (Canter & Alison, 2000), especially those spread over a wide geography, it is not possible to maintain the top-down discipline that is de rigueur for a standing army.

Instead, what Atran (2004) calls a "hydra-headed network" is much more likely to be the norm. The evolving structure of such networks is well illustrated in Chapter 8 by Mullins, and how it can develop into something not far from a business when it involves frequent kidnap activities as described in Chapter 11 by Phillips.

In a detailed study of the al-Qaeda network Sageman (2004) shows just how complex and self-generating terrorist networks can be. These loose networks come about partly because illegal organizations face such challenges to preserving the identification and communication processes that are crucial for the effectiveness of legitimate ones (as Canter, 2000, discusses) that they have to rely on other ways of operating. The indications are that they survive by encouraging and supporting small, independent groups, over which they have very little direct control (Atran, 2004). But this requires that the groups are very much self-defined and self-motivated, rather than being fiercely manipulated by some charismatic leader.

One important implication of this mechanism of autonomous, self-generating groups as a mechanism for carrying out terrorism is that it can be traced back at least to the writings of 19th-century anarchists such as Michael Bakunin (cf. Anarchist Archives, 2006) who saw revolution emerging out of spontaneous secret societies who combine together to overthrow the status quo. The intelligentsia were to articulate the disquiet and aspirations of the masses who would then find their own ways into revolution.

The role of religious ideology

If it is not some particular guru who brainwashes followers, then it has often been thought that it is a general religious ideology that is drawn on to formulate destructive intentions. The fact that all the London and USA attackers were Muslim and that Palestinian suicide bombers are typically Muslim too has led to the assumption in many quarters that there are some inherent seeds in Islam that provide the basis for suicide bombing. Certainly as Sarangi and Canter explain in Chapter 3 there are streams of thought that do interpret the Quran as endorsing violence against non-believers. But the dominant Islamic tradition is nonetheless extremely tolerant.

Even when considering suicide bombers there is nothing new or particularly Islamic about them. There is the ancient Jewish exemplar in the biblical account of Samson bringing the temple down upon the Philistines as a way of escaping from his own degradation and death at their hands. In modern time, as the widely quoted report by Gunaratna (2003) documents, suicide bombing is certainly not limited to Muslim terrorists. The Kurdistan Workers' Party (PKK) that has carried out many suicide bombings in Turkey is anti-religious, drawing on Marxist-Leninist ideology, but with a very strong nationalist, rather than religious, orientation. What Gunaratna (2003) calls "ethno-nationalism", rather than religious doctrine, is what drives the Tamil Tigers to carry out suicide bombings in Sri Lanka and India.

Of course, the most well-known use of suicide as a military means was by Japanese pilots in World War II. This had nothing to do with either a challenge to state oppression or Islam. Yet its parallels to recent suicide bombings has been recognized by some European newspapers referring to these attacks with the Japanese label of 'kamikaze', literally meaning the wind (or spirit) of God.

The use of military personnel as self-destructive missiles in World War II may teach us something of the processes by which people think themselves into this desperate final act. In his detailed study of "Japan's suicide samurai" Lamont-Brown (1997) reveals that Japanese military leaders were initially reluctant to use this tactic that was so wasteful of trained pilots and aeroplanes, but that towards the end of the war they saw no other way of preventing the American fleet from landing troops on Japanese soil. A special airborne 'Divine Thunderbolts Corps' was therefore established. The pilots in this corps were initially drawn from well-trained airmen, who came from strongly nationalist families. They saw themselves as upholding the honour and traditions of their families. But as the war progressed young men with very limited training, from working class backgrounds, were drafted in to carry on the attacks.

The early suicide pilots endorsed a mythology of devotion to the Emperor, who was regarded as a god, such that it was an honour to die in his service. They believed they would be reincarnated as cherry blossom in the nationalist Yasukuni Shrine in Tokyo, such that this flower became their symbol. Those who came after them appear to have been more directly motivated by the dishonour of failure and the pride their family would feel in their success. The shame that would be brought on their family if they came back alive was regarded as unbearable. Certainly through the names of the squadrons, their symbols and rituals the pilots believed that they were 'divine wings' wreaking a terrible toll on the enemy. In fact, once the US Navy got over the initial shock of such apparently senseless attacks, kamikaze assaults proved to be futile in stopping the advance of the US military on Japan. But the determination the Japanese showed to fight to the last breath may have been influential in the decision to drop the atom bomb.

There are doubtless some parallels in present-day suicide bombing, notably a conviction in the great significance of their actions and the often quoted belief in rewards in the after-life. Perhaps of more significance, similar to 'non-military' suicide, is the view that there was no other way for Japan to defend itself against a greatly superior military force. However, the fact that all five of the failed July 21st London bombers were caught alive without any further violence shows that the British situation is very different from the Japanese. For those London suicide bombers, at least, life was preferable to 'honourable' death.

The kamikaze pilots also show us that the concept of 'religious zeal' needs to be treated with caution. The Shinto tradition of which they were a part claimed it was honourable to die protecting the emperor. This has analogies to the Quranic claims that "whoever fights for the cause of God, whether he dies or triumphs, on him we shall bestow a rich recompense" (4:72, Quran – Penguin translation by N. J. Dawood (2003), p. 68). But they are both very different types of belief systems. The tradition of the Japanese emperor as a god was greatly diluted after the war in a way that it is difficult to imagine happening to beliefs in the Prophet and his teachings. It seems more feasible to think of the religious ideology as a skeleton that can be fleshed out in accordance with the experiences and self-image of any given individual.

However, as with any reference to a broad ideology you cannot blame an idea for the people who hold it. Many millions of people endorse fundamentalist Islam without interpreting it as meaning they should commit acts of self-destructive violence. The religion may offer up a belief system on which potential suicide bombers can draw, but it cannot be accounted as the primary cause for their actions. To understand the processes that give rise to suicide bombing, as with all other aspects of terrorism, we need to consider the processes of which the individual is a part and the cognitive and emotional processes within the individual that give rise to a commitment to acts of terrorism.

Terrorism as Process

In his earlier writing Horgan (2005) has developed the important argument that terrorism is not an act but a process of which a person is a part. Moghaddam's (2005) 'staircase' model of terrorism makes a similar point of a person entering into and becoming part of an ever more involving commitment to violence for political or ideological ends. The framework for this is a mixture of first, recognition that the group with which the terrorist identifies is distinct from and threatened by some other external group and, secondly, that there are culturally remembered or experienced causes of grievance that are nursed by the group to which the terrorist belongs. In Chapter 5 Ross reviews the power of these grievances by examining three very diverse terrorist groups in different parts of the world. He emphasizes in particular the roles these grievances play in keeping the group in existence over many years. The grievances become a way of specifying the special, distinct identity of the group and what fuels its antagonism to those who the group see as their enemies. An important point here is that it is not the deprivation or other degrading experiences themselves that are seen as the central cause of acts of violence but the interpretation of these to generate a profound sense of grievance.

The grievance, however, only has to give rise to a few people acting violently before the explosive mix of emotional turmoil and direct experience draws others into the destructive cycle. In Chapter 2 Ferguson and Burgess show how for many people it is the psychological consequences of being part of violence that itself can set up a continuing process of terrorist aggression. For these individuals the world becomes framed in terms of its potential for bloodshed. This has long-term consequences that the authorities ignore at their peril. It can mean that even after the apparently successful peace process, as in Northern Ireland, there are still many people for whom the precipitating factors, direct experience of violence and perceived grievance have not gone away. The possibility of the violence re-emerging will thus still be present for at least a generation.

The perception of grievances and associated routes into terrorism need not be as direct as in Northern Ireland as Williams' case study in Chapter 4 illustrates. Faheem Khalid Lodhi was well established in Australia as an architect without any personal experiences to lead him into acts of violence. It was indirect contact through people he interacted with in his original homeland of Pakistan that seemed to open the way for him to prepare a terrorist attack. There are many parallels here to other terrorists and would-be terrorists in Britain, Spain and the USA. They start to define themselves in terms of a particular social group that is itself defined in terms of feelings of outrage and frustration for which terrorist acts become the focal outlet.

This process of identification with a particular, violent group can take many and often unexpected forms and is currently certainly not limited to jihadi factions of Islam. Borgeson and Valeri in Chapter 10 describe a Christian group that is given little coverage in most reviews of terrorism but which has been responsible, directly or indirectly, for a number of atrocities, most notably the Oklahoma City bombing by Timothy McVeigh. The FBI has certainly identified their network as a terrorist threat that is nationwide across the USA. There are clear parallels to other loosely connected groups that oppose many aspects of the country in which they reside, but of particular significance is how much these groups are defined by a hatred for a common enemy. In the case of the Aryan Nations this has been most overtly the perception of Jewish and various ethnic minorities as diluting and degrading the Christian purity of nations.

As Borgeson and Valeri illustrate, this focus on a perceived enemy has led some of the leaders of the Aryan Nations to seek alliances with groups, notably al-Qaeda, whom many would regard as an obvious adversary for such a militantly Christian group. They define themselves so directly in relation to a common enemy that it reduces the feeling of hatred towards a symbolically less significant enemy. This demonstrates how much of the social psychology of terrorist groups is embedded in the rhetoric of who they are against rather than what their primary objectives are. This can result in the actions of these groups becoming ever more removed from any obvious ideal, or from clear objectives. Their actions centre on survival and their continued definition as a distinct entity.

Such flexibility in allowing their actions to be acceptable to them, provided they facilitate the group's existence, means that the fundamental criminality of their actions can readily overlap with what is more commonly thought of as organized crime. As Vishnevetsky shows in his fascinating account of youth gangs in Chechnya in Chapter 9, organized crime may be the route into terrorism for some individuals. This accords with the issues explored in Chapter 7 by Gupta and his colleagues. They show that distinguishing between terrorists and organized criminals is indeed difficult. There are, however, important albeit subtle differences that need to be determined in order to deal appropriately with the somewhat dissimilar challenges they pose to the social order.

The spread of interactions between terrorism and organized crime is also paralleled in the ways in which terrorist acts drift into state structures, being covertly or overtly supported by national authorities. In this regard the actions of Chechen leader Shamil Basayev, who masterminded the Budennovsk, Dubrovka and Beslan suicidal, hostage-taking raids, as acts against Russian control of Chechnya, would place those actions outside of Richardson's (2006) definition of terrorism. However, most of the processes that can be recognized in the more obviously terrorist groups were present in these violent attacks. This perspective on the Chechen terrorist attacks within Russia is especially useful to explore because it seems that the removal of Shamil Basayev and his replacement in Chechnya by another warlord, Ramzan Kadyrov, has changed the nature of the relationship between Chechnya and Russia.

Kadyrov seems to have achieved a more equitable relationship with the Russians by coalescing what Russell in Chapter 12 describes as the "needs" of the Chechens with the "greed" of those he needs to manage the country. Interestingly this includes weaning the Chechens of the Wahhabi approach to Islam which Basayev used to legitimatize his actions, and instead to support the less aggressive Sufi tradition which had been dominant in Chechnya in earlier times. Thus Kadyrov's activities serve to show the importance for any insurgent groups of how the appropriate actions for dealing with their grievances are interpreted. The less attractive aspect of Kadyrov's dominion is its illustration of how generations of insurgency against oppression provide a landscape in which vicious, totalitarian rule can take root and prosper, suffocating the rule of law.

The Social Psychology of Terrorism

The organizational and economic processes that become an integral part of the survival of terrorist activities, their overlap with organized crime and evolution into tyrannical states inevitably have a form and life of their own that is often undervalued when people write of isolated insurgent groups carrying out single atrocities. Where certain types of criminality are endemic, whether that is due to ideological commitment or criminal greed, then structures emerge that maintain and develop those crimes. These structures can help the criminal activity expand into something much more recognizable as a business. This is particularly true of terrorist groups for whom frequent kidnapping can become a major part of their activities. In Chapter 11 Phillips shows how the requirements of repetitive kidnapping lead to the need for many features that would be recognized in any business, although 'warehousing' and 'selling on' take more chilling meanings than in the conventional world of commerce. A particularly important consequence of this is that once such a 'business model' is in place it can have a self-sustaining quality that may mask the original ideological or political intentions.

The processes revealed when considering state-supported terrorism, as in Chechnya, and the integration with violent crime and such business-like spin-offs as kidnap for ransom draw attention to the complex but significant social processes of which terrorism is inevitably a part. In recent years there has been growing interest in modelling the networks of contacts to which the interactions between terrorists give rise. This may have been of more theoretical value, because of the interesting mathematics it makes possible, than of real practical benefit and has tended to treat terrorist networks as fixed in time. Mullins' examination in Chapter 8 of the growth of the foiled 'Millennial Plot' to bomb Los Angeles airport in 2000, and the 9/11 attack, is therefore salutary in showing that these networks are dynamic entities. They develop and change in various ways, although it is interesting to see that the foiled plot always had a less stable structure than the one that caused such destruction to the Twin Towers and the Pentagon.

Reporting Terrorism

The evolving complexity of terrorist groups with their many tentacles and strands into other areas of illegal activity whilst still professing an ideological or political set of objectives, however vague those objectives may be, makes it extremely difficult for journalists wishing to give a direct, simple coherent account of terrorists and their actions. It is therefore understandable that mass media accounts of terrorist actions will rely heavily on official statements, but these in themselves will inevitably be oversimplified with strong political biases. In the most technical chapter of the present volume, Chapter 13, Danis and Stohl illustrate the possibilities for careful content analysis of newspaper reports. These analyses show the difference in US and UK reporting and how those differences are themselves influenced by the outlet for these reports.

Given that terrorism is fundamentally about making deeds speak, the way in which these deeds are reported and commented upon is crucial to the eventual impact of such acts of violence. However, the differences described in Chapter 13 do alert researchers to the need to get behind mass media reports to uncover the many different and interlinked faces of terrorism.

The Future

The dynamic, evolving and multi-faceted nature of terrorism indicates that it will be an ever-changing menace. It is therefore timely that Sharp Parker, in Chapter 14, reviews what is known of cyberterrorism and its potential. We should remember that just as the kamikaze pilots of World War II presaged the flying of airplanes into the Twin Towers, so the various computer threats that daily plague every one of us have to be taken seriously as possibly open to abuse by insurgents. It is well known that terrorists are already well versed in the use of the Internet to recruit, plan and co-ordinate. The widespread prevalence of Internet-based crime also provides a warning of the opportunities that are possibly available. The particular challenge here, as Sharp Parker points out, is that the international nature of many violent movements directly maps onto the globalization of the Internet. Therefore an international response is especially important in tackling this potential challenge.

Countering the Psychological Precursors to Terrorism

The heart of any attempts to undermine the central psychological processes that feed terrorism has to be to break down the simple division into the terrorist group and the rest. So many commentators draw attention to this issue of social identity that it is remarkable that politicians and educators are not more robust in their overt attempts to undermine any such simple-minded dichotomy. Indeed there are so many processes that support the distinction espoused by terrorists between 'us' and 'them' that without a major campaign to erode its distinctions the divisions are likely to become stronger and simpler.

What major public figures seem to underestimate is that the ingroup/ outgroup division can all too readily be the skeleton which can be fleshed out with a heroic narrative enlivened by justifications for violence. Anyone who has seen the anodyne Danish cartoons of the Prophet that have been cited as the cause for violence and bloodshed around the globe will immediately realise that the cartoons themselves were of far less importance than the narrative in which they were embedded that presents 'the West' insulting 'Islam' and the importance of revenge against such insults.

The human process of categorization is so fundamental that we are usually not aware that we are doing it. This lack of awareness is particularly dangerous when the categories are arbitrary and naïve. In the current climate there is a remarkably simple-minded notion of 'ethnicity' that colours far too many debates. As Marks (2002) amongst many others has made exceptionally clear, there is no biological basis to race and even less to any notion of 'ethnic' group. In broad terms, the closer together any two people live the more likely they are to share genetic material. So there will be some similarities within any population, but despite the superficial distinctions of skin colour or nose shape the major differences between people are in their attitudes and culture, not in their biology.

Any attempts to define individuals in terms of single characteristics, be it religion, country of birth, 'ethnicity', 'race' or even football team supported, rather than any of the many other ways they can be identified serves to foster the basis for the Samson syndrome (Canter, 2006). Education that unpacks the many different overlapping narratives that characterize human history has to be at the forefront in the fight against terrorism. Intending terrorists need to be aware that we are not all Philistines.

Disengagement

Part of the process of disengagement from terrorism, then, is to enrich the understanding of all those involved in the complexities of identity. But the intricacies of the social processes in which any individual is embedded make this more difficult. Both Horgan in Chapter 15 and Moghaddam in the concluding chapter discuss the difficulties of disengagement for people whose whole life and subculture have embraced terrorism. In their different ways these two experts show that the problems of disengagement are integrally linked with the processes that lead people into terrorism initially. These can be the bonds of family and kinship so clearly revealed in Kassimeris' case study of the 17N terrorist group in Chapter 6, or the broader ideological links that Williams discusses in Chapter 4. But as Moghaddam expresses so graphically these are people already well up a staircase who have to find a way down.

They can be helped to avoid entering the processes of terrorism in the first place by setting in motion psychological, political and cultural processes that recognize that terrorism is indeed a many-headed beast. No one discipline can claim to provide an understanding of how groups will emerge that wish to carry out symbolic acts of violence against the state. As is revealed throughout the chapters of the present volume the psychological distinctions that underlie these atrocities are integrated into social and organizational processes. They can only be undermined and their power reduced by dealing with all the different faces of terrorism.

References

Anarchist Archives (2006). *Bakunin's collected works*. Retrieved March 2006, from http://dwardmac.pitzer.edu/Anarchist_Archives/bakunin/BakuninCW.html

Atran, S. (2004). Mishandling suicide terrorism. *The Washington Quarterly*, *27*, 67–90.

Bodansky, Y. (2001). *Bin Laden: The man who declared war on America*. New York: Random House.

Canter, D. (1995). *Criminal shadows*. London: HarperCollins.

Canter, D. (2000). Destructive organisational psychology. In D. Canter, & L. Alison (Eds), *The social psychology of crime* (pp. 321–334). Aldershot: Ashgate.

Canter, D. (2006). The Samson Syndrome: Is there a kamikaze psychology? *21st Century Society*, *1*, 107–127.

Coogan, T. P. (2002). *The IRA*. New York: Palgrave.

Crosby, F. (1982). *Relative deprivation and working women*. New York: Oxford University Press.

Duckitt, J., & Mphuting, T. (1998). Group identification and intergroup attitudes: A longitudinal analysis in South Africa. *Journal of Personality and Social Psychology*, *74*, 80–85.

Gunaratna, R. (2003). *Suicide terrorism: A global threat*. Jane's Information Group, 20 October 2000. Retrieved June 10, 2009, from www.janes.com/security/international_security/news/usscole/jir001020_1_n.shtml

Heap, M., & Kirsch, I. (Eds) (2006). *Hypnosis: Theory, research and application*. Aldershot: Ashgate.

Hickey, E. (2005). *Serial murderers and their victims*. Belmont: Wadsworth.

Horgan, J. (2005). *The psychology of terrorism*. London: Routledge.

Khan, M. H. (2005). *Videotape of Mohammad Sidique Khan*. Retrieved May 15, 2009, from http://news.bbc.co.uk/1/hi/uk/4678837.stm

Lamont-Brown, R. (1997). *Kamikaze: Japan's suicide Samurai*. London: Cassell.

Marks, J. (2002). *What it means to be 98% chimpanzee*. Berkeley, CA: University of California Press.

Merari, A. (1990). *Special oversight panel on terrorism hearing on terrorism and threats to U.S. interests in the Middle East*. Retrieved May 15, 2009, from http://commdocs.house.gov/committees/security/has195240.000/has195240_0f.htm

Moghaddam, F. M. (2005). The staircase to terrorism: A psychological exploration. *American Psychologist*, *60*, 161–169.

Orwell, G. (1933). *The road to Wigan Pier*. Retrieved January 6, 2006, from www.george-orwell.org/The_Road_to_Wigan_Pier/4.html

Richardson, L. (2006). *What terrorists want: Understanding the terrorist threat*. London: John Murray.

Sageman, M. (2004). *Understanding terror networks*. Philadelphia: University of Pennsylvania Press.

Silke, A. (2003). The psychology of suicidal terrorism. In A. Silke (Ed.), *Terrorists, victims and society* (pp. 93–108). Chichester: John Wiley & Sons Ltd.

Smith, H. J., & Leach, C. W. (2004). Group membership and everyday social comparison experiences. *European Journal of Social Psychology, 34*, 297–308.

Soibelman, M. (2004). Palestinian suicide bombers. *Journal of Investigative Psychology and Offender Profiling, 1*, 175–190.

Speckhard, A. (2006). Defusing human bombs: understanding suicide terrorism. In J. Victoroff, & S. Mednick (Eds), *Psychology and terrorism*. Amsterdam: IOS Press.

Walker, I., & Smith, H. J. (Eds) (2002). *Relative deprivation: Specification, development, and integration*. Cambridge: Cambridge University Press.

Youngs, R. (2006). *Democracy and security in the Middle East*. Internal report submitted for publication. Madrid: Fundación para las Relaciones Internacionales y el Diálogo Exterior, from http://www.fride.org/publication/58/democracy-and-security-in-the-middle-east assessed August 21 2009.

2

From Naïvety to Insurgency: Becoming a Paramilitary in Northern Ireland[1]

Neil Ferguson and Mark Burgess

Synopsis: Studies are reviewed that show how exposure to violence has the potential to push people into participating in paramilitary activities. They illustrate that even after peace has been negotiated the social problems do not disappear. They also demonstrate that the conflict may well have caused the perpetrators of political violence to become psychologically harmed since they become victims of their own violent actions. The need to address these problems is discussed in order to reduce the risk of the conflict smouldering on and then reigniting. In conclusion the importance is emphasized of politicians and military leaders reflecting on the lessons learned in Northern Ireland when deciding how to contain or react to terrorism across the globe, regardless of its origins.

For many people living in the UK, the world has become a more fearful and less safe place since the terrorist attacks of 11 September 2001 and the resulting global 'war on terror'. The attacks on the twin towers of the World Trade Center killed over 2,800 people with victims coming from 85 different nations, including Britain which lost 67 citizens, and many more of the casualties had close family ties with the United Kingdom. Since 2001 Britain and the city of London in particular have been the target of terrorist attacks linked to Islamic extremists, the deadliest attack being on the public transport network in London killing 52 people on 7 July 2005. In addition, the British media,

[1] Correspondence concerning this chapter should be sent to Neil Ferguson, Desmond Tutu Centre for War and Peace Studies, Liverpool Hope University, Hope Park, Liverpool, UK. Phone: +44 (0)151 291-3754. Fax: +44 (0)151 291-3773. Email: fergusn@hope.ac.uk

The Faces of Terrorism: Multidisciplinary Perspectives Edited by David Canter
© 2009 John Wiley & Sons Ltd.

politicians and public find certain features of Islamic terrorism exceptionally frightening. In particular the Islamic theological concept of 'jihad' provoked fear and unease among the British public and has received a lot of media attention since 2001. These beliefs in jihad and martyrdom are of particular concern within Britain as they indicate a readiness among Islamic fundamentalists to use human-bomb attacks as weapons in their terror campaign.

This obsession with 'shahid', suicide bombers and the perception that they are particular to Islamic fundamentalism is somewhat misplaced, as these tactics are used by other non-Muslim terror groups and were pioneered by the mainly Hindu, Liberation Tigers of Tamil Eelam (LTTE, a.k.a. Tamil Tigers); even the Marxist and atheist Popular Front for the Liberation of Palestine (PFLP) have employed suicide attacks. In reality suicide attacks have been used throughout history, even the Old Testament of the Bible recounts the story of how a blind Samson purposely pushes down the pillars of the temple causing it to collapse killing over 3,000 people and himself.

Hudson (1999) would argue that martyrdom is and always has been an ideal terrorist tactic and a great benefit to any terrorist organization, because as the suicide bomber dies during the attack they cannot show remorse or guilt for their actions in the future, thus reducing guilt and moral anxiety among remaining group members and their supporters. While Speckhard (2006) adds that a suicide bombing is: (a) inexpensive, (b) highly effective, (c) highly lethal, (d) extremely horrifying, (e) almost impossible to prevent, (f) difficult to trace and (g) if the organization has a large pool of willing individuals who support this tactic, then there is an almost endless supply of 'smart' weapons. Thus while the suicide attack is a highly effective military strategy, it is not an innovative one.

Terror-related bomb attacks on London or other British cities are not a new phenomenon, as republican groups have frequently bombed Britain. Indeed the Real Irish Republican Army (RIRA) caused two car-bomb explosions in London, the first was in Ealing, the second exploded outside the BBC's Television Centre, while a third car bomb failed to fully explode in Birmingham city centre as recently as 2001. These are only the last in a series of numerous bomb attacks which have taken place in the UK since the Provisional IRA expanded their war in the early 1970s.

If we broaden our focus to include Northern Ireland, even the use of human bombs and suicide as weapons in a campaign of political violence are not new to the UK. In 1989–1990 the IRA used a particularly disturbing strategy called 'proxy bombing' in their armed struggle against Britain. During a proxy bomb attack the IRA would force their way into an individual's home, take the family hostage, then force the father with threats that they would kill his family into a van which was packed with explosives, strap him into it and force him to drive the vehicle to an army or police installation, once he arrived at the target they would detonate the explosives remotely, thus turning their hostage into an unwilling human bomb. Irish republicanism has also used suicide and martyrdom as a weapon to bring about political change. The most vivid illustration of this was the second wave of 'hunger strikes' in 1981. During this period IRA prisoners starved themselves to death to demand changes to the status of political prisoners. Reviewing these events from the last couple of decades illustrates that the current experiences of terrorism and the fear it generates are not a new phenomenon, indeed the UK has been dealing with sustained terrorist campaigns since the late 1960s, and the main focus of that violence has been in Northern Ireland.

The State of Northern Ireland was formed when the Anglo-Irish Treaty of 6 December 1921 partitioned Ireland into two nations. Since partition the people of Northern Ireland have suffered significant campaigns of politically motivated violence in almost every decade. However, the latest and most sustained period of violence began in the late 1960s and continued at pace until the ceasefires and peace negotiation in the late 1990s.

Over the duration of the Troubles, as the conflict is euphemistically called, the conflict has been responsible for over 3,700 deaths and over 40,000 injuries, with civilians bearing the brunt of all deaths (53%) and injuries (68%) (Smyth, 1998; Smyth & Hamilton, 2004). The vast majority of deaths have been attributed to paramilitaries (87% of the total; 59% by republicans, 28% by loyalists), and a minority (about 11% of the total) attributed to the security forces (Smyth, 1998). It must be remembered that paramilitary groups in Northern Ireland are not the irregular militias who assist the regular military, as in the common definition of the term. The Northern Irish paramilitary groups such as the Irish Republican Army (IRA) and the Ulster Volunteer Force (UVF) are armed insurgent groups, who are normally viewed as terrorists by their opponents.

Before the peace agreement in Northern Ireland in 1998 there was a global focus on both the Troubles and Irish paramilitary groups leading to Northern Ireland and its paramilitaries becoming the most researched and understood on the planet (Mac Ginty, Muldoon & Ferguson, 2007; Whyte, 1990). Since 9/11 the focus has moved away from Northern Ireland, with the recent fears around Islamic extremism generating a huge demand for information about terrorism and Islamic terrorism. Horgan (2005) illustrates this huge demand by documenting how over 800 books published in English alone were written about the events of 9/11 before the first anniversary of the attacks. This is a huge exponential growth in an area of study which had only a handful of publications in the late 1960s (Rapoport, 1988). A particular fascination has been with the psychology of the terrorist and the 'radicalization' process that transforms normal young men into fanatics determined to kill for political reasons. Unfortunately, as Horgan (2005) acknowledges, this deluge of journals, books and newspaper articles has not necessarily increased our knowledge of these processes to any great degree, as much of the analysis is misinformed, short-sighted and based on unreliable data. For example, Silke (2001) reports that 80% of terrorism studies relied on the secondary analysis of data from journals, books or other media for their findings, with only 13% of data being derived from interviews with terrorists. Silke's (2001) review of the research on terrorism also discovered that only about 20% of all published articles actually provide any new knowledge, while the other 80% simply reiterate and rework old data.

The main reason for the failure of the field of terrorism studies to provide good quality data is due to the lack of active researchers working in the area (see Silke, 2003a), and the reason for the lack of researchers is glaringly obvious, the activity is dangerous, with numerous physical and psychological hazards. However, Northern Ireland and other societies emerging and recovering from sustained insurgent campaigns now offer relatively benign environments in which to research terrorism than say Iraq, Chechnya and Afghanistan do. Northern Ireland is particularly suited for further research as it is located in an English-speaking part of Europe, and the communities have experience of dealing with researchers (Mac Ginty et al., 2007).

Nonetheless there has been a debate about the relevance of this 'old' terrorism to the 'new' terrorism we are now dealing with, and many have been keen to ignore or dismiss analysis based on old terrorism (Horgan, in press). However, Horgan and other terrorism experts (e.g. Benjamin & Simon, 2002; Crenshaw, 2005) have pointed out that the failure to explore pre-2001 terrorism means we lose the ability to appreciate the similarities involved in the process of engagement in terrorism. For instance, research has shown that suicide attacks are predominately driven by nationalism, not Islamic ideology. Pape (2005) argues that every major suicide-terrorist campaign across the globe, whether it is in the Lebanon or Chechnya, aims to compel democratic states to withdraw military forces from the country. Even a glimpse at the complexities of the current conflict in Iraq illustrates that there is a need to understand nationalist-separatist-related terrorism as much as terrorism originating among extremist Islamic groups.

This need to develop terrorism research grounded on quality data combined with the accessibility of Northern Ireland and our experience of researching aspects of the Troubles prompted our recent research to explore the processes involved in joining a paramilitary group (Burgess, Ferguson, & Hollywood, 2005a; 2005b), to what extent ex-combatants perceive there to be potential for future violence in post-agreement Northern Ireland (Burgess, Ferguson, & Hollywood, 2007) and the impact that engaging in terrorism can have for the perpetrators of political violence (Ferguson, Burgess, & Hollywood, in press). This chapter will build on research exploring how normal individuals can follow the road to insurgency and the impact this journey has on them and their attitudes towards the effectiveness of political violence in achieving political goals.

The Road to Insurgency

Research focusing on the reasons why people join armed insurgent groups or commit acts of terrorism has generally explored intra-individual explanations, with terrorists being labelled or diagnosed as mad or sociopathic. They have traditionally been seen as possessing psychological disorders that make them capable of committing murderous atrocities (Horgan, 2003; Silke, 1998). Although this myth of the 'mad' terrorist still exists and is repeatedly recreated in the popular media, there is a growing awareness that this reductionist explanation based on individual abnormality is inadequate and probably no more than wishful thinking (Burgess et al., 2005a, 2005b; Horgan, 2003; Louis & Taylor, 2002; Oberschall, 2004; Silke, 1998; Victoroff, 2005).

A recent and comprehensive review of the research (Victoroff, 2005) suggests that an understanding of violent insurgency requires a more comprehensive analysis. This analysis needs to incorporate intra-individual factors, wider social factors and the dynamics of the conflict. Despite the methodological shortcomings of terrorism research, studies involving individuals from insurgency groups from across the globe have consistently exposed an inventory of factors that increase the likelihood of participation in a campaign of violence. Some of our own previous work has also supported the efficacy of these factors, which include:

(a)   The existence of a grievance or perceived injustice by a subgroup of the population (see Burgess et al., 2005b for first-hand accounts; Crenshaw, 2003). Interestingly, Ferguson, Burgess, and Hollywood's (in press) interviews with former Northern Irish paramilitaries have illustrated how some of the paramilitaries interviewed reflected back and remarked that this 'injustice' that they faced may not have been anything more than myths that were circulating at the beginning of the Troubles, myths that people were naïve enough to accept without question, rather than 'real' experiences of injustice and ill treatment.

(b)   Age and gender. Terrorist acts are generally committed by young males aged 15 to 25 (Silke, 2003b). Research consistently demonstrates that jihadist movements normally recruit and train unmarried males in their late teens or early twenties (Horgan, 2003). Age and gender seem to be the only biological or genetic factors at play in distinguishing potential recruits to armed groups from those less inclined to join (Silke, 2003b). However, the knowledge that young, unmarried men are more likely to engage in politically motivated violence is almost useless for anyone engaged in counterinsurgency, and employing this knowledge in profiling terrorists or for rounding up and interning young men is more likely to be counter-productive.

(c)   The individual's family may have a past involvement with, or show support for the movement, thus promoting membership within the family through historical connections (Burgess et al., 2005b; Crawford, 2003). Speckhard (2006) argues that this is one of the key aspects of the process of drawing in recruits from non-conflict zones and Sageman (2004) believes that strong bonds with family and friends rather than behavioural disorders are the key motivating factor for young Muslims joining the jihad. Brett and Specht (2004) have suggested that apart from actually being in the midst of an active conflict, having family who support an individual's membership is the most consistent factor in joining an armed group.

(d)   High levels of community support for the insurgent group or membership of the group provides high status within the community (Burgess et al., 2007; Post, Sprinzak, & Denny, 2003). Being a terrorist places immense physical, psychological and social burdens on the individual (Burgess et al., 2005b; Ferguson et al., in press); they can be isolated, face death or imprisonment, etc. Yet there are advantages to getting involved in violent resistance through gaining respect and esteem within your community; while membership may also bring financial or sexual rewards as well as increased social status (Silke, 2003b; Horgan, 2005).

(e)   Eventual membership is the result of an incremental process of increasing acts of insurgence (Burgess et al., 2005a). This process may start with relatively mundane behaviour such as stone throwing or spray painting graffiti before progressing to destroying property and finally becoming involved in injuring and killing opponents (Oberschall, 2004). Many of the paramilitaries and ex-combatants we interviewed (Ferguson, Burgess, & Hollywood, 2007) discussed how they would begin on the fringes of the conflict, perhaps running with gangs and getting involved in riots, before being approached by, or approaching armed groups and becoming involved in assassinations or bombings.

(f)   The individual is motivated by vengeance and feels a need to hit back and right wrongs (Burgess et al., 2005a, 2005b, 2007; Crenshaw, 2003; Silke, 2003b; Speckhard, 2006). This is one of the most consistent findings from research dealing with why people engage in political violence (Silke, 2003b). The personal histories of armed insurgents are frequently filled with stories about incidents in which they, their acquaintances or communities are victimized by 'them' and decide that they need to take action, seek revenge and join an armed group.

(g)   To join an armed group involves identifying with the people that the group represents, so prospective members need to perceive themselves as categorically interchangeable with other ingroup members. This heightened identification allows them to become stereotypical ingroup members, taking on the group ideology, culture and values. Social

Identity Theory (SIT; Tajfel, 1978; Tajfel & Turner, 1979) offers a detailed and robust theory from which to explore this process of identification and commitment to group goals and recent research from Northern Ireland has indicated that Protestants or Catholics with high levels of ingroup identification, feel, think and act differently from their counterparts with a weaker strength of identity (Cairns, Kenworthy, Campbell, & Hewstone, 2006; Ferguson, 2009; Tausch, Hewstone, Kenworthy, Cairns, & Christ, 2007) potentially making them more likely to engage in discrimination and violence.

(h) Witnessing violence against family, friends or the wider group an individual identifies with, either first hand or even via the television, as was the case for a member of the UVF we interviewed (see Burgess et al., 2005b), could easily be imagined as victimizing. It could also be imagined that exposure to these events may cause trauma and possibly Posttraumatic Stress Disorder (PTSD). Speckhard (2006) argues that these traumatic events can also cause dissociation (a feeling of separation from the body, thoughts, perceptions and/or emotions), which may cause an individual to become fixated on revenge and the defence of the group regardless of risk to one's life or well-being. Ferguson et al. (in press) also concluded that Northern Irish paramilitaries did demonstrate moral disengagement, detachment and dissociation which are symptoms of perpetration-induced traumatic stress (PITS) (MacNair, 2002, 2005) or indicative of PTSD.[2] This dissociation, traumatization or victimization may then play a key role in motivating individuals to join armed groups as a way of actively dealing with their trauma and negative feelings of victimization.

(i) Research has revealed how in addition to the individual strongly identifying with his or her group, identification with role models who support the actions of the armed group is important in sustaining and committing the individual to political violence. Burgess et al. (2005b) found that some Northern Irish paramilitaries were moved to engage in political violence due to 'idols' in their community openly supporting armed confrontation. After interviews with members of armed Palestinian groups, such as Hamas, Post et al. (2003) reflected how the interviewees had upheld religious figures who espoused violence or revolutionaries such as Ché Guevara as heroes.

(j) Finally, clearly to become a member of an armed group there must be an organization that the individual has the opportunity to join, and that wants his or her membership (Silke, 2003b). Although, it is of course

---

[2] However, it is unclear whether their initial experiences of violence were a cause of these symptoms or whether the violence they had perpetrated as paramilitaries resulted in the trauma and symptoms.

possible for the individual to set up their own armed group, and one of the interviewees (Ferguson et al., 2007) had done just that, or to act as a lone wolf.

Our research supports and adds to this inventory of terrorist induction. Burgess et al. (2005a, 2005b) interviewed eight members of the IRA and UVF and discovered that in addition to this list of risk factors, the interviewees had all instigated their violent activism after a *critical incident*. For all the participants these critical incidents were attacks on themselves, their family or the wider community they identified with. For example, a former member of the UVF decided to become involved in terrorism after he heard of a young man with the same name, age and background as him who had been killed by one of the 22 bombs the IRA exploded on Bloody Friday in 1972. He explains the impact this had on him:

> And I thought, 'That's my fence sitting days over,' and I joined the UVF. And there's so many stories like that where you talk to Republicans or Loyalists and you find out there was a moment. There was a moment when they crossed the Rubicon. (Burgess et al., 2005b, p.26)

This participant's experience is reflected by the actions of a young woman who decided to join an opposing paramilitary group, namely the IRA, after witnessing police and security forces violently engaging a group of protestors:

> ... a lot of [peacefully protesting] women and children would have been beaten with batons and it was just messy. You begin to think, 'this is not good'. ... I decided in '69 when the troubles really began and I'd watched a lot of people being hurt and a lot of friends die for standing up for what they believed in. I quickly, not through anger, but through sadness and fear, decided, 'Ok, I'll take up this cause and I'll try and change'. (Burgess et al., 2005a, p.46)

The experience of critical incidents fuelling recruitment into Northern Irish paramilitary groups was also recognized by non-combatants. In one interview a peaceful civil rights activist remarked how violent confrontation provided people with a critical incident that increased IRA membership:

> It's easy, after Bloody Sunday, for 10 or 20 young fellas to be so angry. They've seen their mates shot and they go down and see about joining the IRA. (Burgess et al., 2005a, p. 46)

These quotes illustrate how the use of military force to tackle problems leads to more violence, creating the destructive spiral that Crenshaw (2003, p. 95) labels the "action-reaction syndrome" fuelling further conflict. It should also be remembered that in these cases the individual was not the target of the aggression, all that was needed was that s/he identified with the person or persons who were subjected to the violence and s/he perceived this assault as an injustice to them and their wider community.

Burgess et al. (2005a, 2005b) also demonstrate that it is not simple exposure to these events that results in taking up arms. Indeed, many of the participants who suffered from indirect and direct violent experiences did not join paramilitary groups. Instead they became involved in peace work, civil protest or simply did nothing. For the interviewees that took action, either peaceful or violent, all reported *periods of reflection* after these critical incidents during which the individual consciously considered how he or she would act to change the status quo, or hit back at those who were threatening their community. This act of reflection is an important consideration as many insurgents project a view that they had no choice, that the sociopolitical conditions forced them to use violence (Crenshaw, 2003). The fact that these individuals do make a conscious decision to engage in terrorism is further demonstrated by the reality that not everyone from an oppressed community engages in terrorism. Only a small section of the populace take up arms regardless of the brutality and oppression they collectively face (Crenshaw, 2003; Silke, 2003b).

Our data adds to a growing understanding of the complexity involved in attributing the causes for terrorism. As noted there are intra-individual causes based on the decision-making processes that combine with demographic characteristics, such as age, gender, employment status, level of education, family and social history. Another important ingredient that is added to this mix involves the dynamics of the violence, with our interviewees reporting that the use of violence on communities will be reciprocated with violence from some members of that community, while other members will offer support and succour. This indicates that terrorism is a likely result of war or violent oppression. Interestingly our findings and the previous findings exploring why people engage in terrorism are similar to research exploring why adolescents join legitimate and illegal armed groups across the globe. Brett and Specht (2004) interviewed 53 adolescent boys and girls from 9 different conflict situations and junior British soldiers; the key factors involved in their interviewees' decision to join an armed group (ranging from the LTTE to the Mojahedin) map very clearly to the antecedent factors listed previously, and also note the importance of *critical moments* in distinguishing those who decide to join an armed group from their peers who do not. These antecedent factors increase the likelihood of becoming involved, but once people have employed violence to bring political change, how does this to relate to the probability that they will support the resumption of violence when they seek further political change.

The Potential for Further Violence in Northern Ireland

Burgess et al. (2007) explored interviewees' views on the likelihood of the peace process succeeding, or of Northern Ireland being drawn back into sustained ethnopolitical violence. The five interviewees were either members or ex-members of the IRA (n = 3) or peaceful civil rights demonstrators (n = 2). The majority of the interviewees felt that reactionary violence had brought about the Northern Ireland peace process and positively changed Northern Irish society with regard to the status of the Catholic minority. This belief that violence brings about positive gains for your group with regard to employment, housing, education, political power and status offers a challenge to the peace process and Northern Ireland's transition from a culture of violence to a culture of co-existence.

Although there have been titanic changes in Northern Ireland since the signing of the peace agreement in 1998, it was important to note that none of the participants viewed post-1998 Northern Ireland as a society at peace, they believed that the conflict was smouldering with the potential to reignite under the right, or should we say wrong circumstances. There was an acknowledgement that the Catholic and Protestant communities were more segregated now than in any previous decade and that this virtual apartheid keeps the potential for further conflict alive (see Shirlow, 2003). Participants also felt that Northern Irish people liked the conflict, as it defined who they were and helped them understand the world, concisely summed up by an ex-paramilitary in that "there is an addiction to conflict here ... I mean people need that in order to be safe and secure" (Burgess et al., 2005a, p. 47).

However, many of the participants thought that political apathy and the growing drug culture in Northern Ireland (see Higgins, Percy, & McCrystal, 2004) would inhibit the ability of the community to organize, re-arm and defend itself effectively in the future.

> For reasons that are best known to themselves, if a person's drugged up to the eyeballs, they aren't going to be out lifting an Armalite rifle or an AK-47 rifle or whatever. They can't defend themselves, never mind attack. (Burgess et al., 2007, p. 79)

These opinions reflect how the protection offered by residential segregation may reduce conflict in the short term, but only keep the conflict simmering in the long term (see Ferguson & Cairns, 1996; Shirlow, 2003). Events such as the widespread unrest on the streets of Belfast in September 2005, recent finds of hundreds of pounds of explosives in August 2007 and again in February and May 2009, the shootings of two soldiers and a police officer in March 2009, and the failed rocket attack on a police patrol in August 2008 clearly demonstrate how little it takes to reignite the flames of conflict, how fragile the current peace process could be and how signing an agreement does not necessarily bring the peace it promises. However, as these events have not caused widespread violence or reignited the Troubles, this indicates that a growing apathy may offer some hope for a longer peace.

All Gave Some, Some Gave All: Terrorism, Trauma and Violence

As mentioned earlier, our paramilitary interviewees, particularly republican paramilitaries, spoke about how having witnessed attacks, assaults, having their home searched and being brutalized by the state and the security forces caused them to join armed organizations. Speckhard (2006) has argued that these experiences induced trauma and dissociation which made their membership of armed groups more likely. However, once they became members of these armed groups they then engaged in violence and killed, attempted to kill or trained others to kill, engaging in what they previously viewed as immoral acts causing perpetration-induced trauma. The interviews with both loyalist and republican paramilitaries illustrate that engaging in politically motivated violence caused them great feelings of guilt and revulsion at what they had to become to bring about political change; indeed many viewed themselves as becoming 'monsters' or unleashing their 'dark side'. For example, this ex-member of the IRA reflects on the impact that joining an armed insurgent group and engaging in politically motivated violence had on him:

> I'm someone that's living in the past, that went through it and is able to recount and tell them the horrors of it. And how much it can take lumps out of your head. Because it has taken lumps out of mine, there's no doubt about it. I have the rest of my life to live thinking on things that I've done and maybe hurt people. And I'm very, very, sorry for it. I never wanted to do it. I don't want any young people to go through that again. And I want them to appreciate life, you know, and get on and be happy and love one another no matter what religion they are.

A number of the paramilitaries discussed their activities with a detachment or demonstrated dehumanization, talking about 'only shooting at uniforms' or how any members of the other community were suitable targets, while a number of the other participants showed no remorse for members of the other side who were murdered. A loyalist paramilitary illustrates this detachment:

> I never have cared about any mans religion, the colour of their skin. If I see them as an enemy, or in opposition to what I want, it doesn't bother me what religion you are, whether you're Protestant, Catholic, black, Chinese

or white, if you were jeopardizing what my goal was, then you know, it didn't bother me to take action against you. So I can kill anybody, it doesn't bother me.

It has been suggested that moral disengagement, detachment and dissociation are symptoms of perpetration-induced traumatic stress (PITS) commonly experienced by combat veterans (MacNair, 2002, 2005) or indicative of PTSD and this loyalist paramilitary's reflection illustrates the stress and guilt caused by perpetrating politically motivated murder:

> Put it to the back of your mind. You know what I mean; people say do you ever think of anything. I said no. See, the more you think about it, it would do your head in. You put something to the back of your head, you put it to the back of your head. There's sometimes like I'm sitting, and things come on TV from 30 years ago. We are sitting watching TV and one minute we're talking away, and next minute something comes on, I just keep quiet. But my missus knows.

Grossman's (1996) study of the taboo subject of humans killing humans sheds light on these findings, his research illustrated that humans have a powerful resistance to killing each other, which the military have spent centuries trying to overcome, so when individuals engage in armed actions and kill at close range, without combat training or being conditioned to kill fellow human beings they have a high propensity to suffer psychological harm, which usually manifests as PTSD symptoms. So while trauma may be one of the antecedent factors involved in the radicalization process, it is most certainly an outcome of engaging in violent extremism, and an outcome that both outlasts the conflict and potentially plays a role in fuelling future violence.

Conclusion

These studies demonstrate how exposure to violence directed towards a particular individual, his or her family, or the wider community s/he identifies with collides with other social and personal factors and creates the potential to push him or her into joining a paramilitary group and engaging in violence against the state or other armed or unarmed groups. They illustrate that even after the peace has been negotiated and the photo call achieved the social problems or conflicting identities bound to the conflict do not disappear, but instead fester and act as breeding grounds for future violence. Additionally, the studies also demonstrate that the conflict may well have caused the perpetrators of political violence to become victims of their own violent actions, leaving them psychologically harmed in the post-conflict space. These problems need to be addressed otherwise the conflict can still smoulder and reignite. The lessons from Northern Ireland are not just lessons for Northern Ireland. Academics, politicians and military leaders would do well to reflect on the lessons learned in Northern Ireland and in other post-conflict societies when deciding how to contain or react to terrorism across the globe, regardless of where it emanates from.

References

Benjamin, D., & Simon, S. (2002). *The age of sacred terror*. New York: Random House.

Brett, R., & Specht, I. (2004). *Young soldiers: Why they choose to fight*. London: Lynne Rienner.

Burgess, M., Ferguson, N., & Hollywood, I. (2005a). Violence begets violence: Drawing ordinary civilians into the cycle of military intervention and violent resistance. *Australasian Journal of Human Security, 1*, 41–52.

Burgess, M., Ferguson, N., & Hollywood, I. (2005b). A social psychology of defiance: From discontent to action. In M. Sönser-Breen (Ed.), *Minding evil: Explorations of human iniquity* (pp. 19–38). Amsterdam/New York: Rodolpi.

Burgess, M., Ferguson, N., & Hollywood, I. (2007). Rebels' perspectives of the legacy of past violence and of the current peace in post-agreement Northern Ireland: An interpretative phenomenological analysis. *Political Psychology, 28*, 69–88.

Cairns, E., Kenworthy, J., Campbell, A., & Hewstone, M. (2006). The role of in-group identification, religious group membership and intergroup conflict in moderating in-group and out-group affect. *British Journal of Social Psychology, 45*, 701–716.

Crawford, C. (2003). *Inside the UDA: Volunteers and violence*. London: Pluto Press.

Crenshaw, M. (2003). The causes of terrorism. In C. W. Kegley, Jr. (Ed.), *The new global terrorism: Characteristics, causes, controls* (pp. 92–138). Upper Saddle River, NJ: Prentice Hall.

Crenshaw, M. (2005, July). 'Old' vs. 'new' terrorism: Have motivations changed? Nevitt Stanford Award Lecture at the International Society of Political Psychology, 28th Annual Scientific Meeting, Toronto, Canada.

Ferguson, N. (2009). The impact of political violence on moral reasoning: Socio-political reasoning in Northern Ireland. In S. Scuzzarello, C. Kinnvall, & K. Renwick Monroe (Eds), *On behalf of others: The morality of care in a global world* (pp. 233–254). Oxford: Oxford University Press.

Ferguson, N., Burgess, M., & Hollywood, I. (2007). *Research interviews with Northern Irish paramilitaries*. Unpublished transcripts.

Ferguson, N., Burgess, M., & Hollywood, I. (in press). Who are the victims? Victimhood experiences in post-agreement Northern Ireland.

Ferguson, N., & Cairns, E. (1996). Political violence and moral maturity in Northern Ireland. *Political Psychology, 17*, 713–725.

Grossman, D. (1996). *On killing: The psychological cost of learning to kill in war and society*. New York: Back Bay Books.

Higgins, K., Percey, A., & McCrystal, P. (2004). Secular trends in substance use: The conflict and young people in Northern Ireland. *Journal of Social Issues*, *60*, 485–506.

Horgan, J. (2003). The search for the terrorist personality. In A. Silke (Ed.), *Psychological perspectives on terrorism and its consequences* (pp. 3–27). Chichester, England: John Wiley & Sons Ltd.

Horgan, J. (2005). *The psychology of terrorism*. London: Routledge.

Horgan, J. (in press). Beyond imagination, exaggeration and distortion: Towards a psychological perspective on terrorism and counterterrorism. In A. Strathern, & P. J. Stewart (Eds), *Terrorism and terror: Imagination and practice*. Duke University Press.

Hudson, R. A. (1999). *The sociology and psychology of terrorism. Who becomes a terrorist and why?* Washington: Federal Research Division.

Louis, W., & Taylor, D. (2002). Understanding the September 11 terrorist attack on America: The role of intergroup theories of normative influence. *Analyses of Social Issues and Public Policy*, *2*, 87–100.

Mac Ginty, R., Muldoon, O., & Ferguson, N. (2007). No war, no peace: Northern Ireland after the Agreement. *Political Psychology*, *28*, 1–12.

MacNair, R. M. (2002). *Perpetration-induced traumatic stress: The psychological consequences of killing*. Westport, CT: Praeger.

MacNair, R. M. (2005).Violence begets violence: The consequences of violence become causation. In M. Fitzduff, & C. E. Stout (Eds), *The psychology of resolving global conflicts: From war to peace: Vol. 2. Group and social factors* (pp. 191–210). West Port, CT: Praeger.

Oberschall, A. (2004). Explaining terrorism: The contribution of collective action theory. *Sociological Theory*, *22*, 26–37.

Pape, R. (2005). *Dying to win: The strategic logic of suicide terrorism*. New York: Random House.

Post, J. M., Sprinzak, E., & Denny, L. M. (2003). The terrorists in their own words: Interviews with 35 incarcerated Middle Eastern terrorists. *Terrorism and Political Violence*, *15*, 171–184.

Rapoport, D. C. (1988). Introduction. In D. C. Rapoport (Ed.), *Inside terrorist organisations* (pp. 1–10). London: Frank Cass.

Sageman, M. (2004). *Understanding terror networks*. Philadelphia: University of Pennsylvania Press.

Shirlow, P. (2003). 'Who fears to speak': Fear, mobility and ethno-sectarianism in the two 'Ardoynes'. *The Global Review of Ethnopolitics*, *3*, 76–91.

Silke, A. (1998). Cheshire-cat logic: The recurring theme of terrorist abnormality in psychological research. *Psychology, Crime and Law*, *4*, 51–69.

Silke, A. (2001). The Devil you know: Continuing problems with research on terrorism. *Terrorism and Political Violence*, *13*, 1–14.

Silke, A. (2003a). Preface. In A. Silke (Ed.), *Terrorists, victims and society: Psychological perspectives on terrorism and its consequences* (pp. xiii–xxi). Chichester: John Wiley & Sons Ltd.

Silke, A. (2003b). Becoming a terrorist. In A. Silke (Ed.), *Terrorists, victims and society: Psychological perspectives on terrorism and its consequences* (pp. 29–53). Chichester: John Wiley & Sons Ltd.

Smyth, M. (1998). Remembering in Northern Ireland: Victims, perpetrators and hier-
archies of pain and responsibility. In B. Hamber (Ed.), *Past imperfect: Dealing with
the past in Northern Ireland and societies in transition* (p. 31). Derry/Londonderry:
University of Ulster & INCORE.

Smyth, M., & Hamilton, J. (2004). The human cost of the Troubles. In O. Hargie, &
D. Dickson, *Researching the Troubles: Social science perspectives on the Northern
Ireland conflict* (pp.15–36). Edinburgh: Mainstream Publishing Ltd.

Speckhard, A. (2006). Defusing human bombs: Understanding suicide terrorism. In
J. Victoroff (Ed.), *Tangled roots: Social and psychological factors in the genesis of
terrorism* (pp. 277–291). Amsterdam: IOS Press.

Tajfel, H. (1978). *Differentiation between social groups: Studies in the social psychology
of intergroup relations.* London: Academic Press.

Tajfel, H., & Turner, J. C. (1979). An integrative theory of intergroup conflict. In
W. G. Austin, & S. Worchel (Eds), *The social psychology of intergroup relations*
(pp. 33–47). Monterey, CA: Brooks/Cole.

Tausch, N., Hewstone, M., Kenworthy, J., Cairns, E., & Christ, O. (2007). Cross-
community contact, perceived status differences, and intergroup attitudes in
Northern Ireland: The mediating roles of individual-level versus group-level threats
and the moderating role of social identification. *Political Psychology, 28,* 53–68.

Victoroff, J. (2005). The mind of the terrorist: A review and critique of psychological
approaches. *Journal of Conflict Resolution, 49,* 3–42.

Whyte, J. (1990). *Interpreting Northern Ireland.* Oxford: Clarendon Press.

3

The Rhetorical Foundation of Militant Jihad

Sudhanshu Sarangi and David Canter

Synopsis: Radical, violent Islam or 'militant jihad' derives its authority from a particular set of interpretations of Islamic texts. An understanding of the essence of these interpretations helps to distinguish the views of militant jihadis from those of moderate Muslims. Important jihadi writings were therefore reviewed to establish a set of criteria that characterize the religious rhetoric of militant jihadis. These criteria are: (a) a dismissal of the dominant, interpretative role of Islamic jurists by emphasizing a literal interpretation of sacred texts with the stated objective of restoring the golden age of Islam (*Salaf*); (b) establish the sovereignty of God and rule by 'Sharia' in the entire world; (c) a clear and uncompromising break with all existing or past forms of man-made systems; (d) to convert non-believers or ask then to accept an inferior citizen status; if they agree to neither, killing them would be justified on the grounds of faith alone; (e) women are inherently less favoured by God and are fundamentally seductive, so they must be segregated and limitations imposed on the interaction between sexes to maintain society's moral fabric; (f) the establishment of Islamic rule is the responsibility of an enlightened vanguard, who must wage a jihad against the domestic apostate rulers and foreign infidel enemies. However, the arguments for the overthrow of the world order through an unlimited, unconditional and violent jihad do not have really thorough roots in Islamic jurisprudence and the great majority of Muslims, who are moderate, do not accept the rhetoric, objectives and methods of the jihadis.

The Faces of Terrorism: Multidisciplinary Perspectives Edited by David Canter
© 2009 John Wiley & Sons Ltd.

Introduction

Islam asks its believers to follow five basic pillars of faith and action (*arkân al-islâm*):

1. There is no deity except Allah and Muhammad is the Prophet of Allah (*shahâdah*)
2. Performing five ritual prayers a day (*salât*)
3. Giving alms (*zakât*)
4. Fasting during the holy month of Ramadan every year (*sawm*)
5. Performing a pilgrimage to Mecca once in a lifetime (*Hajj*).

All Muslims agree on these five pillars of faith and are guided by one essential, immutable and binding scripture – 'the Holy Quran'. However, despite the fact that all Muslims believe in one God, the supremacy of the Quran and offer prayer in Arabic, interpretations and attitudes among the believers of Islam have historically shown a great degree of divergence, not limited to the widely known differences between the Sunni and Shia streams of Islamic faith. Rhetorically one group may call another 'heretics' even justifying punishment and retribution resulting in bloodshed.

Had the jihadi claims that their version of Islam is the only true, legitimate or pure Islam, been merely intellectual articulation or religious discourse, Muslims and non-Muslims could have ignored them, but in recent years jihadi rhetoric has underpinned death and destruction on an unprecedented scale creating concern for the stability and security of the world.

Absence of a proper understanding of the jihadi expression of Islam has led to many misconceptions. First, there is the belief that Islamic Jihad is a new ideology, or that the radical trend originated in the context of the Afghan war (1978–89). In fact the radical tendency can be traced back at least to the writings of medieval jurists like Taqi al-Din Ahmad ibn Taymiyya (1263–1328), 18th century evangelist Muhammad bin 'Abd al-Wahhab (1703–1791) and in modern times Hasan al-Banna (1906–1949), Mawlana Abu'l a'la Mawdudi (1903–1979), Muhammad Ilyas (1885–1944), Sayyid Qutb (1906–1966) and many others. Both of the leaders of al-Qaeda, Osama bin Laden and Ayman al-Zawahiri inherited well-known ideological positions. They are not the intellectual founding fathers of radical Islam.

Secondly, it is often assumed that Islam is a homogenous religion, which has an intrinsic core that motivates Muslims to indulge in violence and disruption or makes them intolerant towards other faiths. Many even believe that we are witnessing, what Huntington (1998) has called "a clash of civilization" in which two monolithic world views are facing each other like prize-fighters. Such a perspective undervalues the many distinctions within the heterogeneity of this vast and multi-faceted world religion, the second largest after Christianity with around 1.5 billion faithful.

Part of the confusion about Islam arises from the fact that as essentially God-fearing people, all of whom respect the central messages of the Quran, most Muslims are loathe to do or say anything that implies a criticism of their religion. Most are therefore reluctant to take sides with those perceived as the enemies of Islam. Those moderates who feel the need to defend Islam, have been trying to explain that the 'jihadi' interpretation is a false or wrong interpretation of Islam and that it is unfair for Islam to be blamed for the belief or the work of a few extremists. However, careful consideration of the fundamentals of Islam does open up the possibility that the jihadi interpretation is neither an accidental nor a false interpretation of Islam. It is just one of a number of possible interpretations of the religion and not the most authoritative.

A crucial principle in Islam stated in Quran II: 256* is: "There shall be no compulsion in religion."

This is taken to mean that ultimately accepting or rejecting an interpretation is left to the conscience of the believers. They alone decide at an individual level what expresses the true will of God. This allows Muslims to subscribe to many alternative positions making the religion far more pluralistic than is often assumed. Within this variety of opinions a majority of Islamic scholars and Muslims the world over do not subscribe to the jihadi interpretation.

A third misunderstanding is to view al-Qaeda as a synonym for militant jihad. Al-Qaeda is neither the first nor the only jihadi organization in the world. The emphasis on al-Qaeda as the core of militant jihad ignores the many other militant Islamic groups that have existed in many non-Western societies over the last century. For example, Egypt has had to cope with violent jihadis for more than 60 years. It was cadres from the previously existing Egyptian groups: Egyptian Islamic Jihad (al-jihad islamiya), Egyptian Islamic Group (jamma islamiyya), who joined with mujahedeens from Arab, Maghreb, South and Central Asia and the Far East to create al-Qaeda in the late 1980s (Gunaratna, 2002; Sageman, 2004). Furthermore, jihadi movements have been active in many countries including Algeria, Indonesia, Chechnya, Pakistan and India and these organizations share similar ideological positions, are equally dangerous and have been responsible for as many or more deaths than those attributed to al-Qaeda.

Although most of the regional jihadi movements are now overshadowed by the dominant presence of al-Qaeda they had no difficulty in supporting or joining al-Qaeda's World Islamic Front for Jihad against Jews, Crusaders and others, created by a fatwa issued on 23 February 1998 signed by Osama bin Laden, Ayman al-Zawahiri, Abu-Yasir Ahmad Taha, Amir Hamzah and Fazlur

*All quotations from the Quran are from the Penguin translation by N. J. Dawood (2003).

Rahman (Bin Laden, 2005), and in accepting al-Qaeda's leadership. The World Islamic Front for Jihad is an umbrella organization of jihadis from Kashmir, Chechnya, Indonesia, Algeria, Morocco, Saudi Arabia, Egypt and Palestine for collaboration and unity. Though, the front appears to exist more as a networking concept and less as an organization with identifiable structures.

A fourth misunderstanding is the attempt to place various movements and groups in the context of regional and national boundaries. Jihad is a negation of the notion of nationalism. It is misleading to assume that a jihadi in Britain will have a different rhetoric or agenda from a jihadi in Egypt, Kashmir or Chechnya. As Sayyid Qutb (2007) has argued, "a Muslim has no nationality except his belief" (p. 118). The word *ummah* in Arabic refers to the Muslim community regardless of differences of tribe and territory and is not related to any issue of national self-determination or the notion of a modern nation state as traditionally understood in Western political theory.

The Jurists and the Activists

Unlike Canonical law, "Islamic law was never supported by an organized power" as Schacht (1991, p. 2) a leading scholar on the subject, has stated. There is no church in Islam and no priesthood of the kind known to Christianity. Islamic law precedes the Islamic state. A mosque is a private (non-state) institution. Thus, in theory at least, no one has any superior authority to interpret the religion. As a result "Islamic law", Schacht (1991, p. 3) argues, was never "uniform at any point of its development." Interpretation of the religion is provided by religious scholars who are called variously *alim* (or *ulama*), *faqih*, *mulla*, *shaykh* or *Imam*. They give their authoritative opinions (*fatwas*) on what is required (*wajib*) to be done, what is forbidden (*haram*), what is recommended (*mandub*), what is disapproved of (*makruh*) or what is merely permitted (*mubah*). Since the jurists do not have the backing of state power it is ultimately left to each individual Muslim to decide from his/her conscience whether a *fatwa* represents the will of God or not. The leading Islamic jurist Khaled Abou El Fadl of the UCLA School of Law has argued convincingly that *fatwas* carry persuasive authority, but they are not mandatory or binding.

Despite being a sacred law, Islamic law was created by a process of rational interpretation to introduce religious standards and moral values. Secondly, Schacht (1991, p. 4) argues it "possesses a pronounced private and individualistic character". During the Umayyad period, about the beginning of the second Islamic century, schools of jurisprudence developed in various important centres of Islam like Iraq and Medina with each school depending on, what Schacht (1991) has described as "their own living tradition". These traditions were established from opinions on important subjects of the day and on a varied degree of emphasis on different roots of jurisprudence or *usul al-fiqh*. Though some of these schools have now become extinct, there are four extant schools called *Madhhab* in Sunni Islam: Hanafi, Maliki, Shafi and Hanbali. Similarly the Jafari and Zaydi schools guide the Shi'as, and the Ismaili school survives among the Ismailis in India (Coulson, 1994; Schacht, 1991; Ziadeh, 1995).

Jurists are trained in the three main sources of Islamic law. First and foremost is the holy Quran, which Muslims believe, represents God's words as revealed to Prophet Muhammad and is a literal oral tradition. The second is the *Sunnah*, which is also an oral tradition that roughly refers to traditions or rule by analogy; what Prophet Muhammad and his four Companions 'said' or 'did not say' or 'did' or 'did not do'. Individual instances of the precedents are reported in the third source, the *Hadith*. Besides studying these sources, jurists are trained in methodologies for considering evidence and general principles of jurisprudence like principles of equity, public interest and general custom. Because of the interpretative nature of legal opinion multiplicity was expected and tolerated with respect. As stated by Ziadeh (1995) the *Hanafis* make liberal use of opinion in their formulations and are often called 'People of Opinion' as opposed to other schools that rely on traditions of the Prophet and are called 'People of Traditions'.

Taken together the three sources of law, all the legal opinions of the different schools of thought, along with procedural law (methodologies for considering evidence) and broad legal principles, are collectively called Sharia. After many years of education in a school of jurisprudence, Fadl (2006) reports that the scholars receive licences or permission (*ijazas*) from several established jurists before being accepted as jurists. Thus, the jurists are carefully trained to interpret the law and are thus nearly always well respected.

The jurisprudential tradition of interpretative law was challenged by the Hanabali jurist Ibn Taymiyya, who lived at a time of the Mongol conquest of the Abbasid Empire in 1258. Taymiyya blamed the fall of the Caliphate on a corruption in Islamic society brought on by interpretative and speculative readings and innovations (*bidah*) as opposed to what he viewed was the desirable method of a simple literal following of the Quran and the Sunnah. He wanted Muslims to restore the glory of Islam and the golden age when Prophet Muhammad and his four Companions ruled over Medina by following the pure form of Islam as represented in the Quran and the Sunnah and practised by the Prophet and his Companions. Taymiyya, thus, led the foundation for a revivalist movement that sought to go back to the fundamentals of the Quran for restoring the golden age of Islam, the *Salaf* (the ancient period when Prophet Muhammad and his four Companions ruled over Medina). This preaching of the *salaf* or *salafiyyah*, as it is called, is the core of the contemporary global Salafi jihad.

Inspired by Taymiyya, the opposition to jurists became a key component of the discourse of modern jihadi activists like Hasan al-Banna and Sayyid Qutb, who argued that the Companions drank from the pure spring of Quran and Hadith unlike subsequent generations who used mixed sources including, as Qutb (2007) writes, "Greek philosophy and logic, ancient Persian legends and their ideas, Jewish scriptures and traditions, other religions and civilizations" (p. 17). The jurists had tried to be creative and intellectual, argued the activists. Faraj (1986), one of the most influential of jihadi ideologues, describes, thus:

> The most reliable Speech is the Book of God, and the best guidance is the guidance of Muhammad, may God's peace be upon him. The worst of all things are novelties, since every novelty is an innovation (*bidah*) and every innovation is a deviation, and all deviation is in Hell. (p. 160)

The activists downplayed the need to seek the guidance of jurists since all can read the Quran and the Sunnah and can understand God's will and decide for themselves (though the activists miss no opportunity to selectively quote from jurists as authorities to support their own claims). They propose that, fundamentally, every individual is equally competent to understand God's will as expressed in the Quran and the Sunnah without unnecessary intellectualization. This readiness for anyone to interpret the *Hadith* and issue a *fatwa* (more so in the age of the Internet) is illustrated by Osama bin Laden and his likes. Bin Laden attended the Management and Economics School at King Abdulaziz University in Jeddah and his deputy al-Zawahiri was trained as a physician; neither had any formal jurisprudential training or the necessary license to issue any *fatwa*.

The literalist view of Islam undermined the guiding role of the jurists and the appropriation of the religious tradition by activists for the purpose of what Kepel (2006) has called "political Islam". The activists were not bound by jurisprudential traditions with regard to procedural law and legal principles like equity and greater public good. Fadl (2006) argues, the activists indulge in 'Hadith-hurling' i.e. widely quoting supporting precedents/traditions in a selective way without considering the broader jurisprudential principles to advocate violence, revenge and disruption; a process, he describes, as a "great theft" of the soul of Islam and a negation of what Islam fundamentally stands for: peace and brotherhood.

Qutb (2007) was opposed to the discourse in Islam being intellectualized, because Islam, he claimed, was for practical guidance that included a political programme. A Muslim was to translate Quranic instructions into action. He argued that the generations after the Companions used the "instruction for academic discussion and enjoyment" (p. 19). In short, Qutb and the activists advocate a philosophy of praxis more commonly associated with Italian Communist Antonio Gramsci (1995). Even before Qutb, Mawlana Mawdudi

(1903–1979), the founder of Jamaat-i-Islami in undivided India and Hasan al-Banna (1906–1949), the founder of the Muslim Brotherhood in Egypt had used Islam for advocating radical political action (Adams, 1983; Kepel, 2006).

As Nettler (1995) points out, the Wahhabi movement and the Saudi state that emerged from that movement have been deeply influenced by the ideas of Hanbali jurist Ibn Taymiyya, particularly the emphasis on a literalist interpretation of the Quran and the Sunnah and the conception of Medina as the model for an Islamic state or *salaf*. Hanbali is the official school of jurisprudence of the Saudi state. The Saudi political and religious elite use their financial power to export their ideas around the world. Osama bin Laden and the mujahedeens fighting in Afghanistan against the Soviet Union enjoyed patronage and official approval of the Saudi state and the Saudi religious elite. Saudi Arabia was also one of the three states to recognize and establish full diplomatic ties with the Taliban regime in Afghanistan; the other two countries being United Arab Emirates and Pakistan. The Wahhabis of Saudi Arabia have funded madrassas, mosques and academic activities to propagate their brand of Islam around the world. Wahhabism has been a clear foundation for militant jihad, though since about 1989, the Council of Senior Ulama of Saudi Arabia has issued *fatwas* supporting the views of the Saudi regime, who are now at odds with bin Laden over the stationing of American forces on Saudi soil in the wake of Operation Desert Storm (1990–91) and the latter has retaliated with *fatwas* issued under the auspices of the Advisory Reform Committee, based in London, declaring jihad against the religious-political elite of Saudi Arabia (Bin Laden, 2005).

The militant jihadis come from many Islamic streams and not only from Wahhabism. The Taliban grew out of the madrassa network of Darul Uloom Deoband, the largest Islamic seminary in the world based in India and Pakistan. Most of the Taliban cadres came from Deoband-affiliated madrassas in the north-west of Pakistan and believed in an extreme form of Deobandism preached in these madrassas and the training camps for Afghan mujahedeens (Rashid, 2002). The Taliban fugitive chief Mullah Umar and the chief of Pakistan-based Kashmiri jihadi group Jaish-e-Mohammad, Maulana Masud Azhar, were the product of the Binouri Madrassa in Karachi, which is the largest Deobandi madrassa in Pakistan. As discussed by Metcalf (1995) the Deobandi madrassas teach *hadith* and the Hanafi legal tradition, while adhering to Sufism for personal transformation with the help of spiritual guidance. But, Rashid (2002) is right in suggesting that the Taliban brand of Deobandism is a rather extreme example of Deobandi Islam.

The ideologues of militant jihad mostly come from the religio-political elite in society and are well educated and articulate. Mawdudi was an influential journalist and editor of *al-Jamiah*. Hasan al-Banna graduated from the Dar al-Ulum College in Cairo, much like Sayyid Qutb after him, and went on to become a well-respected teacher. Qutb was a senior official in the education department in Egypt. Dr Abdullah Azzam, the founder of al-Qaeda, had earned a doctorate in Islamic Jurisprudence from Egypt's al-Azhar university and was a Professor before joining jihad in Afghanistan against the Soviet Union. Osama bin Laden belonged to one of the richest families in the Middle East and went to the Management and Economics School at King Abdulaziz University in Jeddah. Al-Zawahiri went to the Medical School in Cairo University and was a trained physician. The jihadis come from different Islamic traditions, but agree on a simple literal following of the Quran and the Sunnah.

Establishing God's Rule and Destruction of Man-made Systems

The theological foundation of Islam is based on accepting the monotheistic declaration 'La ilha illa Allah' (There is no deity but God) (tawhid). This principle also means that rule and sovereignty or 'hakimiyah' belong only to God (la hukm wa la siyadah ila lillah). Qutb (2007), one of the most representative and influential activists, argues:

> The earth belongs to God and should be purified for Him unless the banner, 'No deity except God', is unfurled across the earth. Man is servant to God alone, and he can remain so only if he unfurls the banner ... no sovereignty except God's, no law except from God, and no authority of one man over another, as the authority in all respects belong to God. (p. 26)

The sacred law (the Sharia) embodies God's will and humans must completely and fully submit to the law. The consistent argument from Ibn Taymiyya to al-Zawahiri is that Muslims have been made weak because they have diverted from God's path, and allowed themselves to be ruled by Western, mixed and man-made laws, in effect, creating *jahili* societies that are ignorant of or have deviated from God's commandments. If Ibn Taymiyya blamed the fall of the Abbasid Empire on the lack of Quranic rule, the later activists blame the defeat in the Six-Day War with Israel in 1967 and the continued 'weakness' of the Muslim *ummah* on the failure to establish Sharia law and forge Muslim unity. They argue that there is no need for human laws since God has already expressed His will in the form of the Sharia and that the attempt by humans to give themselves a law is heretical and is against God's will. Only once a group of people who bow to God alone gain control over society (build a theocratic society) may they formulate practical laws. However, in no case is any rule by another human being or group of persons acceptable because that is *Shirk*, ascribing the attributes, power or authority of God to others besides Him and/ or worshipping others besides Him.

When a prime minister or president is duly elected, submitting to his rule will be *Shirk* and un-Islamic. A revolt against his rule will be an appropriate religious duty. A law cannot become legitimate because it is framed by representatives elected by a majority. Javid Iqbal (1983), explaining what he sees as the Islamic position on democracy, states "In an Islamic state the people are not vested with ultimate sovereignty" and "the only principle operative is the supremacy of Islamic law"(p. 253). Neither any majority nor any minority can have the power to make laws after God has expressed the law in no uncertain terms. Legitimacy belongs to God alone, not humans. The activists neither want Western-style democracy nor Western-style nation states as is brought out in the writings of Mawdudi and Qutb. They want a theocracy in the entire world where there is rule of the Sharia and all human relationships are based on equality subjugated to God alone.

The establishment of God's rule is opposed physically by the enemies of Islam and the goal is, as al-Zawahiri (2006, p. 135) explains, to "topple the Government and establish an Islamic state" and secondly, fight against "the Jewish-US alliance". This two-fold distinction between the enemies is integral to the jihadi rhetoric as is articulated in the writings of Faraj (1986), al-Zawahiri (2006) and others, and analysed by Marc Sageman (2004) amongst others. It is a distinction between firstly the foreign enemy, or 'far enemy': the Infidels (the Crusaders, Zionists and others) who occupy or colonize Muslim land and subjugate Muslims, or prop-up un-Islamic, apostate regimes by proxy; America being described as the 'head of the snake'. Secondly, the domestic apostate rulers, or 'near enemy', who prevent or fail to establish government by Islamic Sharia and collaborate with the Infidel Crusaders, the Zionists and others, repressing Muslims and disseminating Western values.

The early activists were focused on the 'far enemy' and 'imperialism'; but the later activists like Faraj (1986) argued:

> The basis of the existence of imperialism in the lands of Islam are (precisely) these rulers. To begin by putting an end to imperialism is not a laudatory and not a useful act. It is only a waste of time. We must concentrate on our own Islamic situation: we have to establish the Rule of God supreme ....
> There is no doubt that the first battlefield for *jihad* is the extermination of these infidel leaders and to replace them by a complete Islamic Order. From here we should start. (p. 193)

Faraj's (1986) monograph, *The neglected duty*, is a classic exposition of the shift in focus of the jihad movement for which the concept of *takfir* became central. *Takfir*, literally 'pronouncement of unbelief against someone' or loosely, excommunication, was justified on the ground that the domestic rulers had failed to establish *hakimiyah* or sovereignty of God, as explained by Ibraham Karawan (1995), Marc Sageman (2004), Gilles Kepel (2006) and others. This position was a reiteration of Qutb's (2007) characterization of contemporary Islamic society as un-Islamic and Mawdudi's (1998) argument that *hakimiyah* was the only legitimate system. Faraj (1986) argued that the domestic rulers were in apostasy and deserved to be killed.

A further principle derived from the abandonment of man-made systems is the desire to establish Islamic rule wherever possible as a springboard for spreading Islam to the rest of the world, if necessary through *hijra* (migration from a hostile un-Islamic *jahiliyyah* environment, as explained by Esposito (2002)). Many of the jihadis like bin Laden, al-Zawahiri and others migrated to other countries to establish Islamic rule.

The jihadi programme starts with the first objective of establishing a base in the heart of the Islamic world. Al-Zawahiri (2006) argues:

> Armies achieve victory only when the infantry takes hold of land. Likewise, the Mujaheed Islamic movement will not triumph against the world coalition unless it possesses a fundamentalist base in the heart of the Islamic world. (p. 214)

In a letter dated 11 October 2005 to al-Zarqawi, the former head of al-Qaeda in Iraq, al-Zawahiri lays down his programme for the Iraqi resistance in a letter:

> The first stage: Expel the Americans from Iraq.
> The second stage: Establish an Islamic authority or amirate, then develop it and support it until it achieves the level of a caliphate …
> The third stage: Extend the jihad wave to the secular countries neighbouring Iraq.
> The fourth stage: It may coincide with what came before: the clash with Israel, because Israel was established only to challenge any new Islamic entity. (pp. 255–256)

The only time the jihadis came close to pursuing their programme successfully was when they came to power in Afghanistan and Chechnya. The jihadi programme is the same whether it is for regional movements as in Chechnya, Kashmir and Algeria, or the heart of the struggle in Palestine and the Arabian peninsula: control a territory, establish Islamic rule in the territory and export jihad to the remaining part of the world until the rule of God and Sharia is established in the entire world and, as they see it, the 'struggle will continue till the day of the final judgment' i.e. for as long as it takes (e.g. Al-Zawahiri, 2006).

The Surrender of Rationality

The basis of Islamic law making is the well-recognized concept of '*ijtihad*', which means the exercise of independent judgment by a person with sufficient knowledge. The literalist interpretation limits the scope of independent judgment. As Fadl (2006) argues rhetorically, God gave human beings *aql*, the ability to reason. But, if the extremist view of Islamic law is to be accepted:

> God did not leave much space for human beings to apply their rational faculties since God unequivocally resolved most matters for human beings and all that is left is for humans to obey … it would make little sense for God to reward the effort, if all God expects of us on most matters is blind obedience … Muslims become like mechanized robots. (pp. 158–159)

The scope of law making is further limited by the desire to replicate the society of earlier times to the total exclusion of all contemporary systems since the latter embody human creativity and ingenuity. Nothing of the man-made traditions, institutions and the law can be salvaged, if they are contrary to the literalist interpretation of Islam. The *shura* system of theocratic government does not contain a detailed theory of governance and ends up at best as a just and benevolent dictatorship that functions through periodic consultation with a council of religious scholars. Moreover, the argument of an unlikely overthrow of all rules by humans, taken to its logical conclusion, can only lead to anarchy.

The moderates are concerned that extremists are projecting Islam as a system fundamentally against the universal values of democracy and human rights. Fadl (2006) argues that Islam is not opposed to democracy, human rights and a tolerant social culture. But, such reconciliation is possible only if Islam is interpreted keeping in mind the broader jurisprudential principles of equity, historical context and the best interests of human beings (*tahqiq masalih al-'ibad*). For moderate Muslims there is no reason to give up rationality, which formed the basis of a rich and varied jurisprudential tradition of interpretative law, in favour of a literalist construction of Islam which projects the universal values of democracy, human rights and moderation as un-Islamic.

Western Culture and *Jahiliya*

Jahiliya (Newby, 2006, p. 112) is often contrasted with the word Islam to mean all the values that are opposite to Islam, referring to the period before the rise of Islam; a state of ignorance of the divine commandments. It is the antonym of knowledge (*ilm*), good behaviour and kindness (*hilm*). Islam is expected to have a transformative effect on the believer so that the believer emerges from the state of *jahiliya* into a world of wisdom, knowledge and morality.

The state of affairs before Allah revealed the law to Prophet Muhammad was called *jihiliya*. Qutb (2007) used this Quranic concept to characterize not merely ancient times before Islam, but the contemporary world as well. So, both the non-Muslim and contemporary Muslim societies, he called *jahili*. When an individual becomes a believer he has to, Qutb argues, make a complete break from *jahiliya*. He has to accept divine law, oneness of God and complete submission to God. He cannot have compromises or 'give and take' with the *jahili* society. For Qutb the only source of culture, belief and practices has to be pure Quran without any dilution or influence, either Western or Oriental.

The view that there can be hybrids in the form of 'Islamic democracy' or 'Islamic socialism' or that with a slight change the current political and economic systems can become acceptable to Islam, to Qutb, are unnecessary attempts at appeasement, since no such compromise is possible. He argued that even the slightest non-Islamic influence can 'pollute the clear spring of Islam'. Islamic society requires a radical revolution – a clear break with current beliefs, culture and ways. People are not Muslims as long as they live the life of *jahiliya* even if they perform prayer five times a day, fast during Ramadan, offer *zakat* and perform Hajj. Qutb (2007) writes:

> Islam cannot accept any mixing with jahiliyyah, either in its concept or in the modes of living which are derived from this concept. Either Islam will remain, or jahiliyyah; Islam cannot accept or agree to a situation which is half-Islam and half-jahiliyyah …. Command belongs to God, or otherwise jahiliyyah; God's Shariah will prevail, or else people's desires. (p. 130)

Qutb, then goes on to say that "the foremost duty of Islam in this world is to depose jahiliyyah from the leadership of man, and to take the leadership into its own hands" (p. 131). The idea that Western society is superior to the Islamic society despite its *jahili* character is countered by Qutb:

> Look at this capitalism with its monopolies, its usury and whatever else is unjust in it; at this individual freedom, devoid of human sympathy and responsibility for relatives except under the force of law; at this materialistic attitude which deadens the spirit; at this behaviour, like animals, which you call 'free mixing of the sexes'; at this vulgarity which you call 'emancipation of women', which are contrary to the demands of practical life; and at Islam, with its logic, beauty, humanity and happiness, which reaches the horizons to which man strives but does not reach. (p. 139)

Qutb's arguments are nuanced when it comes to Western science and scholarship. Islamists accept that Muslim society needs to learn the pure sciences like physics, engineering, medicine, mathematics and biology in which the West has made significant progress. But Muslims must keep away from liberal arts like political science and philosophy, since they contain un-Islamic ideas and are sinful. They must even keep away from any aspect of science like

Darwinian theory of evolution and Freudian psychoanalysis which are not based on a strict empirical foundation and are opposed to Islamic beliefs.

Further, any learning on matters of faith, religion, morality and value must be from Muslims since the non-believers always conspire to turn the believer away from the latter's faith.

> Many among the People of the Book wish, through envy, to lead you back to unbelief. (Quran 2:109).
> You will please neither the Jews nor the Christians until you follow their faith. (Quran 2:120)

Qutb (2007) and other activists argue that Western science fought with the Church and therefore there is hostility between religion and science in the Western world, which is turning the West against Islam as well. But Islamic science is a part of faith and does not question faith.

The Islamists argue that there is a deliberate conspiracy for Western cultural invasion through art forms, fashion, media and the market, all of which are controlled by the West so that Muslims are separated from an appropriate puritanical cultural life. They fear that through these invasions the West will make sure that Muslim society cannot get away from *jahiliya* and will consequently remain weak and away from the *Salaf*. Muslim society must insulate itself from all such pernicious influences and cultural invasions.

As with other fundamentalist religions, such as ultra-orthodox Jews, or the Amish in Pennsylvania, the Islamists believe they must insulate Muslims from the global village by blocking TV channels, the Internet, most art forms and by ensuring 'intellectual insularity'. Fadl (2006) argues that the extremists have a desire just to be different as a way of assertion against modernity. For example, toothpaste is un-Islamic, which puritans claim, should not be used because Prophet Muhammad did not use it. The logic is Muslims must do everything possible to maintain a separate identity. The Islamists alienate themselves from modernity by imagining a perfect past. Fadl (2006) writes: "The more alienating modernity became, the more they idealized the past; and more idealized the past, the more undesirable the modern age became" (p. 174).

Dealing with Non-believers

The second part of the declaration '*La ilha illa Allah*' (There is no deity except Allah) is the declaration '*Muhammadar Rasul Allah*' (Muhammad is the Messenger of God). Muslims believe that Allah sent 124,000 prophets for guidance ending with Prophet Muhammad with whom the chain of prophethood and messengership ends and religion stands perfected for the entire universe. Like the great majority of religions Islam claims the only way to salvation. Therefore, it is said that people guided by the Abrahamic prophets like Moses and David and Jesus should convert to Islam and follow the latest and the best law rather than old laws that stand abrogated by the will of God. The only way to save non-Muslims and Muslims who do not practice Islam from being damned is to convert both to true Islam and make them follow the Sharia.

Activists like Qutb, Faraj and others use the believer–non-believer dichotomy to turn the world into one of permanent conflict and war and this dichotomy lies at the core of the jihadi rhetoric. A territory in which Islamic rule is established (rule of the Sharia) becomes the abode of Islam or *dar al-Islam* and the rest of the world is *dar al-Harb* or *dar al-Kafir* (the abode of infidels). So long as Sharia rule is not established even a Muslim land cannot be called *dar al-Islam*.

A Muslim can have only two relationships with *dar al-Harb*: peace with a contractual agreement or war. But even peace with contractual agreement ends on an agreed date or because of violation of contractual obligations, thereafter the relationship is only of war. A non-Muslim, if he declines to accept Islam will be given a different status as a citizen called *dhimma* status. He will not be entitled to hold senior posts in the government or the army, his place of worship will be lower than a mosque and he will pay a poll tax, called *jijiya*, though he will be exempt from paying *Zakat*, which will be compulsory for Muslims. If he refuses to be converted to Islam or violates his *dhimma* status he will be at war with the Islamic state.

Moderates like Fadl (2006) argue that the Quran does not dichotomize the world into *dar al-Islam* and *dar al-Harb*. The only distinction made is between the abode of the hereafter and the abode of earthly life. In fact, the moderates cite a set of verses from the Quran that talk about respect for people of the scriptures (Christianity, Judaism), often referred to as *Salam* verse,

> Be courteous when you argue with the People of the Book, except with those among them who do evil. Say: 'We believe in that which has been revealed to us and which was revealed to you. Our God and your God is one. To Him we submit. (Quran 29:46)

In case of any disagreement with people of other faiths, Muslims should act to assure their opponents that their disagreement is not personal, and that Muslims do not bear a grudge or enmity toward their opponent and the appropriate response is to wish their opponents the bliss of peace (Quran 25:63; 28:55; 43:89).

As argued by Fadl (2006) and the moderates, the Quran does not preclude the possibility that peoples of other faith, who adhere to their religion, may also attain salvation and does not support any arrogance on the part of Muslims in dealing with non-Muslims. The dispute, if any, is to be resolved by God and not humans:

> It is no concern of yours whether He will forgive or punish them. They are the wrongdoers ... He pardons whom He will and punishes whom He pleases. God is forgiving and merciful. (Quran 3:128–29)

The reaction of the jihadis to the moderation of the *Salam* verses is to recite the first part of the sword verse:

> When the sacred months are over, slay the idolaters wherever you find them. Arrest them, besiege them, and lie in ambush everywhere for them. (Quran 9:5)

The sword verse is frequently quoted by the jihadis to justify killing of non-Muslims on the grounds of faith alone. The second part of the verse, which they do not quote, says "If they repent and take to prayer and render the alms levy, allow them to go their way. God is forgiving and merciful."

There are many religions that call upon their believers to take to proselytizing, but in modern times no one talks about proselytizing with a sword. Islam also has a set of verses that advocate toleration:

> Believers, Jews, Sabaeans and Christians – whoever believes in God and the Last Day and does what is right – shall have nothing to fear or regret. (Quran 5:69)

A large number of other verses in the Quran advocate toleration and respect for people of other religious faith (e.g. Quran 2:62, 22:34, 3:199), but the jihadis disregard these verses or claim that they are not relevant to our times and have been 'abrogated' by God during jihad. Fadl (2006) argues that anything the jihadis find inconsistent with their rhetoric is dismissed so that they can avoid responsibility for acting in a manner inconsistent with the Quran. The Quran contains both the sword verses and the *salam* verses and it is a matter of emphasis and interpretation by believers, which one to advocate.

Status of Women

The coming to power of the Taliban regime in Afghanistan unveiled to the world one of the worst forms of patriarchy and forced segregation of women. The jihadis had shown how women are treated in the righteous Islamic State under the rule of the Sharia and the Muslim *ulama*. The status of women in Afghanistan under the Taliban, which pursued an extreme form of Deobandism, was very close to the puritanical Wahhabi conservative standpoint on women, though the Taliban took the puritanical logic to hitherto unseen extremes. The main features of the extremist position on women are:

Firstly, God favoured men and women unequally since He wanted them to perform different duties in life. Any violation of the principle of inequality is a rebellion against God. God favoured men more than women and women should accept their status as the will of God.

Secondly, while equality is denied to women, dignity and justice are ensured.

Thirdly, women are inherently seductive and unless men are protected from being seduced by women and vice versa, moral fabric in society will be torn apart or there will be what is called *fitnah* in society. *Fitnah* refers to a state of discord and also a trial or temptation that takes believers away from the ways of God. Unless men are protected from sexual lust they will be seduced and land up in hell. So, to protect men from being damned restrictions have to be imposed on women and on inter-mixing of sexes. Thus, by wearing the *hijab* and keeping away from the public, women can be protected from the lustful eyes of men and from being exposed to molestation and rape. Respect for women requires women not becoming objects of lust and desire for men other than their husbands by maintaining modesty in clothing and manners. These ideas connect with the view that family is the basis of society and the basis of the family is the division of labour between husband and wife. There is no greater work for women than bringing up children for which God specifically favoured women. Looking after children is the duty God gave to women and they must perform this duty faithfully.

The jihadi discourse claims moral superiority of Islamic society for the greater respect that women receive and for the preserving of family as an institution for the moral upbringing of society. Qutb (2007) claims:

> ... if the relationship between man and woman is based on lust, passion and impulse, and the division of work is not based on family responsibility and natural gifts; if woman's role is merely to be attractive, sexy and flirtatious, and if woman is freed from her basic responsibility of bringing up children; and if, on her own or under social demand, she prefers to become a hostess or a stewardess in a hotel or ship or air company, thus spending her ability for material productivity rather than in the training of human beings, ... then such a civilization is backward from the human point of view, or '*jahili*' in the Islamic terminology. (p. 98)

Much of the conservative view on the status of women is influenced by the preaching of Abd al-Wahhab (1703–1791) and subsequent generations of Wahhabi Mullahs. The rhetoric is a compilation of all that can be said demeaning women: confining them to the home, placing them under the veil and justifying the dominance of their male relatives. These practices are regarded as essential to maintain the moral fabric of society.

On the other hand, the view of moderates like Fadl (2006) on the role of woman is to understand Islam in its historical context as a reform movement and to say that there is no restriction on further reform consistent with the essential principles of Islam as a religion that cares for humanity and strives for morality and beauty. They argue that one of the first acts of the Prophet was the prohibition of female infanticide. But, generally women were given various rights as a response to demands raised by them before Prophet Muhammad during the course of the latter's leadership over the *umma*.

Many of these changes were revolutionary in the medieval historical context. For example, in place of maintaining harems, men were asked not to marry more than four women. Buying and selling of women was declared immoral and sexual desires were brought within the institution of family for the stated reason of providing women with greater economic security. Women were given maintenance rights. '*Idda*' (the waiting period for a woman after divorce before she can remarry) was limited to twice, i.e. men can no longer make women wait more than twice before re-marrying. The purpose of the reform measures was to ensure that women are not repressed and are allowed to pursue the ways of God. Whenever women raised issues of repression before Prophet Muhammad he responded in a manner to stop repression. Several verses in the Quran make clear that men and women are to be treated as equal (Quran 3:195, 4:124, 16:97, 33:35, 40:40, 49:13, etc.).

> Those who submit to God and accept true Faith; who are devout, sincere, patient, humble, charitable, and chaste; who fast and are ever mindful of God – on these, both men and women, God will bestow forgiveness and a rich recompense. (Quran 33:35)

To the extremists' claim that the Islamic state should compel and coerce all women to wear the veil and maintain modesty, the moderates argue that the veil is not Islamically mandated. It should be a woman's autonomous decision whether to wear the veil or not, and that her choice should be respected. The Quran preaches that there ought to be no compulsion in religion. Toleration is fundamental to Islam. The use of force to segregate women, preventing them from a basic education or prohibiting them from contributing to productive activity are all 'compulsions' and hence not Islamic.

It is nonetheless misleading to suggest that the moderates have a totally Western egalitarian view of women. They still expect women to maintain a level of modesty and family value, but they do not want to keep women away from education and the workplace. They cite the case of Aisha, one of Prophet Muhammad's wives who led troops into battle and played an important role in interpreting the religion after the death of the Prophet. Even though polygamy is permitted in the Quran in the context of a warring medieval society, with the condition that a man must be able to afford it, polygamy is neither mandatory nor a religious duty. Tunisia has made polygamy illegal on Islamic grounds, i.e. Islam's egalitarian core, and Turkey has banned it as part of secularism and modernity. Most other Muslim societies have used various religious interpretations to restrict polygamy, though they have not been able to declare it illegal altogether like Tunisia and Turkey.

Jihad and Terrorism

The revival of the *Salaf*, the establishment of the rule by the Sharia, the clear break from *jahiliya*, overthrowing the rule by humans, are the duty of all human beings on whose behalf a vanguard assumes responsibility. The preferred method of the vanguard is *dawah* (peaceful missionary preaching) so that people can be transformed out of *jahiliya* to accept the rule of God alone. But *dawah* threatens the established domestic as well as international order, making repression of the vanguard inevitable. The jihadis argue that even when the vanguard has an electoral victory as with al-Gama'a al-Islamiyya in Algeria in 1992 or Hamas' victory in the 2006 Palestine election; it will not be accepted by the world order. Thus, a pre-requisite for the revival of the *Salaf* is the annihilation of all physical opposition from: (a) domestic apostate rulers repressing the vanguard; (b) infidels sponsoring the apostate regimes by proxy or by occupation; and (c) the Crusaders, the Zionists and others who have declared war against the Muslim *ummah*. So, in defence the vanguard has to fight against all oppositions and launch an armed struggle, which they call 'jihad' using a Quranic concept.

The initial focus of the jihad movement was the 'defence of Muslim Land' from occupation by non-Muslims. Dr Abdullah Azzam (2008), Jordanian religious scholar of Palestinian descent and founder of al-Qaeda and one of the founders of Hamas, who is generally described as the "Emir or Godfather of global jihad" (Esposito, 2002, p. 7), issued a *fatwa* against the Russians after they invaded Afghanistan in 1979 titled "Defence of the Muslim Lands: the first obligation after *Iman*". *Iman* refers to "both an inner state" and an "outward expression" as a "proof of faith" (Newby, 2006, p. 100). Azzam's *fatwa* was supported by Abd al-Aziz bin Baaz, then Chief Mufti of the Council of Senior Ulama of Saudi Arabia. So, jihad is a fundamental religious duty of all Muslims, almost a sixth pillar of faith. Azzam (2008) starts his *fatwa* with a quotation from Ibn Taymiyya: "The first obligation after *Iman* is the repulsion of the enemy aggressor who assaults the religion and the worldly affairs" (p. 1).

The position that jihad is a duty to fight foreign occupation, as argued by Azzam, is different from the primary focus of the Egyptian groups like the Egyptian Islamic Jihad and Egyptian Islamic Group on the apostasy of domestic rulers and *takfir*. Faraj, for example, in *The neglected duty*, extensively quotes

Ibn Taymiyya's *fatwas* to declare war against the Egyptian regime. He finds the current rulers no different from the invading Mongols that Taymiyya was concerned about. Faraj (1986) writes:

> The Rulers of this age are in apostasy from Islam. They were raised at the tables of imperialism, be it Crusaderism, or Communism, or Zionism. They carry nothing from Islam but their names, even though they pray and fast and claim to be Muslims .... It is a well-established rule of Islamic law that the punishment of an apostate will be heavier than the punishment of an infidel .... For instance, an apostate has to be killed in all circumstances .... The Mongols and their likes – the equivalent of our rulers today .... Whosoever doubts whether they should be fought is more ignorant of the religion of Islam. (p. 169)

Osama bin Laden and the al-Qaeda were influenced by the Egyptian groups and the latter's ideologues like Qutb and Faraj. Osama bin Laden's 23 August1996 *fatwa* titled "Expel the Polytheists from the Arabian peninsula" includes *takfir* and apostasy of the domestic rulers as the first justification and allowing the occupation by infidels as the second justification for jihad against the Saudi regime. Bin Laden (2005) gives the following justification:

1. Its suspension of the rulings of the Islamic law and replacement thereof with man-made laws, and its entering into a bloody confrontation with the righteous scholars and pious youth. May God sanctify whom He pleases.
2. Its inability to protect the land and its allowing the enemies of God to occupy it for years in the form of the American Crusaders, who have become the principal reason for all aspects of our land's disastrous predicament. (p. 28)

Jihad against the Infidels is based on the dichotomous division of the world, into two perennially warring abodes: the abode of Islam (*dar al-Islam*) and the abode of the Infidels (*dar al-Harb*), and people into believers and non-believers. This dichotomous division, as explained by Fadl (2006), is derived not from the Quran or the Sunnah, but from the work of classical Islamic jurists, who came up with this distinction to deal with the requirements of a medieval world where countries in Europe, the Middle East and Asia went to war routinely, signed peace treaties and plundered the weak. Some classical jurists even thought up other abodes like the abode of non-belligerence or neutrality (*dar al-sulh*, or *al-'ahd*) and *the* abode of justice (*dar al-'adl*). But, these divisions, relevant to medieval times, have become the basis for declaring jihad against non-believers in the modern world.

The jihadi view on the sword verse urging the killing of non-believers on the grounds of faith alone is in disregard of the *Salam* verses that preach toleration and peace. Islam regards killing of one human being as the killing of the entire humanity and, as with the Old Testament, proclaims that saving the life of one is saving the life of all humanity (Quran 5:32). The holy Quran says:

> Show forgiveness, speak for justice, and avoid the ignorant. (Quran 7:199)

Fadl (2006) argues that the jihadis "entirely ignore the Quranic teaching that the act of destroying or spreading ruin on this earth is one of the gravest sins possible – *fasad fi al-ard*, which means to corrupt the earth by destroying the beauty of creation" (p. 237). Even going by the jihadi logic it is expected that non-believers have to be given the option of conversion or accepting *dhimma* status, before declaring an offensive jihad.

The primary focus of the jihad against the Infidels is the state of Israel, which is said to have been created as part of a conspiracy to perpetually occupy Palestine, specifically Jerusalem and the al-Aqsa Mosque. The defeats of the Arab world in the wars against Israel in 1948 was projected by Hasan al-Banna, the founder of the Muslim brotherhood, as resulting from weakness of the Muslim *ummah* because of not following the true Islam of Prophet Muhammad and his Companions. The defeat in the Six-Day War in 1967 of the combined forces of Egypt, Syria, Jordan and Iraq at the hands of Israel marked a decisive shift in the polemics of the jihadi movement. Firstly, the claim of the Arab nationalists that they were prepared to "throw Israel and those behind Israel into the sea" (al-Zawahiri, 2006, p. 64) the third time there was a war (the first two wars were in 1948 and 1956) came to be ridiculed by the jihadi ideologues, who also argued that peace efforts with Israel would be futile. In Azzam's words: "Jihad and the rifle alone: no negotiations, no conferences, and no dialogues" (quoted in Esposito, 2002, p. 7).

The government of Gamal Abdel Nasser had in the mid-1960s arrested activists of the Muslim Brotherhood in their thousands and executed its top leaders like Qutb in order to suppress the Islamic activists. After the war Nasser was discredited on the Arab streets and blamed for the defeat. The jihadis like al-Zawahiri (2006) claim "the death of abd-al-Nasir … was also the death of his principles" (p. 51). Anwar Sadat, after succeeding Nasser, released many of the Islamic activists and tried to appease the Islamists by projecting himself as the 'Believer President'. But, subsequently Sadat signed a peace treaty with the state of Israel with the mediation of the Americans (the Camp David peace deal, 1979). There were several attempts by the activists to capture power and create an Islamic state in Egypt as part of which Sadat was assassinated on 6 October 1981. Since then the Egyptian state has left no stone unturned in suppressing the jihadis and even the Egyptian Islamic Jihad has now made peace with the Egyptian regime. But the anti-Zionist character continues to be fundamental in the justification of jihad against the Infidels.

The initial rhetoric against the West was that the West had created and supported Israel. The situation changed when the Soviet Union occupied

Afghanistan. Jihadis from all over the Arab world reached Pakistan and joined the Afghan war in the 'jihad to defend Muslim land'. For a while the West was not the principal focus. Once the jihadis defeated a superpower with the largest ground force and American forces made a hasty retreat in Somalia in 1993, the jihadis claimed that God was on their side. The regional movements in Israel, Kashmir, Morocco, Sudan, Chechnya, Indonesia, etc. were now intensified. For the jihadis the world was their stage, they had arrived and the war was now against the world order led by "the United States and the global Jewish Government" (al-Zawahiri, 2006, p. 125).

In 1998 bin Laden and others issued a *fatwa* (Bin Laden, 2005) which is significant not merely because it provided a broad base for the jihadi movement by the creation of the World Islamic Front for Jihad against the Jews, Crusaders and others, but also because it made a case for an all-out, unrestricted offensive war, moving beyond the notion of jihad to defend Muslim land. The *fatwa* begins with the sword verse and goes on to state the most aggressive intent:

> To kill the Americans and their allies – civilians and military – is an individual duty incumbent upon every Muslim in all countries, in order to liberate the al-Aqsa Mosque and the Holy Mosque from their grip, so that their armies leave all the territory of Islam, defeated, broken, and unable to threaten any Muslim. This is in accordance with the words of God Almighty. (bin Laden, 2005, p. 61)

The killing of civilians/non-combatants: women, even people of old age and children, almost any one, can now be part of jihad. The argument, as al-Zawahiri (2006) makes clear is that civilians have willingly voted for their governments and are accountable for the misdeeds of their governments. Further, civilians pay taxes that fund the so-called 'war against terror' and occupation of Muslim lands that has led to the death and repression of Muslim men, women and children. Al-Qaeda's further justification, as best represented in the writings of al-Zawahiri (2006), is "the need to inflict the maximum casualties against the opponent, for this is the language understood by the West, no matter how much time and effort such operations take" (p. 223). Beginning with the notion of jihad to defend Muslim land the rhetoric now is for an all-out, no-holds-barred offensive jihad 'to kill the Americans and their allies – civilians and military' and to take revenge for Muslim deaths, without any further conditionality or limitation. This killing is declared a religious duty.

The call for jihad, including the so-called martyrdom missions (generally called suicide missions) also involves the fulfilment of the personal desire to make one eligible for God's munificence. A death for an Islamic cause, jihadis argue, entitles a believer to privileges and rights. Since death is unavoidable, it is preferable that a believer dies fighting for Islam and receives the rewards of

God rather than waiting for death to come on its own. In fact, the martyr does not die and is treated with care and respect in God's garden. Among the verses of the Quran quoted frequently by the jihadis are the following:

> Never think that those who were slain in the cause of God are dead. They are alive, and well provided for by their Lord; pleased with His gifts and rejoicing that those they left behind, who have not yet joined them, have nothing to fear or regret; rejoicing in God's grace and bounty. God will not deny the faithful their reward. (Quran 3:169–171)

The martyrs are treated with milk, honey and grapes and enjoy eternal youth with virgins (Quran 55:54–56; 56:12–39). The jihadis justify their activities in the name of defending Islam; at the same time it becomes an individual religious duty, which will entitle the jihadi to the benefits of God's generosity and the promised heaven. The critique of the jihadi articulation by the moderates is not the secular rationalist assertion that there is no evidence for life after death or that there is no heaven. The moderates argue that the activists have no competence to issue *fatwa* and that global jihad has no Islamic justification. Further, accepting someone in heaven is a decision that can be taken by God alone in the Hereafter and that there are several ways to attain the garden and jihad is not the only way. Fadl (2006) argues that the Quran uses the term *qital* to describe war, which can never be holy; it is either justified or unjustified. But, either way, war is not a desirable activity. The Quran teaches peace and moderation, tolerance and the avoidance of war. There are many verses in the Quran that preach peace and toleration rather than war and bloodshed. The Quran says:

> If they incline to peace, make peace with them, and put your trust in God. (Quran 8:61)

In fact, moderate jurists like Fadl (2006) contend that Islamic law treats attacks on non-combatants in order to terrorize, including kidnapping, hostage taking, mutilation and torture, as the crime of *hiraba* (waging war against society) which is specifically prohibited. "In the modern age", Fadl writes, "terrorism is the quintessential crime of corrupting the earth" (p. 237).

Recent Developments

The jihadi objective is still the establishment of a Muslim state in the heart of the Islamic world, and to progressively revive the fallen Caliphate and the glory of the *Salaf*. However, the focus of the movement has shifted away from the 'near' enemy to the 'far' enemy. As al-Zawahiri (2006) writes,

The Crusaders alliance led by the United States will not allow any Muslim force to reach power in the Arab countries .... Confining the battle to the domestic enemy, (within the Arab states), will not be feasible in this stage of the battle" (p. 201).

Jihad is now projected as a universal battle against the United States and its allies, Israel, Russia, India and international organizations like the United Nations, the Western multinational corporations, the international communications and data exchange systems, the international news agencies and satellite channels and even international relief agencies (al-Zawahiri, 2006, p. 201). Moreover, contemporary jihad makes no distinction between combatants and non-combatants despite the view of a majority of Muslim scholars that Islam cannot be interpreted to justify such an unlimited and universal terrorist movement, particularly indiscriminate killing of civilians.

The focus on the far enemy is a result of the US-led 'global war on terror' as much as a realization that global jihad now faces domestic opposition. The Council of Senior Ulama of Saudi Arabia, headed by the former Chief Mufti bin Baaz, was targeted for condemnation by Osama bin Laden in a statement issued on 29 December 1994, in which bin Laden accuses bin Baaz of allowing state repression and further that "this has not only happened in your knowledge and with your silence, but as a result of your judicial decrees" (Bin Laden, 2005, p. 5). Bin Laden and al-Qaeda continue to fight the Saudi regime and the Saudi Wahhabi religious elite.

In Egypt imprisoned leaders of al-Gama'a al-Islamiyya or in short Jamma Islamiyya (Egyptian Islamic Group), which began a violent campaign in the 1970s based on the concept of *takfir* and whose leader Abu-Yasir Rifai Ahmad Taha was one of the signatories to the 1998 *fatwa* forming the World Islamic Front (Bin Laden, 2005, p. 69), denounced violence in 1997 and announced a unilateral cessation to violent operations on religious grounds (al-Zawahiri, 2006; Sageman, 2004). The Jamma had carried out large-scale violent attacks in the 1990s resulting in the imprisonment of more than 20,000 activists. The Egyptian Government refused to enter into any dialogue with the Jamma, which was crippled by the imprisonment of its top leaders and migration of many out of Egypt. But, over a period of time the peace initiative has produced an active theological dialogue, particularly with the Azhari seminary. In 2001–2002 the Jamma published a series of four books entitled 'Correction of Understanding', which lay down the foundation of what is called a 'new theology' that supports a non-violent approach to Islamic movements (Salwa, 2006). As might be expected, former Egyptian jihadi leaders like al-Zawahiri (2006) have criticized the peace initiative.

After 2001, Pakistan, a country ruled for a long time by a military-mullah alliance and supporting jihad in Afghanistan and Kashmir, joined the US-led war on terror. The jihadis, in retaliation, have carried out three unsuccessful attempts to kill General Musharaf and have started a violent campaign against the security forces, particularly in the north-western tribal areas, now under the control of the Pakistani Taliban. The moderate parties have come together to partially restore democracy and to fight terrorism; in the process Benazir Bhutto was killed. The religious political parties were routed in the 2008 Pakistan general elections.

On 25 February 2008 the Darul Uloom Deoband, the largest Islamic seminary in the world, held an anti-terrorism conference, which was attended by 6,000 Deobandi *Imams*. At the end of the conference the Deobandis issued a *fatwa* stating that terrorism is not Islamic:

> Islam is the religion of mercy for all humanity. It is the fountainhead of eternal peace, tranquillity, security. Islam has given so much importance to human beings that it regards the killing of a single person the killing of the entire humanity, without differentiation based on creed and caste. Its teaching of peace encompasses all humanity. Islam has taught its followers to treat all mankind with equality, mercy, tolerance, justice. Islam sternly condemns all kinds of oppression, violence and terrorism. It has regarded oppression, mischief, rioting and murdering among the severest sins and crimes. (Declaration of All India Anti-Terrorism Conference, p. 1)

Conservative Islam was never the favoured religion of the masses, who were condemned as '*jahils*' (ignorant people) by the elite. Consider the following examples. Fundamentalists prohibit all forms of singing and dancing. Watching TV is considered un-Islamic except when Islam is being preached. Reading a story book or watching a play or a movie is un-Islamic since they are lies. Offering a flower to a lady is un-Islamic. Standing up in honour of someone is un-Islamic since no one except God should be honoured. Muslims are forbidden from clapping since no one except God should be praised. Celebrating a birthday, including that of Prophet Muhammad is prohibited. Masses of Muslims do not conform to the puritanical standards of the extremists and go about life with ease. Many subscribe to highly tolerant versions of *Sufi* Islam.

The politico-religious elite represented by the *ulama*, the academia, the political dispensation and the armies, be it in Saudi Arabia, Egypt or Pakistan, all have now distanced themselves from the jihadi articulation of Islam. The Wahhabis, the Azharis and the Deobandis, though essentially conservatives, denounce the jihadi interpretations and espousal of violence. There are many possible ways of interpreting Islam. The global jihadi version is one particular interpretation that originated in a particular theological, geo-political and historical context. But, the issue is why some individuals find the jihadi version attractive even when they have many other alternative ways of making sense of Islamic faith and identity.

Concluding Considerations

As with all fundamentalist interpretations of faith, or faith-like ideologies, there are profound paradoxes and internal contradictions in the global jihadi perspective. It claims to be based on a direct reading of the sacred texts, unhindered by intellectualization, but requires that it is the interpretation and *fatwas* issued by jihadi leaders that are to be taken as offering the true meaning of the Quran. The arguments are defended by reference to the 'sword verses' in the Quran, but disregard the 'peace verses'. Many aspects of Western scholarship and science are decried, but those that can be directly used for military benefit are accepted. The interpretations of the Quran that assign women and non-believers to inferior status are accepted but the principles of Quranic jurisprudence that recognize human rights and equality are ignored. Religious objectives are interpreted as geo-political goals.

Perhaps of most significance in our secular, non-intellectual age is that the arguments for violence and destruction are played out in the rhetoric of religious discussions that are rooted in the interpretation of early mediaeval texts. The parallels to the debates of the Spanish Inquisition, or the Talmudic discussions that laid the groundwork for Judaism in the Middle Ages, are everywhere to be seen, with the exception that those essentially European debates were founded in a confident acceptance that they were the world order, rather than the search to return to an earlier world order hundreds of years later, which seems to be the essence of present-day jihadism.

The general upsurge in fundamentalism across many religions over the last quarter of a century, in parallel with the demise of the great atheistic ideologies like communism, has been widely documented. It is reflected, to take two well-known examples, in the spread of creationism across Christian groups and the growth in ultra-orthodox communities in Israel. But what singles the jihadi movement out from all of these is its embrace of violence with the aim of comprehensively changing the character of the state and the world order into a basically theocratic global system. Other religious movements are possibly concerned with transforming individuals or even working as an effective pressure group within the system to advance a set of policy objectives using peaceful or democratic methods. The identification of the weakness of Arab nations in the face of Western military prowess as being due to a lack of following of proper Islamic principles seems to be a crucial aspect of the central militancy of the jihadi belief system. It is interesting to note that those Muslim states that are gaining in self-confidence are the ones leading the challenge to the rhetoric of the sword verses.

Religion has different degrees of impact on day-to-day life in modern society. Muslim societies are possibly influenced by religion far more than the modern Western societies. But, to be religious or even Islamic is one thing;

advocating jihad is entirely another. We have argued that it is possible for a Muslim to pursue alternative ways of understanding Islam while keeping a safe distance from global jihad. The question therefore arises as to why the followers of violent jihad apparently accept the arguments and *fatwas* of the activists when many alternatives are open to them? Is the answer to be found in some other more personal processes (e.g. the influence of tribal customs of taking revenge) that are mediating the interpretations and the acceptance? And are these psychological processes what we should be considering? We need to have a clear grasp of the personal as well as rhetorical issues in thinking about any process of disengagement.

References

Adams, C. J. (1983). Mawdudi and the Islamic State. In J. L. Esposito (Ed.), *Voices of resurgent Islam*. New York: Oxford University Press.

Al-Zawahiri, A. (2006). *His own words* (Trans. Laura Mansfield). USA: TLG Publications.

Azzam, A. (2008). *Defence of the Muslim land: The first obligation after Iman*. Retrieved April 21, 2008 from www.religioscope.com/info/doc/jihad/azzam_defence_1_table.htm

Bin Laden, O. (2005). *Messages to the world: The statements of Osama bin Laden*, edited and introduced by Bruce Lawrence. London: Verso.

Coulson, N. J. (1994). *A history of Islamic law*. Edinburgh: Edinburgh University Press.

Esposito, J. L. (2002). *Unholy war: Terror in the name of Islam*. Oxford: Oxford University Press.

Fadl, K. A. (2006). *The great theft: Wrestling Islam from the extremists*. New Delhi: HarperCollins Publishers India.

Faraj, A. A. (1986). *The neglected duty*. New York: Macmillan Publishing Company.

Gramsci, A. (1995). *Further selections from the prison notebooks*. London: Lawrence & Wishart.

Gunaratna, R. (2002). *Inside Al-Qaeda: Global network of terror*. London: C. Hurst & Co. (Publishers) Ltd.

Huntington, S. P. (1998). *The clash of civilizations and the remaking of the world order*. London: Touchstone Books.

Iqbal, J. (1983). Democracy and the Modern Islamic State. In J. L. Esposito (Ed.), *Voices of resurgent Islam*. Oxford: Oxford University Press.

Karawan, I. A. (1995). Takfir. In J. L. Esposito (Ed.), *The Oxford encyclopaedia of the modern Islamic world* (Vol. 4, pp. 178–179). New York: Oxford University Press.

Kepel, G. (2006). *The trail of political Islam*. London: I. B. Tauris & Co. Ltd.

Mawdudi, S. A. (1998). *Jihad in Islam*. Pakistan: Islamic Publication (Pvt.) Limited.

Metcalf, B. D. (1995). Deobandis. In J. L. Esposito (Ed.), *The Oxford encyclopaedia of the modern Islamic world* (Vol. 1, pp. 362–363). New York: Oxford University Press.

Nettler, R. L. (1995). Ibn Taymiyah, Taqi al-din Ahmed. In J. L. Esposito (Ed.), *The Oxford encyclopaedia of the modern Islamic world* (Vol. 2, pp. 165–166). New York: Oxford University Press.

Newby, G. D. (2006). *Concise encyclopaedia of Islam*. Oxford: Oxford University Press.

Qutb, S. (2007). *Milestones*. New Delhi: Islamic Book Service.

Rashid, A. (2002). *Taliban: Islam, oil and the new great game in Central Asia*. London: I. B. Tauris & Co. Ltd.

Sageman, M. (2004). *Understanding terror networks*. Philadelphia: University of Pennsylvania Press.

Salwa, E. (2006). *The militant Islamic group in Egypt (1974–2004)*. Cairo: Maktabat al-Shuruq al-Duwaliyya.

Schacht, J. (1991). *An introduction to Islamic law*. Oxford: Oxford University Press.

Ziadeh, F. J. (1995). Sunni School of Law. In J. L. Esposito (Ed.), *The Oxford encyclopaedia of the modern Islamic world* (Vol. 2, pp. 456–462). New York: Oxford University Press.

Statements

Declaration of All India Anti-Terrorism Conference, Darul Uloom Deoband, 25 February 2008. Retrieved April 30, 2008 from www.indianmuslims.info/documents/declaration_all_india_anti_terrorism_conference.html

4

Case study – The Puzzling Case (from a Western Perspective) of Lone Terrorist Faheem Khalid Lodhi

Clive Williams

Synopsis: Lone terrorists will continue to pose a challenge for intelligence analysts, particularly before they perpetrate an offence. The main lead to these types of individuals will come from their contact with others, behavioural patterns and attempts to purchase or access terrorism-related materials. This article examines the case of Australian citizen Faheem Khalid Lodhi to consider whether there are indicators that might alert us in the future to similar-minded individuals. A major concern from a counterterrorism point of view is that it took several years from the time of radicalization for Lodhi to be identified as a potential terrorist threat to Australia.

Introduction

In August 2006 Pakistani immigrant Faheem Khalid Lodhi, who had earlier been convicted in Sydney, Australia, of three terrorism-related offences, received a sentence of 20 years' imprisonment. Prior to his arrest in April 2004, Lodhi had no recorded convictions, either in Australia or Pakistan.

Throughout the lead-up to the trial, and subsequently, people expressed surprise that a professional migrant like Lodhi, with good prospects and everything that most Australians value to live for, would want to risk it all by engaging in terrorism. (More recently, the cases of the attempted London bombings and the Glasgow airport attack have involved immigrant or visiting professionals, also with similar excellent prospects.)

The Faces of Terrorism: Multidisciplinary Perspectives Edited by David Canter
© 2009 John Wiley & Sons Ltd.

Lodhi's case certainly goes against our experience of previous migrants to Australia. Often fleeing from turmoil or security threats in their home countries, they were keen to build a new life for themselves and their children. Countries of origin in the past 30 or so years have included Pakistan, Vietnam, Lebanon, South Africa, the Balkans and Zimbabwe.

Post-1990, with the rise of militant Islam, problems have sometimes arisen in Australia with the Islamic sons of migrants, particularly after they have been radicalized by charismatic preachers, or been back to their parents' home countries, such as Pakistan or Lebanon. There have also been problems with some poorly educated first generation migrants to Australia who have found it difficult to obtain employment other than menial work.

This article focuses on the case of Lodhi, and examines indicators that might lead to early identification of a potential security threat posed by professional migrants with an Islamic background.

Lodhi's Background

Faheem Khalid Lodhi (Urdu: خالد لودهى فہيم; also know as Abu Hamza) was born around 1969–70, at Sialkot in the Punjab region of Pakistan. He comes from a well-established family. His father is in his seventies and his mother is about 70 years of age. They continue to live in Sialkot, where his father is now retired. Lodhi's father was previously employed at the Pakistan airport, and later worked as a trained legal practitioner in Lahore. Lodhi has three sisters and two brothers. A 39-year-old brother lives and works in Sydney as a teacher. He has an uncle, an electrician, who also lives in the Sydney region.

Lodhi completed his secondary schooling in Pakistan before training as an architect at Lahore University over a period of five years. He finished that degree at about the age of 24 and, after a brief period of indenture with an architectural firm, commenced his own general practice in Lahore, which continued until 1997.

After a brief visit to Sydney, he decided to emigrate to Australia, and this occurred in 1998. He later obtained Australian citizenship. Upon arrival in Australia, Lodhi set about obtaining qualifications to enable him to practice as an architect. He applied for registration with the New South Wales Architects Registration Board and enrolled at the University of Sydney where, over the next 18 months, he completed a number of additional subjects. He graduated in 2000 with a Bachelor of Architecture from the University of Sydney.

Lodhi married in 1999 in Pakistan. This was an arranged marriage and it was not until 2000 that his wife was able to join him in Australia. She is a qualified medical practitioner in Pakistan. Since arriving in Australia she has been undertaking additional studies to obtain registration as a doctor in New South Wales. There are no children from the marriage.

Lodhi also undertook further professional training at the Ultimo College of Technical and Further Education where he obtained certificates in Quality Management and Total Quality Management. At the time of his arrest in April 2004, he was in the process of completing a Masters Degree in Construction Management at the University of New South Wales.

In addition to working with architects Thomson Adsett & Partners, Lodhi was employed in 2004 by Bishop Hitchcock & Irvine, an architect's firm in Alexandria, Sydney. He was working there at the time of his arrest. Since Lodhi's arrest and conviction, his wife has remained loyal and supportive. His wife, brother and uncle have frequently visited him in prison.

Association with Others

Willie Brigitte

The case against Lodhi relied in part upon an alleged conspiracy involving French citizen Willie Brigitte. Brigitte was convicted in France on 15 March 2007 on a charge of "associating with a group with a view to preparing an act of terrorism" and received a nine-year sentence. Prosecutors accused Brigitte of planning to attack the Lucas Heights nuclear research facility outside Sydney and military installations.

Brigitte arrived in Australia on 16 May 2003 and was deported on visa violation charges five months later.

Lodhi had apparently never met Willie Brigitte prior to his arrival in Australia. All he knew – from instructions given to him which he had marked in his diary – was the flight number, arrival time and a description of the Frenchman: "Black hair, goatee, glasses". When Brigitte walked through the arrival gates, Lodhi was waiting for him. The trial documents allege that, using false names, Brigitte and Lodhi sought to obtain 10 chemicals that could be used to make explosives, conducted research on vital infrastructure such as military bases and power stations, and researched military tactics and how to make bombs.

In the documents which were tendered in court, police claim that Lodhi, the alleged attack mastermind, lied to the Australian Security Intelligence Organisation (ASIO) on 19 occasions before admitting to his activities. Lodhi allegedly told ASIO that he collected Brigitte from the airport and met him on at least 10 other occasions. Lodhi had keys to Brigitte's flat, looked at maps with him and had talked to him about his (Brigitte's) marriage to Australian woman Melanie Brown. He told ASIO that he knew Brigitte as "Jabrille".

Lodhi also allegedly told ASIO he downloaded images of military facilities and later dumped them, used a false name to buy a map of the electricity grid and a mobile phone, and was in phone and email contact with Sajid Mir. (Sajid Mir is often mentioned by Muslims living in Western countries as their contact person with Pakistani terrorist group, Lashkar-e-Taiba.) Lodhi told ASIO of a meeting between Brigitte and Abdul Rakib Hasan, who at the time worked for a halal butcher in Lakemba, Sydney.

Lodhi had been in Pakistan with Sydney medical student Izhar ul-Haque, who was charged with separate terrorism-related offences. Ul-Haque told police that Lodhi said to him, "Jihad is a good thing". Izhar ul-Haque has since been acquitted because the records of interview were deemed inadmissible.

For his part, Brigitte had a name and a mobile phone number passed on to him by his Pakistani minder, Sajid. This was the same minder he met when he trained for jihad in Pakistan, hoping to fight the Americans in Afghanistan. After he was deported back to France, Brigitte identified his Sydney contact as Lodhi from a series of photographs shown to him by French authorities.

Over the next five months from May 2003 the pair allegedly met regularly to plot a terrorist attack on Australia's energy supply network. The prosecution also alleged that Lodhi had used a false name to open a mobile phone account to call Brigitte.

According to the prosecution, Brigitte's subsequent interrogation sessions in France revealed that he went to Australia to plan a bombing attack. The prosecution alleged Lodhi trained with banned terrorist group, Lashkar-e-Taiba, in Pakistan and acted as Brigitte's local contact in Australia. But Brigitte was not called as a witness and there is no independent confirmation that he has made such admissions. The Lodhi jury was told that Brigitte was "unavailable". It is also possible that Brigitte would not have been a co-operative witness.

Ibrahim Ahmed al-Hamdi and Arif Naharudin

Magistrate Price approved the giving of evidence via video-link by alleged terrorists held in custody in the United States and Singapore. However, the first of these witnesses, Ibrahim Ahmed al-Hamdi, admitted under cross-examination that United States authorities had stopped asking him to testify in other cases because he had been discredited.

Speaking from a Kentucky prison, al-Hamdi acknowledged that he had lied and fantasized when giving evidence about conditions in a Lashkar-e-Taiba camp in Pakistan. Al-Hamdi, who is originally from Yemen, is serving 15 years for weapons possession and visa breaches. He was arrested in February 2003 and charged with conspiracy to commit a terrorist act in Chechnya. That was dropped by the Federal Bureau of Investigation (FBI) on a plea bargain on condition he gave evidence against former associates.

In an apparent move to prevent the second video witness, Arif Naharudin, from being similarly discredited, Howe, the government's barrister, applied for and was granted a second set of suppression orders, also on the basis of confidential affidavits that were only shown to the defence in censored form. Howe obtained 'public interest immunity' from disclosing details of Naharudin's interrogation in Singapore – where he has been held for two years without charge – as well as an order blocking any public cross-examination of the witness.

Howe tendered two additional 'open' affidavits from Australian Federal Police Commissioner Mick Keelty and ASIO Director-General Dennis Richardson. These stated that their terrorism investigations would be "seriously compromised" if the information was disclosed to Lodhi's defence. But Boulten, Lodhi's barrister, told the court there was ample reason to assume that the suppressed information related to allegations of favourable treatment similar to that received by American detainees.

Izhar ul-Haque

Lodhi had earlier been charged with attempting to recruit Izhar ul-Haque, a 21-year-old (in 2003) medical student, to Lashkar-e-Taiba, while being 'reckless' as to whether Lashkar-e-Taiba was a terrorist organization. This charge was later dropped.

Police allege that Lodhi gradually persuaded ul-Haque to go to Pakistan and train with Lashkar-e-Taiba. Ul-Haque told police that Lodhi took him to a Lashkar-e-Taiba camp in Lahore and to his family home. On ul-Haque's return to Australia he continued his relationship with Lodhi, who asked him to keep his mobile phone number written in code.

According to the documents, Lodhi's admissions were made during interviews with ASIO in October and November 2003, after Willie Brigitte was deported.

Sajid Mir

Documents obtained by The Sydney Morning Herald newspaper after an application to Central Local Court provided the first confirmed link between Lodhi, Brigitte and a man in Pakistan known as 'Sajid'.

It also emerged that when police raided Brigitte's flat in 2003 they allegedly seized images of United States landmarks, a map of Australia marking nuclear power reactors, uranium mines and military bases, articles on the Australian Special Air Service in Afghanistan, and a receipt indicating Sajid had sent Brigitte €2000.

Brigitte allegedly told his French interrogators he was involved in planning a terrorist attack in Australia. He has told authorities that he met Sajid at the Lashkar-e-Taiba camp in Pakistan. Sajid, whom investigators have not yet located, was responsible for every foreign jihadist at the camp.

Evidence from Yong Ki Kwon

Witness Yong Ki Kwon testified via video-link from the United States at Lodhi's committal hearing in Sydney's Central Local Court. Kwon, who is serving an 11-year sentence for a terrorism offence, told the court he met Brigitte at a Lashkar-e-Taiba training camp in Pakistan in late 2001. However, he said he had never met Lodhi.

Shortly after the September 11th attacks he flew to Pakistan to "learn about combat activities". Under questioning from prosecutor Geoffrey Bellew he said, "I intended to … do anything I could to help the Muslim fighters".

He then travelled to a Lashkar-e-Taiba base in Lahore before hiking into the mountains where he met Brigitte, known by the alias Sala Hudin. "I remember him telling me he used to live in France and that all his Muslim brothers had left France", he said.

He said that Brigitte, with whom he had shared a room at one stage, was impatient to fight for jihad. "I remember him telling me there was only one Sheik and that's Osama bin Laden."

Kwon said he had met another unidentified Australian with the alias Abu Asad, who was planning to return home.

> He said to get to Lashkar-e-Taiba camp he had to get a reference letter from some Sheikh in Australia … He said his uncle had gone to a Lashkar-e-Taiba camp and had gone back. I remember seeing the group [Abu Asad's] doing combat manoeuvres, crawling and rolling …

The 45-day basic training course included use of AK-47s, M16s, light machine guns, pistols and rocket-propelled grenades. "We learnt how to take them apart and put them back together and [then we'd] go out and shoot a couple of rounds", Kwon said.

Trainees also learnt reconnaissance, camouflage, escape tactics, cryptic talk and target practice. "They'd make us hike up the mountains and spy on the other [Lashkar-e-Taiba] camps, sometimes infiltrate them without being seen and report back", Kwon said.

Defence lawyer Philip Boulten, Senior Counsel, attempted to discredit Kwon, saying that he had lied when questioned about his movements by the FBI in March 2003. The witness admitted lying and later plea bargaining with the FBI, pleaded guilty to lesser charges in exchange for information.

The AFP first interviewed Kwon about his terrorism connections in December 2003. He said he hoped that by giving evidence in Lodhi's case and several cases involving former friends, he could get his sentence further reduced.

The Investigation

Months before Lodhi's arrest his computer at the Sydney architectural firm was examined. Lodhi reportedly accessed a government planning website to obtain satellite images of city buildings and transport infrastructure. The website, called iplan, is publicly available to facilitate the work of urban planners, architects and others.

The prosecution further alleged that Lodhi dumped aerial photographs of Sydney military installations, including the Holsworthy army base, in a park rubbish bin near his home. Surveillance is said to show Lodhi dumping aerial images of Australia's military bases in a bin, suspected to be a 'dead drop'.

He is also accused of faxing an inquiry to a chemical company about purchasing urea nitrate – a fertilizer that can be used to make explosives – using a false company name and a false name to obtain a mobile phone number.

In raids on Lodhi's home and workplace in October 2003, police say they seized a disc containing four United States military training manuals on explosives and weapons, more than 600 files relating to Islamist extremism, handwritten notes for purchasing a false passport, and poems on martyrdom.

ASIO says it found 15 pages of notes written in Urdu in the top drawer of Lodhi's work desk. These allegedly reveal that Lodhi was ordering chemicals which were potential ingredients for making explosives, and include instructions on how to make chemical fires, petrol bombs, poison, cyanide gas, invisible ink, sulphuric acid, hand grenades, and a timing device for explosives. There were also notes on intelligence procedures.

Lodhi's intended targets were believed to be the national electricity supply system, and three Sydney defence installations: Victoria Barracks, Sydney naval base HMAS Penguin, and Holsworthy Barracks.

Conviction Charges and Trial Outcomes

Lodhi was convicted on three charges:

- On or about 3 October 2003 at Sydney the offender collected documents, namely two maps of the Australian electricity supply system, which were connected with preparation for a terrorist act, namely bombing part of the system, knowing the said connection – a maximum sentence of 15 years' jail.

- On or about 10 October 2003 the offender, intentionally did an act in preparation for a terrorist act, namely he sought information concerning the availability of materials capable of being used for the manufacture of explosives or incendiary devices – a maximum sentence of life in jail.
- On or about 26 October 2003 the offender possessed a document containing information concerning the ingredients for and the method of manufacture of poisons, explosives, detonators and incendiary devices connected with the preparation for a terrorist act, knowing the said connection – a maximum sentence of 15 years' jail.

Lodhi received 10 years on the first count, 20 years on the second and 10 years on the third, to be served concurrently. The jury found that the accused was not guilty in respect of a fourth charge that on or about 24 October 2003 the offender made a set of aerial photographs of certain Australian defence establishments, so Lodhi was acquitted of this charge.

Motivation

Justice Anthony Whealy commented that Lodhi had "the intent of advancing a political, religious or ideological cause, namely violent jihad" and to "instil terror into members of the public so that they could never again feel free from the threat of bombing in Australia".

Psychological profile

Lodhi did not publicly enunciate reasons for his actions and maintained his innocence throughout the trial. He informed Tim Watson-Munro, a Consultant Forensic Psychologist, that he is a devout Muslim. He told the psychologist that his renewed interest in his faith occurred at about the time of his marriage. Prior to that, he claimed that his interest in religion had been "fairly laissez-faire".

Lodhi also stated to the psychologist that after his marriage he felt a strong need to have a greater structure and focus in his life, and it was in this context that he had become more dedicated to the spiritual aspects of his life. From that time onwards, he regularly attended his local mosque and he did the same during his major visits to Pakistan after 2000.

Watson-Munro concluded that there was nothing in Lodhi's prior history, nor emerging from his discussions with him, to indicate a violent disposition, nor were there any features of an antisocial personality. Lodhi told Watson-Munro that he came to Australia to better his life and that at no time had he felt any antipathy towards this country. There were no symptoms of depression and no indications of depressive illness at the time of psychological assessment.

Watson-Munro observed that determining whether Lodhi might pose a risk upon his release was a difficult assessment to make in the light of Lodhi's continuing claim to be innocent, notwithstanding the jury's verdict.

The psychologist noted, however, that there was no previous involvement with the police or courts; rather there was a history of a hardworking devout man who was well supported by the members of his family who were in Australia. All of these matters, Watson-Munro considered, were positive prognostic indicators.

Finally, Lodhi told the psychologist of the difficult system of incarceration he was enduring, due to his classification as a high security 'AA' inmate. Notwithstanding these difficulties, it was assessed that he appeared to be coping quite well with his situation.

Judge's closing comments

The sentencing judge, Justice Anthony Whealy, noted that Lodhi had, throughout his life, demonstrated and maintained a solid and prodigious work ethic. He added:

> May I now pass to a consideration of the subjective features of the offender.
>
> First, there is the undoubted fact that he is, by all accounts, a person who has hitherto led a blameless life. He is a person who comes from a favourable and strongly supportive family background and who has no criminal background or antecedents whatsoever. These features of the offender's life and circumstances are clearly matters that may be brought to account in his favour for the purposes of the sentencing process.
>
> But I have to say that these favourable circumstances make it difficult to understand why a young man of excellent personal background, with a considerable professional work ethic, would have contemplated and carried out the very serious criminal actions that have brought him to his present position in these proceedings.
>
> The offender has, of course, maintained his innocence throughout the trial and continues to do so during this sentencing hearing. I can gain no meaningful insight into the circumstances which have transformed him from an otherwise respectable member of the community to a dangerous terrorist whose views are coloured by notions of the most extreme and fundamental kind.

It may be that the offender's deep embrace of religion about the time of his marriage resulted in his embracing extremist views. This is perhaps no more than speculation on my part but, even if it were true, it does not explain why or how the dangerous intentions underlying the offender's actions were ignited.

It has always been my understanding that Islam does not enjoin the killing of innocent people. Moreover, violent warfare is regarded by true Islam as a matter of last resort. It is subject to rigorous conditions laid down by the sacred law. The term 'jihad' literally means struggle. The greatest form of jihad is the inner struggle of the soul, which is to be waged against selfish desires for the sake of the attainment of inner peace.

Indeed, these concepts were the very concepts of jihad espoused by the offender during his trial. But it is clear from the jury's verdict and the findings I have made that they are not the true reflection of this man's inner thoughts and beliefs. The extremist views, which he must in truth be taken to have espoused, are not representative of the true nature of his Islamic religion. Rather they are a distortion of it.

As I say, these reflections, made in an endeavour to gain insight into the reasons, which may have led a young man of previous excellent character into the path of serious criminal misconduct, are perhaps speculation. The truth is I can gain little, if any, insight into the offender's mind in this regard. The consequence is, however, that I can make no allowance in his favour for remorse and contrition. There plainly is none.

The offender was perfectly entitled to maintain his innocence both during the trial and thereafter. This does not mean that his penalty is to be in any sense aggravated or increased. But it does mean that I can make no allowance on his behalf for contrition and remorse. Equally, it makes it difficult for the sentencing court to form any view as to whether the imposition of a significant penalty on the offender will result in his reform and rehabilitation.

The best I can do is to repeat the opinion expressed in Mr Watson-Munro's report suggesting that the absence of any previous violent disposition, the absence of any features of an antisocial personality, and the strongly supportive background of the offender's family are positive factors in his favour. These matters entitle the Court to express some cautious hope that, in time, the offender's extreme views may dissipate and that rehabilitation may not be beyond him.

Sentencing

Lodhi was convicted by the New South Wales Supreme Court jury in June 2006 on three out of four counts of terrorism. On 22 August 2006 Lodhi was sentenced to a maximum of 20 years in jail, with a 15-year non-parole period and minimum 15 years to be served. Lodhi, who is still classified as a high security 'AA' prisoner, will be eligible for parole in 2019.

Conclusions

The Consultant Forensic Psychologist seems not to have thought to explore beyond the conventional framework for psychological examination of any offender, notwithstanding Lodhi's social background or the social and religious influences that had led him to consider perpetrating terrorist violence in his new Australian environment.

It seems unlikely that Lodhi emigrated to Australia in 1998 with the intent of creating an opportunity to engage in a terrorist attack on his new homeland.

It seems instead that his subsequent visits to Pakistan, as with many young Pakistanis from Western backgrounds (such as the London 7/7 bombers), caused him to undergo a 'born again' religious experience. As a result, he was prepared to give up prospects of what would be regarded by most Australians as a promising career and satisfying professional lifestyle for a risky venture that would almost inevitably lead to a lengthy jail term, professional ruin, and stress on his marriage and family relationships in Australia.

Much more work obviously needs to be done with surviving Western-based Islamist extremist professionals to gain a better understanding of what motivated them to mount terrorist attacks against a Western society – particularly if they claim, as in Lodhi's case, not to harbour any particular antipathy towards it.

An obvious future line of research will be to compare the professionals involved in the United Kingdom London and Glasgow incidents of June 2007 with Lodhi, once the trial process has run its course, to look for common factors and indicators.

Bibliography

Kapisthalam, K. (2006). *The truth about Lashkar-e-Taiba*. Retrieved June 10, 2009, from www.hartwilliams.com/hd8/blog/2006_03_05_A%20Holy-Owned%20Subsidiary

New South Wales Supreme Court, *R v. Lodhi* (2006). NSWSC 691. Hearing dates 19/04/06–19/06/06; 29/06/06; 13/07/06; Judgment date 23 August 2006.

O'Brien, N., & Symons, E-K. (2007). Aussie attack planner revealed. *The Australian*, 16 March.

Wilson, J. (2005). Lashkar-E-Toiba: new threats posed by an old organization. *Terrorism Monitor*, 3, 24 February. Retrieved June 10, 2009, from www.jamestown.org/single/?no_cache=1&tx_ttnews%5Btt_news%5D=27599

5

The Primacy of Grievance as a Structural Cause of Oppositional Political Terrorism: Comparing Al-Fatah, FARC, and PIRA[1]

Jeffrey Ian Ross

Synopsis: This chapter applies the structural components of a previously developed causal model to three well-known and different campaigns of oppositional political terrorism: Al-Fatah, FARC, and PIRA. By doing so, the reader will have a better understanding of the causal dynamics of oppositional political terrorism. After the history of each group is provided, each of 10 basic structural factors is applied to the terrorist organizations. The evidence points to the powerful and longstanding effects of grievance to sustain the longevity of the group.

Introduction

Over the past five decades researchers, policymakers, practitioners and pundits have identified numerous kinds of terrorism. Part of the struggle, in trying to understand the phenomenon of terrorism has been coming to some sort of consensus with respect to a proper definition, and then developing typologies that are analytically meaningful. Nevertheless a considerable amount of ground has been covered with these important building blocks in the field of terrorism studies. For example, Alex Schmid has developed a consensus definition (1983), which while modified by him (Schmid & Jongman, 1988) and

---

[1] Special thanks to David Canter, Claire Delisle, Glen Feder and Dawn L. Rothe for comments on this chapter.

The Faces of Terrorism: Multidisciplinary Perspectives Edited by David Canter
© 2009 John Wiley & Sons Ltd.

others (Ross, 1993; Ross & Gurr, 1989), seems to have considerable scholarly currency.

Additionally, Mickolus' typology of terrorism (1981), breaking it down into four types based on whether there is government involvement and if it involves or affects citizens of more than one country, has widespread utility. One of the hallmarks of Mickolus' typology is the identification of oppositional political terrorism. This kind of political violence/crime subsumes domestic, transnational, international and state-sponsored terrorism. Here the state and its allies are targeted for political violence. This term also distinguishes these kinds of actions from state terrorism, which consists of political violence/crimes committed by governments against their own people. Over the past four decades, not only have researchers struggled with conceptual aspects of the field, some have advanced explanations for the causes of terrorism.

Few researchers, however, have developed a general causal model or theory of the causes of oppositional political terrorism. In fact, in recent times there has been some noticeable opposition, if not hostility, connected to the notion that there may be "root causes of terrorism" (Newman, 2006). Nevertheless, these analyses have produced an important and necessary knowledge base from which to conduct a further study. Among their accomplishments are: the identification of important causal variables; specification of factors which are important in the stages of terrorism (i.e. Crenshaw, 1981; Johnson, 1982, ch. 8); description of individual factors in a historical context (i.e. Targ, 1979); partial development of a typology of causes (i.e. Crenshaw, Johnson); deduction of factors from more general theories of conflict (e.g. Hamilton, 1978); identification of processes which are contributing and sufficient (Gross, 1972); specification and empirical testing of relationships among some of the variables (e.g. Hamilton); and, the construction of models on the causes and sequences of terrorism (e.g. Gross; Hamilton). Merits aside, these works suffer from a series of problems that include, but are not limited to, the absence of a comprehensive theory or a model of terrorism (Ross, 1993, 1999).

Objective

A causal model of oppositional political terrorism would allow us to better specify the factors which contribute to terrorism and may help counterterrorist experts to minimize the frequency and intensity of this form of political violence. In terms of sequencing, it is easier to study structural factors because it is less resource intensive than a psychological approach. For the latter, it is usually necessary to interview participants (in the field, in prison, and in other places where access is difficult or dangerous).

It also follows that each type of terrorism has a different pattern of causation. Terrorism is principally a response to a variety of subtle, interacting, ongoing, and changing psychological and structural factors manifested by perpetrators, and audiences (i.e. victims, public, business community, government). Thus, the relative importance of each independent variable depends on the context, which includes: the type of perpetrator, terrorist act, target, country, audience, and time period.

A considerable diversity exists among terrorists, their organizations, and the context in which they operate. However, if analysts are to move beyond case study analysis (with the subjects often chosen at random), it is imperative that generalizations be made. In an effort to address these concerns Ross (1993) developed a structural causal model of oppositional political terrorism. The proposed model is general enough to accommodate a variety of different individuals, groups and contexts.

The model incorporates 10 basic structural factors, divided between precursors and precipitants, and is used to explain the rise of oppositional political terrorism. This model has been applied in whole or in part to the Québécois separatist-related terrorism (Ross, 1995a); the relationship between protest and terrorism in connection with the Gulf Crisis/Conflict (1990–1991) (Ross, 1995b) and has been extended to integrate psychological factors (Ross, 1999).

It is also recognized that many of these variables are necessary but not sufficient as causes, and that not all factors identified need to be present for terrorism to occur. The variables are, from least to most important: modernization; type of political system; level of urbanization; social, cultural and historical facilitation; organizational split and development; presence of other forms of unrest; support; counterterrorist organization failure; availability of weapons and explosives; and, grievances. In short, all terrorism depends upon a grievance. This simple idea, often overlooked by other writers, is crucial because it focuses our attention on the moral outrage that precedes one's search for an extremist network where conspiracies are formed. Without first appreciating the power of grievance, we can never fully understand the dynamics that individuals and groups are subject to in their decisions to engage in terrorism.

Case Selection

This chapter applies the structural components of the causal model developed to three different campaigns of oppositional political terrorism. Although several terrorist groups were possible candidates for inclusion, the organizations selected are geographically distinct, with slightly different objectives, and are well known to the general public, counterterrorism experts, and scholars alike. Moreover, they are still in operation at various levels of intensity. In most respects, our approach conforms to what is typically called a 'most-similar' systems design (Lijphart, 1971, 1975). In short, this method restricts comparisons made among entities which share several commonalities in order to make generalizations which are relatively valid.

First, the Palestinian-Israeli conflict has spawned a number of terrorist organizations, including al-Fatah, the Popular Front for the Liberation of Palestine (PFLP), the Popular Democratic Front for the Liberation of Palestine General Command (PFLP GC), the Abu Nidal group, and Hamas fighting for the creation of a separate homeland for the Palestinian people. One of the earliest established, most well known, and largest groups is al-Fatah (or Fatah for short). Formed in 1957, this organization, originally led by Yasser Arafat, has been responsible for 233 incidents, with 1,462 injuries, and 463 fatalities (TKB database, retrieved February 21, 2008). In 1972, although Fatah officially announced that it would no longer engage in terrorism, it still supports other groups, such as the al-Aqsa Martyrs' Brigade (referred to in some circles as the armed wing of Fatah), which engages in suicide bombings.

Second, the Revolutionary Armed Forces of Colombia (FARC), established in 1964, is one of the oldest terrorist organizations in South America. They want to replace the existing government of Colombia with a regime run on Marxist-Leninist principles. Since their inception, this group has been responsible for 656 incidents, resulting in 1,373 injuries, and 703 deaths (TKB database, retrieved February 21, 2008). In 1984, after countless deaths and injuries to police, the military and non-combatants, the Colombian government began to negotiate with FARC, with hopes of transforming this organization into a respectable political party. Although some members of FARC conceded with government requests, others remained steadfast in their approach and tactics to further the mission of the group. One of the consequences of detente, however, was that disgruntled members of Colombia's military started an unofficial war against the legitimate FARC candidates. In 2002, FARC resumed its terrorist campaign against the government. They are reported to have about 170,000 members (Holmes, Gutierrez de Pineres, & Curtin, 2007).

Third, in Northern Ireland where the state's legitimacy is contested by the minority nationalist (Catholic) population, the Irish Republican Army (IRA) waged an armed struggle from 1969–1997. Irish republicanism has a long history of opposing the British presence in Ireland, but it was not until 1968, with the advent of the civil rights movement, that the IRA was re-activated in response to repressive laws, police actions and Protestant antagonism. The Provisional IRA (PIRA), which emerged in 1969 as a result of a split in the ranks of the 'Official' IRA, carried out numerous attacks in Northern Ireland, England and elsewhere to motivate the British to leave Northern Ireland. The peace initiative of 1993 led to the Irish Peace Process. The last decade has seen the signing of the Good Friday Agreement, disarmament of the Provisional IRA and a new form of devolved consociational power sharing between the nationalist and unionist representatives. Since its origins, the IRA has been accused of 84 incidents of terrorism (TKB database, retrieved February 21, 2008). Although the TKB database indicated that the IRA's terrorism has resulted in 140 injuries, and 29 deaths (retrieved February 21, 2008), according to the Conflict Archive which is available on the Internet, and Malcolm Sutton's *An index of deaths from the conflict in Ireland 1969–1993*, there have been 3,524 deaths related to the Troubles (1969–2000) plus about 30,000 injuries. It is said that the IRA is responsible for half these deaths (Sutton, 1994).

The case studies that follow examine the history of these three groups and reviews the relevant structural components that led to their establishment.

Al-Fatah

On 29 November 1947, the United Nations passed Resolution 181, which effectively partitioned Palestine (occupied by the British since the fall of the Ottoman Empire in World War I, circa 1918) into two states: a Jewish one (Israel), and a Palestinian one for the Arab majority living in the area. Although the plan was accepted by the Jewish Agency (responsible for monitoring the negotiations), it was rejected by the Palestinians and the neighbouring Arab states acting on the Palestinians' behalf. Violence between Arabs and Jews broke out in Palestine. On 14 May 1948, the British removed their troops. Israelis, through the efforts of their army, the Israeli Defense Force, immediately consolidated their power and repressed the Palestinians living within their borders (Chomsky, 1983; Morris, 2001). Many moved to the neighbouring countries of Egypt, Lebanon, Syria and Jordan.

In 1957, Yasser Arafat and approximately 20 other individuals from different clandestine Palestinian groups formed al-Fatah in Kuwait (Hart 1984; Iyad 1981; Mishal 1986). They were influenced by the success of the Algerian revolution, in which nationalists used an urban guerrilla campaign to successfully force the French out of Algeria. Over time, Fatah – also known as the National Palestine Liberation Movement – has become the "largest, oldest, and most influential Palestinian resistance organization" (Long, 1990, p. 36). Fatah has approximately twelve to fifteen thousand fighters and numerous support personnel (Livingstone & Halevy, 1990, p. 72). Fatah focuses on Palestinian nationalism; it does not support any particular political ideology or religious doctrine, despite the fact that many of its leaders are Muslims (Long, 1990, p. 36). It has received resources from "Arab governments, criminal activities, and profits from its extensive portfolio and other business activities" (Livingston & Halevy 1990, p. 72).

During its history Fatah has maintained offices throughout the world, particularly in the Middle East, Europe and Asia. At the time of this writing it appears that their only known headquarters is in the West Bank. This terrorist organization is broken down into subunits, one of which, known as the Western Section, "was headed, until April 1988, by ... Abu Jihad. It is an operations body set up to promote armed struggle ... in the occupied territories. Once headquartered in Amman, Jordan", and for a while in Baghdad, "it has about four hundred members. Since the death of Abu Jihad, Yasser Arafat has assumed full control of the Western Section" (Livingstone & Halevy, 1990, p. 73).

In 1964, with the support of other Arab countries, Egypt established the Palestine Liberation Organization (PLO), the governing body of the Palestinian people. In June 1967, the neighbouring Arab countries of Egypt, Lebanon, Jordan and Syria waged a combined military attack against Israel. In what is popularly known as the Six-Day War, the Israelis not only thwarted the aggression on their own territory, but also took control of additional land in the Arab countries, securing the Gaza Strip, the Sinai Peninsula, Golan Heights, East Jerusalem, and the West Bank (also known as the Occupied Territories). Fatah gained control of the PLO in 1968 after the setbacks of the Six-Day War and the Battle of Karameh (Jordan) (March 1968), during which they made several military gains against an encroaching Israeli army.

In the 1960s and 1970s, both as a source of revenue and for political reasons, Fatah trained some Middle Eastern, European, African and Asian terrorist groups, who then committed violent actions in support of each other's causes. Many Middle Eastern countries, including Saudi Arabia, Kuwait and other Persian Gulf states, provided aid to Fatah during this time.

In September 1970, fearing a loss of political power, Jordan's King Hussein expelled high-ranking Palestinians living in his country. What made this all the more strange was that Palestinians and Jordanians are ethnically very similar. Moreover, many were Jordanian citizens. The majority relocated to southern Lebanon, where Fatah established a strong presence that they used to their advantage to attack northern Israeli settlements.

At several points in time during its existence, Fatah committed terrorist actions alone or had one of its subunits commit violence against Israel targets. For example, the breakaway group Black September was born out of the ashes of the Jordanian expulsion. This organization planned and committed several spectacular terrorist events, including "the murder of eleven Israeli athletes at the 1972 Munich Olympics and of two American diplomats, Ambassador Clio Noel and his deputy chief of mission, Curtis Moore, in Khartoum in March 1973" (Long, 1990, p. 38).

Shortly after the 1973 Yom Kippur War, during which Egypt and Syria backed by a coalition of Arab states, attempted but failed to retake the land lost in the 1967 conflict, prominent Palestinian terrorist organizations lost confidence in the Egyptians' and Syrians' ability to serve as their advocates. Fatah announced it would cease engaging in international terrorism, particularly hijacking, because they believed that it was not helping their cause and blamed the sporadic attacks which happened after this declaration to be the work of offshoot organizations (Halevy & Livingston, 1990). In 1974, in a signal that both he and his organizations were achieving international legitimacy, Arafat addressed the United Nations. This was coterminous with the dissolution of Black September (Dobson, 1974).

In the mid-1970s, the Israelis (bolstered by United Nations forces) set up a security zone inside Lebanon on Israel's northern border. Starting in 1975, however, and lasting until 1990 – with factions such as Maronite Christians, (represented by the Phalange), Shiite Muslims, Hezbollah, Druze and members of the PLO – a bloody civil war took place in Lebanon.

In 1979, the governments of Israel and Egypt (with the assistance of then-US President Jimmy Carter) signed the Camp David peace accord. The PLO (and by extension Fatah) recognized that it would have to deal with Israel directly and engage in some sort of compromise.

In June 1982, however, Israelis became exhausted with cross-border attacks by Hezbollah and Palestinian factions, and invaded Lebanon beyond the security zone. Within days Israeli tanks made their way to Beirut. During the occupation, the Phalange, a Lebanese political party and militia primarily composed of Maronite Christians, (who were loosely under the control of the Israeli army), made its way into the Sabra and Shatila refugee camps in Beirut, ostensibly to root out Palestinian gunmen. Instead, the Phalange massacred 460 to 800 individuals, 35 of whom were women and children.

In May 1983, the United States brokered an agreement for the Israelis and Palestinians to leave Lebanon, and for American, French and Italian peacekeepers to maintain order. Palestinian fighters relocated to Algeria, Iraq, Tunisia, Yemen and other Middle Eastern countries (Mishal, 1986). Meanwhile, "Arafat and the PLO leadership had to be evacuated to Tunis" (Laqueur 2003, p. 102). Although the relocation of the PLO headquarters to Tunis would make it more difficult for Israelis to attack, it also meant that the leadership became increasingly out of touch with what was happening 'on the street' in Palestinian areas. This also paved the way for the creation of the Intifada, largely an autonomous outgrowth of the day-to-day frustrations of living under Israeli occupation.

Starting in 1987, many Palestinian activists living in the Occupied Territories engaged in what was called the Intifada (Schiff & Ya'ari, 1989). The Intifada primarily consisted of youths attacking Israeli soldiers in the Gaza Strip and in the West Bank with rocks and stones. When the Israeli army overreacted by injuring and killing participants, many of the world's media outlets were present to broadcast the army shooting what appeared to be defenceless youths. In the furore of the times, an Islamic fundamentalist group called Hamas (a wing of the Muslim Brotherhood) was born. Although Hamas, established in 1972, was originally a self-help organization (providing welfare and social services to needy Palestinians), in 1997 it started engaging in terrorism (Mishal & Sela, 2002). Since that time, Hamas and Islamic Jihad, (another Islamic fundamentalist terrorist organization which derives its name from the Islamic word and practice 'Holy War') have carried out numerous suicide attacks against the Israeli army and Israeli civilians, inside both the Occupied Territories and Israel proper. These two splinter groups of the Muslim Brotherhood want to establish an Islamic country in these areas and do not recognize Israel's right to exist as a sovereign state (http://news.bbc.co.uk/1/hi/world/middle_east/978626.stm). Not only are they seen as a threat to Israel, but also to the leadership of the PLO, and many Western countries because they are perceived to be more violent and less susceptible to negotiation.

In April 1993, the PLO and Israeli Government signed the Declaration of Principles (also known as the Oslo Accords). The Oslo Accords set out a number of agreements to foster peace between the two groups and the normalization of relations with the other Arab countries. Among the concessions were that Fatah would give up terrorism, and that the Israelis would permit the Palestinians limited autonomy in the Gaza Strip and West Bank. Both Israeli Prime Minister Yitzhak Rabin and Palestinian leader Yasser Arafat received the Nobel Peace Prize for this accomplishment. According to the plan for limited Palestinian autonomy, the Palestinian National Authority (PNA or PA for short) was formed in 1994 to administer the Gaza Strip and West Bank, with Arafat as its head.

Despite the accords, it has been alleged that Fatah financially and politically supports armed factions or wings such as Force 17, the Hawari Special Operations Group, Tanzim and the al-Aqsa Martyrs' Brigade. In 1998, things looked promising for peace; a deal brokered by US President Bill Clinton, called the Wye River Accords, was signed by Arafat and Israeli Prime Minister Benjamin Netanyahu. Essentially, per the accords, the Palestinians were going to crack down on terrorism, Israel would return land to Palestinians, and Palestinians in Israeli prisons would be transferred to the PNA. This was popularly seen as a land-for-peace deal. Due to increased tension, however, in 2000 a second Intifada began, coupled with suicide bombings in crowded areas (e.g. buses, markets, etc.) in Israeli cities.

According to Newman (2003), "Hamas and Jihad are responsible for attacks on Israeli citizens on the West Bank and Israel proper" in discos, restaurants, bus stations and shopping malls (p. 155). Israeli retaliation for the attacks killed a great number of people. "Equally for most Israelis", Newman points out, "the failure of Arafat to clamp down on Hamas and Jihad was a clear indication that the renewed violence was taking place with the tacit approval of Arafat … . While this may have been true at the beginning of the al-Aqsa Intifada, by 9/11, Arafat lacked total control over all the Palestinian factions and he would have been unable to prevent every suicide bombing" (2003, p. 155). In fact, by the summer of 2001, the popularity of Fatah and the PA had

finally been eclipsed by Islamic fundamentalist and other Palestinian nationalist groups (Newman, 2003, p. 156).

In the wake of 9/11, the United States has continued in its efforts to broker
a new peace agreement. About a week after 9/11, "Bush forced [Israeli Prime
Minister] Sharon and Arafat to agree to a ceasefire and it was announced that
if the ceasefire held for 48 hours, Foreign Minister Shimon Peres would reopen
peace talks with the Palestinian Leader" (Newman, 2003, p. 157).

In March 2002, the Israeli Defense Forces occupied the West Bank; surrounded the city of Ramallah (West Bank), and at various points in time
encircled Arafat's compound, which was heavily affected by shelling. Several
assassinations and assassination attempts have been carried out against the
leadership of al-Aqsa Martyrs' Brigade and Hamas. Between 2000 and 2004
suicide bombings took place on a regular basis inside Israel. Since 2005, there
has been a very significant decrease in suicide bombings (although many have
been foiled). They are no longer regular occurrences.

On 11 November 2004, two weeks after being transported to a hospital in
France because he was suffering from an intestinal disorder, Arafat slipped into
a coma and died. Many international leaders hoped that Arafat's death would
pave the way to increased peace in the Israeli-Palestinian conflict. Since then,
there have been some serious changes in the leadership of both the Israelis and
Palestinians. On 6 January 2006 Prime Minister Ariel Sharon suffered a major
stroke and it is unlikely that he will fully recover. In his place the deputy Prime
Minister Ehud Olmert has assumed power. Later that month (26 January 2006)
Hamas won the general election for the Palestinian parliament claiming 76
seats to Fatah's 43, and with 13 going to smaller parties and independents.

After Arafat's death the leadership of Fatah was assumed by Farouk
Kaddoumi, a veteran of the organization since 1960. Most of his activities have
been conducted while in exile (outside of the West Bank and Gaza). He has
held senior positions in the PLO, but is opposed to the Oslo Accords, and the
PNA. He is often in conflict with the PNA.

Revolutionary Armed Forces of Colombia (FARC)

Three so-called narco-terrorist groups operate in Colombia: the United
Self-Defense Forces of Colombia (AUC), the National Liberation Army (ELN),
and the Armed Forces of Colombia, or Fuerzas Armadas Revolucionarias
de Colombia (FARC). FARC is the largest, best trained, and most deadly
of the three. FARC is an extreme, left-wing, communist-inspired group with
a reported membership of twelve to eighteen thousand (Simonsen &
Spindlove, 2004, 341; www.farcep.org). Established in 1964, this group is led
by Manuel Marulanda (formerly known as Pedro Antonio Marin, a.k.a.

Tirofijo ("Sureshot") who is in his seventies, and six others, including senior military commander Jorge Briceño, a.k.a. Mono Jojoy. Although its origins are murky, the group first came to public attention in 1966 "as the military wing of the Colombian Communist Party" (Simonsen & Spindlove, 2004, p. 341).

Part of the reason for FARC's success is that it has developed a loyal following among Colombia's poor, especially the peasants and indigenous people who live in relatively remote rural areas (Stafford & Palacios, 2002). In some respects, FARC is better described as a guerrilla organization that uses terrorism to further its objectives (e.g. Chaliand, 1983; Marighela, 1971). However, because of its killing of civilians it should be considered a terrorist organization. This group has accumulated significant resources through the drug trade (i.e. coca, opium and marijuana), either through cultivation or through providing security for traffickers (Ehrenfeld, 1992).

Its primary objective is to overthrow the Colombian Government. Other demands include increased equality, a reduction in unemployment, land reform, an end to privatization, and a redistribution of wealth. FARC is also anti-American; it believes that the United States is an imperialist country, especially because of its intervention in Colombian affairs. Ironically, FARC wants Colombia to legalize drugs. They argue that this would reduce the violence and negative effects of these illegal substances. Because of its connection with drug trafficking, FARC maintains links to criminal gangs in Ecuador, Panama and Venezuela.

FARC engages in kidnapping, extortion, bank robbery and drug trafficking in order to finance the organization, but in terms of pure terrorism, it has been responsible for assassinations, bombings and the hijacking of an airliner. It focuses on a wide range of targets including the police, military, politicians and civilians. FARC's attacks on government targets has led to the development of death squads, paramilitary organizations that engage in extrajudicial killings and disappearances, as well as torture of actual or suspected members of the terrorist organization or their sympathizers. Most of its violence has been confined to Colombia; rarely has FARC engaged in terrorism outside the country.

In the later 1980s, FARC established the Patriotic Union (UP), a political party, but the UP fell victim to right-wing death squads sponsored by drug lords and members of the Colombian military. Apparently, some three thousand UP members were killed, including its 1990 presidential candidate, Bernardo Jaramillo Ossa (http://news.bbc.co.uk/1/hi/world/americas/1746777.stm).

In 1998, as a concession to sit down to peace talks, Colombian President Andrés Pastrana granted FARC a 42,000-square kilometre safe haven, which was essentially their base of operations. The negotiations proceeded slowly as FARC continued to build up their resources (through gun running, coca production, smuggling, etc.). In the meantime, the group kidnapped and killed several politicians including Ingrid Betancourt, a leading and well-liked presidential candidate. In 2001, Pastrana once again began talks with FARC about a peace treaty: However, "as negotiations became bogged down, the Pastrana government threatened to end the deal that had created a demilitarized zone" (Simonsen & Spindlove, 2004, p. 341). In February 2002, the government ended the talks, revoked the political status of FARC, issued warrants for the arrest of its leaders, and instructed Colombia's military to retake the area occupied by FARC. The military offensive called 'Operation Black Cat', used both aircraft and helicopters (Simonsen & Spindlove, 2004, p. 341).

From 2002 to 2004, FARC has been under constant attack by the mounting police and military attacks ordered by President Alvaro Uribe Velez. According to a recent Associated Press story, "Colombian forces have captured or killed top regional commanders with noms de guerre 'El Negro Acacio', who oversaw much of the group's coca operations, 'Martin Sombra' who is alleged to have guarded hostages, including three US contractors, and 'Martin Caballero'. In January, [2008] FARC leader Ricardo Palmera, better known as Simon Trinidad, was sentenced to 60 years in prison in the United States" (Muse, 2008).

In February 2008 FARC members were attacked by the Columbian army just inside the Ecuadorian border. In the raid Raul Reyes, considered the second in command in the FARC organization, and 17 other members were killed.

During its 40+ years of existence, FARC has also developed enemies beyond Colombia's national government, including the National Liberation Army (ELN), the smaller of the two main Marxist terrorist organizations in Colombia. FARC seems to have very little international support and thus must rely on its own illegal businesses to support itself (www.ict.org.il/inter_ter/org.cfm; http://www.farcep.org/pagina_ingles).

Provisional Irish Republican Army (PIRA)

The IRA struggle is centuries old (Bell, 1997; Toolis, 1997). In order to understand this conflict, one needs to be familiar with the history and the political and economic role of Ireland. The Irish Catholics' desire for autonomy from British rule has waxed and waned due to a variety of circumstances. At certain points in history, the effort has appeared to have a religious basis; at other times, it has aired grievances that are simply economic and political (i.e. the subjugation of Catholics to Protestant and British rule). This has prompted some analysts to suggest that the conflict has ethnic, rather than religious roots (Bruce, 1993, 1995).

A few highlights are in order. After a popular rebellion led by such notable figures as Michael Collins, the Irish Free State (now known as the Republic of

Ireland) was established in 1921. This encompassed 26 out of 32 counties; the remaining 6 northern counties were partitioned, remained under British protection and are called Northern Ireland (referred to as Ulster by unionists and loyalists). In particular Ulster is a province of Ireland that has nine counties including the counties of Monaghan, Cavan and Donegal. The Six Counties (Northern Ireland) are FATDAD: Fermanagh, Armagh, Tyrone, Derry, Antrim and Down). Generally the republicans/nationalists refer to Northern Ireland as "the Six Counties" or "the North" or "the North of Ireland," while their unionist/loyalist counterparts refer to it as "Northern Ireland" or "Ulster". (Republicans do not recognize the legitimacy of the statelet so they never refer to it as Northern Ireland.) Since the creation of Northern Ireland in 1920, the minority Catholic population on its territory has endured difficult living conditions, including inadequate housing, high unemployment and disenfranchisement (White, 2003, p. 86). Since 1968, close to 3,600 individuals have died in this conflict. The dead include not only British military, but also police officers (particularly Royal Ulster Constabulary (RUC)) and innocent civilians (Sutton, 1994).

During the 1960s, partially inspired by the civil rights movement in the United States, both Protestants and Catholics began to press for improved housing conditions and educational opportunities. But the repression by the Northern Irish Government exacerbated matters: "Catholics were not allowed to demonstrate … if they attempted to do so, they were attacked by loyalists while the RUC and its reserve force known as the B Specials, both largely made up of Protestants, looked on without attempting to stop the violence, and at times joined in. At the same time no attempts were made to stop Protestant demonstrations. The Catholics believed the RUC and B Specials were in league with the other anti-Catholic unionists in the North" (White, 2003, p. 87). Catholics (nationalists) and Protestants (loyalists) were essentially at each others' throats (Talbot, 2003, p. 335).

In August 1969, riots erupted in Belfast and Londonderry/Derry (Londonderry is what Protestants call it, Derry is what nationalists call it). Local police were relatively ineffective against this kind of civil disturbance. As a result, the British Government increased the numbers of soldiers stationed there. The army – interpreting the situation as a colonial war – quickly allied itself with the Protestants, which only served to polarize the population (Hocking, 1988). The British military also uncritically allied itself with the RUC. The army would surround Catholic neighbourhoods, break down doors, and throw tear gas and smoke bombs, all in a combined effort to draw out terrorists and their sympathizers. The Catholics wanted the army out, and many Protestants believed that they could act with impunity against the Catholics (White, 2003, p. 88). As a result of this sectarian violence, the Irish Republican Army (IRA) reconstituted itself and started engaging in terrorist actions. In December 1969, the IRA split into the 'Officials' and the

'Provisionals'. Confusion was rampant, as both organizations had military and political wings (Silke, 1999). Then in January 1972, during a peaceful civil rights parade in Derry/Londonderry, 13 unarmed civilians were shot dead, while 14 others were wounded by British paratroopers. This event, popularly referred to as Bloody Sunday, galvanized many Irish Catholics against the British presence in Northern Ireland.

In the summer of 1972, the 'Official' IRA declared a ceasefire. It placed its energy into supporting Sinn Fein, the political party established to seek independence for Northern Ireland from Great Britain. Since that time, "the term IRA was used for the organization that had developed from the 'Provisional IRA'" (Simonsen & Spindlove, 2004, p. 78). Membership in the IRA increased to approximately fifteen hundred to two thousand members during the 1970s and dropped to three to five hundred after the 1994 ceasefire was signed (Simonsen & Spindlove, 2004, p. 78).

In 1973 the British Government passed the *Northern Ireland (Emergency Provisions) Act*, which allowed the military greater powers of search and detention of terrorist suspects. The army could enter anyone's house at any time during the day without obtaining a warrant. During the same year, PIRA launched a campaign of bombings on the British mainland in cities including Brighton, Guildford and London. Since then, violence in Northern Ireland has "intensified in cyclical waves: in 1972; in 1974; in the early 1980s; in the late 1980s; and in the early 1990s" (Talbot, 2003, p. 335). Talbot says, "Loyalists have indulged in significant sectarian violence, attacked the Royal Ulster Constabulary (RUC) and the Army and have also assassinated Republican leaders. After early sectarianism, PIRA targeted primarily British state representatives, the RUC, the Army, Unionist and British politicians, and the British Royal Family. However, by the early 1990s Republican and Loyalist paramilitaries had become engaged in a mounting series of 'eye for an eye' type sectarian murders" (Talbot, 2003, p. 335).

PIRA has received financial support, weapons and intelligence from countries such as Libya, Spain and the former Soviet Union, along with aid from formerly communist Eastern bloc countries. It has received finances through its aid organizations located in the United States (Adams, 1986), extortion and bank robberies. PIRA has established safe houses in Europe and in 2002 it was discovered that they were training FARC members in bomb-building techniques.

Over the last decade-and-a-half, several positive steps have occurred in the longstanding conflict (Dingley, 1999). In 1985, the United Kingdom and the Republic of Ireland signed a peace agreement regarding the governance of Northern Ireland. Known as the Anglo-Irish Peace Accord, "the agreement seeks to bring to an end to terrorism by establishing a joint system of government for the troubled area" (White 2003, p. 90). In 1998, the PIRA signed a peace agreement with Great Britain popularly known as the Good Friday (or

Belfast) Agreement, and in the following year, power-sharing governance was established in Northern Ireland with the institution of the New Assembly. Although devolution of powers were withdrawn by London on two occasions, the Assembly has been up and running again since 2007. The second suspension was a result of allegations that the IRA continued to engage in gun smuggling and spying on its political opposition. In 2001, the PIRA began to decommission its weapons and in 2002, Martin McGuinness and Gerry Adams (respectively the PIRA and Sinn Fein leaders) were offered seats in the British Parliament. They refused, as acceptance would necessitate signing an oath to the Queen of England, which they virulently opposed. Things went from bad to worse when in December 2004 the IRA was accused of the $50 million robbery of a bank in Belfast, and in January 2005 the IRA was allegedly involved in a pub brawl in which a Catholic man was stabbed to death in Belfast.

In July 2005, shortly after the suicide bombings in London's Tube (subway) allegedly caused by Islamic fundamentalists, and amongst scepticism from leading Northern Irish Protestants, the IRA formally declared that it will give up its three-decade-long violent struggle to unite with the Republic of Ireland and achieve its goals through peaceful means (Frankel, 2005).

Comparisons

Making comparisons among the three terrorist groups is not easy. They have different ideologies, capabilities and geographic and political circumstances. For example, whereas the PIRA and Fatah are nationalist-separatist organizations, FARC has a Marxist-Leninist ideology. Nevertheless, some insights can be garnered from comparing the degree to which the structural causes previously outlined are applicable to each group.

Permissive causes

1.   *Modernization* (i.e. facilitates better access to vulnerable targets, destructive weapons and technology, mass media, recruits, audiences, conflicts with traditional societies, and improved networks of transportation)

All three countries in which these organizations predominantly operate have different levels of modernization (Huntington, 1968). Determining just how 'modern' the host countries are is not so clear-cut. Short of utilizing chemical, bacterial, radiological, and nuclear weapons (CBRN), all three groups have tried to acquire and use sophisticated technology, including weaponry and communications. The majority of their most significant attacks have occurred in urban locales, and their leadership is usually highly educated and trained professionals.

2. *Type of political system* (i.e. terrorism is facilitated in prosperous democracies)

The majority of Palestinians (and by extension, Fatah members) live under Israeli rule (ostensibly a parliamentary democracy). Those Palestinians who live in the West Bank are living under conditions of martial law imposed by the Israelis. Otherwise, the vast Palestinian diaspora – those who have emigrated to other countries – live under a wide variety of political systems. PIRA live disproportionately under British rule, also a parliamentary democracy (with symbolic remnants of a monarchy), which as of early 2005 had draconian anti-terrorism legislation (such as the *Prevention of Terrorism Acts 1974, 1989, 2005*). The Colombian political system is in a state of flux (Stafford & Palacios, 2002); Colombia signed a new constitution in 1991 that was supposed to usher in new, expanded political participation. Although currently a presidential system with direct elections, the system is characterized by political patronage and clientelism.

3. *Level of urbanization* (i.e. cities are more likely than rural environments to facilitate terrorism)

Our three case-study groups operate in areas with different levels of urbanization. Although it has frequently carried out terrorist attacks in the cities of Colombia, particularly Medellin, FARC has conducted its activities primarily in rural and generally remote locations, drawing a disproportionate number of their fighters from those areas. According to Holmes et al. (2007), "By the end of the twentieth century, the FARC had 67 rural and 4 urban fronts" (p. 250). PIRA and Fatah have flourished in cities (and in the case of Fatah, refugee camps scattered throughout the Middle East and occupied territories where they recruit), though they also draw their supporters and membership from the smaller towns and enclaves throughout their respective country.

Precipitant causes

1. *Social, cultural and historical facilitation* (i.e. shared attitudes, beliefs, customs, habits, myths, opinions, traditions, and values that permit the development of nationalism, fanaticism, violence and terrorism in a subgroup of a population)

Since these terrorist struggles have endured for a considerable amount of time, they have numerous social and cultural traditions and a rich history on which to draw. PIRA need not look further than the Republic of Ireland for a constant reminder of what the power of political violence can accomplish.

PIRA also has many members who have achieved international notoriety (e.g. Bobby Sands and the hunger strikers of the 1980s). FARC is born out of the bloody civil war that engulfed Colombia during the 1950s and the tumultuous history of the Colombian Communist Party. Holmes et al. (2007) have even suggested that FARC "has deeper historical roots, beginning in the 1920s and the 1930s, in the early agrarian conflict of poor agricultural workers against the large landed estates" (p. 250). And Fatah can trace its origins to the British mandate (i.e. the occupation of Palestine starting at the beginning of the 20th century), and the acknowledgement that its Arab allies might not be able to come to its aid as demonstrated in their overwhelming defeat during the 1956 Sinai war. In addition to numerous publications that these groups have produced, and in some cases radio stations, all three of these terrorist groups have developed websites to manage their public image and to disseminate information and propaganda to members and supporters. (Although the IRA does not have a website, Sinn Fein, the political party, has a comprehensive website.)

2.   *Organizational split and development* (i.e. conflicts between moderate and the more extreme wings of an anti-government organization)

Although Fatah never broke away from a larger group, it certainly has led to many splits not only in its own organization, but in the PLO. Similarly, PIRA has encouraged divisions due to its approach to the conflict; "in the fall of 1997 one faction accepting the new Good Friday Agreement, and the other, a newly formed splinter of PIRA, the Real IRA … continuing armed resistance to the British occupation of Northern Ireland" (Simonsen & Spindlove, 2004, pp. 74–75). The Continuity IRA is another such group. Their connection with the political wing of Sinn Fein is undoubtedly confusing; understanding the platforms and objectives of the respective subdivision is difficult at best. As for the relationship between Continuity IRA and Real IRA (which are both very tiny), the way that Sinn Fein explains it is that they are ALL Republicans but that those in CIRA and RIRA, though they share the same objective as Adams and his allies, their strategies differ in that Sinn Fein and the Provos are committed to pursuing a strictly political path while these two groups still advocate armed struggle. FARC itself was the result of organizational development, having grown out of an alliance between liberals and communists after the civil war that engulfed Colombia between 1948 and 1958; later, FARC stimulated the growth of several new leftist guerrilla or terrorist organizations, including the ELN and the EPL.

3.   *Presence of other forms of unrest* (i.e. provides learning opportunities, legitimizes the resort to violent actions, and heightens grievances)

Colombia, like Northern Ireland, has been wracked with all sorts of labour difficulties and criminal violence. According to the Henning Center for Labor Relations, since the mid-1980s, 3,800 union leaders and activists in Colombia have been assassinated by far-right paramilitary organizations (www.henning-center.berkeley.edu/gateway/colombia.html). Colombia has also been subject to violence and other forms of human rights violations by the military and right-wing paramilitary groups. Labour unrest is also a bone of contention for Palestinians. They are typically underpaid and a source of cheap labour for some Israeli businesses who care to hire them.

4. *Support* (i.e. providing finances, training, intelligence, false documents, donations or sales of weapons, explosives, composite materials, provision of sanctuary or safe housing, propaganda campaigns, ideological justification, public opinion, legal services, or a constant supply of recruits)

Fatah has been helped by wealthy Palestinians, Arab states, Eastern bloc countries and the former Soviet Union. FARC has made a considerable amount of money through kidnappings, assassinations and working for the drug cartel, especially as the cartel's strong arm. Recently it has been alleged that Hugo Chavez's government in Venezuela has helped FARC. PIRA has allegedly received training and weapons from Libya, and has engaged in kidnappings and robberies (banks and post offices) for needed funds, and Fatah has been involved in several kinds of criminal activities, including drug trafficking, extortion and protection services.

5. *Counterterrorist organization failure*

At various times, the Colombian, British and Israeli national security and intelligence agencies that monitor terrorist groups have failed to detect terrorist cells and actions. With each security lapse, these government entities try to improve policies and procedures. In most cases, new approaches are put into place, just as terrorist organizations are constantly looking for holes in the existing security systems.

6. *Availability of weapons, explosives, and materials*

In recent years Fatah has been accused of making its own bombs, while other weapons are stolen and smuggled from Israel or Egypt. They have acquired "rocket-propelled grenades, machine guns, rockets and mortars" (Lavie, 2007). Meanwhile, Hamas has been building Katyusha rockets and firing them on Israel; whether they pass this technology on to Fatah or their splinter groups is unknown. Alternatively Qassam rockets are being launched from Gaza into places like Sderot. Often these are used against Israelis. There is some credible evidence of co-operation between PIRA and FARC, in terms of sharing bomb-making expertise (Rowan, 2002). Otherwise it has been alleged that gangs in Central American countries are helping to facilitate the trafficking of weapons to FARC. The IRA have got access to arms from a number of different sources including the sympathetic (or profit-hungry) arms dealers in the United States, continental Europe, and the government of Muammar al-Gaddafi, of Libya.

7. *Grievances*

Although things are complicated by geography (i.e. the state of Israel lies between the West Bank and the Gaza Strip), Fatah seeks to establish a sovereign homeland for the Palestinian people, a group that has been disproportionately under Israeli control since the partition. FARC wants a complete communist revolution in the state of Colombia, and PIRA wants the British Army (and Government) to leave Northern Ireland, which would then allow the Irish nationalists to establish a separate country. The entire republican movement (Sinn Fein and the IRA) want to end the British presence in Ireland but recognize that they need to work politically to achieve a united Ireland as opposed to a separate country. Undoubtedly over these groups' respective histories, concessions have been given by their host country and other world powers (capable of doing so). But the fact remains that the level of perceived grievances is sufficiently high to sustain the different terrorist organizations.

Conclusion

By reviewing the history and motivations of these terrorist groups, we can determine similarities and differences in causal patterning. Although selected elements of all the 10 previously reviewed factors can be found in all of the 3 terrorist organizations, not all had them in equal amounts.

In the case of Fatah, it appeared that grievances, combined with the presence of other forms of political unrest (the constant cycle of violence between Israel and its Arab neighbours during its first 30 years of existence), and support by a variety of constituencies was important in the maintenance of this organization. With respect to the FARC, grievances combined with support, access to weapons and explosives clearly helped this organization endure frequent Colombian Government attempts to displace it. Finally, in the PIRA case, grievances, along with support, access to weapons and explosives has helped this organization endure and weather splits and disaffections.

In sum, what this analysis points to – the trait they share most in common – is the powerful effect of grievances. While the other factors are important, none can sustain an organization without the perception of some sort of hurt, insult or damage to an organization, religion, culture, race or ethnicity; a wrong that is widely felt, longstanding and unresolved. These grievances have been a source of contention despite changes in leaders and generations and accommodation by the states in which these groups operate. Unless some sort of meaningful change is made by the countries where they started, these conflicts will persist and possibly worsen. New generations will carry on the struggle and both sides (victims and perpetrators) will suffer injury, senseless property destruction and death.

References

Adams, J. (1986). *The financing of terrorism*. New York: Simon & Schuster.

Bell, J. B. (1997). *The secret army: The IRA* (3rd rev. ed.). New Brunswick, NJ: Transaction Publishers.

Bruce, S. (1993). Fundamentalism, ethnicity, and enclave. In M. E. Marty, & R. S. Appleby (Eds), *Fundamentalisms and the state* (pp. 50–67). Chicago: University of Chicago Press.

Bruce, S. (1995). Paramilitaries, peace, and politics: Ulster loyalists and the 1994 truce. *Studies in Conflict & Terrorism, 18*, 187–202.

Chaliand, G. (1983). *Guerilla strategies: A historical anthology from the Long March to Afghanistan*. Berkeley: University of California Press.

Chomsky, N. (1983). *The fateful triangle: The United States, Israel, and the Palestinians*. Boston: South End Press.

Crenshaw, M. (1981). The causes of terrorism. *Comparative Politics, 13*, 379–99.

Dingley, J. (1999). Peace processes and Northern Ireland: Squaring circles. *Terrorism and Political Violence, 11*, 32–52.

Dobson, C. (1974). *Black September*. New York: Macmillan.

Ehrenfeld, R. (1992). *Narco-terrorism*. New York: Basic Books.

Frankel, G. (2005, July 29). IRA says it will abandon violence. *The Washington Post*, p. A1, A18. Retrieved May 18, 2009, from www.washingtonpost.com/wp-dyn/content/article/2005/07/28/AR2005072800427.html

Gross, F. (1972). *Violence in politics: Terror and political assassination in Eastern Europe and Russia*. The Hague: Mouton.

Hamilton, L. C. (1978). *Ecology of terrorism: A historical and statistical study*. Unpublished doctoral dissertation, University of Colorado.

Hart, A. (1984). *Arafat: Terrorist or peacemaker?* London: Sidgwick & Jackson.

Hocking, J. J. (1988). Counter–terrorism as counterinsurgency: The British experience. *Social Justice, 15*, 83–97.

Holmes, J. S., Gutierrez de Pineres, S. A., & Curtin, K. M. (2007). A subnational study of insurgency: FARC violence in the 1990s. *Studies in Conflict & Terrorism, 30*, 249–265.

Huntington, S. P. (1968). *Political order in changing societies*. New Haven, CT: Yale University Press.

Iyad, A. with E. Rouleau (1981). *My home, my land*. New York: Times Books.

Johnson, C. (1982). *Revolutionary change*. Stanford, CA: Stanford University Press.

Laqueur, W. (2003). *No end to war: Terrorism in the twenty-first century*. New York: Continuum.

Lavie, M. (2007, June 8). Fatah seeks weapons deal with Israel. *The Independent*. Retrieved February 28, 2008 from www.independent.co.uk/news/world/middle-east/fatah-seeks-weapons-deal-with-israel-452250.html

Lijphart, A. (1971). Comparative politics and the comparative model. *American Political Science Review*, 65, 682–93.

Lijphart, A. (1975). The comparable-cases strategy in comparative research. *Comparative Political Studies*, 8, 158–75.

Livingstone, N. C., & Halevy D. (1990). *Inside the PLO*. New York: Quill/William Morrow.

Long, D. E. (1990). *The anatomy of terrorism*. New York: Free Press.

Marighela, C. (1971). *Handbook (mini-manual) of urban guerrilla warfare*. In C. Marighela (Ed.), *For the liberation of Brazil*. London: Penguin.

Mickolus, E. (1981). *Combating international terrorism: A quantitative analysis*. Unpublished doctoral dissertation, Yale University.

Mishal, S. (1986). *The PLO under Arafat*. New Haven, CT: Yale University Press.

Mishal, S., & Sela, A. (2002). *The Palestinian Hamas: Vision, violence and coexistence*. New York: Colombia University Press.

Morris, B. (2001). *Righteous victims: A history of the Arab-Zionist conflict, 1881–2001*. New York: Vintage.

Muse, T. (2008, March 1). Senior Colombian rebel commander killed. *Associated Press*. Retrieved May 18, 2009, from www.usatoday.com/news/world/2008-03-01-colombia_N.htm

Newman, D. (2003). The consequence or the cause? Impact on the Israeli-Palestine peace process. In M. Buckley, & R. Fawn (Eds), *Global responses to terrorism: 9/11, Afghanistan and beyond* (pp. 153–164). New York: Routledge.

Newman, E. (2006). Exploring the 'root causes' of terrorism. *Studies in Conflict & Terrorism*, 29, 749–772.

Ross, J. I. (1993). The structural causes of oppositional political terrorism: Towards a causal model. *Journal of Peace Research*, 30, 317–329.

Ross, J. I. (1995a). The rise and fall of Québécois separatist terrorism: A qualitative application of factors from two models. *Studies in Conflict & Terrorism*, 18, 285–297.

Ross, J. I. (1995b). The relationship between domestic protest and oppositional political terrorism in connection with the Gulf conflict. *Journal of Contemporary Criminal Justice*, 11, 35–51.

Ross, J. I. (1999). Beyond the conceptualization of terrorism: A psychological-structural model of the causes of this activity. In C. Summers, & E. Markusen (Eds), *Collective violence: Harmful behavior in groups and governments* (pp. 169–194). Lanham, MD: Rowman & Littlefield.

Ross, J. I., & Gurr, T. R. (1989). Why terrorism subsides: A comparative study of Canada and the United States. *Comparative Politics*, 21, 406–426.

Rowan, B. (2002, June 13). Analysis: Colombia and the IRA. *BBC*. Retrieved March 4, 2008, from http://news.bbc.co.uk/1/hi/northern_ireland/2043323.stm

Schiff, Z., & Ya'ari, E. (1989). *Intifada: The inside story of the Palestinian uprising that changed the Middle East equation*. New York: Touchstone.

Schmid, A. P. (1983). *Political terrorism: A research guide to concepts, theories, data bases and literature*. New Brunswick, NJ: Transaction Publishers.

Schmid, A. P., & Jongman, A. J. (1988). *Political terrorism: A new guide to actors, concepts, data bases, theories, and literature* (Rev. ed.). New Brunswick, NJ: Transaction Publishers.

Silke, A. (1999). Rebel's dilemma: The changing relationship between the IRA, Sinn Fein, and paramilitary vigilantism in Northern Ireland. *Terrorism and Political Violence, 11,* 55–93.

Simonsen, C., & Spindlove, J. R. (2004). *Terrorism today: The past, the players, the future* (2nd ed.). Upper Saddle, NJ: Pearson Prentice Hall.

Stafford, F., & Palacios, M. (2002). *Colombia: Fragmented land, divided society.* New York: Oxford University Press.

Sutton, M. (1994). *Bear in mind these dead … An index of deaths from the conflict in Ireland 1969–1993.* Belfast: Beyond the Pale Publications.

Talbot, R. (2003). Northern Ireland and the United Kingdom. In F. Shanty, & R. Picquet (Eds), *Encyclopedia of world terrorism* (pp. 335–342). Armonk, NY: M. E. Sharpe.

Targ, H. R. (1979). Societal structure and revolutionary terrorism: A preliminary investigation. In M. Stohl (Ed.), *The Politics of Terrorism* (2nd ed., pp. 119–143). New York: Marcel Dekker.

Toolis, K. (1997). *Rebel hearts: Journeys with the IRA's soul.* New York: St. Martin's Griffin.

White, J. (2003). *Terrorism: An introduction* (4th ed.). Belmont, CA: Wadsworth.

6

Case Study – The 17th November Group: Europe's Last Revolutionary Terrorists

George Kassimeris

Synopsis: The self-proclaimed Revolutionary Organization 17 November (Επαναστατική Οργάνωση 17 Νοέμβρη), also known as 17N (or N17), named after the final day of the 1973 Athens Polytechnic uprising, was a Marxist organization that assassinated 23 people in 103 attacks on US, diplomatic and Greek targets. It was brought to an end in 2002 when a bomb went off prematurely implicating its carrier. The subsequent trial is reviewed to reveal the characteristics of the organization.

The Demise of 17N

It was 10.25 am on Saturday, 29 June 2002 when the extraordinarily long run of luck of Europe's most elusive group, the Revolutionary Organization 17 November (17N), finally ran out. A strong blast ripped through the warm evening air near the ticket office of Hellas Flying Dolphins in the port of Piraeus. One man was seriously injured in the face, hands and chest. It seemed that the bomb he was carrying, concocted from alarm clocks, common detonators, 9-volt batteries and dynamite had gone off prematurely. Port authorities rushed to the scene and the man was taken to the emergency unit of the nearby Tzanneio hospital.

Early reports speculated that the bomber was a member of one of the country's smaller terrorist groups such as the Revolutionary Cells or Popular Resistance which had been relatively active of late. But the contents of a rucksack (a. 38 handgun and two hand grenades) found near to the injured man,

The Faces of Terrorism: Multidisciplinary Perspectives Edited by David Canter
© 2009 John Wiley & Sons Ltd.

soon identified a Savvas Xiros, and proved much more tantalizing. Three days later, Police Chief Fotis Nassiakos announced that the. 38 Smith and Wesson had been identified as the gun stolen from a police officer killed by 17N on Christmas Eve 1984 and was the same weapon that had subsequently been used in the assassinations of shipowner Costas Peratikos and prosecutor Costas Androulidakis as well as a number of other incidents involving the group. A member of the terrorist organization, often referred to as *organossi phantasma* or phantom organization, which had acted with impunity for 27 years, was suddenly in police custody.

Xiros' arrest marked the beginning of the end for the 17N. From his hospital bed and apparently fearing for his life, the icon painter and – as it turned out – a senior 17N gunman, Xiros gave the prosecutor in charge of the anti-terrorism investigation critical information that fuelled a chain of arrests that led to the dismantling of the group in less than a month.[1] Xiros later declared that he had been drugged and tortured into offering his confessions but his hospital testimony formed the cornerstone of the state's case against 17N.

In December 2003, after a marathon nine-month trial – the longest in modern Greek history – held in a purpose-built courtroom in Athens' largest maximum-security prison, Korydallos, a three-member tribunal convicted 15 members of the group while another 4 defendants were acquitted due to lack of sufficient evidence. The court upheld the state prosecutor's recommendation for 21 life terms and a 25-year sentence for accused leader and chief ideologue, Alexandros Giotopoulos, while the group's operational leader, Dimitris Koufodinas received 13 life sentences and 25 years in jail. Other life sentences plus 25 years were handed down to Savvas Xiros (6 life terms), his brother Christodoulos (10 life terms), Vassilis Tzortzatos (4 life terms) and Iraklis Kostaris (4 life terms). Five other members: Vassilis (the younger of the Xiros brothers), Costas Karatsolis, Patroklos Tselentis, Sotyris Kondylis and Costas Telios received the maximum 25-year sentence. Telios, who had handed himself in and was diagnosed with severe psychiatric disability, was the only convicted member to receive a suspended sentence and walk free pending an appellate trial, on the condition that he reported to his local police precinct monthly and did not leave the country. Only four convicts received less than the maximum 25 years: Thomas Serifis (17 years), Dionysis Georgiadis (9 years), and 8 years each to Nikos Papanastasiou and Pavlos Serifis.

---

[1] The information supplied by Xiros led also to the discovery of the group's main arsenal in three flats in central Athens. The flats – one of them rented by Xiros himself contained a number of the 60 anti-tank rockets stolen by 17N from an army base in northern Greece in 1989, the typewriter used to produce the group's early communiqués, 17N's red flag with the trademark five-pointed star as well as grenades, wigs, communiqués, and posters of Ché Guevara, Karl Marx and Aris Velouhiotis, a Greek World War II resistance fighter. One of the weapons, a G-3 rifle, was used to kill the group's last victim, the British defence attaché in Athens, Stephen Saunders, who was shot dead in June 2000 as he drove to work.

Who Were the Terrorists?

In the case of armed groups such as the Italian Red Brigades, telling the stories of three or four members would most probably be insufficient to gain an understanding of what led the group to behave as it did mainly because the organization itself consisted of more than a handful of adherents. But in the case of 17N, a comparatively very small group with a more defined rank-and-file structure, such an approach might work. The fact is that in spite of the testimonies of 508 people and of more than 900 hours of court hearings, the history of the foundation of the group still remains unclear.[2] Yet, the sheer longevity of the entire 17N terrorist experience should raise three particularly intriguing and intertwined questions: 'who were these people?', 'where did they come from?' and, more crucially, 'what kept them inside terrorist organizations for so long?' Studies of Europe's most enduring ideological terrorist groups have shown that organizations relied heavily for their strength and survival over many years on the existence of a clear moral identity characterized by solidarity, strong emotional bonds and a quasi-religious devotion to an ideological cause (see, for example, Franceschini, 1988; Jamieson, 1990). In the case of 17N, three of the terrorists were brothers, two were cousins and one was godfather to the others' children. In other words, blood bonds, so important in Greek society, reinforced trust and silence, helping to explain the group's operational continuity and remarkable resistance to infiltration. At the same time, however, the fact that 17N's members were so few and so close to each other also meant that once its structure cracked it crumbled like a 'house of cards', to use the phrase of veteran US State Department terrorism analyst, Dennis Pluchinsky.[3] Back in the early 1990s, Pluchinsky had prophetically written that:

> [T]he Achilles heel for 17N may be the absence of any known supporter or sympathizer base. In essence, unlike the RAF and DEV SOL, 17N has not demonstrated an ability to reorganize after police arrests. The group may be susceptible to a police 'knockout punch' – like AD and the CCC. 17N appears to be a small, possibly single cell, self-sufficient group that could become demoralized and unravelled with the arrests of one or two of its members. (Alexander & Pluchinsky, 1992)

Which is exactly what happened on 29 June 2002 with the premature detonation of the bomb Savvas Xiros was carrying in Piraeus.

---

[2] See "17N: I Diki den Edose apandisseis" [17N: The trial failed to provide answers] in *Kathimerini tis Kyriakis*, 30 December 2003.
[3] As Dennis Pluchinsky put it to me, "I have never seen a terrorist group unravel so quickly".

Alexandros Giotopoulos

"*It was not a fair trial, not even a trial but rather a tasteless piece of theatre. The part of the decision that concerns me was dictated by the Americans.*"

Alexandros Giotopoulos was convicted as "the clear mastermind and leader" of 17N. The state prosecutor characterized him as "the root of evil both before and after his arrest" and proposed a sentence that amounted to 2,412 years which is what Giotopoulos eventually received. Giotopoulos' defence team maintained throughout the trial that physical evidence was scant and that his conviction was basically the product of testimonies by other accused 17N members, a violation of the Greek criminal code's provision which specifically states that the testimony of a guilty person alone cannot be sufficient in establishing guilt.[4]

Son of a prominent Trotskyite theoretician and activist of the pre-World War II era, Giotopoulos studied in France during the years of the Colonels' junta, where in 1969 he helped found the radical 'May 29' movement, which advocated armed rebellion against the Greek military regime. According to Andreas Staikos, a friend and fellow group member, "May 29 was inspired by Cohn Bendit's March 22 group, and was a totally conspiratorial organization that included six members; its exclusive aim was to overthrow the Greek dictatorship".[5] In 1971 Giotopoulos and Staikos were found guilty by the Greek authorities of creating an armed organization and were sentenced in absentia to five years in jail. Giotopoulos remained in Paris where he founded a new group, the Popular Armed Struggle (LEA), which from its inception was divided over how to direct its energies.[6] Giotopoulos was in favour of aggressive acts of urban guerrilla warfare and split from the group with a small clique of others. Staikos remembered Giotopoulos as somebody with "a very disciplined mind, combining good arguments with rhetorical and discursive capabilities. And he had a good knowledge of Marxist and revolutionary theory. Theory was his bread and butter".[7]

Returning to Athens after the fall of the Colonels' regime in 1975, Giotopoulos came, according to Greek police sources,[8] into contact with members of Greece's other prominent urban guerrilla group, Revolutionary Popular Struggle (ELA), and attempted unsuccessfully to persuade them to sign on to a plan to abduct the CIA's Athens station chief, Richard Welch. Welch was eventually shot dead outside his home, on 23 December 1975, by

---

[4] On the case of the defence, see *Kyriakatiki Eleftherotypia*, special supplement entitled "I Ora tis Krissis: I Megali Diki tis 17N" [Judgement time: The big trial of 17N].
[5] Andreas Staikos interview with *Athens News*, 2 August 2002.
[6] Ibid.
[7] Ibid.
[8] Author's interview with anti-terrorism officer, Athens, 10 September 2002.

17N. Giotopoulos, whose fingerprints were identified by Greek police in two of 17N's Athens hideouts, maintained throughout the trial that he had no involvement whatsoever with 17N. In denying all 963 charges against him, Giotopoulos asserted that "the picture painted of him as the [17N] leader was a police fabrication" and that the main reason why he was put behind bars was because "the Americans, the British and their collaborators in the Greek government wanted that".[9] According to Giotopoulos, the charges were nothing more than "a cheap fabrication by the Americans and British signed by [Greek] prosecutors and former provincial police, and based on confessions taken in a hospital intensive care unit from people [that is Xiros] destroyed by psychotropic drugs and blackmail".[10] Giotopoulos also denied that handwritten corrections on drafts of 17N proclamations were his own as the state prosecutor had charged and claimed that his fingerprints, found in 17N safe houses, including a left thumbprint on a mobile phone manual, were transferred by the police onto movable objects.

Giotopoulos not only denied any participation in 17N but also put a great deal of effort into arguing that 17N must have been a horizontal cell organization with no leadership. At the same time, Giotopoulos placed the group's actions in a political environment, which, in his view, necessitated armed intervention in daily life. From his point of view, 17N activity was not terrorism but "an armed political struggle with the aim of toppling the capitalist regime in favour of an anti-bureaucratic form of socialism that would give power to the people".[11] Giotopoulos also seemed to believe that resorting to armed violence was a reasonable and calculated response to certain social and political circumstances. As such, he saw militant opposition as the only effective form of political pressure against American hegemonism and an unresponsive regime. According to Giotopoulos's analysis, it was the

> perpetuation of the dependence on the USA, the reproduction of huge economic inequalities and the total absence of a basic welfare state together with the low level of workers' income and the disappearance of agricultural income which drove young people to take up arms against representatives of dominant circles, place bombs against symbolic targets and violently clash with repressive mechanisms.[12]

Giotopoulos' attempts to link American hegemonism to long-standing domestic problems were reminiscent of 17N's Welch communiqué whereby 17N writers had argued at the time that American presence on national soil

[9] Korydallos prison court chambers, 6 March 2003.
[10] Ibid.
[11] Pre-trial Giotopoulos interview with the central Greece provincial newspaper, *Lamiakos Typos*, 5 October 2002.
[12] Ibid.

was the root cause of Greece's underdevelopment and responsible for its perpetuation.[13]

Giotopoulos also attacked what he called "the official Left" for failing to address certain social problems arising from a fundamental conflict between the dominant and the exploited classes in Greek society. Chronically bankrupt and lacking credibility the left, Giotopoulos argued,

> was and remains incapable of expressing the hundreds of thousands of people struggling. ... And it was not surprising that in such circumstances, 17N and other armed organizations found fertile ground to grow – effectively capitalizing on the absence of a credible leftist alternative.[14]

Whenever he spoke, Giotopoulos used language that was direct and condescending. He heaped insults on target figures like the state prosecutor, Christos Lambrou (who called Giotopoulos' denials "phoney and hypocritical, because he knows everyone and is behind everything"), and co-defendant, Patroklos Tselentis, who had identified him in his testimony as "the leader of the group and its ideological brain as well as the author of its proclamation".[15] Giotopoulos described Tselentis as "a small, pathetic little man" who chose to co-operate with the authorities telling lies so he could benefit from the benevolent provisions of the counterterrorism law.[16]

Overall, Giotopoulos' court testimony shed no light on any major issues concerning the group's prehistory, motives, purposes and notions of political power, though he spoke (in the few times when he chose to speak) with an authority rivalled only by that of Dimitris Koufodinas. When asked by Chief Judge Margaritis if he would find the courage like his co-defendant Koufodinas to accept responsibility for his past actions, Giotopoulos' characteristic reply was: "that's exactly what I would have done, had I actually been the leader".[17] However, one cannot but be struck by Giotopoulos' overall stance. Even if one puts aside the ludicrousness of his claim that he was framed in an Anglo-American conspiracy because of his activity against the 1967–74 Greek dictatorship, the strongest impression was that he relied up to the end on a heavy dose of defiance and mystique as if such mystique would somehow efface criticism. Having adopted throughout an almost Blanquist stand in denouncing the hearing as a travesty of justice ("the decision is ridiculous, the entire world is laughing") and bombastically calling "today's Greece" a "modern colony of

---

[13] The Welch communiqué, dated December 1975, charged that "US imperialism [was] the Number One enemy of the people" and held the Americans responsible for "decades of innumerable humiliations, calamities and crimes" inflicted upon the Greek people.

[14] Giotopoulos interview with *Lamiakos Typos*.

[15] See below the court profile and testimony of Patroklos Tselentis.

[16] Ibid.

[17] Korydallos prison court chambers, 16 March 2003.

the United States", Giotopoulos, like the group he led, refused to the very end to modify his ideological rigidity and doctrinal inflexibility and tried to construct a 'language' with which to publicize his political existence, claim legitimacy and pose as a representative of the entire community.

Dimitris Koufodinas

"Our main weapon is the truth and the truth is always revolutionary."

The history of 17N terrorism ended on 5 September 2002 when the group's leader of operations, Dimitris Koufodinas turned himself into the police after two months on the run. Koufodinas, who had vanished immediately after the explosion at Piraeus port, pulled up outside police headquarters on Alexandras Avenue in a taxi at 2.35 pm, dressed in jeans, a black T-shirt, sunglasses and a jockey cap. "I am Dimitris Koufodinas and I have come to turn myself in", he told the stunned duty officer before being taken to the 12th floor of the anti-terrorism squad. Xiros told anti-terrorism officers days later that he had urged Koufodinas to flee the scene. Koufodinas, who had more than 24 hours to get away before police realized that Xiros was connected to 17N, ran first to one of the gang's hideouts in Pangrati where, according to police sources, he destroyed evidence before going on the run.[18] In a statement read out by his lawyer, Koufodinas, declared that he willingly gave himself up,

> to undertake the political responsibility of all 17N actions. I deny my guilt in the actions attributed to me the way they are in the indictment. The value that determined my personal course was my faith in the construction of revolutionary movement and my vision for a socialist society. I express my solidarity with all those who are in detention, justly or unjustly with regard to this case. For every fighter, dignity is a basic value and a title of honour.[19]

Dimitris Koufodinas was born in 1958 in the village of Terpni, 45 kilometres from the city of Serres in northern Greece. Terpni was, as it remains today, a typical Greek northern village that prides itself on the ordinariness of its daily life and the unexciting decency of its people. In 1971, when Koufodinas was 13, his father moved the family to Athens at a time when the Greek capital was in turmoil because of the Colonels' dictatorial regime. Metapolitefsi, the 1974

---

[18] Author's interview with anti-terrorism officer, Athens, 10 September 2002.
[19] On how the Greek media reacted to the Koufodinas unexpected surrender see, for instance, *Kathimerini* and *Ta Nea*, 6 September 2002, and *Kyrikatiki Eleftherotypia* and *To Vima tis Kyriakis*, 8 September 2002. See also "Deka apantisseis gia to grifo Koufodina" [Ten answers for the Koufodinas puzzle] in *Eleftherotypia*, 12 September 2002, and "Greece's most wanted surrenders" in *The Guardian*, 6 September 2002.

transition from dictatorship to democracy, seems to have had a strong impact on Koufodinas' early political formation. The 1974 transition, it has to be emphasized, was not the result of a clear and sharp break with the Colonels' junta but the product of a whole range of compromises and negotiations between elite-level political actors and the military. Metapolitefsi, or "junta by another name" as 17N called the transition in several communiqués, had a formative influence on Koufodinas' politicization and his early involvement in student politics confirms this. A member of PASOK's Socialist PAMK youth movement from secondary school, Koufodinas intensified his activism when he enrolled in 1977 at Athens University to read Economics. Koufodinas is remembered by secondary school friend, Nikos Giannopoulos, who testified in court, as a "someone whose depth and intellect were impressive for his age and who could have, had he stayed on course, landed himself at a later stage an important job in party politics or the state bureaucracy".[20] Another friend from his days of student activism, remembered Koufodinas as a "calm, articulate young man with guts and ideological consistency".[21] Family relatives also described Koufodinas as "somebody who never liked upsetting people".[22] Koufodinas broke his family ties in 1983, almost a year before the attempted assassination of US Army Sergeant Robert Judd which, according to the indictment, was Koufodinas' operational debut with the group.[23]

Dimitris Koufodinas does not fit the stereotype of terrorist as wild and irrational fanatic.[24] Never in the nine months of court proceedings did Koufodinas raise his voice above the pitch of natural conversation and his every gesture and every word were controlled and measured. Although Chief Judge Margaritis systematically asked him for "answers to questions that would provide this court and Greek society as a whole with a clearer picture",[25] Koufodinas stubbornly resisted the temptation to say anything substantial (and possibly incriminating) about his comrades or the inner workings of the organization.[26] In his court testimony Koufodinas declared:

---

[20] Nikos Giannopoulos in his court testimony, Korydallos prison chambers, 25 July 2003.

[21] *Metro* magazine journalist, Nikos Vafeiadis in his court testimony, Korydallos prison chambers, 26 July 2003.

[22] Cited in *Eleftherotypia*, 9 September 2002.

[23] Judd was attacked by two men on a motorcycle at a traffic stop as he was driving a shipment of diplomatic mail to the US Air Force base at Athens Hellenicon airport. The attackers pulled alongside Judd's car and it was Koufodinas, according to the charge sheet, who fired with 17N's .45-calibre signature weapon five rounds against him. Judd, instinctively, accelerated, jumped the median strip and sped away.

[24] See "O antrhropos pou pire tin efthini" [The man who took responsibility], in *Kyriakatiki Eleftherotypia*, 30 November 2003, and "Esosse tin … timi tous" [He saved … their honour], in *Ta Nea*, 8 December 2003.

[25] Court proceedings, Korydallos prison court chambers, 23 July 2003.

[26] "He had the look of a man who knew something damaging about everyone of his co-defendants", a Greek political commentator who was also covering the opening of the 17N trial said to me.

I won't do what you would want me to do. I won't even bother entering your logic. Our morality doesn't accept logics of co-operation and squealing. I will say nothing about my role in connection with the organization. I won't even begin to tell you in which operations I had or did not have a role. And I will say nothing about any of my co-defendants. This is my stand and I will hold to it until the end, irrespective of any personal cost.[27]

Described by several 17N members in their testimonies of summer 2002 as the key link between the group's historic leadership and the operatives, Koufodinas acknowledged before the court responsibility for 17N's entire legacy but he refused at any stage of the proceedings to recognize that his group had been completely wrong in their analysis of Greek society. On the contrary, Koufodinas declared that he remained confident of ultimate victory even though he accepted that as far as the organization's operations were concerned 17N was finished. Koufodinas argued that from a historical perspective and given "the revolutionary movement's course in this country, the end of 17N's story [had] yet to be written".[28]

Koufodinas believed that 17N and 17N alone continued to represent in Greece a pure and undefiled Marxist-Leninist faith, dismissing the universal designation of them as terrorists and of their actions as terrorism. Challenging the court's tendency to depict their activities as acts of senseless barbarity devoid of any serious political content, Koufodinas argued that "this present court does not wish and cannot put 17N on trial for what 17N really was".[29] In his view, 17N "was, as the group had persistently stated from the very beginning, an organization of simple, popular fighters. And since it came from the guts of the populace, it was the populace's voice that 17N listened to, and it was the populace's own interests that it tried to serve".[30]

Fighting imperialism and capitalism

Going back to the group's armed debut in 1975 and the assassination of the CIA's station chief in Athens, Richard Welch, Koufodinas tried to explain where 17N drew inspiration and motivation from for its campaign. (On 17N's tactics, targets and operational evolution between 1975 to1980, see Kassimeris (2001, pp.72–75).) "In December '75", he stated, "a group of fighters decided to execute CIA's station chief in Athens". In the words of Koufodinas there

---

[27] Court proceedings, Korydallos prison chambers, 24 July 2003.
[28] Letter to *Eleftherotypia* newspaper, 10 September 2002.
[29] Court proceedings, Korydallos prison chambers, 24 July 2003.
[30] Ibid.

couldn't be a more clear and justified action. CIA's station chief was and remains the long hand of American power in our country. Running a fifth column of a few hundred agents occupying neural posts inside the government, the state bureaucracy, the army, the political parties and the media, he controls and directs the political, social and economic life of our country in relation to the interests of the USA. The Greek people know full well what the CIA is all about, and the role it has played since the Civil War. [The role it had played] in every election, especially the 1961 election of rigging and violence; in the assassination of [Greek MP] Lambrakis, and the military junta and the tragedy of Cyprus. Why has the Cyprus dossier not been opened yet? Whatever happened to your justice and your democracy? Why so much selectivity for what is a crime and who is really a criminal? Who let the [junta] torturers walk free? Was it the people or was it your independent justice? For the Greek people know exactly why the CIA's station chief in Greece was executed. What they don't know is who exactly was behind this action and that is thanks to a campaign of disinformation, distortion and disorientation by the government, the political parties and the media. When the campaign of 17N began, a campaign of disinformation began with it and still continues to this day.[31]

Throughout, Koufodinas tried to conceal the fact that as a group 17N possessed little capacity or inclination for organizing mass action. The group, he conceded with over-due proletarian modesty, "never considered itself to be the centre of revolution nor did it consider that its modes of action were the only appropriate ones"[32], confirming the view that even if a revolutionary situation had arisen in Greece, the group would have lacked the organizational strength to exploit it since it was neither a guerrilla force nor an effective popular political movement. Koufodinas, however, described 17N as an organization of

the revolutionary left, a part of the left which believes that the present-day social system cannot ease social inequalities simply because it provokes and accentuates them. A system that cannot solve the problem of unemployment simply because it creates unemployment and needs to do so. A system that cannot efface war and conflict simply because it feeds on both. A system that cannot support the equal development of all nations simply because it relies on the unequal treatment and exploitation of the backward, underdeveloped countries. A system that doesn't care about the ecological damage that it causes to our planet. And a system that shows no respect for different cultures and different races simply because it obeys the God of money and profit.[33]

Such a system, Koufodinas asserted, "couldn't be reformed, couldn't be democratized nor could be humanized: it had to be overthrown through a

[31] Court proceedings, Korydallos prison chambers, 24 July 2003.
[32] Ibid.
[33] Ibid.

socialist revolution".[34] At the same time, however, he recognized that finding a political route to it had been "for the past two centuries the central issue within the left and the main area of contention between reformist and revolutionary left".[35]

Commitment to ideology as a guide for political action pervaded Koufodinas' court testimony. Advocating revolutionary violence as an ideological response to declining radicalism and reformism, Koufodinas deplored "all those who had turned their back on revolutionary activism out of sheer opportunism and bourgeois convenience".[36] In Koufodinas' analysis, "the difference between those who had chosen the path to revolution and those who hadn't was neither a theoretical nor an abstract one" since choosing the path of revolution meant "choosing to fight for the poor, the weak and the exploited".[37] At the same time in an attempt to impose retrospective historical significance to what 17N was and did, Koufodinas claimed that,

> the left which 17N belonged to was the left of Lenin, Ché Guevara and Velouchiotis; the left of the October, Spanish, Chinese and Cuban revolutions; the left of the anti-colonial revolutions in Algeria and Vietnam, the left of May '68 and November '73; the left of urban guerrilla warfare.[38]

One of Koufodinas' most insistent themes during the nine months of the trial was 17N's "struggle" against "American military imperialism". In combative tone, Koufodinas presented the attacks of the group against US targets as a challenging response to American bullying and barbarity on Greek soil and in the region as a whole. American imperialism, he added, had brought nothing but chaos and butchery not only in Greece but in most parts of the planet and "the only way left to the people of the world to resist was 'asymmetric guerrilla warfare'".[39] For 17N's operational chief, asymmetric guerrilla warfare was premised on the prototype guerrilla assumption that a sustained rate of small-scale military operations could generate a degree of coercive psychological pressure disproportionate to their destructive consequences. Koufodinas was convinced that asymmetric guerrilla warfare would sooner rather than later result in the creation of "many Vietnams and that could prove the Achilles' heel of this arrogant hyper-armed empire".[40] In this context, Koufodinas also said that for the past 27 years, 17N had made it its central task "to discredit and humiliate the mythologized [US] secret services,

[34] Ibid
[35] Ibid.
[36] Ibid.
[37] Ibid.
[38] Ibid.
[39] Ibid.
[40] Ibid.

quash and crush their image as the formidable Hollywood super agents, some-thing which explains their hysterical rage and vindictiveness against us".[41] The condescending language Koufodinas used to describe the US intelligence services was reminiscent of 17N's 1999 provocative "Come and get us, if you really can" communiqué released a week after reports in the Greek media that US intelligence had provided the Simitis government with a list of 17N members.[42]

For Koufodinas, present-day Greece was not very far ideologically from the post-civil war Greece of the 1960s. One did not have to be a historian of modern Greece, he said, in order to recognize that the deep polarizations, running from top to bottom of Greece's inequality-riven society were the product of "a state that used scandalous taxation and banking systems to direct the capital made by many to the pockets of the few, driving the country into economic decline, stagnation and today's inevitable de-industrialization".[43] There was no shadow of doubt in Koufodinas' mind that Greece was run by thieves and that the people mainly responsible for turning the Greek polity into a kleptocracy were the country's established political elites. Having declared that Greek politicians on all sides had cheating in their bloodstream, Koufodinas also made plain that he particularly deplored the fact that the parties of the left had long been "assimilated by the present political regime, and had in fact become the regimes' left-side crutches, selling out struggles and letting the achievements of past decades go to waste".[44]

From Marx to Velouchiotis

The resort to violence was for Koufodinas a reasonable and calculated response to a resigned, defeatist and inept left which reneged on its own principles. "But beyond this left", Koufodinas argued, "there also exists the anti-regime left, the left which refuses to turn the other cheek too; the left which believes that the solution against the deep flaws of the system and the political, social and cultural crisis can only be a revolutionary solution".[45] Taking his theme further, Koufodinas paraphrased from Karl Marx's *Das Kapital* and *The Communist Manifesto* in order to rationalize 17N's campaign of violence and argue that according to Marx, violence of that kind was not terrorism.[46]

---

[41] Ibid.
[42] "We have but one answer to all these reports", said the eight-page communiqué to *Eleftherotypia* newspaper, "Come and get us, if you can". See *Eleftherotypia*, 16 March 1999 and *Athens News*, 17 March 1999.
[43] Court proceedings, Korydallos prison chambers, 24 July 2003.
[44] Ibid.
[45] Ibid.
[46] Ibid.

The strategies of guerrilla groups of Latin America, the Tupamaros in particular, were also employed by 17N's operational leader to explain how the group came to see the use and practice of organized military force as an effective instrument of policy. Koufodinas seemed to agree with the strategic approach that, for groups like 17N, a sophisticated understanding of the utility of the military instrument and how it can best be exploited in a psychological sense was of catalytic importance if the political goals of the group were ever to be fulfilled. When 17N commandos, Koufodinas said, "raided the Vyronas police station and the National War Museum making off with anti-tank weapons and bazookas, and the same when they entered the Sykourio military warehouse stealing 60 rockets, grenades, bullets and other explosives and all this without firing a single bullet, they demonstrated that 17N was not only a self-appointed group but also a group that had the appropriate resources at its disposal to engage in revolutionary armed struggle".[47]

For Koufodinas, one could say anything one liked about 17N, except that they were something other than what they always claimed to be and showed themselves to be in all of their actions. 17N's activities, he further argued, "had the very same characteristics as the activities of the [Greek] resistance".[48] Koufodinas did not attempt to present himself as a modern-day Aris Velouchiotis, the charismatic guerrilla leader and founder of ELAS (the Greek People's Liberation Army), but it quickly became apparent that he idolized him. "When Aris entered a village and gave a speech in the village square under the nose of the Germans with his armed partisans in formation, he was both demonstrating that armed resistance was possible and cultivating the ground for further activity".[49] By linking ELAS' military aims and practices to those of 17N, Koufodinas wanted to show that the group's armed struggle taking place "in a country which has experienced humiliation, exclusion, state-terrorism, the absolute power of plutocrats, policemen and military judges" was merely defensive.[50] 17N attacked targets, Koufodinas said,

> which symbolized imperialism and capitalism. And, yes, we did manage to terrorize them if you consider that Washington spent more on protection for its Athens embassy than it did anywhere else in the world. [And if you consider] that the security services of big countries in the West kept on sending their best experts and kept on offering astronomical sums of money for information that would lead to an arrest; that the Greek big industrialists and tycoons would build fortresses and have armies of bodyguards. All these people – and we're talking about a few thousand of them – were really terrorized by us and for that we are very proud.[51]

[47] Ibid.
[48] Ibid.
[49] Ibid.
[50] Ibid.
[51] Ibid.

Koufodinas also denied charges that 17N had held the country to ransom by terror. 17N violence was, as he put it, very carefully controlled and discriminate and "the majority of the Greek people did not go to sleep every night fearing that their lives were in danger from 17N".[52] For Koufodinas, it was the regime's violence instead which "provoked fear and terror in the entire population and it was the violence of the state security mechanisms which caused loneliness and human degradation".[53] 17N's operations chief also charged that "the regime used the term 'terrorism' to cover up the reality of its own violence and attempt at the same time to defame the [group's] popular anti-violence".[54]

Koufodinas took this theme further by dealing with the question of how far the military instrument could be manipulated to achieve the group's political goals. Declaring that 17N had "rightly been characterized by many as an orga-nization of moderation", he went on to explain that the group was never under any illusions about "the movement's level of development and that was pre-cisely why it did not declare total war on all fronts".[55] Although he failed to acknowledge directly the fact that the military means at the group's disposal were always limited, Koufodinas observed that 17N "never made full use of all available resources because the group did not want to rush things and also because it never confused its goals with reality and violence with present politi-cal circumstances".[56] According to Koufodinas, it was "within this logic that 17N made no attempts to attack at the heart of the Greek state so there could be no exaggerated polarization"[57] which would have (even though Koufodinas refused to admit so) precipitated the group's undoing as proved to be the case in Italy with the Red Brigades.[58]

'Armed propaganda', 'revolutionary violence' and 'political results'

17N leadership was influenced by the BR view that military actions "are intended as armed propaganda", and that violence was used to both "illustrate new pos-sibilities of political action and secure some form of political recognition" (Moss, 1983, p. 85). To Koufodinas it was clear that every single armed action was an effective instrument of propaganda aimed at building momentum and gaining

[52] Ibid.
[53] Ibid.
[54] Ibid.
[55] Ibid.
[56] Ibid.
[57] Ibid.
[58] In 17N's *Manifesto 1992*, the communiqué writer acknowledges that it would never have been able to survive and avoid capture had the group not drawn lessons from the Red Brigades' experi-ence. See *Manifesto 1992*, dated 17 November 1992.

support. 17N's operations chief further argued that the propaganda value of a military action was determined by the type and nature of that action. Armed action, he said, could only carry the group and the movement forward to its objectives if the selection of target was one that "spoke for itself and also one that ordinary people immediately understood and identified with".[59] Mapping out certain parameters of 17N's strategic formulation, Koufodinas insisted that the target selection must also be such that "exposes and de-legitimates the regime without having any negative political or material consequences for the workers and the mass movement".[60] Koufodinas saw 17N military activity as

> inextricably linked to the wide popular masses and their everyday problems and therefore strikes were directed against targets like the tax system of the swindler state or against the regime of public hospital doctors whose lack of ethos and humanity forced patients into spending huge sums to see big-name doctors and attend private clinics. 17N's activities also had symbolic value. It selected target-symbols of power and authority in every political, economic and social sphere: representatives of institutional mechanisms and of imperialistic hegemony and capitalist exploitation, corrupted politicians and civil servants, thieves of social wealth and public property.[61]

Koufodinas was equally emphatic about the 'political results' of 17N's activities. In his words, 17N's actions were generally seen as "just social defence against" agents of anti-national interest such as the plutocratic oligarchy whose "deeds were causing serious social damage".[62] Koufodinas asked the judges somewhat sarcastically "whether society or individual members of that society should have the right to defend themselves against such acts of heavy social cost, especially when your own institutional mechanisms have been doing nothing about it".[63] As far as Koufodinas was concerned, 17N "functioned as a counterbalance against such an all-powerful regime while articulating at the same time the message that some people still resist and will always continue to resist".[64] For him, "17N actions against the powerful mechanisms of the regime had a rejuvenating effect on the Greek populace's sense of dignity and pride".[65] Koufodinas' point was to show that 17N actions were "judged by the Greek people on the basis of their past humiliating, oppressive and exploitative experiences, as actions of self-defence and popular justice. And this is why 17N's actions were met with social and popular acceptance".[66]

[59] Court proceedings, Korydallos prison chambers, 24 July 2003.
[60] Ibid.
[61] Ibid.
[62] Ibid.
[63] Ibid.
[64] Ibid
[65] Ibid.
[66] Ibid.

Koufodinas repeatedly rejected media claims that the group were psychotic ideologues fighting a hopeless war. To Koufodinas it was clear that "an armed revolutionary", was not a "maniac of violence, a lunatic, a lover of guns and killings".[67] Treating the court to a philosophic *tour d'horizon*, 17N's operations chief argued that a revolutionary "chooses violence as a direct response through political analyses".[68] "And once he has chosen to go down that path", Koufodinas added, "he has the obligation, if he is true to himself and to his ideas, to go all the way".[69] Koufodinas presented the armed revolutionary as someone "whose life choices are actually made against his personal interests".[70] As someone "who, having to overcome his strong instincts for self-survival, seeks a closer encounter with a biologically unreasonable existence – unreasonable simply because he is in danger of losing his freedom".[71] Rather than advancing the view that a revolutionary's existence began to have meaning only once he joined a group in which he belonged and had faith, Koufodinas argued somewhat paradoxically that "this actually happens at the point when the fighter is forced to experience a deep and unbearable contradiction between love for life and the necessity for action against it".[72] At the same time, Koufodinas did not want to be seen to be retreating behind the defence that the fighter had to "pay a very high price of pain for this contradiction", as he phrased it. The price was undoubtedly high, he added, but this was compensated by the fact that the fighter was "taking part in a struggle against protogenic violence – violence that denies man his inner essence, dehumanizes him and ultimately sinks him into barbarity".[73]

Unlike Alexandros Giotopoulos, the group's chief ideologue who denied participation in 17N, Koufodinas as one of the leaders and chief organizer of the group took responsibility for the entire 17N experience and sought to defend their violent actions by placing them in the political and historical context of the period. An emblematic personality of 17N terrorism Dimitris Koufodinas embraced the view that Greece's "self-negating democracy" necessitated exactly the kind of political violence that they had undertaken. Unapologetic to the end about the group's murderous record, Koufodinas told the court that death was fundamentally not a moral problem but a political one and therefore "labels such as assassins and deplorable killers that people place upon us, cannot really define our actions".[74]

---

[67] Ibid.
[68] Ibid.
[69] Ibid.
[70] Ibid.
[71] Ibid.
[72] Ibid.
[73] Ibid.
[74] Court proceedings, Korydallos prison chambers, 24 July 2003.

Savvas Xiros

"I am distressed for every murder, for every tear, for every sob, for all the mourning I have caused."

While Koufodinas tried in court to explain that the starting point and motive for all 17N actions had always been the group's political beliefs and its vision of a better world, Savvas Xiros spent his limited (because of his multiple injuries) energies trying to convince everybody inside and outside the courtroom that his hospital testimony (which implicated most of the other defendants) was the result of torture and psychotropic drugs.[75] Claiming that he was forced by the anti-terrorism authorities to give names and denounce the terrorist group he once served, Xiros said that he was "held illegally for 40 days in contravention of every law, with my eyes constantly bound, without sleep for days, tied with tight ropes and chains, under constant interrogation with no sense of time and under conditions of psychological violence and with threats of extradition [to the US] and against my life".[76] Marinos Pittaridis, the doctor who looked after Xiros at Evagellismos Hospital and saved his life, saw things differently. This is how he described the whole episode and it is worth quoting his words in full:

> The security inside but also outside the hospital was unprecedented. Surrounded by police the hospital felt more like a high-security prison than a public hospital. Everyday we had to go through countless checks. Our name, our position in the hospital, our daily tasks were checked. What time we went in, what time we left. The truth is that it took a while for the doctors and staff to win the trust of the anti-terrorist squad officers. In their eyes, those first days, we were all suspect terrorists.
>
> When Savvas Xiros was brought into the intensive care unit, we did not know what 'type' of terrorist he was, meaning what terrorist group he was

[75] In his hospital testimony, Xiros stated that "this present day, I consider myself not a member of 17N but a victim of that organization. I therefore ask to be tried with leniency and that's why I went beyond what I was asked, giving a very detailed testimony. I regard my testimony as a public confession before God and his people. I ask forgiveness from all those I hurt and particularly the relatives of the victims without thinking for a minute that an apology is sufficient".

[76] Ibid. On solely legal grounds, Xiros' defence raised questions about the circumstances of his client's weeks of detention and interrogation in room 1031 of Evagellismos hospital without a lawyer present before being charged. Xiros' lawyer, Giorgos Agiostratitis maintained that "our constitution provides that from the arrest of anyone charged with crime, they must be brought before a judge within 24 hours. If the person charged is incapacitated, the judge goes to the hospital. Only in this case, he went 70 days later. Either the person charge is medically able to present himself to the judge or the investigating judge can go to the hospital and conduct the questioning in the presence of a lawyer. Otherwise, if the person charged is sick and unable to move and a judge does not come to see him, the questioning that took place should have not taken place". Author's interview with Giorgos Agiostratitis, Athens, 14 October 2002.

from. We were kept in the dark. Until we learned from TV who Savvas Xiros was, we never imagined that he could be a 17 November member. As a doctor I felt a huge responsibility to make sure that everything that could be done to save him was done. I'm pretty sure that if Xiros hadn't made it, there would have been plenty of people out there accusing us of not trying hard enough.

When you do a job like mine, the first thing you must have is neutrality. You must never confuse emotions and duty. Never discriminate. From the very first moment, I tried to push away the thought that the patient in that intensive care unit was a terrorist who had spread death. For me he was just another patient who you have to try to keep alive. Savvas Xiros has tried to make excuses to his comrades for what happened but the truth is that he and only he wanted to talk. And he didn't talk because we gave him medication that makes you talk – such medication doesn't exist anyway – but because he was really scared that they would come after him and kill him. I remember trying to calm him down telling him not to worry, that it's all over and him saying to me: is it really, or is this the beginning?

When he began talking to the anti-terrorism prosecutor, Yiannis Diotis and the chief of the anti-terrorism squad, he would talk non-stop till the early hours of the morning. I asked him several times if he wanted me to intervene so he wouldn't have to talk for so long but every time I asked him, he would say: No. Let me talk; let me get it out of the way.[77]

In his 4 March 2003 "not guilty" plea, which was read out by the court's president given Xiros' poor eyesight following the explosion, the son of an Orthodox priest from Salonica challenged the court's jurisdiction stating that he considered "the court not competent to judge this case, because it is called upon to judge political acts, which only the people and history are competent to judge".[78] Xiros also said in his prepared testimony that the central goal of the court was "to defame our struggle and every other type of social struggle and terrorize in advance all those who might consider similar actions in the future".[79]

It is a risk to try to penetrate the mental processes of a 17N terrorist with involvement in 85 terrorist acts in the space of 17 years but Xiros became something of tragic figure inside the Korydallos court. His tragedy stemmed from his inability or even refusal to come to terms with his guilt for what happened and it was the tension between guilt and reality that ran through every section of Xiros' testimony. Unable to reconcile himself to his own failures and sensitive to the charge that he informed on his comrades, Xiros blended fact with fiction, past and present, delivering his arguments with plenty of polemic

[77] Author's interview with Marinos Pittaridis, Athens, 19 May 2003.
[78] Court proceedings, Korydallos prison chambers, 4 March 2003.
[79] Ibid.

but very little conviction. There can be no question that he was the man whose hospital testimony resulted in the dismantling of 17N and led to the arrest of most of his comrades. However, from the moment Koufodinas decided to surrender and Xiros found himself reunited with him and the rest in Korydallos prison, he tried to exorcize, if not delete, the reality of his previous actions with contradictory statements and rants about plots, threats, psychotropic medicines. Xiros' hard-fought but pointless battle in rebuilding his 17N terrorist image finally ended in repentance and remorse. Asking for forgiveness from the families of his victims, the religious icon painter said in a handwritten letter distributed to the Greek media the day after he received six life sentences, that he was "distressed for every murder, for every tear, for every sob, for all the mourning and pain"[80] he had caused.

Patroklos Tselentis

"The moment I heard of Savvas' injury, I thought the group's time is up. From that moment on, I was ready and determined about everything. A part of my life had collapsed."

Known inside the group as "Film" for his love of photography and cinema, Patroklos Tselentis was arrested on 25 July 2002 and became 17N's biggest pentito[81] after Savvas Xiros decided to retract his original hospital confession. Tselentis' police confession and subsequent court testimony were central to the state's case against the group's two main leaders Giotopoulos and Koufodinas. "Every act of the group", Tselentis told the court, "was known to and prepared by Giotopoulos and Koufodinas".[82] Tselentis and Koufodinas went to the same university in Athens and it was Koufodinas who inducted him into the group in 1983 where Tselentis lasted until the autumn of 1988 having participated in 11 operations, the last being the 17N raid of an Athens police station in August 1998.

---

[80] On Xiros' full statement and his contradictory, if not tormented, nine months in Korydallos courtroom see *Eleftherotypia*, 17 December 2003.

[81] As in Italy, Greek anti-terrorism legislation encouraged voluntary collaboration and co-operation with the authorities and the renunciation of terrorist aims and methods. In Italy the penitence law was introduced in May 1982. In order to benefit from it, the *pentito* had to make a full confession of all crimes committed, and second she/he had to make an active contribution towards the prevention of further acts of terrorism. It was then up to the judicial authorities to decide on the relevance of the evidence provided, how much a prison sentence could be reduced. Patrizio Peci was the Red Brigades' biggest *pentito* and in his book *Io L'Iinfame* [I, the Vile One] he listed all the reasons for his decision.

[82] Court proceedings, Korydallos prison chambers, 30 July 2003.

In court, Tselentis spoke in a monotone but with regret[83] and discernible remorse about the murders he and the other 17N terrorists had committed, prompting the prosecutor to praise him for his straightforward stance in co-operating with the authorities. "The fact that you chose to side with the good and the legal", said the prosecutor, "honours you and will help you be at ease with your conscience for the rest of your life".[84]

Most people, and terrorists are generally no exception, do not ordinarily engage in reprehensible conduct until they have justified to themselves the morality of their actions. According to Tselentis, towards the end of 1987, he could no longer justify 17N's activities or his direct role in those activities and became disillusioned.[85] Running rapidly out "enthusiasm", to use his own phrase, Tselentis told the court that a point was reached when

> it became very obvious that our actions and particularly our communiqués did not have the impact I had hoped they would. I could see that our initia-tives were, in fact, distancing us from solutions instead of bringing us closer to them. I could also see society changing whereas we, I and the other group members, were stuck in the past. My biggest problem, however, was that I could no longer comprehend the obsessiveness on the part of some members for constant violent activity. This, in the language of the left, is called mili-tarism. There was, in other words, a need for violent activity being carried out constantly but for no objective reason.[86]

Tselentis tried to explain why, "in spite of the fact that [he] disagreed with all this and could see that it was going nowhere",[87] he still did not go to the police. "There can be only one answer to this", he said.[88] Calm and articulate, Tselentis went on to argue that "a member of such a group is a conscious member. He fervently believes that what he does is the right thing, is morally accepted. He feels, in many ways, that part of society condones his stance".[89] Extremely sensitive to the fact that he might be branded as a traitor, Tselentis went out of his way to clarify that he would never set himself up as a scourge and a whistle blower. Tselentis told the court that, for reasons which may readily be guessed, it would never be him, reneging on his own principles. To Tselentis it was clear that "you don't betray people who are willing to sacrifice their lives for what they believe in even if you have come to disagree with

---

[83] "Court president, judges, prosecutors, I must first of all ask forgiveness of society, of those who co-operated with and trusted me, of those who loved me" were Tselentis's first words in his court testimony. Court proceedings, Korydallos prison chambers, 30 July 2003.
[84] Ibid.
[85] Ibid.
[86] Ibid.
[87] Ibid.
[88] Ibid.
[89] Ibid.

them".[90] The 17N pentito took his argument further by saying that it was one thing to disagree with comrades who pursued unrealizable goals by means of unrealistic strategies and another to give them over to "police authorities whose methods and tactics, as everybody knows, have never inspired popular confidence".[91]

Tselentis did not avoid discussing the crucial issue of morality. To the question of how could he be perfectly willing to participate in assassinations of people but not find the courage to bring a solution to that problem, Tselentis' reply was: "cowardice". Wrestling with himself "because of my past, I tried to expiate for all the things I had done. I tried to become a model citizen, trying to help, to the degree that I was able, all the people around me who could do with my help".[92] "I joined the Army," he told the court, "got married and tried to start again, tried to lead a normal life".[93]

Tselentis, in stark contrast to Koufodinas and Giotopoulos who had nothing to say first-hand about the group's inner workings, told the court that the 17N leadership would gather on the fourth of each month in cafeterias to discuss tactics and future targets! As he explained, the logic behind such gatherings in public places was that the more public the place the less suspicion it would arouse. "We always made sure that we picked big, crowded places with lots of noise so we could talk without being overheard by other people".[94] Providing the court with a brief organizational profile of 17N, Tselentis said that "every attack would take on average two years to prepare for and each communiqué to follow the attack would be thoroughly discussed among 17N members with the final touches being put in place three to four weeks before the actual operation".[95] According to Tselentis, the group had numerous (more than three at a time) hideouts with arms and explosives but each member responsible for a hideout was given no details about the rest.

Tselentis also spoke at length about the personalities of Alexandros Giotopoulos and Dimitris Koufodinas. Tselentis described Giotopoulos as someone "very confident, well educated with a strong personality and robust rhetorical abilities. Someone who commanded my respect from the moment I first met him".[96] When asked by the state prosecutor about Giotopoulos' motives and what drove him to his crimes and the reasons that pushed him towards the terrorist activity that he is accused of, Tselentis said that he had "little doubt that the man he met then, did everything that he did for ideological reasons", before adding that "in the end, power in whatever form always

[90] Ibid.
[91] Ibid.
[92] Ibid.
[93] Ibid.
[94] Ibid.
[95] Ibid.
[96] Ibid.

brings about arrogance, decadence and degeneration".[97] The 17N pentito took issue with Giotopoulos' dogmatic intransigence. "I could see", he told the court president, that "he stubbornly refused to accept that his view of the world was mistaken".[98] Asked to make a brief comparison between the 17N's ideologue and its chief organizer, Tselentis asserted that Giotopoulos and Koufodinas couldn't be further apart. Giotopoulos was "cultured and elitist, in a class of his own" whereas Koufodinas was "a simple but diligent and moralistic man, who was also in some ways socially diffident. He was insular and had difficulties in mixing with other people".[99]

The gulf between the two men could be seen from their reactions to Tselentis' damaging court testimony. Whereas Giotopoulos' language was deliberately condescending and was used to attack Tselentis ("pathetic little man"), Koufodinas gently admonished his "former fighter and former friend, for choosing to go down the path of collaboration".[100] "Patroklos Tselentis", said Koufodinas nodding with that peculiar mixture of indifference and frowning solemnity,

> found himself at the hands of the institutions he fought against when in 17N, but has now come to accept and support them. He decided to collaborate, to tell what these agencies want him to say, to hurt and slander the group and its members. However, he will soon discover that after choosing the path of collaboration, there's no turning back. After he has said whatever he thinks he needs to say that can be of benefit to him, after he speaks damagingly against all his co-defendants, after he has distorted the truth and defamed the organization, they will then be forced to lie even more before abandoning him like a used lemon rind to face society's contempt.[101]

Up to the end of his testimony, Tselentis repeated mechanically (it obviously mattered enormously to him) that when he left in the autumn of 1988, no member of the group tried to force him to change his mind. Before concluding his testimony Tselentis, went on to challenge Koufodinas' most insistent theme during the trial which was that 17N's armed struggle was merely defensive:

> The only thing I can say is that this is not the way. And such practices lead to tragic results. The group members get cut off from society, take decisions outside society and their very own existence inside conspiratorial organizations has tragic consequences not only for society itself but also for themselves. Savvas Xiros is a tragic case. And the same applies to Dimitris Koufodinas. Beyond their tragic victims, they are tragic victims themselves.[102]

[97] Ibid.
[98] Ibid.
[99] Ibid.
[100] Ibid.
[101] Ibid.
[102] Ibid.

Terrorism as a Way of Life

"Why did you kill my husband?" Dora Bakoyiannis – Athens mayor at the time and widow of 17N victim, Pavlos Bakoyiannis, who was assassinated in 1989 – asked Dimitris Koufodinas. "Read our proclamation", came the laconic reply from him. "It sets out the reasons very well."[103] This type of remark was typical of 17N thinking and underlined the fact that the group's conception of the political arena was not one where men and women are invited to choose freely between competing ideas and visions through argument and debate, but one characterized by a series of immovable truths to which people should owe allegiance. It was Koufodinas' philosophy of the gun that for almost three decades underpinned 17N's campaign of terrorism. Ignoring the fact that violence "should not take the place of the political purpose, nor obliterate it" (Paret, 1986, p. 200), 17N continued the sporadic killing and wounding of high-profile targets as the most effective way available to crystallize public disaffection with the regime and embed itself in mainstream consciousness.

How will history judge 17N? What was 17N after all? 17N was, according to Giotopoulos' defence lawyer, Yiannis Rachiotis, "an organization very different" from the rest of the left and from other armed groups that operated in Western Europe.[104] For Rachiotis, "the [Greek] left as we all know was, until 17N's emergence, on the defensive".[105] Offering a left-slanted interpretation of history Rachiotis said that 17N epitomized "the attacking left, the hunted left that finally decides to become the hunter", seeking to restore a sense of proportion and balance.[106]

History, however, will judge 17N as a failed group. Irrespective of Rachiotis' readings and despite attempts by group members to justify their actions as an extension of a historically defined Greek communist tradition and a quest for national independence and nationhood, 17N was never an authentic revolutionary group but a clandestine band of disillusioned armed militants with a flair for revolutionary rhetoric and symbolism for whom terrorism had become a way of life, a career. It was not even "a variable of the movement gone crazy", to use the phraseology of Italian 'terrorist-philosopher' Antonio Negri.[107] If Koufodinas' apologia confirmed one thing it was that he and the majority of his 17N comrades lived in a closed, self-referential world where terrorism had become a way of life from which they found it impossible to walk away. Koufodinas' stubborn refusal throughout the trial to confront reality made him speak like a man whose entire sense of life revolved around the belief that

[103] Court proceedings, Korydallos prison chambers, 1 April 2003.
[104] Court proceedings, Korydallos prison chambers, 13 March 2003.
[105] Ibid.
[106] Ibid.
[107] See interview with Negri in *The Independent*, 17 August 2004.

destiny had somehow granted him this extraordinary privilege that he must guard well and pass on at some historical point. In that sense, 17N had been impervious to political logic since it did not matter to them that their fantasy war with the Greek establishment and the Americans was pointless and doomed to failure – as long as 17N 'intervened' and 'resisted'.

Beyond this, however, there is no evading the fact that Alexandros Giotopoulos, Dimitris Koufodinas and Savvas Xiros succeeded in running rings round the Greek authorities primarily because they took advantage of the fact that Greece's national counterterrorism effort was conducted for more than two decades against a background of polarization, confrontation and rivalry between the police and the intelligence services, between government and opposition, between different sections of the Greek society. (On Greece's poor anti-terrorism efforts, see Kassimeris (2001, pp. 152–198).) No national consensus, no compromise, no co-operation. Greece was fortunate enough not to have suffered anything comparable to Italy's *anni di piombo* (years of lead) and 17N unlike the Red Brigades, never held a nation to ransom through terror but it did come closer than anyone else in the country's 30-year history of post-1974 democracy to making the Greek state appear naïve, inept and politically powerless. There are several lessons to be learned from this misadventure for both the Greek state and society. Greece can, in fact, be used as an excellent case study of what *not* to do when dealing with terrorism.

Could 17N still make a come back in some other form? The group's head of operations, Dimitris Koufodinas, was right when he said that 17N as a terrorist organization was finished. Yet, he was equally correct in saying that, "perhaps, in 10 to 15 years' time, a new generation of fighters for the people might relaunch the struggle".[108] Ideologically, Koufodinas and Co. have come to the end of the line with the group's logistical and financial apparatus having been dismantled. Yet, the dismantling of 17N does not mean the final elimination of terrorism in Greece. European experience has shown that when a major terrorist organization gets cracked, after a period of time a new generation of terrorists emerge who tend to lack the operational capabilities and scope of the group they aspire to imitate but that does not render them less dangerous. In fact, a new group calling itself Revolutionary Struggle,[109] with a string of 17N-style bomb and rocket attacks since October 2004 (less than a year after the 17N verdict) have provided worthwhile proof, if proof were really needed, that terrorism was, is and will continue to be a technique used by aggrieved groups which cannot see or refuse to see any other way of influencing political developments by conventional means. Disturbing though the truth may be, Greece before 9/11 lacked the political will to sustain a determined counterterrorism

---

[108] Court proceedings, Korydallos prison chambers, 24 July 2003.
[109] See 'Terrorism has returned to Greece' in *Wall Street Journal Europe*, 24 June 2005, and 'New terrorists, same old mistakes' in www.opendemocracy.net, 25 January 2007.

campaign thus allowing 17N to become a permanent, almost accepted fixture in Greek national life. This should never be allowed to happen again.

References

Alexander Y., & Pluchinsky, D. (Eds) (1992). *Europe's red terrorists: The fighting communist organizations* (p. 48). London: Frank Cass.

Franceschini, A. (1988). *Mara Renato ed Io: Storia dei fondatori delle BR*. Milano: Armando Mondatori Editore.

Jamieson, A. (1990). Identity and morality in the Italian Red Brigades. *Terrorism and Political Violence, 2*, 508–20.

Kassimeris, G. (2001). *Europe's last red terrorists: The Revolutionary Organization 17 November* (pp. 72–75). New York: New York University Press.

Moss, D. (1983). Analyzing Italian political violence as a sequence of communicative acts: The Red Brigades 1970–1982. *Social Analysis, 3*, 85.

Paret, P. (1986). Clausewitz. In P. Paret (Ed.), *Makers of modern strategy: From Machiavelli to the nuclear age* (p. 200). Oxford: Oxford University Press.

7

Terrorism and Organized Crime: A Theoretical Perspective[1]

Dipak K. Gupta[2], John Horgan and Alex P. Schmid

A terrorist without a cause (at least in his own mind) is not a terrorist.

Konrad Kellen[3]

Synopsis: A definitional distinction between terrorist groups and organized crime is provided that is based on their respective behavioural precepts. A microeconomic model is developed from this basic distinction. This puts diverse observations of the real world within an analytical framework. Thus, while a large body of case studies has painted a complex and seemingly counter-intuitive picture of links between terrorist groups and criminal organizations, this model lends a helping hand in sorting them out in a more systematic way. By delving deeply into the basic benefits and costs we are able to understand the reasons for certain links to exist or not exist between terrorist groups and organized criminals. Future research testing hypotheses based on this model will allow us to formulate appropriate policy parameters not on the basis of prejudice and unfounded beliefs but on the solid bedrock of empirical evidence.

Introduction

In popular imagination the nexus between terrorist groups and transnational organized crime syndicates are often taken as granted. Their unholy alliance

---

[1] Study partially funded by a grant from the US Institute of Peace.
[2] I am deeply in debt to Christopher Clague for his help. The remaining errors are ours.
[3] Kellen (1984, p. 10), quoted in Hoffman (1998, p. 43).

The Faces of Terrorism: Multidisciplinary Perspectives Edited by David Canter
© 2009 John Wiley & Sons Ltd.

opens up many frightening scenarios. Reflecting this collective concern, the journalistic media has painted an ominous picture of organized crime collaborating with the terrorist groups. In fact, a quick search by the two terms, 'terrorism' and 'organized crime' in the newspaper databases shows an incredible amount of ink spilled on the issue.[4] Over the past decade, as threats of terrorism have grown, a number of intelligence and national security agencies along with many heads of state and top-level policymakers have become concerned about the prospect of transformation and convergence of the twin scourges of our global society. Such concerns found their expression in 2001, merely two weeks after the attacks of 9/11, when the Security Council of the United Nations adopted a resolution noting "… with concern the close connection between international terrorism and transnational organized crime, illicit drugs, money-laundering, illegal arms trafficking, and illegal movement of nuclear, chemical, biological and other potentially deadly materials …".[5]

Unfortunately, despite this impressive volume of publications, there is hardly an attempt to place the discussion within a theoretical framework of behavioural perspective.

Although there is a great deal of speculation regarding the nefarious nuptial, records of painstaking studies paint a complex connection between the two. In fact, a number of more careful investigations have found a much more nuanced picture of the relationship between the two. The purpose of this paper is to put this growing literature into perspective by developing a simple behavioural model of engaging in the two kinds of activities. On the basis of this we will draw a number of hypotheses, which will be evaluated in the light of the currently available empirical literature on terrorist and organized crime groups.

Any attempt at examining the relationship cannot escape the need to define the two extra-legal organizations. However, despite some heroic attempts (Schmid & Jongman, 1988), the general consensus is that there is no universally accepted definition of terrorism. However, based on the large number of publications, we can offer a working definition of terrorism, which would include such characteristics as attacks against a civilian population by an organized group, intention of achieving some political or religious objectives, perpetrated by non-state actors (see Hoffman, 1998). Similarly, despite wide-ranging differences in opinion (see Naylor, 1997, p. 6; Naylor, 2002, pp. 14–18; Reuter, 1983, p. 75), it is generally argued that an organized crime may be defined with the help of attributes such as an established hierarchy,[6] durability

---

[4]A search by the two terms in an academic database (Pro Quest search) since September 2001 yields nearly 2,000 hits, mostly in newspapers and popular magazines. A similar Google search shows over 5 million entries.

[5]US Security Council Resolution # 1373 (9/28/2001).

[6]It is important at this point to note that there is a distinction between organized groups and clusters.

of organization, and involvement in criminal activities to make financial gains or positions of power for the core members of the group.[7]

For this study, we will accept the outlines of the two definitions given above and will add an important behavioural distinction between the two. Although both terrorist groups and organized criminal groups reside outside the perimeter of the legal structure of organized societies, there is a marked difference in the core motivation between the two. Hoffman (1998, p. 43) correctly points out: "… the terrorist is fundamentally an altruist: he believes he is serving a 'good' cause designed to achieve a greater good for a wider constituency. … The criminal, by comparison, serves no cause at all, just his own personal aggrandizement and material satiation." Similarly, Jamieson notes (2005, p. 165): "Organized crime and terrorism are correctly viewed as quite distinct phenomena. Essentially, the terrorist is a revolutionary, with clear political objectives involving the overthrow of a government or status quo, and a set of articulated strategies to achieve them. Organized crime actors are inherently conservative: they tend to resist political upheaval and seek conditions of order and stability, those more conducive to their business activities."

Thus, through their activities, a terrorist group attempts to achieve public goods, the benefits of which must be shared with the entire community irrespective of an individual's participation in the endeavour to procure it.[8] Therefore, a terrorist group, by definition must be *primarily* altruistic in its aims. In contrast, a criminal gang does not operate out of any higher callings. Their predominant motivation is the provision of private and/or quasi-public goods, which are shared only among the core members of the gang.

This importance of this distinction between the two groups becomes manifestly clear when we consider their respective strategies. A terrorist group undertakes violent activities to communicate with their base, their adversaries and their clients (Schmid & de Graaf, 1982). As a result, many of these acts, as Combs (2006) points out, mix violence with drama. Through these 'propaganda by deed' political dissident groups claim responsibilities and gain prominence. In

---

[7]For a detailed discussion of the definitional issues, see the UN Centre for International Crime Prevention (2002), pp. 6–7. Also, in this context, it is important to note that for organized crime it is worthwhile to distinguish between a group and a cluster. A cluster is an assemblage of small groups, which are often treated as if they form a single entity. For instance, the Russian Mafia or the Sicilian Mafia may give the impression of a single entity, but they are composed of many small groups, often at odds with each other. However, for this study, this distinction is somewhat less important.

[8]The concept of public goods was introduced by Samuelson (1965) and these are defined with two important attributes, *excludability* and *exhaustibility*. Public goods are for the enjoyment of every member of the community, regardless of their level of involvement in the effort at procuring these goods. Thus, if tax dollars pay for clean air, a destitute person who does not pay any taxes is free to enjoy the benefits of a clean environment. Second, the benefits of public goods do not get exhausted with the increase in the number of users. Therefore, when a new child is born, we do not worry about her share of the clean air (see Baumol & Blinder, 1985, pp. 543–44).

contrast, a criminal group, by its very nature, is secretive and tries to work under the broader radarscope of the state apparatus. To gain public attention is not part of their primary motivation. Jamieson (2005) thus points out that while a terrorist group would strive to upset the political status quo and invite anarchy and chaos in the process, a sophisticated organized crime group would like to work within the political system by infiltrating it with bribery and threat. They would, therefore, like any other commercial venture, want to promote the status quo, unless of course the state is directly targeting them.

Since the two groups have divergent objectives the state is also likely to be asymmetrical in it response. Terrorism poses a political as well as a general threat to the state authorities. These acts are violent, often spectacular and their randomness brings insecurity to the entire population. In contrast, organized crime activities target only certain sections, which are often considered to be at the fringe of society. Given this important distinction, it is safe to assume that, in general, the state would react much more sharply facing threats of terrorism than acts of crime.

Defining Linkages

Since the two groups are interested in two different objectives, it seems reasonable to assume that similar to any other normal activity they will be tempted to get involved with both. Specifically, we can broadly define the areas of collaboration and transformation between terrorist groups and organized crimes as follows:

1) A terrorist group engages in non-political criminal activities, such as bank robbery, gun running, human trafficking, drug dealing, etc. to sustain its political goals.
2) A terrorist group episodically collaborates with organized crime groups to purchase or transport weapons (including weapons of mass destruction) and/or operatives.
3) A terrorist group collaborates on a sustained basis with an organized crime gang(s) to engage in criminal activities to raise money to carry out its political agenda.
4) A criminal group collaborates on a sustained basis with terrorist groups to engage in acts of political violence and terrorism. In other words, criminal groups metamorphose into political groups.

A number of studies are gathering information on these four types of possible collaborations. We would like to propose a behavioural model, on the basis of which, we can predict the contours of such a relationship.

The Model

To recapitulate, although there are many points of similarities between a terrorist group and an organized crime group, the fundamental distinction rests with their goals. A terrorist organization's primary objective is the political, such as a change in the government, independence for a part of a country, or the establishment of a new social order based on a certain political or religious view. By nature, these are public goods. If these goals are attained, the benefits emanating from them will flow to every member of a community regardless of participation. In contrast, a criminal gang is not interested in attaining political goods. Instead, they aim for quasi-public goods, which benefit only the members of their group. This is an important distinction and, for this reason, Dishman (2001, p. 46) correctly points out that "drug barons and revolutionary leaders do not walk the same path to success".

We hypothesize that a group can participate in two kinds of activities. The first aims at procuring public goods, benefiting the entire community and the second, quasi-public goods, promoting welfare of only the members of the group. We further assume that public goods are achieved through altruistic acts of terrorism, whereas the quasi-public goods are acquired by taking part in criminal activities.

$$\text{Max } U = \pi_p(P) + \pi_q(Q) \tag{1}$$

Where U = Utility derived by a group by engaging in the two types of activities

P = Public goods (benefits to the entire community regardless of participation)

Q = Quasi-public goods (benefits to the group members and its leadership)

π_p = Relative weight placed by the organization on achieving public goods (P)

π_q = Relative weight placed by the organization on achieving quasi-public goods (Q)

Since a group can engage in procuring either a public or a quasi-public good, we write: $\pi_p + \pi_q = 1$

Since a terrorist group is defined by its primary need to procure public goods, we can see that for it, $\pi_p > \pi_q > .5$. Gupta (2005) has argued that not all terrorist organizations are the same in the putative relative importance they place on ideological goals. While groups like al-Qaeda and Hamas operate from a strong ideological position, others, such as the Abu Sayyaf and the FARC in Colombia tend to be much more interested in making money for their core membership. Thus those rare groups, which are purely ideological, will have weights of $\pi_p = 1$; $\pi_q = 0$. However, for criminal groups, $\pi_p < \pi_q$ and those which are purely criminal, $\pi_p = 0$; $\pi_q = 1$. And for those groups that operate from mixed motives, the relative weights for the two are greater than 0. Since it is impossible to be a pure altruist (Andreoni, 1990), we can conjecture that while terrorist organizations would operate from a mixed motive $(1 > \pi_p > .5)$, for most criminal groups such confusion of objectives is rarely present. The relative strength of this ideological position of a terrorist group reflects the importance it places on its activities. Thus while engaging in criminal activities may be less risky and more remunerative (especially for the core group members), in choosing the appropriate mix, the leadership must weigh in the risks of loss of political legitimacy as a result of their close association with criminal activities.[9]

When a group participates in extra-legal activities, it risks being apprehended and punished (C). These coefficients are externally given to the terrorist groups as a result of deliberate public policies adopted by the governmental authorities and implemented by the law enforcement agencies and the military.

Thus for the two activities, a group faces the relative cost (TC) as:

$$TC = c_p P + c_q Q = \overline{C} \tag{2}$$

We assume that a group has the capability $(\overline{C})$ to absorb a finite amount of cost incurred as a result of their extra-legal activities.[10] This cost figure incorporates the negative sanctions imposed by the state authorities.

Thus based on our discussion, we can write the maximand as:

$$\text{Max } U = \pi_p P + \pi_q Q + \lambda\left(\overline{C} - c_p T - c_q Q^2\right)$$

The first order condition shows preference for the two activities:

$$\frac{\delta U}{\delta P} = \pi_p - \lambda c_p = 0 \tag{3}$$

[9]The importance of the support of the client base is well recognized in the literature. For instance Bloom (2004) demonstrates the close association between popular support for suicide bombing among the Palestinian population in West Bank and the Gaza Strip and the staging of suicide bombings by the Hamas, the PIJ and other dissident groups. Similarly, Kalyvas and Sanchez-Cuenca (2005) argue how a group must choose its strategies based on the cultural, religious and political sensitivities of their base.
[10]For a similar assumption, see Enders and Sandler (2005) p. 36.

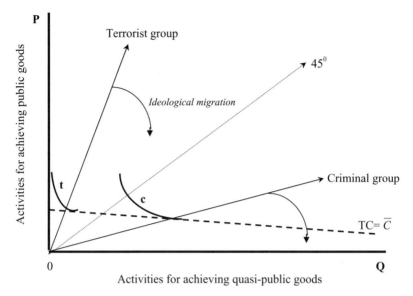

Figure 7.1. Transformation of Groups

and,

$$\frac{\delta U}{\delta Q} = \pi_q - \lambda C_q = 0 \tag{4}$$

Our formulation yields the familiar maximization principle of marginal utility from an activity being equal to its marginal cost. However, this simple formulation allows us to develop a number of important hypotheses, which can help us understand the complex findings of various case studies. We have presented the geometric version of our model in Figure 7.1.

Figure 7.1 pictorially depicts our arguments. In this diagram, the vertical axis measures the utility that a group derives from obtaining public goods, while the horizontal axis indicates the utility of quasi-public goods. The 45 degree line shows an equal preference (.5) for the two goods. Any position above this line implies that a group derives a greater utility from achieving a unit of public goods than from a unit of quasi-public good, while the positions below show the opposite. We may recall that we assume that a group obtains public good through terrorist activities and quasi-public goods by being engaged in criminal endeavours. Thus a hypothetical terrorist group will typically demonstrate a position shown by the indifference map (t). In contrast, a criminal organization will choose its optimal mix along the indifference map (c).

The dashed line TC is analogous to a budget constraint, within which a group must choose a combination of the two activities in order to maximize its utility. We may note that the slope of the cost curve presupposes a higher cost imposed by the state for engaging in terrorist activities.

Hypotheses and Empirical Evidence

Our simple model gives us some interesting insights into our stated problem. The problem with conducting research in the murky area of interaction between terrorist groups and criminal organizations is the secret nature of the two. Furthermore, terrorist organizations because of their political goal, attempt to portray a 'squeaky-clean' appearance. On the other hand, their protagonists, the government and their political rivals, in order to undermine the political legitimacy in the eyes of their constituents attempt to paint the two with the same brush. As a result, the supportive evidence for our model must come from secondary sources of published reports. On the basis of this logical formulation, we can draw the following hypotheses:

Hypothesis 1. *Due to its financial need to carry out political activities, a terrorist group will operate from a mixed motive with a varying degree of commitment toward public good and quasi-public good.* As Gunaratna (2001) and others have shown, in order to sustain themselves, every terrorist organization must operate a sideline of legal and illegal activities to raise money. A sophisticated terrorist group, like any other organization must have division of labour. Within its organizational structure, even the most ideological group must include those whose primary task it is to raise money. As a result, a terrorist group would always have the proclivity to veer off toward pure criminality.

Hypothesis 2. *Despite widespread fear, the actual collaboration between a terrorist group and an organized crime group would be rare and, when there is such a rapport, it will be episodic rather than sustained and long term.* In 2002, a study commissioned by the United Nations Centre for International Crime Prevention (CICP) asked governments of 40 countries to indicate whether there were evidences of collaboration between the two groups (Dandaurand & Chin, 2004). The results indicated that only 22% of the groups engaged in sustained levels of collaboration both internally and externally. A full 30% of the groups showed no link whatsoever (see Figure 7.2). Based on this evidence, the study (p. 28) noted that "The nature of the links between the two types of groups seemed to be primarily logistical and financial, denoting the presence of alliances of convenience. It tended to be operational, in those relatively rare instances where there were also some

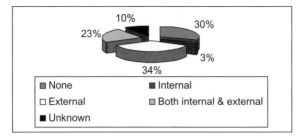

Figure 7.2. Co-operation between Terrorist and Organized Crime Groups

ideological and political links between the two groups".[11] Thus, Schmid (2005, p. 8) points out: "… terrorism – that peculiar mix of violence, politics, and propaganda – should not be confused with mainly profit-driven organized crime. The vague narco-terrorism formula with its implicit call to fuse the 'war on drugs' and the 'war on terror' might offer a misleading intellectual roadmap to address the problem of terrorism. For that a broader definition is required". Similarly, Dishman (2001, p. 45) concludes that "In fact, little evidence suggests that Mafia groups and terrorists are interested in pursuing collaborative arrangements with each other to traffic contraband or commit other crimes".

Hypothesis 3. *As the ideological needs become less sharp, the group will tend to veer toward criminal activities or, toward obtaining quasi-public goods.* The strong ideology of the collective maintains a group's status as a terrorist organization, dedicated to the betterment of the entire community. However, when such a position weakens, as a result of changing political reality, a terrorist organization, in order to maintain its position turns toward organized crime. As a result, its violence often turns toward its own community in terms of vigilantism. This hypothesis is most evident from the cases of the IRA and the ETA (Alexander, Swetnam, & Levine, 2001). The political realities of the two embattled regions changed, which caused both the groups to turn inward and toward vigilantism (Silke, 1998, 1999) and criminal activities (Horgan & Taylor, 1999, 2003).

Hypothesis 4. *A terrorist group would be highly likely to develop 'in-house' capabilities for raising money through various extra-legal ways rather than be associated with a known criminal organization for its own reputational needs.* The end of the Cold War period saw a significant reduction in the proxy warfare by the two superpowers by providing help to the terrorist groups in order to weaken the governments of the rival's client states. The events

[11]Yvon Dandaurand & Vivienne Chin (2004, April), *Links between terrorism and other forms of crime.* A report submitted to Foreign Affairs Canada. Vancouver: International Centre for Criminal Law Reform and Criminal Justice Policy.

of 9/11 may have either raised awareness regarding 'playing with fire' or have made it difficult for a number of Islamic nations, notably Saudi Arabia, Libya, and possibly Pakistan, in supporting extremists.[12] As a result, it is natural for the terrorist groups to seek funding for their operation through other means. Therefore, facing the dire financial needs many of them have developed 'in-house' capabilities of criminal activities (Dishman, 2001; see also Horgan & Taylor, 1999, 2003).

Hypothesis 5. *Unless the leadership of a terrorist group is vigilant, even when ideological issues are sharp, there is a high likelihood of its moving closer to criminal activities at the risk of losing its political legitimacy within its client base.* Given the natural allure of money and criminal activities, it is not surprising that a terrorist group may show metamorphosis into a criminal organization. One of the best examples of this is perhaps the Abu Sayyaf group in the Philippines (Rogers, 2004). Despite its professed allegiance to the Islamic cause, which, for a while brought it close to al-Qaeda, the group quickly revealed itself as a criminal organization. Sageman (2004, p. 44) reports that as soon as Osama bin Laden came to know of the true nature of the Philippino Islamic group, he cut off their relationship. This example clearly demonstrates the need of the group leadership to be vigilant against any slide toward criminality.

Hypothesis 6. *Under strong and stable governmental control, where there exists a large difference in the two costs, a group that starts off as highly ideological, when it develops 'in-house' capabilities for raising money, is likely to splinter into various groups, many with a greater emphasis on criminal behaviour. Conversely, where governmental control is weak (a failed state), with the costs of two activities being the same, the distinction between the two groups will be blurred.* Given the different relative preferences for public goods over private or quasi-public goods, there is little incentive for either of them to get into a sustained level of relationship.

Hypothesis 7. *It will be extremely rare for a criminal group to turn to terrorism for the attainment of public goods. Even when a criminal group might start out with some goals of attaining public goods, it will quickly revert back to becoming almost entirely a criminal enterprise.* Although it is rare, a criminal group can sometimes engage in altruistic behaviour. The fables of Robin Hood provide a vivid example of such duality of objective. In recent years, some groups, such as the Medellin Cartel, headed by Pablo Escobar made efforts to improve the lives of the poor people living in the area. However, their devotion toward providing public goods was short-lived at best. The case of the Italian Cosa Nostra provides another example in support of this hypothesis. After the invasion of Sicily by the Allied Forces during World War II, the help of the Mafia was recognized. As a reward for their support, members of the Mafia were not only allowed to carry weapons, they were

---

[12]For an explanation regarding our doubts about Pakistan, see Haqqani (2005).

installed as mayors and law enforcement officials all over western Sicily. This process of political legitimization helped their expansion in the immediate aftermath of the war (Jamieson, 2005, p. 167) not only in Italy but also in the United States. However, this opportunity to be part of the legitimate political process was soon abandoned in favour of making money. They demonstrate the clearest case, where a criminal group was given an unprecedented opportunity to become a legitimate political force but quickly reverted back to their familiar ways.

Hypothesis 8. *In those cases where a criminal group might target an entire society, its goals would still remain the attainment of quasi-public good without upsetting the status quo. A criminal organization would choose such an option only as a last resort, when faced with a decisive move by the government to eliminate it.* There are a number of examples of criminal gangs using terrorist tactics and targeting an entire society. In those cases where a group might target an entire society, its goals would still remain the attainment of quasi-public good without upsetting the status quo. For instance, the Italian Mafia started its campaign of car bombing in 1993, where it targeted a television personality, bombed a train, and planted bombs that damaged among other cultural icons, the Uffizi Gallery in Florence. Yet, these acts, although superficially similar to many other acts of terrorism, were different in one important area. The aim of this campaign was not altruistic; it did not purport to change the Italian society. It simply wanted to frighten the government into ceasing its law enforcement activities. Therefore, given this important distinction, these attacks cannot be classified as terrorism. When a criminal gang uses violence, it is to disrupt an investigation or an interdiction. Through selective use of violence, they try to dissuade the authorities from pursuing them (Williams & Savona, 1995).

Discussion and Policy Implications

The relationship between terrorist organizations and organized crime is often a matter of myth, misperception and ad hoc reasoning. Facing political challenges from groups that use extra-legal methods of protest, every government attempts to portray dissident organizations as common criminals. Such accusations aim at the political legitimacy of these groups. Similarly, some criminal groups also drape themselves in the cloak of political idealism. In this chapter, we have attempted to sort through the confusion by providing a definitional distinction between terrorist groups and organized crime based on their respective behavioural precepts. From this basic distinction, we have formulated a model by using the standard tools of microeconomics.

The advantage of using a theoretical model is its ability to put the diverse observations of the real world within an analytical framework. Thus, while a large body of case studies has painted a complex and seemingly counter-intuitive picture of links between terrorist groups and criminal organizations, this model lends a helping hand in sorting them out in a more systematic way. By delving deep into the basic motivations of benefits and costs we are able to understand the reasons for certain links to exist or not exist. The second advantage of an analytical model is its ability to provide us with testable hypotheses. We strongly make the case for further empirical research to test the veracity of our proposed hypotheses. A lot of public policies have been adopted by the highest national and international bodies based on the illusory perception of frightening scenarios. The third advantage of our model rests with its ability to allow us to formulate appropriate policy parameters not on the basis of prejudice and unfounded beliefs but on the solid bedrock of empirical evidence.

References

Alexander, Y., Swetnam, M. S., & Levine, H. M. (2001). *ETA: Profile of a terrorist group*. Ardsley, NY: Transnational Press.

Andreoni, J. (1990). Impure altruism and donations to public goods: A theory of warm-glow giving. *Economic Journal, 100*, 464–77.

Baumol, W. J., & Blinder, A. S. (1985). *Economics: Principles and policy* (3rd ed.). San Diego, CA: Harcourt Brace Jovanovich.

Bloom, M. (2004). Palestinian suicide bombing: Public support, market share and outbidding. *Political Science Quarterly, 119*, 61–88.

Combs, C. (2006) *Terrorism in the Twenty-First Century* (3rd ed.). Upper Saddle River, NJ: Prentice Hall.

Dandaurand, Y., & Chin, V. (2004, April). *Links between terrorism and other forms of crime*. A report submitted to Foreign Affairs Canada. Vancouver: International Centre for Criminal Law Reform and Criminal Justice Policy.

Dishman, C. (2001). Terrorism, Crime, and Transformation. *Studies in Conflict & Terrorism, 24*, 43–59.

Enders, W., & Sandler, T. (2005). *The political economy of terrorism* (p. 36). Cambridge: Cambridge University Press.

Gunaratna, R. (2001). The lifeblood of terrorist organizations: Evolving terrorist financial strategies. In A. P. Schmid (Ed.), *Countering terrorism through international cooperation* (pp. 182–85). Milan: ISPAC.

Gupta, D. K. (2005). Toward an integrated behavioral framework for analyzing terrorism: Individual motivations to group dynamics. *Democracy and Security, 1*.

Haqqani, H. (2005). *Pakistan: Between mosque and military*. New York: Carnegie Endowment for International Peace.

Hoffman, B. (1998). *Inside terrorism*. New York: Columbia University Press.

Horgan, J., & Taylor, M. (1999). Playing the 'green card' – Financing the Provisional IRA: Part 1. *Terrorism and Political Violence, 11*, 1–38.

Horgan, J., & Taylor, M. (2003). Playing the 'green card' – Financing the Provisional IRA: Part 2. *Terrorism and Political Violence*, 15, 1–60.

Jamieson, A. (2005). The use of terrorism by organized crime: An Italian case study. In T. Bjorgo (Ed.), *Root causes of terrorism: Myths, reality and ways forward* (pp. 164–177). London: Routledge.

Kalyvas, S., & Sanchez-Cuenca, I. (2005). Killing without dying: The absence of suicide missions. In D. Gambetta (Ed.), *Making sense of suicide missions* (pp. 209-232). Oxford: Oxford University Press.

Kellen, K. (1984). *On terrorists and terrorism*. N-1942-RC. Santa Monica, CA: RAND Corporation, December 1982.

Naylor, R. T. (1997). Mafias, myths, and markets: On the theory and practice of enterprise crime. *Trans-national Organized Crime*, 3, 2–18.

Naylor, R. T. (2002). *Wages of crime: Black markets, illegal finance and the underworld economy*. Ithaca: Cornell University Press.

Reuter, P. (1983). *Disorganized crime: Illegal markets and the Mafia*. Cambridge: MIT Press.

Rogers, S. (2004). Beyond Abu Sayyaf. *Foreign Affairs*, Jan-Feb, 15–28.

Sageman, M. (2004). *Understanding terror networks*. Philadelphia: University of Pennsylvania Press.

Samuelson, P. A. (1965). *Foundations of economic analysis*. New York: Athenium Press.

Schmid, A. (2005). *Links between terrorism and drug trafficking: A case of 'narco-terrorism'?* Paper presented at the International Summit on Democracy and Security, 8–11 March, Madrid.

Schmid, A. P., & de Graaf, J. (1982). *Violence as communication: Insurgent terrorism and the Western news media*. Beverly Hills, CA: Sage Publications.

Schmid, A. P., & Jongman, A. J. (1988). *Political terrorism: A new guide to actors, authors, concepts, data bases, theories, and literature*. New Brunswick, NJ: Transaction Books.

Silke, A. (1998). The lords of discipline: The methods and motives of paramilitary vigilantism in Northern Ireland. *Low Intensity Conflict & Law Enforcement*, 7, 121–156.

Silke, A. (1999). Rebel's dilemma: The changing relationship between the IRA, Sinn Fein and paramilitary vigilantism in Northern Ireland. *Terrorism and Political Violence*, 11, 55–93.

UN Centre for International Crime Prevention (2002). *Glossary of money laundering terms*. Available at www.unodc/money_laundering_glossary.html#m/

Williams, P., & Savona, E. U. (1995). Introduction: Problems and dangers posed by organized crime in the various regions of the world. *Transnational Organized Crime*, 1, 25.

Further Reading

Akerlof, G. A., & Kranton, R. E. (2000). Economics and identity. *Quarterly Journal of Economics*, 125, 715–54.

Anderson, B. (1983). *Imagined communities*. London: Verso.

Anderson, T. S. (2004). Transnational organized terror and organized crime: Blurring the lines. *SAIS Review*, 24, 50–52.

Banerjee, S. (1980). *In the wake of Naxalbari: A history of the Naxalite movement in India*. Calcutta: Subarnarekha.

Boorman, S. A., & Levitt, P. R. (1980). *The genetics of altruism*. New York: Academic Press.

Collier, P. M., & Hoeffler, A. (2004). Greed and grievance in civil war. *Oxford Economic Papers*, 56, 563–584.

Coogan, T. P. (2002). *The IRA*. New York: St. Martin's Press.

DeNardo, J. (1985). *Power in numbers: The political strategy of protest and rebellion*. Princeton, NJ: Princeton University Press.

Ghosh, S. (1975). *The Naxalite movement*. Calcutta: Firma K. L. Mukhopadhyay.

Gupta, D. K. (1990). *The economics of political violence: The effects of political instability on economic growth*. New York, NY: Praeger.

Gupta, D. K. (2001). *Path to collective madness: A study in social order and political pathology*. Westport, CT: Greenwood Publishing.

Gupta, D. K. (2002). Economics and collective identity: Explaining collective action. In S. Grossbard-Shechtman, & C. Clague (Eds), *The expansion of economics: Toward a more inclusive social science*. Armonk, NY: M. E. Sharpe.

Gupta, R. K. (2004). *The crimson agenda: Maoist protest and terror*. New Delhi: Wordsmith.

Juergensmeyer, M. (2000). *Terror in the mind of God: The global rise of religious violence*. Berkeley: University of California Press.

Kenney, M. (2003). From Pablo to Osama: Counter-terrorism lessons from the wars on drugs. *Survival*, 45, 187–206.

Konet, R. (2001). Sexual fantasies of a suicide bomber. Retrieved January 14, 2005, from www.israelinsider.com

Morgan, R. (2002). The demon lover syndrome. *MS*, 13, 17.

Post, J. (2005). The socio-cultural underpinnings of terrorist psychology: When hatred is bred in bones. In T. Bjorgo (Ed.), *Root causes of terrorism: Myths, reality and ways forward* (pp. 54–69). London: Routledge.

Rapoport, D. (1992). Terrorism. In M. Hawkesworth, & M. Kogan (Eds), *Routledge encyclopedia of government and politics* (Vol. 2, p. 1067). London: Routledge.

Ray, R. (2002). *The Naxalites and their ideology* (2nd ed.). New Delhi: Oxford University Press.

Robins, R. S., & J. Post (1997). *Political paranoia: The psychopolitics of hatred*. New Haven, CT: Yale University Press.

Sanderson, T. M. (2004). Transnational terror and organized crime: Blurring the lines. *SAIS Review*, 24, 49–61.

Satz, D., & Ferejohn, J. (1994). Rational choice and social theory. *Journal of Philosophy*, 91, 71–87.

Schmid, A. P. (1996). The links between transnational organized crime and terrorist crimes. *Transnational Organized Crime*, 2, 40–82.

Sen, A. K. (1977). Rational fools: A critique of the behavioral foundation of economic theory. *Philosophy and Public Affairs*, 6, 317–344.

Sen, A. (1980). *An approach to Naxalbari*. Calcutta: Institute of Scientific Thought.

Slater, P. J. B. (1994). *Behaviour and evolution*. Cambridge, UK: Cambridge University Press.

8

Terrorist Networks and Small Group Psychology

Sam Mullins

Synopsis: As a first step towards creating models of terrorist group development over time, approaches to characterizing the ways in which behaviour and
changing social structure are related are described. The emphasis is on the
lifespan of these groups and the theoretical interpretations that increase understanding of terrorist behaviour.

Within the field of terrorism studies the term 'network' is most often used in
reference to the organizational level of analysis, (e.g. McAllister, 2004; Mishal
& Rosenthal, 2005), and it tends to be used simply to give vague accounts of
the dispersed and non-hierarchical nature of al-Qaeda and Islamic terrorism
in general. This reaffirms the fact that such a large and ever-changing social
movement essentially has no objective structure, whilst at the opposite end of
the spectrum the individual level of analysis may be too idiographic to be of
practical utility. The group level of analysis, although still extremely challenging is therefore likely to be the most productive in furthering our understanding of terrorism, and this is confirmed by the fact that relatively small groups
represent the 'front line' of terrorism, which law enforcement and security
agencies must deal with on a daily basis.

Practitioners, as much as academics, recognize that social environments play
a key role in facilitating processes of radicalization and decisions to engage in
acts of terrorism. The importance of social settings such as mosques, youth clubs
and gyms is a recurrent theme throughout the *Report of the Official Account of
the Bombings in London on 7th July 2005*, (House of Commons, 2006), which
hypothesizes that "Mentors may first identify individuals from within larger
groups who may be susceptible to radicalisation; then 'groom' them privately

The Faces of Terrorism: Multidisciplinary Perspectives Edited by David Canter
© 2009 John Wiley & Sons Ltd.

in small groups until individuals begin feeding off each other's radicalisation" (p. 31). Meanwhile Sageman (2004) points out that social bonds precede ideological commitment, and that a combination of social isolation and group cohesion contributes to escalation of ideology, although outsiders to the immediate group may be necessary to serve as 'bridges' to terrorist organizations for the purposes of training and resources.

What becomes apparent is that the vital component in the process of becoming a terrorist is spontaneous group interaction with one's peers, rather than planned, systematic 'brain-washing' and indoctrination. Furthermore, the importance of spontaneous group interaction in the absence of direct top-down influence is amplified by the emergence of distinct 'self-starter' groups, which rely on the Internet and other freely available material both for ideological and operational information, thereby negating the need for formal links to larger organizations (Kirby, 2007).

However, despite this recognition there is still a need for further detailed study of the exact nature of emergent terrorist groups or cells. Since social structure, (patterns of interactions between actors in a network), affects opportunities for, and limitations upon behaviour (Wasserman & Fauss, 1994), a particularly useful way of increasing our understanding of these groups is to study their structure.

Moreover, whilst final group-structure is of interest in exploring operational functionality, (e.g. Krebbs, 2002), it is dynamic changes in structure over the course of a group's development that temporally correspond with changes in individual and group psychology. Therefore systematic analysis of terrorist-group structural development will increase understanding of the psychology of radicalization and of these groups' behaviour, which in turn will inform counterterrorism and intervention strategies. The present study attempts to lay the foundations for this approach by way of an exploratory dynamic usage of the usually static analytical tool, Social Network Analysis (SNA), to model the development of two well-known groups of Islamic terrorists.

Methodology

Multiple undirected association matrices were constructed using Excel, with one matrix for each change in social structure. Three levels of association were used: 0 to indicate a lack of association, 1 to indicate acquaintanceship/friendship, and 2 to indicate a strong friendship or family bond. Strength of association was judged based on both qualitative and quantitative factors, taking into account psychological, affective and pragmatic criteria as well as length of time of association. Thus bond-strength can vary for different reasons and also interacts with time so that same-strength ties may hold different meanings depending on how long they last for. Excel matrices were analysed using Ucinet, (Borgatti, Everett, & Freeman, 2002), to produce a series of network diagrams for both groups, which served as visual aids for theoretical interpretation, with layout being determined by a combination of applying Ucinet's spring-embedding function and manually adjusting node positions to give perceptual consistency across each sequence. Formal network measures were not employed due to the highly interconnected nature of the networks, rendering these measures of limited utility. References to 'behavioural centrality' refer to places and/or people that are known to have emerged as integral to the functioning of the group. Thus a particular location may be behaviourally central if it is frequented more than other locations, and a person may be behaviourally central by acquiring an established presence within the group.

The Millennial Plot

The so-called 'Millennial Plot', (Sageman, 2004), involved a plan to bomb Los Angeles airport, which was discovered when a character named Ahmed Ressam was arrested with explosives in his car while trying to enter the USA from Canada. Figure 8.1 is an approximation of the social situation that Ressam,

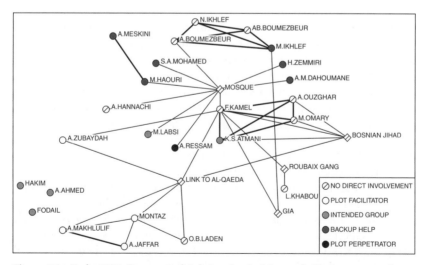

Figure 8.1. Early 1994: Ressam and Labsi arrive in Montreal. There are several pre-existing associations amongst members of the group as it existed then. The mosque serves as an indirect link for what in reality were most likely direct associations between other future group members.

and another conspirator, Mustapha Labsi, separately entered into six years earlier at the beginning of 1994.

Immigrating like this to a new country can be understood as a time of self-reconstruction, (see Kidwell, Dunham, Bacho, Pastorino, & Portes, 1995), and social bonding is likely to be important to this process. Not surprisingly, Ressam was drawn to other similar young men in the community and at the local mosque and as Carley (1990) points out, continued interaction would increase this homogeny through shared information. These men happened to be involved in relatively petty crime, which Ressam was happy to indulge in, and as he would soon find out, this criminal activity was organized in order to support Islamic terrorism. It is also significant that Ressam met and forged an alliance with another newcomer in Mustapha Labsi because by acting together consistently over time they could be taken far more seriously by the existing group. In addition to this, given that Ressam and Labsi had no other competing social memberships, this would increase 'fit' and accessibility of self-categorization with specific reference to this group (Voci, 2006), thereby facilitating socialization into the group once accepted.

Acceptance of the group's norms and values was further facilitated by the social situation that emerged as the two newcomers were surrounded by higher status group members including the ostensible leader of the group, Fateh Kamel and his comrades from Bosnia. Thus upward social comparison was inevitable and as Ressam and Labsi found themselves living with experienced mujahedeen at the behavioural centre of the network, the range of social comparison was constricted and the process of emulation was enhanced.

Interestingly, Ressam and Labsi must have been aware of the group's terrorist associations from quite early on and yet they were not deterred by this, which implies that they were either sympathetic or indifferent to violent jihad without having first developed a profound sense of collective identity, although specific group membership was clearly highly valued. In fact self-categorization as a Muslim was initiated by non-religious concepts in that by joining in with the rest of the group in derogating an outgroup in the West, Ressam and Labsi were defining themselves in terms of what they were *not*. This then leads to the question of what they *were*. They definitely saw themselves as group members, and since ideal group members identified with the wider Muslim collective, (as perceived from their own ideological standpoint), elements of this identity were gradually absorbed. The combination of occupying relatively central positions within the group whilst simultaneously lacking established status thus acted as a catalyst for absorbing more militant group members' ideology and there would be a need to justify occupation of these positions through expression of group-identity. Repeated verbal expression of group values would in turn lead to gradual internalization of those values and a desire to act upon them in order to further secure group membership.

However, there does not seem to have been any significant effort made to pursue terrorist activity until such time as the existing social order was disturbed by Abderraouf Hannachi, who had been in Montreal some years earlier and returned in 1997 from training at al-Qaeda camps in Afghanistan. In terms of social comparison Hannachi represented something of a paradox. Because he was not an established group member there was a degree of downward comparison but because he had achieved something in line with the group's values there was also a degree of upward comparison from group members who had not received terrorist training. Hannachi essentially had a more rightful claim to a central position within the group than Ressam and Labsi and he was therefore a threat to their sense of identity, motivating them to earn their group membership by acting upon their beliefs. Hence Ressam and Labsi took the plunge and accepted Hannachi's offer of arranging for them to do as he had and train in Afghanistan. Accompanied by the experienced Karim Said Atmani they received a boost to their confidence and embarked on the adventure they had fantasized about, resulting in a segment of the group's core breaking away.

Atmani then left Ressam and Labsi and was later arrested, removing him from the equation. The two friends then found themselves part of a five-man cell during training, along with Hakim, Fodail and Abu Ahmed. Being organized like this from above may have caused initial friction, (Tuckman's (1965) 'storming' and 'norming' in preparation for performing), but conspiring together for 11 months in remote areas of Afghanistan, working towards a shared clandestine goal, would have facilitated bonding and a transition from group to team. The conditions experienced during training in fact very much resemble descriptions of groupthink, whereby such factors as directive leadership and high group cohesion lead to illusions of invulnerability and a preference for extreme options, (Janis, 1982), and in this sense groupthink is desirable for the trainers of terrorists.

Following training Ressam was left isolated, however, due to travel restrictions placed on the other members of the team. Despite this he chose to push ahead with the operation, enlisting help from members of his old network in Montreal. This decision can be understood not only in terms of heightened ideological commitment and expended effort, but also in terms of the fact that social isolation translates into threat, increasing the salience of social identity and ingroup/outgroup bias and serving as motivation to form a coalition with others in order to overcome that threat (Navarette, Kurzban, Fessler, & Kirkpatrick, 2004). Hence coalitional psychology may explain the resilience of disrupted networks as much as does ideological commitment. Acting as the central co-ordinator of the plot, Ressam shared different amounts of information with his new co-conspirators so that the final group resembled a classic wheel organizational structure, (see Figure 8.2), and in fact at this point traditional measures of centrality do identify him as a key figure.

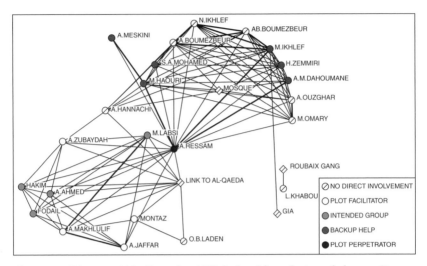

Figure 8.2. February 1999 – December 1999: Isolated from the intended group, Ressam utilizes previous contacts for help.

It would appear then that the Millennial Plot had become one man's personal quest to carry out an act of terrorism and that Ressam must therefore have internalized his conditions of worth, (Rogers, 1961), and become extremely committed to his group's cause. However, his transformation may not have been so complete. Ressam had experienced a rapid growth in the number of his associations, almost all of whom were of higher status than him, and yet despite this he had still occupied a fairly central position within the group. Combined, this would be somewhat overwhelming, making Ressam liable to agreement and vulnerable to social pressure, and this is supported by the Canadian authorities' dismissal of the group as a mere "bunch of guys" (Sageman, 2004, p. 101). In addition there were no plans to make the operation a suicide mission and therefore no evidence of depersonalization, and Ressam's only plans for afterwards were to return to Algeria as if he had completed a rite of passage. In fact becoming attached to an actual operation may well have come as a surprise since Hannachi had simple gone away to train and returned back to the community having attained status. This does not in any way rob Ressam or others of full responsibility for their actions; however, it does imply an incomplete grasp of the consequences of those actions. In fact the impersonal, indiscriminate nature of terrorism is ideal for permitting this and therefore for attracting disaffected youth wishing to strike out at an indistinguishable enemy. In addition, Ressam's case also demonstrates the cumulative nature of decision making in that although it may be very tempting to focus on the final, pivotal decision to carry out an act of terrorism, that decision may effectively be pre-made as part of an ongoing chain of 'smaller' decisions that lead up to it.

The September 11th Hamburg Group

Of nineteen September 11th hijackers, three came from a group of eight friends based in Hamburg. This group was very similar to the Montreal group in terms of centring around a local community mosque in the early stages, and in terms of the degree of similarity between group members, most of the Hamburg friends having recently immigrated to Germany to attend university. It is important though, that in contrast to Montreal, the Hamburg group was religious from the outset and therefore not immediately defined as deviant.

In terms of the psychology of attitude change and persuasion, although the group's teacher or mentor, Mohammed Belfas was a perceived expert and therefore a believable source of information, attending his study group in the first place was based on the assumption that it would yield useful information and so group members were simply being given information which confirmed and expanded upon their existing beliefs, rather than being persuaded into accepting an entirely new ideology.

The steady growth rate of the Hamburg group is also of interest; newcomers joined individually and were introduced to the rest of the group, maintaining a full-clique structure but again with internal alliances, as particular members shared different levels of similarity and each individual's relationship to the rest of the group was more or less unique. Thus, for example, Ramzi bin al-Shibh exchanged knowledge and social support with the rest of the group on an equal basis while Said Bahaji and Zakariya Essabar both traded conformity for social acceptance. In addition, the periods of time in between admissions, although in part dependent upon availability of candidates, seems to suggest the need for time to manage relations within the group, and might also be thought of as probation periods for newcomers, promoting a high level of group stability and security. As an aside, this might also have implications for the timing of infiltration strategies since the acceptance of newcomers may in part depend upon group stability, which is affected by other recent admissions.

This ongoing structural group stability would be conducive to the development of an equally solid sense of group identity, which in the case of the Hamburg group was accompanied in tandem by an increasingly profound sense of wider collective identity. Social structure and developing ideology are clearly related and this relationship helps explain both conformity and radicalization. In a socially enclosed environment alternative beliefs and influences are avoided, and then based on the simple fact that human communication requires new information, (the 'informativeness principle', Olson & Zanna, 1993); interactions within such an environment cannot remain stagnant for long. This creates pressure towards ideological advancement, which is likely to be accepted where group membership is highly valued. Thus structural and ideological progression may parallel each other and create a cycle of

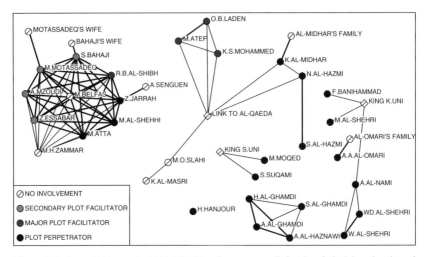

Figure 8.3. Late 1998 – early 1999: The Hamburg group (left side of plot) has developed into an extremely cohesive singular unit, committed to violent jihad. Despite this overall cohesion there are still important internal alliances.

radicalization: as beliefs become more extreme, the group becomes more isolated and membership becomes more important, so escalation of beliefs is interdependent with structural isolation and escalation of group commitment. However, this also implies a build-up of pressure and a need to express group identity.

Having reached a critical stage of development towards the end of 1999, the Hamburg group – as in Montreal – was also influenced and given the opportunity to act upon their beliefs by outsiders, and again the group divided in preparation for action, with Atta, al-Shehhi, bin al-Shibh and Jarrah making the first trip to Afghanistan where they were quickly selected for 'The Planes Operation' (The 9/11 Commission Report). And although this initial division may have been simply for practical reasons, it was the beginning of a permanent rift, including between the group and their original mentor, Belfas, whom they distanced themselves from in order to maintain security. The point of departure between a group and their mentor where there is one, may be indicative of later stages of group development and preparation to act as well as being the final step in moving along a continuum from compliance to 'conversion'.

The process of division, however, is likely to leave the group vulnerable for both practical and psychological reasons, especially where individuals become isolated from the rest of the group. This helps explain Ziad Jarrah's later reluctance as he nearly pulled out of the operation in the absence of close ingroup social support while based in the US, only re-committing himself to the mission following a face to face conference with Ramzi bin al-Shibh, the man who had first introduced him to the group. Similarly, Nawaf al-Hazmi of the Saudi group of hijackers was left in a very vulnerable situation when his companion Khalid al-Midhar left the US to be with his family, subsequently significantly compromising the security of the operation by befriending and sharing information with outsiders. Of course in Jarrah's case, he also retained strong social bonds outside the group to his sweetheart, Aysel Senguen, and such enduring external bonds may exert a gravitational pull away from the group and their objective. Al-Midhar, who left al-Hazmi, was the only other hijacker aside from Jarrah to demonstrate this pull away from the group after he had failed flight school, but then given the choice between living with his family (and experiencing loss of face), or dying with his friends, he chose the latter. Given that several of the September 11th hijackers requested to contact family in the days leading up to the attack (The 9/11 Commission Report, p. 245), it is clear that significant external ties will always remain important even when apparently severed, and may be used as a social 'safety net' in times of crisis. But the social gravity of the peer group remains supreme as long as there is a working social support system in place.

Furthermore, despite developing an intense group and collective identity to the point of 'depersonalization', (evidenced by the commitment to 'martyrdom'), particular internal friendships and allegiances remained vitally important. This is reflected in the particular form of group division, specifically with regards to the Hamburg group but is also seen throughout the final September 11th teams, with pre-existing friendships and family ties forming the basis of each team of hijackers despite claims of objective selection criteria. That such 'trivia' as friendship and family can dictate the final structure of a team of highly 'professional' suicide terrorists speaks volumes for the true power of micro-level social ties.

It is unfortunate that more is not known about the Saudi hijackers' social circumstances leading up to their departure for Afghanistan and subsequent participation in what became 9/11. Almost doubtlessly some of them were directly involved with radical preachers and for some this may have been combined with social uprooting from their home province or country but this in itself is not particularly informing. It seems most of them arrived for training in small groups and then worked together before being selected by bin Laden for this highly important mission. Being hand-picked by such an iconic figure and becoming one of the chosen few would instil a sense of camaraderie, melding the group together, but the group as a whole never had much chance to 'set' as it was continuously broken down and moved around and this helps explain the lasting importance of dyadic relationships throughout the operation as seen in the final teams.

Finally, for the hijackers who had been based in America for a year before the remaining participants arrived, these new faces, relatively fresh from

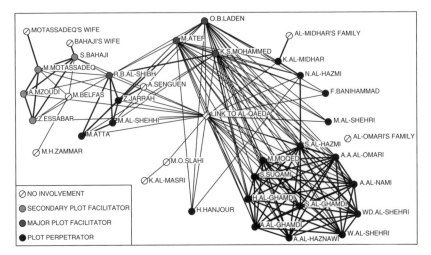

Figure 8.4. Summer 2000 – early 2001: A permanent rift has set in amongst the Hamburg group as Atta, al-Shehhi and Jarrah train in the US, with bin al-Shibh acting as a vital liaison. Particular friendships are also important within the Saudi group (right side of plot), and for most, external family ties are severed.

training and still highly motivated would have provided a boost to their own motivation and strengthened their resolve.

As Sageman, (2004, p. 156), concludes, although the Hamburg group's collective identity was embroiled in an acute sense of 'outgroup' hatred toward the West, it was this sense of collective identity fuelled by group bonding and friendship that ultimately drove 19 men to murder nearly 3,000 strangers, killing themselves in the process.

The Groups Compared

At first glance there is a great deal of similarity between these two groups, (see Table 8.1), in terms of most of the development times involved and in terms of the apparent importance of weak-tie disturbances to upsetting the existing social order and serving as an ideological accelerant. The size of both immediate groups is certainly also comparable; however, the Montreal group was part of a slightly larger extended network and this is related to the various qualitative differences (see Table 8.2).

A very important distinction between the Montreal and Hamburg groups relates to the focus of the group's ideological starting point as either primarily criminal or religious; because of this terrorism was essentially framed or defined

Table 8.1. Quantitative comparison of the Millennial and Hamburg groups

Group Features	Millennial Plot	Hamburg Group
No. In Immediate Group[*]	7–14	8
No. In Operation From Group	1	4
No. Intended From Group	3	4–8
Total No. Intended	6	20
Total Operation No.	3 (50%)	19 (95%)
Average Joining Age	{28}	22.5
Age Of 'Mentor'	34	50
Age Of WTD[**]	47	37
Time 1: 1st Contact To Train	4 years	4 years
Time 2: 1st Contact To WTD	3 years	>3 years
Time 3: From Full To WTD	1 year	Few months
Time 4: From WTD To Train	<1year	1 year
Time 5: Time in Afghanistan	11 months	2–3 months
Time 6: From Train To Op.	1 year 8 months	1 year 10 months
Time 7: End Train To Op.	9 months	1 year 7 months
Time 8: 1st Contact To Op.	<6 years	<6 years

[*] Group size depends upon how the group is defined. For the Montreal group not all ages are known therefore the value given is an estimate based upon known ages of just eight network members.

[**] Weak-tie-disturbance.

Table 8.2. Qualitative comparison of the Millennial and Hamburg groups

Group Features	Millennial Plot	Hamburg Group
Recent immigrants	Yes	Yes
Education	High school/college	University
Original group setting	Criminal	Religious
Social influence	Distributed	Distilled
Pre-existing associations	Yes	No
Growth	Sporadic	Gradual
Full-clique structure	Yes	Yes
Internal alliances	Yes	Yes
Overall structure over time	Clustered	Singular
DPA[***]	Yes	Yes
Religious by time of op.	Yes	Extremely
Suicide/intended	No	Yes
Success	No	Yes

[***] Division-preceding-action.

in different ways as either lying on the extreme end of a continuum of criminal and risk-taking behaviour, or on the extreme end of a continuum of religious and political activity. This then affects development of group and social identity because crime has less overt relevance to the wider collective and necessitates more links outside of the group, while religion facilitates the development of a collective identity analogous to specific group identity, and allows greater social isolation. A related structural issue is whether there are pre-existing associations at the start of a group's development, which was seen in Montreal but not in Hamburg, and which is likely to set the tone for the way in which the group grows over time, ranging from more sporadic to more gradual and steady, with stabilization periods in between new admissions. The nature and structure of a group as it begins may therefore affect the way it grows and the overall structural emphasis that the group takes on over time as either being more clustered or singularly cohesive. Together this affects a difference in group members' individual narratives and conceptualizations of their acts, which in turn has an effect on the formation of group and collective identity.

Structurally of course both groups did seem to have full-clique structure involving all-member interaction, which is an important part of the cycle of radicalization, but they also showed internal alliances despite that overall cohesion, and in both groups these alliances seemed to guide processes of division-preceding-action.

Similarly, both groups did seem to have individual mentors – Kamel in Montreal and Belfas in Hamburg – but Kamel was quite often absent and so the social influence in Montreal was more distributed amongst other higher status group members who served as role models, while Belfas served as a single particularly influential figure at the start of the group's development, then allowing the group to spontaneously develop his ideas. When a group is allowed to do this, the group then takes ownership of those ideas and becomes fully committed to them, rather than trying to live up to the ideas of others, and while the end result may be equally lethal, suicide tactics seem more likely when both ideological and structural factors combine to promote maximum group cohesion.

Concluding Remarks

To be able to understand the behaviour of groups and of their individual members it is necessary to have an appreciation of the lifespan of those groups and of the ways in which behaviour and changing social structure are related. Modelling group development over time is a useful aid to theoretical interpretation and a potentially useful tool for increasing understanding of terrorist behaviour. The present study represents an exploratory step towards developing this system of research, and the following have each been identified or reiterated as being of significance:

- Relationships between ideology and structure
- Distribution of social influence (single/multiple mentors and models)
- Growth processes (gradual vs. sporadic)
- Structural emphases over time (singular vs. clustered)
- Full-clique structure and isolation
- Internal alliances
- WTDs as ideological accelerants and motivation to act
- DPA and increased vulnerability.

Broadly speaking these can be grouped into three key overlapping areas of research:

- Group starting points
- Growth and development
- Preparation for action.

The more groups are studied in this way with consideration for the wider context within which they exist, the greater the chances of cross-comparison, generalization and ultimately prediction. In particular, if meaningful overt cues can be identified in these groups, such as distinct stages of development or patterns of preparation for action, these will hold the potential to be applied in counterterrorism risk-assessment and intervention. Of course this is dependent upon the development of a valid and reliable methodology that can be applied at least retrospectively if not in real time. Issues that are fundamental to this progression include rules for including or excluding nodes, elaboration on the meaning of different strengths of association, and rules for their application, definitions and measurements of 'social isolation' and 'behavioural centrality' and further exploration of the utility of existing network terms and measurements. Finally, application of methodology is dependent upon available data, which varies enormously in its quantity and quality, and yet the dynamic application of SNA to the study of terrorist groups holds great promise for comprehending and combating terrorism and for an understanding of group behaviour more generally.

References

Borgatti, S., Everett, M., & Freeman, L. (2002). *Ucinet 6.109 for Windows: Software for social network analysis*. Harvard, MA: Analytic Technologies.

Carley, K. (1990). Group stability: A socio-cognitive approach. *Advances in Group Processes*, 7, 1–44.

House of Commons (2006). *Report of the Official Account of the Bombings in London on 7th July 2005*. Ordered by the House of Commons to be printed 11 May 2006. London: The Stationery Office.

Janis, I. (1982). *Groupthink: Psychological studies of policy decisions and fiascoes* (2nd ed.). Boston, MA: Houghton-Mifflin.

Kidwell, J., Dunham, R., Bacho, R., Pastorino, E., & Portes, P. (1995). Adolescent identity exploration: A test of Erikson's theory of transitional crisis. *Adolescence*, 30, 785–793.

Kirby, A. (2007). The London Bombers as 'Self-Starters': A case study in indigenous radicalization and the emergence of autonomous cliques. *Studies in Conflict & Terrorism*, 30, 415–428.

Krebbs, V. (2002). Mapping networks of terrorist cells. *Connections*, 24, 43–52.

McAllister, B. (2004). Al-Qaeda and the Innovative Firm: Demythologising the network. *Studies in Conflict & Terrorism*, 27, 297–319.

Mishal, S., & Rosenthal, M. (2005). Al-Qaeda as a Dune Organisation: Toward a typology of Islamic terrorist organisations. *Studies in Conflict & Terrorism*, 28, 275–293.

Navarette, C., Kurzban, R., Fessler, D., & Kirkpatrick, L. (2004). Anxiety and intergroup bias: Terror management or coalitional psychology? *Group Processes and Intergroup Relations*, 7, 370–397.

Olson, J., & Zanna, M. (1993). Attitudes and attitude change. *Annual Review of Psychology*, 44, 117–154.

Rogers, C. (1961). *On becoming a person*. Boston: Houghton Mifflin.

Sageman, M. (2004). *Understanding terror networks*. Philadelphia: University of Pennsylvania Press.

Tuckman, B. (1965). Developmental sequence in small groups. *Psychological Bulletin*, 63, 384–399.

Voci, A. (2006). Relevance of social categories, depersonalization and group processes: Two field tests of self-categorization theory. *European Journal of Social Psychology*, 36, 73–90.

Wasserman, S., & Fauss, K. (1994). *Social network analysis*. Cambridge, MA: Cambridge University Press.

9

Case study – Youth Gangs and Terrorism in Chechnya: Recruitment, Activities and Networks[1]

Michael Vishnevetsky

Synopsis: In this chapter the participation of young people in terrorism in Chechnya is analysed. It outlines the ways in which two groups of 14- to 18-year-olds became involved, what types of action they participated in, and their positions in the terrorist networks. Factors that were conducive to their terrorist activities are identified. The role of violence in youth gangs, and relationships between youth gangs and organized crime are examined. The data were collected from open sources during fieldwork in Russia. The results show that the activities of the two groups differed in terms of their violence and motivations, and were influenced by the presence or absence of connections to a larger group of adult terrorists.

Introduction

Currently, a 'war on terror' is being waged by world governments such as in the US and Russia. This war contributes, however, to the radicalization of young people and their involvement in violence and terrorism. In this way terrorism has the capacity to sustain and regenerate itself, bypassing

[1] I would like to express my gratitude to Professor Susanne Karstedt, my PhD supervisor, for comments on this chapter, and to Professor Hans-Jörg Albrecht, Director of the Max-Planck-Institute for Foreign and International Criminal Law in Freiburg, Germany, and Professor Uriy Antonyan, Chair of Research at the Moscow Institute for Humanitarian Education (IGUMO) for supporting my research.

counterterrorist measures and even thriving on them as they create a wider recruitment base for future terrorism. The lives of the young people who join terrorist activities are in danger, and their personal development does not reach its full potential. Understanding the problem of the involvement of young people in terrorism is therefore essential in order to minimize the damage and risk of terrorism, and the potential negative outcomes of the war on terror.

This research examines the terrorist involvement of young people in a war zone and tries to identify the ways they were recruited, their actions and relations with wider terrorist networks. The subjects of this research are two groups of young people aged between 14 and 18 years old, who were for a brief spell of time involved in severe violence and terrorist activities in Chechnya in 2001. The data were compiled from open sources – newspapers – and from court documents in scientific archives. The results of this research can contribute to the understanding of similar contexts where the war on terror is involved. This chapter starts with a brief outline of research on the participation of young people in organized violence, such as war and similar conflicts, and gangs worldwide. This is done in order to set the participation of young people in crimes of a terrorist nature into a wider theoretical context of participation of young people in violence. Following this, an outline of the history of Chechen terrorism and the war on terror is given in order to provide the background for the research. Finally, the two groups are presented and analysed according to the dimensions developed.

Young Soldiers, Terrorists and Violent Youth Gangs

The age of young people involved in armed conflicts may typically range from 10 to 18 (Brett & Specht, 2004; Dowdney, 2005). Young terrorists are a subgroup of young people involved in violence. They normally act in environments without an ongoing war (Berko, 2004). Young people who participate in war or war-like local conflicts are often referred to as 'child soldiers'. However, in conflict zones where the distinction between the state of war and peace is vague, for example, in Chechnya, the boundaries between young terrorists and soldiers are blurred.

The typical background characteristics of child soldiers are poor families with difficulties, such as single-parent families or families with domestic violence. Often relationships between the children and parents in those families are poor as well. Adolescents do not receive normal schooling before and after they join military groups and become involved in violence, and suffer from other problems related to economic deprivation, such as hunger and living in overcrowded housing (Brett & Specht, 2004, p. 41; Dowdney, 2005, pp. 66–69). Brett and Specht (2004) studied the lives of young participants in a variety of armed conflicts and found that a number of factors may instigate the involvement of young people in violent action in a war zone. The physical insecurity related to their presence in the midst of violence is one of these factors, i.e. adolescents join armed groups in order to protect themselves by becoming soldiers (Brett & Specht, 2004, pp. 40–41; see also Dowdney, 2005, pp. 83–84). There is also economic motivation to join, since soldiers do not starve while the rest of the population in war zones often do (Brett & Specht, 2004, p. 41; Dowdney, 2005, p. 79). Some young people join armed groups guided by ideological conviction, or feeling the need to fight an oppressive regime (Brett & Specht, 2004, p. 27). Frequently young people follow their friends and family members who already participate in violence. Adventurous experiences are also quite attractive prospects for young people.

Berko (2004)[2] interviewed Palestinians of different age groups who were supposed to become suicide bombers and failed to commit acts of suicide terrorism. A number of factors were identified as significant in the process of recruitment of young people into terrorism. Revenge, i.e. the desire to avenge Israelis, was repeatedly stated as a reason to become a suicide bomber. Machismo or the need to bolster one's masculinity was also an important factor for young men. Religious reasons, i.e. the wish to reach paradise, were important for both young men and women. Berko described two cases of one 11- and one 15-year-old who were supposed to be suicide bombers (Berko, 2004, pp. 184–197). The 11-year-old boy had been asked by an experienced adult member of a terrorist organization to deliver a bomb to an Israeli road block. The second case shows that recruiters and the would-be terrorists may be of the same age. A 15-year-old high-school student was recruited by his classmate who was connected to a terrorist organization. The recruiter asked this young man to become a suicide bomber, and he agreed. The recruiter praised the bravery of the recruited youngster. When he was asked why he would not become a suicide bomber himself, the recruiter answered that he was scared to commit an act of suicide terrorism. Then the recruiter received money from the organization for this recruitment and about US$ 30 was given to the recruited youngster.

Berko's research shows that the involvement of very young people in terrorist activities is possible, and that recruitment is decisive in these cases. In my fieldwork on Chechnya, one of my interviewees, a retired Lieutenant-Colonel of the Russian armed forces who had served in Chechnya for eight years during the wars and was commanding a special force intelligence unit reported the story of a very young boy who set off a bomb at a Russian military road block in Chechnya. This is his account:

[2] All translations from the Hebrew and Russian languages are by the author.

... That's upbringing. He has three classes of schooling. I saw such children in Chechnya. I am his enemy, doesn't matter what happens. I gave him a chocolate ... as in the first war we used to feed children, gave them canned meat, chocolates. So he came to one of our posts, [and] our people said – 'Musa has come!', – [he was] a child, an eight-year-old perhaps, and ... yes, – [he] brought a hand grenade. [He] asked where the commander was, [and] said he wanted to thank him. The commander stepped forward. He blew up both of them, [i.e.] the commander and himself. Children run around, one puts a mine under an armoured personnel carrier and so on.

The Western world, in particular the United States, has experienced youth violence as part of youth gang activities. A large body of research provides knowledge about recruitment, training and relations to wider society. The concept of a gang, however, is contested, and there is no agreement on a single definition. In fact, there are dozens of definitions (Ball & Curry, 1997; Decker & Van Winkle, 1996; Spergel, 1995). One of the definitions has been developed by the *Eurogang* research network. According to Eurogang: "A street gang is any durable, street-oriented youth group whose involvement in illegal activity is part of its group identity" (Van Gemert & Fleisher, 2005, p. 12). This definition focuses on a street gang; however, the main characteristics of a gang as identified here are: (1) durability; and (2) the significance of a group's involvement in criminal activity, independent of whether this is violent or not. Klein (1995) also argues that the criminal component of group activity must be included in the definition of a street gang. The focus of his research is on street gangs, although according to Klein, there are other types of gangs as well. Klein mentions skinheads and racist groups, bikers, and also includes terrorist groups amongst the types of gangs which do not fit the characteristics of a street gang (Klein, 1995, p. 22). Klein goes on to describe the use of young people as assassins by the Colombian Medellin drug cartel, or "... the dreaded *sicarios*, who shoot their victims from motorcycles that speed away" (Human Rights Watch, 1994, p. 2), and refers to them as terrorist gangs. It is important to note that during this time, Colombia was in a state of war against its drug cartels, and on the brink of civil war, and consequently these young people acted in a social environment not much dissimilar from the situation in Chechnya.

Typically, gang members are young males from low socio-economic backgrounds (Oehme III, 1997; Spergel, 1995). Often gangs are formed within ethnic minorities and immigrant communities, as in the US in the first half of the 20th century where ethnic Irish, Jewish, Polish and Italian gangs emerged (Grennan, Britz, Rush, & Barker, 2000; Klein, 1995, p. 70). Gang members are normally adolescents or young adults (Decker & Van Winkle, 1996). Sometimes, however, they stay in a gang for long time, well into their thirties and even longer (Decker & Van Winkle, 1996; Klein, 1995; Spergel, 1995).

The reasons for joining a gang may vary for individuals. According to research that includes self-reporting by gang members, they seek protection from other gangs; the respect of their peers and communities, i.e. honour; and financial opportunities that were unavailable before membership in a gang (Decker & Van Winkle, 1996; Esbensen & Peterson-Lynskey, 2001; Lien, 2001). Although most have different combinations of reasons for joining, the actual joining is often facilitated by the fact that a friend or a relative is already a gang member. Decker and Van Winkle (1996, p. 66) found that 29% of their respondents reported that they joined a gang because a friend or a relative had been a member. According to Esbensen and Peterson-Lynskey (2001), 30% joined because their brothers or sisters had been gang members, and 46% followed a friend into the gang. Klein identifies a number of factors predicting gang involvement: low self-esteem, defiance against parents, deficits in contacts with adults, and perceptions of barriers to jobs and other opportunities are amongst these (Klein, 1995, p. 80).

In terms of background factors that are conducive to the emergence of gangs, Spergel (1995) emphasizes social disorganization besides poverty, and specific ethnic cultural traditions. Social disorganization may be the result of immigration, or other "population change and movement" (Spergel, 1995, p. 69). Lien (2001) underlines the importance of the community in the process of gangs' emergence: "The gang is a side-effect of a local community that does not work the way it should" (Lien, 2001, p. 171). Like Spergel, Anderson (1998) suggests that environmental conditions such as poverty and the lack of legitimate prospects for the future are important factors that drive young people in American poor inner-city neighbourhoods towards gangs.

Criminal activities of gangs

Only some of the activities of gangs are illegal. In fact, most of their time gang members participate in legal activities, i.e. 'hanging out', drinking alcohol and playing sports. However, criminal activities are an essential part of gang life. These activities typically include fighting with other gangs, which often involves the use of different kinds of weapons, petty crime (e.g. shoplifting), and selling narcotics. According to Klein (1995), gangs members are "… highly versatile in their criminal offenses" and "… disproportionately violent when compared with the activities of other youth groups or individual persons" (p. 75), but "… most gang members' behaviour is not criminal, and most gang members' crimes are not violent" (p. 29). As such, violent crimes, which are also at the core of gang activities, are more of an exception than a rule. However, it is this exception that is to be observed in the involvement of young people in terrorism.

In summary, criminal activity systematically committed by a group of young people is an essential part of the life of a youth gang. Young soldiers and gang members are typically poor and often join for economic reasons, i.e. in order to improve their economic situation. Ideological reasons may also be important in the motivation of young soldiers to join violent activities. Revenge can be decisive for young terrorists, soldiers and gang members. Friendship and kinship facilitate recruitment into a gang, and also for young soldiers and terrorists. The presence of armed groups opens up avenues for young people to join the military and paramilitary groups. There are accounts of organized crime groups which recruit young people as assassins, bodyguards, etc., and young soldiers and terrorists also act in the service of organized armed groups, for example, paramilitary groups as the arm of drug cartels, militias and different terrorist groups. Social disorganization and a community "that does not work the way it should" are seen us essential pre-conditions to the emergence of gangs. Young soldiers, terrorists and gang members have a number of characteristics in common, and common factors facilitate their involvement.

Terrorism and the War on Terror in Chechnya

The Russian-Chechen wars

Russian-Chechen relations are characterized by violence, conflict and coercion. Conflicts and wars that were the result of Russian expansion in the Caucasus (Akhmadov, 2006; Seely, 2001) and took place from the 17th to 19th centuries, and continued into the 20th century as well. In 1991 the Soviet Union collapsed. All 15 member republics of the USSR such as Russia, Ukraine and Kazakhstan gained independence. However, the autonomous republics such as the Checheno-Ingush had a different legal status within the USSR and were part of Russia. Thus according to the Russian Government's plans all the autonomous republics within the Russian Federation were supposed to stay within the federation and constitute the new independent state of Russia or the Russian Federation. Chechnya was the only autonomous republic within Russia that declared its full independence from Russia in 1991.

In 1994 the government of President Yeltsin sent troops into Chechnya in order to force the republic back into the federation. This was the beginning of the first Russian-Chechen war which lasted from 1994 to 1996. Chechnya led by President Dzhokhar Dudayev fought for its independence. The war ended in 1996 with the Khasavjurt peace accords where it was decided to postpone the decision on the official status of Chechnya for five years, i.e. until 2001. However, this plan was not realized because the second Russian-Chechen war started in 1999. In September 1999 a series of apartment building bombings took place in the cities of Bujnaksk in Dagestan, and Volgodonsk and Moscow in Russia. Chechen terrorists were accused of these acts that claimed 300 dead and 700 wounded. Moreover, in the same month a force of Chechen, Dagestani and foreign militants invaded Dagestan. The invasion was led by Shamil Basayev and Samir Saleh Abdullah Al-Suwailem, a.k.a. Khattab, and its aim was to establish a radical Islamic state in Chechnya and Dagestan. The terrorist acts and the invasion of Dagestan started the second Russian-Chechen war in September 1999. In 2000 the Russian Government announced its military victory, but the end of the war, however, transformed the military engagement into a counterterrorist operation, which has been ongoing ever since. The counterterrorist operation is characterized by severe human rights violations against the locals by the Russian federal forces. These include indiscriminate bombing of villages, random arrests of men, torture and killing of the detained, murders by death squadrons, stealing and destroying the property of the local residents including arson attacks on their houses, and rape of both men and women (Politkovskaya, 2007). Currently Chechnya is ruled by a pro-Moscow Chechen government and it is a republic within the Russian Federation. The republic is a so-called restricted area within Russia which implies restricted media coverage and limitations on visits to Chechnya. However, it is possible to assert that the human rights violations of the local population have not stopped and are continuing under the patronage and with the involvement of the new Chechen Government (Human Rights Watch, 2006; Politkovskaya, 2006, 2007).

Chechen terrorism

According to Murphy (2004), eight acts involving Chechen terrorists took place between 1991 and 1994. These acts used terrorist tactics, primarily taking hostages for ransom and hijacking planes and buses with passengers. They claimed 4 dead and 19 wounded, and millions of US dollars were paid to the terrorists as ransom. One of these terrorist acts, i.e. the hijacking of a civilian plane in November 1991, was carried out as a protest against the Russian presence in Chechnya. Other acts mainly involved taking hostages for ransom. More than 60 terrorist acts both inside and outside Chechnya were committed by Chechens between 1995 and 1999, and more than 80 between 2000 and 2004 (Murphy, 2004). Murphy lists more than 150 terrorist acts of all kinds with proven or probable links to the Chechens that took place between 1991 and 2004. The siege of the Dubrovka Theatre in Moscow in October 2002 and the taking of hostages in a school in Beslan, Northern Osetiya in September 2004 were the most outstanding of these events and were widely covered in the international press. Acts of suicide terrorism began in 2000 and are ongoing since then. According to Speckhard and Akhmedova (2006, p. 13), 28 events of suicide terrorism took place between 2000 and 2005.

After the military engagement of Russia in Chechnya transformed into a counterterrorist operation in 2000, the separatist movement began to transform too. Being pushed into the mountains by the federal and local governmental forces, they went underground. Currently, terrorism in Chechnya consists of a network of so-called '*jamaats*', or small secret groups, which are often comprised of militant Islamists or Wahhabis. The network is clandestine and it has connections to *jamaats* outside Chechnya, i.e. in Dagestan, Ingushetiya, Karachaevo-Cherkesiya and other Northern Caucasian republics (see the website of the underground kavkazcenter.com).

The situation of young people in Chechnya

The wars caused a massive loss amongst the Chechen population and ruined the infrastructure of the republic. Pictures of the destruction of Grozny, the Chechen capital, during the first and second war were widely covered by the international press (see bbc.co.uk, 2000). According to various estimates, the loss of the Chechen population during the wars is estimated at between 65,000–77,000 individuals from a population of approximately 1,000,000 before the wars (Cherkasov, 2001; NovayaGazeta, 2005), affecting many households and families, and consequently children and young people (see below). Extremely high unemployment – 74.2% in 2005 (Sherbakova, 2007), and severe deficiencies in education and health provision followed the wars in Chechnya. Psychological traumatization of the Chechen population seems to be widespread (Speckhard & Akhmedova, 2006). A generation of children who have witnessed violence all their lives has grown up in Chechnya (Baiev, with Daniloff & Daniloff, 2004; Shekochikhin, 2003). According to the research conducted in 2006 by UNICEF, 73% of the children who took part in this research "often experienced traumatic events"; 62% "often remember war"; and 59% "often flinch when they hear unexpected noise" (UNICEF, 2006).

As in other war zones, socio-economic conditions caused by the ongoing war and violence influence families, individuals and in particular young people (Brett & Specht, 2004; Dowdney, 2005). Physical insecurity surrounds the young people in war zones; schooling is often unavailable; poverty and starvation are widespread. The situation in Chechnya is no different from other war zones in this regard. According to the official statistics of the Chechen Ministry of Labour, there are 1,381 orphans, 19,531 semi-orphans, 24,157 handicapped and mutilated children, and 246 children who were mutilated in the course of the counterterrorist operation which has been ongoing since 2000 (regnum.ru, 2007). The Chechen Government has confirmed that "a significant part" of the Chechen population lives in poverty which also "negatively influences the well-being of the Chechen children" (regnum.ru, 2007). In order to alleviate the situation of children affected by the war the Chechen Government has set up several programmes targeting children and young people in need. These include sub-programmes on the 'Social protection of mutilated children'; 'Improving the situation of orphans and children without parental supervision'; 'Education and upbringing'; and 'Prevention of crime committed by adolescents'. The very fact that such programmes were developed by the Chechen Government suggests that the situation of many young people in Chechnya is highly problematic, including significant involvement in criminal activities. This is also confirmed by Politkovskaya (2007), and here is one of her accounts concerning Chechen children and their families:

> ... We are met there [in Avtury village with 19,000 local residents] by a petite, toy-like boy; he is a first class school pupil, who does not go to school. Poverty... the boy does not have clothes, the family is that poor. His mother is always ill – confined to bed. There are four children [in the family], and in addition to everything else unidentified people in camouflage and masks came and took away his father... [who was] a tractor driver and is handicapped. (Politkovskaya, 2007, p. 134)

Method

The data for this study were collected during fieldwork in Russia as part of a larger study of Chechen groups of a terrorist nature. Data collection was based on open sources, and this followed a methodology applied in previous studies, with Sageman (2004) being one of the more well-known examples. I mainly relied on the archive of the Moscow Institute for Humanitarian Education (IGUMO). This archive houses a collection of newspaper and scientific articles, and prosecution and court documents that are based on systematic retrieval from open sources by the research team of the Institute and led by Professor Uriy Antonyan. The research team also interviewed detained Chechen terrorists and conducted a series of psychological tests with them. The archive was used as part of their study on ethno-religious terrorism in Russia (Antonyan, 2006). A series of three articles on young Chechens who were involved in terrorist activities that were published in the *Kommersant* newspaper in the Russian language in 2001 and 2002 were found in this archive, and they provide the database for this chapter. Expert interviews were conducted as well, including the interview with the former Lieutenant-Colonel of the Russian armed forces mentioned above. The newspaper articles appeared in the *Kommersant* on 29 September 2001, and 22 and 24 May 2002. These *Kommersant* articles covered two youth groups, which according to their place of origin and operation are called the 'Chernorechie group' and the 'Grozny group'. The articles were written on the occasion of the killing of the leader of one of the groups by the police and the two trials of the arrested members of these groups. They also provided background material on the family of the young people and gave an account of their activities. The articles were written by journalists Timur Samedov, Aleksandra Larintseva and Sergey Kisin and are referenced respectively.

Youth Groups and Terrorism in Chechnya

The 'Chernorechie Group'

This group was comprised of 4 young Chechen men, one of whom was 16 and the others were 17. The leader of the group, 16-year-old Kazbek Zaurbekov was born in the village of Gojty, near Grozny, in 1985 and had grown up there. It is unclear when exactly he became a member of the Arbi Barayev Group, but he must have been hardly older than 14 when he was recruited. The Arbi Barayev Group was part of Arbi Barayev's network that constituted a large terrorist-criminal organization that took hostages for ransom, committed terrorist acts against the Russian federal forces, the police forces of the bordering republics, for example, Ingushetiya, local police and civil authorities, collaborators with the Russians, and against Chechen religious leaders and elders. Arbi Barayev, born in 1973, had become one of the Chechen field commanders in charge of the Islamic Regiment for Special Purposes in the first Russian-Chechen war. He was awarded the rank of Brigadier-General for his war activities (Dupin, 2001; Trebin, 2003). After the war Barayev became the leader of his own network that was comprised of his armed group, and of smaller, satellite groups, like the Chernorechie group (Samedov, 2001).

Although Kazbek was no older than 15, he was directly attached to Arbi Barayev. Kazbek was involved in the killing of Chechens who collaborated with the Russian federal forces, local religious clerics and elders (Larintseva, 2002; Samedov, 2001). Notwithstanding his young age Kazbek was well regarded and enjoyed a high level of authority amongst the paramilitaries and terrorists in Grozny (Samedov, 2001). About the beginning of 2001 he received an order from Arbi Barayev to create his own group comprised of young people that would be part of the Arbi Barayev network (Larintseva, 2002; Samedov, 2001). Kazbek was appointed 'emir', i.e. terrorist leader, of Chernorechie, a suburb of Grozny. Following the order he recruited three 17-year-old pupils at a school in Chernorechie. The group received weapons and funding directly from Arbi Barayev. The Chernorechie group can be characterized as a locally embedded group, whose members were directly recruited by another young person who was already a member of a large terrorist-criminal network and with experience in violence.

The Chernorechie group was active between May and July 2001, barely three months, during which time it committed three terrorist acts. Their first act was a brutal murder of an elderly Russian who lived in Grozny. According to the newspaper report from the trial, the group members admitted that they had committed this murder motivated by ethnic hatred towards Russians (Larintseva, 2002). The next act was a double murder of two Chechen women, a mother and her daughter. Both women traded in the Chernorechie market and there were rumours that they sold drugs and that the daughter used to go out with the Russian federal soldiers (Larintseva, 2002). The third act was committed against two Chechen policemen who were returning home from work. The members of the group were waiting for the policemen and opened fire on their car as it passed by. No one was killed, but the policemen and the driver of another car were severely wounded.

The Chernorechie group dissolved in August 2001 when three of the group members were arrested after one of them, 17-year-old Dzhambek Dzhamaldinov, had told his grandmother about his involvement in the shooting of the police car. She informed his mother, who was a police officer in Grozny, and both women convinced him to surrender himself and report to the police. He gave the names and whereabouts of the other group members which led to the arrest of two others. The police did not manage to arrest Kazbek Zaurbekov, the leader of the group nor the rest of the group members. He was killed by the police near Grozny a month later in September 2001, when he resisted arrest and opened fire.

Dzhambek was sentenced to five years in a prison colony. His mother, who had reasonably decided that her child would be safest in this situation even in a Russian prison, worked as an Inspector at Human Resources in a Grozny police department. At the trial she expressed this and placed it in the context of in the environment of war and violence prevailing in Chechnya:

> Our children in Chechnya don't have any choice nowadays, anyone can become a gang member because of fear or stupidity, and then the way is either to cemetery or prison. And no one considers that the boys have had a wartime childhood.

This statement corresponds with Brett and Specht (2004):

> Living in a context of armed violence influences young people to use armed violence themselves. It creates feelings of insecurity, and an atmosphere in which violent behaviour is considered legitimate and is linked to the ready availability of weapons. (p. 12)

In the case of this group, the existence of armed groups in Chechnya that were ready to recruit very young people provided the adolescents with the opportunity to join violent action. The wartime childhood of the young men had trained them that violence might be legitimate, and the existing terrorist groups could also provide further legitimation like ethnic hatred, which also targeted the army that was seen as an army of occupation. The recruiter, in this case Kazbek Zaurbekov, had acted on demands, if not on orders of a terrorist network, and made use of these conditions when recruiting members for the group.

Whilst the leader, Kazbek, clearly had a history of violent behaviour, not all members of the group were known to be violent. He allegedly had murdered more than 10 people before founding the group, and had been involved in a number of murders of heads of municipalities and local administration (Samedov, 2001). At the trial 17-year-old Artur Magomadov asked not to be punished severely. His aunt Faima Magomadova testified to his mostly non-violent behaviour: "Artur has always been a gentle boy, who trusts other people and is easily influenced by other people". Artur himself "was answering the questions very quietly and unconfidently", and then "put his face into his hands and began crying". He was sentenced to seven years in a prison colony. It seems that Artur's trust and gullibility had facilitated his recruitment by Kazbek Zaurbekov. The mother of another member, Usman Rasayev, commented to the newspaper on the final verdict for her son: "They gave him eight years for nothing!" (Larintseva, 2002). We do not know here whether she referred to facts or believed that her son was not actively involved in the killings, or if she thought that her son had taken part in a kind of legitimate and warlike violence. However, his involvement in such a group is hard to reconcile with doing 'nothing', and this statement might show the impact of the war-like situation on the normative evaluation of violence.

It is important to note that the group was active for a very short time, and committed lethal violent acts of a terrorist nature only, which were fuelled and motivated by ethnic hatred. They did not participate in any other type of criminal activities. Their victims were either Russians, as in the first case, had relationships with Russians or collaborated with them, as in the second and third cases. As such the pattern of their activities resembles those of groups active in occupied countries or standing up against an army of occupation. Larintseva (2002) reported that according to the Russian Federal Security Service similar groups of young people related to the Arbi Barayev network were active also in other areas of Grozny. It is unclear whether they received orders or were directed towards the victims they targeted, or selected them on their own. Nonetheless, there are common characteristics with the use of young people as assassins by the Colombian Medellin drug cartel, which point to such an interpretation. The Chernorechie group can be clearly characterized as a terrorist gang.

The 'Grozny Group'

This group was comprised of three Chechen youngsters, one of whom was 14 years old and two others were 18 years old. The group was active from January to March 2001, again no longer than three months. According to the newspaper report on the trial of two group members (Kisin, 2002), one of them, 18-year-old Khasanbek Sajdulayev had boasted to his friend, 18-year-old Rustam Khajdarov, that he had killed a Russian elderly woman in order to avenge his relatives and friends who had been wounded by the actions of the Russian forces in the war. In this conversation, Khasanbek had suggested creating a group that would attack Russians living in Grozny. Rustam agreed and brought in another 14-year-old friend, Roman Mazhiyev. Clearly they started their activities quickly (Kisin, 2002).

The group committed a series of attacks on elderly ethnic Russian people in Grozny, including robbery, torture and murder. They used to take a private taxi, drive around the city and look for Russian elderly people standing on their balconies. Recognition and identification was facilitated by physical appearance. They used false documents, pretending to be police officers, to force entry into the homes of their Russian victims. They battered and tortured their victims, and demanded their valuables and other possessions. At some point they also began to use firearms in their raids, and killed three of their victims. According to the newspaper report from the trial, the group members admitted that they committed the attacks because they were motivated by ethnic hatred towards Russians; however, they also admitted to having been motivated by money and other valuables that were in the possession of their victims. This group dissolved in March 2001 when Rustam Khajdarov and Roman Mazhiyev where arrested by the police. Khasanbek Sajdulayev fled and was not apprehended.

These attacks do not fall easily into the framework of terrorist activities. Certainly some ideological motives were present, but these reveal more communality with hate crimes than with a clear political motivation, as given in the definition of terrorism by Laqueur:

> … terrorism has been defined in many different ways, and little can be said about it with certainty except that it is the use of violence by a group for political ends, usually directed against a government, but at times also against another ethnic group, class, race, religion, or political movement. (Laqueur, 1999, p. 46)

The group does not have any political objectives, and is very much based on the personal revenge of its initiator and perhaps of two other members. Clearly, the motives of enrichment and access to money and consumer goods were an equally driving force, if not the most important one.

During its very short life time, this group did not start with lethal violence like the Chernorechie group did. Instead, it developed the use of violence, starting with less serious assaults and ending up with a triple murder. Only in the course of these events, they also acquired more lethal weapons and moved towards the use of firearms, while the Chernorechie group was obviously equipped from the start by the adult terrorist network. The motives of their action were neither unambiguously ideological nor only informed by enriching themselves. They selected particularly helpless victims, namely elderly people, in contrast to the more ideologically driven selection of collaborators and supporters by the Chernorechie group. The group members were not linked to any other criminal and terrorist group or organization and initiated and developed their activities independently. With the exception of the rather weak ideological component of their activities, i.e. ethnic hatred and revenge, the activities of this gang can be compared to the activities of youth gangs elsewhere in Russia. These gangs are typically territorial and use extreme violence in order to obtain property, and defend their territory and the honour of the gang members. Extortion, robbery, rape and homicide are amongst their activities (see Petrov, 2007; Ureva & Iluhina, 2007).

Conclusion

These groups were gangs, as they used severe violence and were involved in illegal activities, which constituted an essential part of their group identity. They were clearly territorial in the sense that they mostly originated from a small suburb and neighbourhood, and had defined areas for their activities. It is important to note that both groups committed their crimes close to their homes and neighbourhood, just like young gang members do. All group members knew each other previously from school and neighbourhood. Both groups differ in terms of their connections to terrorism and terrorist networks. The Chernorechie group was led by a youngster experienced in severe violence who had been a member of a large terrorist organization. He acted on behalf and at the command of the leader of this organization when he founded his own group and started its activities. The gang was connected to a large terrorist-criminal network, and was funded and armed by the leader of this organization. The young leader recruited the other gang members and led them into violent action. The fact that they were all of the same age demonstrates that recruitment was similar to that reported by Berko (2004) on suicide bombers. The second gang was initiated by a young man without any connections to other terrorist organizations, though obviously inspired by vague representations of terrorist ideologies. This group seems to have much more in common with street gangs as described by Klein (1995). Like these, their activities were sporadic and they were not normally systematically involved with organized criminal groups of adults. However, connections of friendship were decisive in the recruitment process. The importance of friendship in the recruitment process is identified by both research on gangs and young soldiers.

The connection of the Chernorechie gang to a large terrorist-criminal organization may define it as a 'terrorist network gang', i.e. a gang which was initiated and supported by a larger network, and served the interests of the larger network. Being a 'network gang' not only enabled the activities of the group in terms of funding and weapons but also defined the direction of its activities. This group did not seek to obtain valuable possessions from their victims but committed terrorist acts that were designed to spread fear amongst the Russians and their collaborators. As such they committed classical terrorist acts, whilst the second group only acted upon a faint copy of terrorist political ideology, in this case ethnic hatred. The second group might be defined as an 'independent gang', since it managed its own logistics and defined its activities, and did not seek any connections with terrorist organizations.

Both groups had a short lifespan of three months. It can be suggested that the inexperience of the young gang members did not enable them to establish efficient ways of action, i.e. such that would allow longer periods of activity. As the mother of one of the Chernorechie group members stated, the fact that the boys had a wartime childhood was central to their involvement. The environment had provided them with a direct and indirect motivation and broad ideological justification to use lethal violence against Russians. The ongoing war in Chechnya made firearms easily available and its use a common feature of daily life. It caused disorder both in terms of adult supervision over adolescents, and policing and community control over youth groups, which allowed the formation of these gangs in the first instance. It also provided the young people with a worthwhile reason to join violent action, for example, to contribute to the struggle against the occupants or to avenge their relatives and friends. These factors facilitated the emergence of youth gangs in Chechnya.

Are these young men terrorists? At an individual level, only Kazbek Zaurbekov may be firmly classified in this way as he had a 'career' in violence, and was an esteemed member of a large terrorist-criminal organization which was demonstrated by his appointment to 'emir'. Other gang members were new to violence, and did not become hard-core terrorists as they were not involved in any sophisticated activities, for example, complex logistics; did not have the experience and skills to be efficient terrorist gang members, for example, to conduct underground activity; and did not have any elaborated ideological vision. Finally they were all still very young. At a group level, however, the Chernorechie group can be classified as a terrorist gang, whilst the Grozny group can be located somewhere between criminal, hate and terrorist gang. Clearly, the war on terror led by the Russian armed forces had given rise to both groups in terms of the selection of victims and the type of violence used against them. The disorganization of society had also facilitated the emergence of both gangs, and the everyday violence and human rights abuses by the Russian armed forces might also have contributed to lure these young people into activities which in the end overwhelmed them.

References

Akhmadov, Y. (2006). *Istoriya Chechni s drevneishih vremen i do kontza XVIII veka* [The history of Chechnya from ancient times and until the end of the XVIII century]. Retrieved August 23, 2006 from www.chechnyafree.ru/index.php?lng=rus&section =bookhisrus&row=8 [in Russian].

Anderson, E. (1998). The social ecology of youth violence. In M. Tonry, & M. H. Moore (Eds), *Youth violence* (Vol. 24). Chicago/London: The University of Chicago Press.

Antonyan, U. (Ed.) (2006). *Etnoreligiozniy Terrorizm*. Moscow: Aspekt Press [in Russian].

Baiev, K. with Daniloff, R., & Daniloff, N. (2004). *The oath: A surgeon under fire*. London: Pocket Books.

Ball, R. A., & Curry, G. D. (1997). The logic of definition in criminology: Purposes and methods for defining 'gangs'. In G. L. Mays (Ed.), *Gangs and gang behavior*. Chicago: Nelson-Hall Publishers.

bbc.co.uk (2000, 10 February). *In pictures: Grozny in ruins*. Retrieved August 23, 2007, from http://news.bbc.co.uk/2/hi/europe/638309.stm

Berko, A. (2004). *Ba Derekh le Gan Eden: Olamam shel Mihablot ve Mihablim Mitabdim ve Sholheiem*. Tel-Aviv: Miskal [in Hebrew].

Brett, R., & Specht, I. (2004). *Young soldiers: Why they choose to fight*. Boulder, Colorado: Lynne Rienner Publishers.

Cherkasov, A. (2001). *Demography, the loss of the population and migration in Chechnya. The critics of sources*. Report of the 'Memorial' Human Rights Organization. A talk at the conference in Stavropol, Russia, September 2001. Retrieved August 29, 2006, from www.memo.ru/hr/hotpoints/N-Caucas/misc/numbook.htm [in Russian].

Decker, S. H., & Van Winkle, B. (1996). *Life in the gang: Family, friends, and violence*. Cambridge: Cambridge University Press.

Dowdney, L. (2005). *International comparison of children and youth in organised armed violence*. Retrieved August 21, 2007, from www.dreamscanbefoundation.org/ NeitherWarnorPeace.pdf

Dupin, S. (2001). Arbi Barayev pogib smertju 'strashnyh'. *Kommersant, 109* [in Russian].

Esbensen, F. A., & Peterson-Lynskey, D. (2001). Young gang members in a school survey. In M. W. Klein, H-J. Kerner, C. L. Maxson, & E. G. M. Weitekamp (Eds), *The Eurogang Paradox: Street gangs and youth groups in the U.S. and Europe*. Dordrecht/ Boston/ London: Kluwer Academic Publishers.

Grennan, S., Britz, M. T., Rush, J., & Barker, T. (2000). *Gangs: An international approach*. New Jersey: Prentice Hall.

Human Rights Watch (1994). *Generation under fire: Children and violence in Colombia.* Retrieved August 21, 2007, from www.hrw.org/reports/1994/colombia/gener2. htm#militias

Human Rights Watch (2006). *Situacija s pytkami v Chechenskoj Respublike.* Retrieved May 18, 2007, from www.hrw.org/russian/reports/russia/2006/memo.html [in Russian].

kavkazcenter.com (2007). Retrieved June 19, 2007, from www.kavkazcenter.com

Kisin, S. (2002, 24 May). Starikov ubivali za to, chto oni ne chechncy. *Kommersant, 87* [in Russian].

Klein, M. W. (1995). *The American street gang: Its nature, prevalence, and control.* Oxford: Oxford University Press.

Laqueur, W. (1999). *The new terrorism: Fanaticism and the arms of mass destruction.* New York: Oxford University Press.

Larintseva, A. (2002). Nedetskiy Prigovor detskoy bande. *Kommersant, 85* [in Russian].

Lien, I-L. (2001). The concept of honor, conflict and violent behavior among youth in Oslo. In M. W. Klein, H-J. Kerner, C. L. Maxson, & E. G. M. Weitekamp (Eds), *The Eurogang Paradox: Street gangs and youth groups in the U.S. and Europe.* Dordrecht/ Boston/London: Kluwer Academic Publishers.

Murphy, P. J. (2004). *The wolves of Islam: Russia and the faces of Chechen terror.* Washington, DC: Brassey's.

NovayaGazeta (2005). *Arifmetika Poter. Otveti ne shodjatsa.* Retrieved August 29, 2006, from http://2005.novayagazeta.ru/nomer/2005/94n/n94n-s16.shtml [in Russian].

Oehme III C. G. (1997). *Gangs, groups, and crime: Perceptions and responses of community organizations.* Durham, NC: Carolina Academic Press.

Petrov, G. (2007). Delezh asfalta. *Ogoniok, 6.* Retrieved August 9, 2007, from www. ogoniok.ru/4982/3/ [in Russian].

Politkovskaya, A. (2006). *Karatelnyj Sgovor.* Retrieved August 6, 2007, from http://2006. novayagazeta.ru/nomer/2006/74n/n74n-s11.shtml [in Russian].

Politkovskaya, A. (2007). *Za Chto.* Moscow: Novaya Gazeta [in Russian].

regnum.ru (2007, 10 May). *Razrabotana programma 'Deti Chechni' na 2007–2010 gody.* Retrieved June 14, 2007, from www.regnum.ru/news/district-nkavkaz/ chechnya/825050.html [in Russian].

Sageman, M. (2004). *Understanding terror networks.* Philadelphia: University of Pennsylvania Press.

Samedov, T. (2001). Zastrelen samyj molodoj emir. *Kommersant, 178* [in Russian].

Seely, R. (2001). *Russo-Chechen conflict 1800–2000: A deadly embrace.* London/Portland: Frank Cass.

Shekochikhin, U. (2003). *Zabytaya Chechnya: Stranitsi iz voennyh bloknotov.* Moscow: Olimp [in Russian].

Sherbakova, E. (2007). Regioni Rossii silno razlichajutsja po urovnju zanjatosti, bezrabotitsi I ispolzovaniju rabochej sily. *Demoscope Weekly, 277–278.* Retrieved June 19, 2007, from http://demoscope.ru/weekly/2007/0277/barom05.php [in Russian].

Speckhard, A., & Akhmedova, K. (2006). The new Chechen Jihad: Militant Wahhabism as a radical movement and a source of suicide terrorism in post-war Chechen society. *Democracy & Security, 2,* 1–53.

Spergel, I. A. (1995). *The youth gang problem: A community approach*. New York/ Oxford: Oxford University Press.

Trebin, M. P. (2003). *Terrorizm v XXI Veke*. Minsk: Kharvest [in Russian].

UNICEF (2006). *Chechenskaya Respublika: Vazhno ne tolko vosstanovit infrastrukturu, no i zalechit dushevnye rany*. Retrieved August 21, 2007, from www.unicef.org/ russia/ru/emergency_programme_6094.html [in Russian].

Ureva, I., & Iluhina, O. (2007). Ulyanovsk: tolko fakty. *Ogoniok*, 6. Retrieved August 9, 2007, from www.ogoniok.ru/4982/2 [in Russian].

Van Gemert, F., & Fleisher, M. S. (2005). In the grip of the group. In S. H. Decke, & F. M. Weerman (Eds), *European street gangs and troublesome youth groups*. Oxford: AltaMira Press.

10

The Enemy of My Enemy is My Friend[1]

Kevin Borgeson and Robin Valeri

Synopsis: A brief history of the Aryan Nations is provided and some of the major tenets of their Christian Identity are presented. The role of Christian Identity within the Aryan Nations is discussed. The chapter then examines ongoing changes in the Aryan Nations, one of the most notorious hate groups in American history, focusing on its growing alignment with one of its former enemies, followers of Islamic Jihad.

Since 11 September 2001 America's concerns about terrorism have largely focused on countering threats from groups outside the United States. However, many of the most infamous terrorist attacks in the United States, including the Oklahoma City bombing by Timothy McVeigh, bombings of abortion clinics by Eric Robert Rudolph, and the mass murder committed by Buford Furrow, have been committed by Americans. These individuals were or are either adherents of Christian Identity, members of the Aryan Nations, or both. A recent article in *Intelligence Report* (Blejwas, Griggs, & Potok, 2005), states that over the last decade there have been an estimated 60 terrorist acts within the United States committed by individuals in hate groups. According to the report most of these domestic terrorist acts have religious underpinnings.[2]

---

[1] A somewhat different version of this chapter appeared in the *Journal of Behavioral Sciences*, 2006, October.

[2] During the interviews members of the Aryan Nations referred to the Muslims they had contact with as 'Islamic Jihadist' because they did not want to reveal the identities or locations of these individuals or groups. For the purpose of this chapter the authors will use the same terminology.

The Faces of Terrorism: Multidisciplinary Perspectives Edited by David Canter
© 2009 John Wiley & Sons Ltd.

Through ethnographic research, the impact of this alignment on changes within the Aryan Nations, especially the religious beliefs of its members, as well as changes between the two groups will be explored. Finally, social psychological theories of prejudice, social identity, and intergroup relations will be used to explain Aryan Nations members' hatred toward Jews and their willingness to work with a former enemy, Islamic Jihadists, to accomplish a shared goal, defeating Jews.

The research for this chapter was gathered over a series of four years beginning in August 2001, approximately one month before 11 September and ending in August 2005. Non-participant observations of rallies, annual meetings and press conferences were conducted. During this time qualitative interviews were also conducted with approximately 25 members of the Aryan Nations.

A Brief History of the Aryan Nations and Christian Identity

Richard Butler founded the Aryan Nations in 1973. Butler was born in Bettet, Colorado, a town located 30 miles east of Denver. His family, who were Presbyterian, lived there for only a few years before moving to the 'Four Corners country' where they lived until 1923. After his family lost their ranch they moved to Denver, Colorado and then moved again in 1931 to California. Upon completion of high school Butler attended Los Angeles City College. During World War II, Butler served in the air force and was a flight engineer in India for 18 months.

Butler returned to the United States in 1946 and began an 18-year career of "operating a machine plant for the production and precision machining of automotive parts and engine assemblies and aircraft parts" (Butler, 2001). It was at this point that Butler and his wife began attending churches of different denominations. To Butler, the religion being preached "wasn't Americanism it was communism to me, we wanted to find a church that taught something that we believed, something that resonated within us" (Butler, 2001). During this time Butler also became involved in the anti-communist movement. He served on the California Committee to Combat Communism. This committee wanted to remove communists from teaching in schools. Their proposal, although it made it onto voter ballots, did not receive enough votes to pass. However, Butler's anti-communist stance became a strong one. During this time Butler began to associate communism with the Jews and came to the realization that he wasn't fighting a foreign government, but a larger moral force, the children of Satan – the Jews.

A former navy commander enlightened Butler that he was not combating communism but Judaism. During this period Butler was introduced to Dr

Wesley Swift and indoctrinated into anti-Semitic beliefs. Butler was instantly impressed with Swift's oratory skills and the way in which Christian Identity made sense of the Bible. Christian Identity, which has been the backbone of the Aryan Nations movement, has a central core of 'religious beliefs': pre-Adamic man, the Serpent Seed, House of Israel, Jesus, and Armageddon.

Pre-Adamic man. Christian Identity adherents believe the earth was created before the chapter of Genesis in the Bible. According to Christian Identity adherents, during this time minorities were created and were to be subservient to whites. Additionally they believe that whites are superior to all others because they are from 'the seed of Adam'.

The Serpent Seed: The Two-Seedline Identity. According to this tenet Eve had sex with both Adam and the Devil on the same day. As a result of these two unions, Eve gave birth to two infants, one from Adam, whose descendants are today's Anglo-Saxons, and the other from the Devil, whose descendants are today's Jewish people (Walters, 2001). This core belief of Christian Identity establishes Jews as descendants of the devil 'the serpent seed of the Devil' thus beginning a battle for the 'true blessing of God'. They believe that the battle is still going on today.

House of Israel. For Aryan Nations members, nationality defines Israel, Israel being the chosen people of God. For Christian Identity proponents, this nationality, those who are the chosen people of God are the 'Anglo-Saxon, Germanic and Scandinavian nations'.

Jesus. According to Christian Identity Jesus is not a Jew but the Messiah who is to bring back whites' dominance on the planet.

Armageddon. Armageddon is coming, and will take place in America, where whites will rise up and destroy all Jews and rule the world.

In 1961 Butler officially joined the church serving under Swift's tutelage for a decade. Butler was given access to Swift's library and Dr Swift, along with Bertrand Comparet, groomed Butler to become a pastor in the Christian Identity faith. For Butler, who was seduced by Christian Identity's outlook that the white race is the true Israel, "the lights started coming on, everything started to make sense" (Butler, 2001). The cold war was not with the communist, but the true anti-Christ, the Jew. These beliefs would fuel Butler's ambitions in life. He saw it as his destiny to learn all he could about the evil Jew.

Butler also became obsessed with the Aryan heritage, which would lead to his fascination with Hitler and National Socialism. From the teachings of Dr Swift, Butler learned that the word Aryan is stigmatized and that this stigma was a direct result of the Jews controlling the media as well as the financial, educational and all other major institutions in the United States. By having this control, Swift and Butler believed, the Jews were able to have mind control over those living in society. The representation that we receive from

K-1 through college all these things we read in comic books as youngsters, it presents one view of life. It doesn't present our view of life, the Aryan view; it presents the non-Aryan view of life. Therefore, we are told being Aryan is bad through this medium and everyone believes it because it is in print. We have lost our ability to think for ourselves. That is what you are supposed to learn in college. Most of the time we are indoctrinated instead of educated. (Butler, 2001)

"From 1964 through 1973, Butler was a marketing analyst. In 1968 he became a senior manufacturing engineer for Lockheed Aircraft Co. at their Palmdale, California plant, where extensive development was under way for the L-1011 aircraft" (Twelve Aryan Nations).

Swift, who had fought diabetes and kidney problems for years, "… died in the waiting room of a Mexican clinic of an apparent heart attack on October 8, 1970" (Barkum, 1997, p. 68). Upon Swift's death there was no immediate successor within the movement because "there were so many potential successors in a movement that had no mechanisms for establishing leadership, let alone succession" (Barkum, 1997, p. 69). This problem would continually plague the movement.

Butler believed he should be Swift's successor and began conducting the weekly lectures. However, attendance at the church services began to shrink. Due to Butler's lack of enthusiastic services he received " no encouragement from the church board" and Swift's daughter claimed that the church membership "began to decrease" (Barkum, 1997, p. 70). Wanting to run a church his way, as well as missing the Northwest, Butler set out to move the Church of Jesus Christ Christian to Hayden Lake, Idaho. Although Butler claimed to be part of the Church of Jesus Christ Christian, Michel Barkum (1997), the author of *Religion and the radical right*, claims that the church never granted Butler a charter.

Becoming tired of the in-fighting, Butler decided to create his own political arm of the Church of Jesus Christ Christian – the Aryan Nations. Butler moved to Coeur d'Alene, Idaho where he originally purchased 50 acres of land, then sold off 30 acres, and built the 'compound' of hate on the remaining 20 acres (Butler, 2001). Butler also created one of the most recognized hate symbols of the right wing neo-Nazi movement. According to Butler this symbol has much religious significance:

It is a four-square path form. It is from Numbers 2 mainly. It is a shield of faith with the crown of Jesus Christ at the top, the three spirits: the Father, Son, and the Holy Spirit, the sword of truth coming from that crown. The four-square path form is talked about in Numbers 2. We have the twelve tribes of Israel represented on the four corners coming into the center of this resurrection. The swastika and the sword of truth, that is the holiest of holies … the red, white and blue are the royal colors of the race. (Butler, 2001)

Although Butler was a racist, most people in Hayden, Idaho accepted him for who he was and went about their daily business. "Hayden Lake town folk had no qualms about Butler. They called him 'Reverend' or 'Dick' and chatted with him whenever he stopped by the Owl Café" (Flynn & Gerhardt, 1989, p. 55).

In June 1978 Butler went to the bottom of his property and placed a sign that read "Aryan Nations". It was at this time that "the political arm of the Aryan Nations was announced to the world, and if they weren't listening, they soon would" (Flynn & Gerhardt, 1989, p. 55). In the 1980s the Aryan Nations committed a number of domestic terrorist acts in the United States. From 1983 to 1984 the Order, a 'secret' splinter group of the Aryan Nations, was allegedly operating without Butler's knowledge. The Order committed Brinks truck robberies that netted them US$ 4.1 million and began an elaborate counterfeiting ring to bring money into the terrorist white supremacy movement in the United States. This group had such an influence on the Aryan Nations as well as on the white supremacist movement in general, that white supremacist Internet sites frequently depict members of the Order as martyrs to the movement and encourage others to continue the work of the Order, committing similar terrorist activities as a means of funding the movement. In 1984 twenty-three Order members were caught and stood trial. In 1985 they were found guilty of racketeering charges and given sentences that "ranged from 40 to 100 years" (Timeline).

However, terrorist activities did not stop after the sentencing of the Order. As shown in Table 10.1, terrorist activity actually increased.

Prompted by his declining health, Butler decided he needed a successor to the Aryan Nations should he die or something happen to him. Butler appointed a few people as the 'new leaders'. However, these new leaders eventually all left the organization because they were not satisfied with the direction that the members wanted to go. In late October 2000, in-fighting within the movement

Table 10.1. White Supremacist terrorist activity (Timeline)

1986	Aryan Nations member David Dorr bombed the Coeur d' Alene court house to send a message to the government that they would not stand for interference with their cause.
1992	The 'Bob Mathews Brigade' is arrested for their plot to kill civil rights leaders.
1993	Chevy Kehoe is arrested for creating a copy of the Order, called the Aryan Peoples Republic which became linked to several bank robberies and five homicides of prominent people.
1992–1996	The Aryan Republican Army (also called the Order II) is formed and goes on to commit 22 bank robberies to help fund terrorist activity.
2003	Several members of the Aryan Nations were arrested on the east coast for creating a small drug ring to help fund the terrorist right.

increased. Some members of the Aryan Nations, because they wished to expand their membership to other like-minded brethren in the world, began to distance themselves from the view that Christian Identity should serve as the sole religion of their movement. Other members maintained that Christian Identity should remain the sole religion of the Aryan Nations. Things became more complicated in October 2004 when Richard Butler passed away. It was at this time that some leaders began to advocate more strongly that people of the Muslim faith should be let in as members of the Aryan Nations, since both religions have a "hatred for Jews".

Recent Changes within the Aryan Nations

Anti-Jewish sentiment

According to Kathleen Blee (2002) women who join organized racist groups learn to become anti-Semitic. Although most Aryan Nations members interviewed for this project were male, Blee's assertion is relevant because most of the interviewees started off in other organized groups hating blacks, not Jews.[3] It was their journey into hate that allowed most of them to "come to the realization that the Jews are to blame for most of the world's problems".[4] Take for instance this quote from a man who joined the Aryan Nations after belonging to several other white supremacist organizations:

> I have been in several organizations over the years – skinheads, Klan, you name it. The problem is they have it all wrong. They want you to believe that the blacks and Hispanics are to blame for society's problems, they aren't. They are too dumb to figure it out. Once I realized that, I figured somebody bigger had to be behind all the problems in the US. It wasn't until I met [a friend] that I began to understand that the Jew was behind most of it, and they are using the blacks and Christians to get their agenda across.

Part of the transformation in their target of hatred is a direct result of their belief in a Jewish conspiracy. For members of the Aryan Nations, the Jewish people serve as scapegoats and are to blame for a host of problems. Results of these interviews reveal a belief in a Jewish conspiracy, specifically a 'Jewish-controlled government'[5] and a 'Jewish-controlled media'.

[3] The average person in the movement has been in approximately three hate groups before joining the Aryan Nations.
[4] Interviews were conducted with members of the Aryan Nations who were guaranteed anonymity. Interviews were conducted between August 2001 – December 2005.
[5] Some members refer to this as Z.O.G., Zionist occupied government.

One of the most frequently expressed beliefs among interviewees was that Jewish people working in the World Trade Center knew in advance of the planned attack and therefore did not go to work on that day. One member stated that the number of people in the buildings did not add up, and the only way that could happen was if the Jews who worked in the building told other Jews not to go into work that day.

> ... just like the number, six thousand ... six thousand people died in the World Trade Center bombings ... that's not true because just recently the number's down to three thousand seventy ... three thousand seventy ... now you take that building between what ... quarter to nine and nine thirty or quarter after nine ... in the morning, do it ... do the ... just think about how many people usually generally work? ... worked in them buildings ... fifty thousand a building I believe the number was ... now nine o'clock in the morning, quarter after nine ... nine thirty, whenever it happened to be. I don't remember now ... figure in how many were there, approximately how many were there on any other given day, then factor in how many were there and how many were killed and how many had a ... really had a chance to get out of the building ... out of the area before the buildings came down ... you know and I know you could do all of that by factoring you know an average you know and the numbers aren't gonna jive even that six hundred ... even that six thousand that was only like twenty-five people a floor you know and I was told by people that work there ... or had worked there in the past you know electricians or whatever ... .

Another common view is that Jews control the media. In the Aryan Nations, media is a buzzword for 'Jew'. Most members cling to a stereotype that started with the Protocol of the Elders of Zion, which stated that Jews have a secret desire to control most social institutions like the media, banks, schools and the government. One of the first conspiracies that one of the authors (Borgeson) was subjected to upon entrance into this area of research was that the Jewish-controlled media covered up the Jews' involvement in 9/11:

> How come immediately after 9/11 there was pictures floating around of Jews dancing on top of buildings? And within minutes the pictures were never seen again? That's because the mainstream Jew media wanted them hushed up so no one knew they were behind it. Are those conspiracies? No, I think they're actual fact.

The Aryan Nations as a Christian-based Organization

One important distinction made by most interviewees between Jews and non-Jews is religion. According to the interviewees, religious differences make Jews intrinsically different. The Aryan Nations is based on Christianity. Racism and anti-Semitism, for most Aryan Nations members, have been justified through Christian Identity, the cornerstone of the Aryan Nations movement for over 25 years. Members of Christian Identity believe the real chosen people (the Twelve Lost Tribes) are the white Anglo-Saxon races of the world. Christian Identity adherents believe that there is currently a battle between good and evil taking place on this earth, and that all whites must unite against the Jews to get their chosen rights back when Jesus returns. For most members race and anti-Semitism are so tied in with Christian Identity, that to step back from the religion is seen as becoming soft on race and anti-Semitism, which the founder of the organization – Richard Butler – believed in:

> I believe that the Identity message is the only religion that should be allowed. You can't let a bunch of sand niggers into the organization – you are supposed to be about the Aryan race. Last time I looked, they sure the hell were not Aryan and they shouldn't be allowed to even be in this country.

The above quote reflects two important beliefs. The first, that Christian Identity is the only religion. Consequently people with any other religious ideology should not be allowed to join the Aryan Nations. The second, that all Muslims are black and therefore should not be allowed to join the Aryan Nations. When the above interviewee was informed that not all Muslims are dark skinned, he replied:

> I haven't seen any. And even if there is some that are white, they should be shot for deserting their race. Whites are the chosen descendants of the Bible, and whites need to wake up and reclaim back our heritage from the children of Satan.

As the above quote demonstrates, race is inherently tied to Christian Identity. According to the interviewee people of the white race should be Christian. Whites who do not adhere to a Christian faith are traitors to their race. Christian Identity is so tied into the belief system that some adherents – as in the quote below – see the addition of any other religion, in this case Muslims, as part of the Aryan Nations mission as a sin, which should not be tolerated:

> Because if they were to interview me, like you are now, they would find out that we do not let anyone in the organization that is not Christian. Period. There are a lot of groups out there that claim to be Identity, but they will let anyone join as long as they are open to the message. That is not good enough because all down through scripture every time we have aligned ourselves with heathens, pagans or unbelievers God has taken his blessing off of us and we have failed.

Changing religious views

For some members of the Aryan Nations, it is not the specific beliefs of Christian Identity that are important to the cause but the religious justification. One member expressed this by stating: "I could never hate someone for the sake of hating them. I base my views on the Bible. The typical race-hating thing gets you nowhere". As a result of this change in position on diversity of religion, Aryan Nations leadership has decided to allow Muslims into their organization. As a matter of fact, they say that by allowing different religions they are living up to the 'mission statement' of founder Richard Butler:

> As was the stance of the founder, Pastor Richard G. Butler, Aryan Nations was developed as an institution of Aryan Virtue, along with the Aryan Brotherhood, which coalesced as a splinter within the prison systems, becoming the foremost means of protection for Aryans whose freedom has been confiscated. Pastor Butler's conception was never an Identity-only organization, and it is not today; however, as people in the past visited the 'Church of Jesus Christ ~ Christian' in Hayden, Idaho, it was all too clear that the group's nucleus was the Identity belief, as it still is today.
>
> [T]he decision was made to make the Aryan Nations two distinct entities, the first being the Aryan Nations proper, and the second, the Tabernacles of the Phinehas Priesthood, the biblical wing of this organization, this was done because many Identity adherents sought their own group to themselves, while our views and systems were attracting the most virulent and therefore the most worthwhile membership, although they were not necessarily Biblical Believers. Butler would not turn these men away, and neither will we.

In response to the flood of emails the organization received, those in charge of the Internet posted a clarification notice describing their non-religious stance; as well as their belief that the Islamic Jihadeen is biblically supported:

> There has been a little misunderstanding as to what our perspective is as far as an alliance with Islamic Jihadeen, and our own Phinehas Priests. There are some out there who would like to imply that we are now an Islamic fundamentalist organization, and this is erroneous, our organization is not for the support of any religion; however, based on the history of the Aryan Nations, the rules and conduct are based on Biblical Law, and the general view of the bulk of this organization is the acceptance of Aryan Messianic Identity, or other forms of what is called 'Christian Identity' in most circles.

Responses to the above two postings reflected such great interest in the Aryan Nations by non-Christian Identity members that the leaders of the Aryan Nations are planning to make liaison appointments of different religions within the organization.

Shared hatred

When asked why the Aryan Nations was aligning itself with Islamic Jihadists, interviewees were quick to point out that the current Christian Identity movement was dead, and that the movement lacked spine:

> The white Christians in today's movement don't have the fervor that the Muslims have. They wouldn't lay down their life for a cause. As a matter of fact, throughout most of the movement, there have been very few people who would lay down their life and be a martyr. If we could instil that pride back into our race the Jews wouldn't have a chance against us. We would be fighting with such veracity they wouldn't be able to stop us.

In response to the dying Christian Identity movement in America, Aryan Nations members began to develop a camaraderie with those that they felt had more 'spine', Islamic Jihadists:

> There is a strong brotherhood with Muslims. Doesn't matter where you live, you are going to go to the aid of another Muslim. It is the way that Christianity used to be before they brought it to the whole world. That was our religion, the white races, for His children on the earth.

As the Aryan Nations began to branch out in its religious denominations, they began to see that they shared similar group characteristics: analogous moral values, perceived media persecution and hatred for the United States Government.

The following quote reflects the belief that adherents of Islam have moral values similar to those of the Aryan Nations:

> Further, seeing the errors of the past, we have taken this approach with alliances to Islamic adherents, because we find their standards of morality to be nearly analogous to our own, and their resolve to uproot and destroy the fallen tree of the Garden, the satanic 'Jew', to also be analogous to our own desires and devotion. In this sense, Islam is our ally. ... Islam has not been dishonored as much by 'Jew'ish incursion, therefore Islamic Jihadeen have safeguarded the purity of the very instinct for self-preservation for which we hold the most vociferous esteem.

The quote then continues with a statement which reflects the belief that the Jews control the media and as such are able to present a negative view of Muslims.

> The 'Jews' have used their control of the media to portray the Islamist as a wild animal, the subhuman of the world, as they preach the virtues of them-

selves along with all races and false creeds that are ignoble enough to collaborate with them. Whereas the Aryan realizes that Ishmael was blessed by Yahweh, and prophesied to always be the fist in the face of his enemy. Ishmael's descendants are among the Arabs and Israelites today, and far be it from us to say that Yahweh was wrong, and the 'Jews' are truthful.

The next part of the message explains why followers of Islam are the allies of the Aryan Nations.

The Ishmaelite is our ally because he is the fist that takes the first strike against Satan's spawn, the 'Jew'. The Aryan is the knock-out punch, the Children of Yahweh will destroy His enemies, and Ishmael will stand aside his brother Isaac and receive his share of the glory and honor. What Yahweh has blessed, is blessed as far as Ishmael, and what Yahweh has cursed and condemned to death, as far as the demonic seed falsely known as the 'Jew', all of the spiritual sodomites of this world along with their minions of deceived Zionist collaborators, all of their horses and all of their men will not put humpty dumpty 'the Jew' back together again.

Then the message goes on to reassure those members of the Aryan Nations who believe Christian Identity is at the centre of the organization of its importance while asserting that members of other religions will be welcomed into the Aryan Nations.

The Tabernacles of the Phinehas Priesthood will remain the Biblically based foundation of the Aryan Nations; however, membership of the Aryan Nations will continue to welcome Islamists and adherents to other moral religions into our ranks. There is nothing new being done within the Aryan Nations, all of our brothers and sisters were always welcome to join our ranks, and as it was in the past, the Biblical views of the Aryan Nations conception will remain the basis of our structure.

Lastly the message explains that the two groups view jihad somewhat differently, but both still show superiority over those of the Jewish faith:

There is one differentiation that the Islamic Believer must accept that is not necessarily Islamic, and this is our modus operandi regarding Jihad. Islamic Jihad is the cleansing of Islamic controlled lands, once the land is decontaminated; the Jihad is over, on the other hand, our Jihad is more specific, and it is strictly and primarily for the extermination of the satanic 'Jew', worldwide, we see no borders, nor boundaries. Any country found to be allowing the 'Jew' to exist, will be at the receiving end of this Jihad, they will find no sanctuary, as the freedom fighters of Islam have been denied sanctuary even from their own 'brothers'. Whoever harbors or aides the 'Jew' will be considered a 'Jew', thus receiving the same fate, or worse. Aryan Nations respects no borders, nor any political system that will collaborate or hide our enemies, the genocide of satanic 'jewry' is the foremost thrust of our Jihad, and this is the main purpose of the Aryan Nations.

Both groups also share a vile hatred for the United States Government. Their loathing is based on the conspiratorial belief that the 'Jewish-run United States Government' is trying to control citizens of both countries.

The US is trying to destroy their (Islam) religion. They (US) have twisted their words to suit their cause (world domination for Jews). The Jewish-run government is trying to control Islam, like they did to us. For those we talk to, they want to go back to 'true Islam'. You see they are like those in Identity – we say 'true Christianity'. We both have a lot in common, and we shouldn't fight with each other. We both are forms of religions; biblically we should not be fighting because we both recognize one God.

By drawing parallels between how the United Sates has treated their own group and how the United States is handling Islam, the Aryan Nations leadership believes that it can help jihadists – because the Aryan Nation has already "gone through what they are currently going through".

Hate, social identity, and Christian Identity

An examination of Christian Identity from the perspective of either the Duplex Theory of Hate (Sternberg, 2005) or Social Identity Theory (Tajfel, 1978; Tajfel & Turner, 1979, 1986; Taylor & Louis, 2005) reveals that Christian Identity serves an important function for the political activity of the Aryan Nations by providing the rationale for hate and/or prejudice and a means of socializing people in these beliefs.

According to Sternberg's (2003, 2005) Duplex Theory of Hate, hate is neither the opposite of love nor the absence of love but is related in a psychologically complex manner to love. Similar to love there are three components to hate: intimacy, passion and commitment. However, unlike love, the basis for hate is the negation of each of these three components. Just as there are love stories there are hate stories which explain why the hated individual or group should be avoided, feared and viewed with contempt (Sternberg, 2005). Sternberg suggests that hate stories achieve this through five steps: by revealing the target as anathema; by uncovering the target's plot or plans against the ingroup; by exposing the extent of the target's power; by demonstrating that the target has put its plan into action; and by revealing the extent to which the target has succeeded in achieving its goals. Christian Identity accomplishes this by portraying Jews as less than human, as deceitful, and therefore deserving of contempt.

The Serpent Seed tenet of Christian Identity, by identifying Jews as the offspring of the Devil, provides a clear rationale as to why the Jews are worthy of hatred. According to Christian Identity, the Jews are not God's chosen people; the true inheritors, as stated in the Bible, are "the White Anglo-Saxon Germanic people of the world". Christian Identity adherents believe the Jews are trying to deceive the world into thinking that the Jewish people are the true inheritors of God's promises, rather than the Anglo-Saxon race. Thus the plot by the Jews to deceive the world is revealed. According to Christian Identity, over the centuries the Jews have not only misinterpreted the Bible but have successfully deceived millions into believing that they are the chosen people. This is clear evidence that the Jews are a powerful group, have translated their plot into action, and are achieving success in accomplishing their goals. Finally, and as demonstrated in the preceding quotes, members of the Aryan Nations believe that the United States, because of the current tide of political correctness combined with the liberal teachings in schools, provides a fertile ground for the Jews to spread their world-dominating agenda. Thus, Christian Identity preaches the core elements of hate. It not only teaches its followers that the Jews are worthy of hatred and fear because they are the offspring of the Devil, but also teaches that Jews should be hated and feared because they have been successful at deceiving millions and, given the current political climate, will continue to be successful in gaining world domination.

Similarly Social Identity Theory, specifically Taylor and Louis's (2005) view that social identity is key to understanding the behaviour of terrorists, suggests that Christian Identity provides the foundation for prejudice toward Jews. According to Social Identity Theory our self-image is composed of our own personal identity as well as our social identity. One's social identity is derived from the individual's membership in various groups. Tajfel and Turner (1979, 1986) suggest that individuals, because they are motivated to evaluate themselves positively, are also motivated to evaluate the groups to which they belong positively. Essential to the evaluation process is a comparison between groups. According to Social Identity Theory this comparison will be biased in such a manner that the ingroup compares favourably to the outgroup.

Taylor (1997, 2002) departed from traditional views of the self by proposing a model of the self-concept in which collective identity has psychological priority over both collective esteem and personal identity, which in turn has priority over personal esteem. According to Taylor, in order for an individual to determine his/her unique attributes and thus develop a personal identity, the individual must have a norm or reference that serves as the standard of comparison. This norm is derived from an individual's group. Thus an individual's social identity, or in Taylor's terminology, an individual's collective identity provides the basis for comparison. Thus personal identity, or the establishment of one's unique attributes, derives from one's collective identity and personal or self-esteem is an evaluation of one's personal identity just as collective esteem is an evaluation of one's collective identity.

Taylor and Louis (2005) propose that members of terrorist groups look to their collective identity not only to determine the group's beliefs, values and behaviours, but also as a basis for establishing their own personal identity. While Social Identity Theory posits that our social identity derives from our various group memberships, Taylor and Louis propose that it is an individual's cultural, or in some cases religious group, because of its pervasiveness throughout the individual's life, that takes precedence over other groups in shaping identity. For an individual whose religion is central to their life, their social identity as a member of that religious group, not only provides them with religious beliefs but also a shared history, valued goals and the steps for achieving those goals. Taylor and Louis further explain that for terrorists, their collective identity and the norms of their ingroup are constantly salient, because of their minority status within their own society as well as their chronic orientation toward the conflict with the outgroup. As a result ingroup norms play an especially powerful role in shaping the terrorist's beliefs and behaviours.

For members of the Aryan Nations, Christian Identity has served as a strong basis for the group's collective identity. Christian Identity, as described previously, clearly explains who should be hated, Jews, and why they should be hated, because they are the offspring of the Devil. These beliefs provide the foundation for leadership within the Aryan Nations to promote violence toward Jews or Jewish-controlled institutions.

Taylor and Louis also explain the role of the outgroup in defining the identity of the terrorists. Of special relevance to this chapter are two points made by Taylor and Louis. First, the ability of the terrorist group, in this case the Aryan Nations, to identify an evil enemy as the source of their suffering clearly places blame for any disadvantages on the external source, in this case the Jew. Secondly, Taylor and Louis suggest that terrorist groups, when faced with a low probability of achieving positive outcomes for the ingroup, may come to view achieving negative outcomes for the enemy as benefiting the ingroup. Thus terrorist acts, although they may not directly benefit one's own group may be seen as an end in themselves.

Somewhat related to this is research by Struch and Schwartz (1989) which examined the attitudes of Israeli citizens toward an ultra-orthodox religious sect. In addition to standard measures of ingroup bias these researchers also included measures of aggression. Results revealed positive correlations between perceived conflict of interests and aggression as well as between intergroup value dissimilarity and aggression. Finally, the positive correlation between perceived conflict of interest and aggression was strongest for those groups of Israelis who themselves identified strongly with some religious (but not ultra-orthodox) group. These findings, taken together with Taylor and Louis's proposition that hurting the outgroup may be an end in itself, may suggest that some Aryan Nations members, because they have strong religious beliefs, see themselves as inherently and vastly different from Jews and in conflict with Jews, may be more disposed to an alignment with Islamic extremists because they see this alignment as leading to the commission of terrorist activities against Jews.

Group position as the basis for prejudice toward Jews

According to Blumer (1958) a "sense of group position" is the basis for prejudice. Blumer suggests that prejudice can best be understood from a relational perspective, i.e. where one's own group should stand in the social order in relation to another group. According to Blumer (1958) the dominant group believes that it is superior to the subordinate group, that the subordinate group is intrinsically different from them, that its own group, the dominant group, has proprietary claim over certain rights or resources, and that the subordinate group desires a greater share of these rights and resources. Blumer further explains that the feelings of superiority over and distinctiveness from the subordinate group provide the basis for the dominant group's aversion toward the subordinate group and that the feeling of proprietary claim to rights and resources, coupled with the belief that the subordinate group is encroaching on these resources together create the dynamic force behind prejudice.

If Blumer's framework of prejudice is applied to the beliefs of the Aryan Nations it is clear to see that members of the movement see themselves as both superior to and intrinsically different from Jews. This is especially evident in the core belief of Two-Seedline Identity in which Aryans are seen as descendants of Adam while Jewish people are viewed as descendants of the Devil. Additionally, based on the tenets of Christian Identity, Aryan Nations members have proprietary claim not only to the United Sates but to the world because they view themselves as the rightful inheritors of the planet. However, interviewees consistently expressed the fear that the Jews were slowly encroaching on their resources, specifically Jews were taking over the United States, its government, media and financial institutions, and brainwashing the public. As stated by Blumer, it is this belief that the subordinate group, the Jews, are trying to take what rightfully belongs to the dominant group, the Aryan race, which creates the dynamic force for prejudice.

Shared goals and reducing prejudice toward Muslims

Gordon Allport in *The Nature of Prejudice* (1954) provides recommendations for the reduction of prejudice. These recommendations, because they share the idea of bringing together members of different groups, have come to be known as the contact hypothesis. In Allport's view, for intergroup prejudice to be reduced through contact certain situational conditions are necessary. Specifically, prejudice is likely to be reduced when contact between the groups is prolonged and focuses on achieving a shared goal, status between the groups is equal, and the new policy of integration is officially or institutionally supported.

An example of reducing prejudice through these means is provided by a classic study conducted by Sherif and colleagues (Sherif, Harvey, White, Hood, & Sherif, 1961). In this study stereotyping and prejudice were first created between the Eagles and Rattlers, groups of boys at summer camp, and then were later reduced by creating situations in which the two groups needed to work together to solve a problem, repairing the camp's water system and fixing a broken-down truck.

While Sherif and colleagues findings suggest that given the right conditions, prejudice can be reduced through contact, it is also possible that efforts to unite the Aryan Nations and followers of Islamic Jihad could result in factionalism or horizontal hostility (Blake, Shepard, & Mouton 1964; Brewer, 1999, 2000; Brown & Wade, 1987; Deschamps & Brown, 1983; White & Langer, 1999). Research by White and Langer (1999) suggests that horizontal hostility can arise when members of a minority group believe that the addition of new members will devalue the ingroup identity by making it less distinctive. Similarly, research by Brown and colleagues (Brown & Wade, 1987; Deschamps & Brown, 1983) suggests that people do not always react positively when boundaries between their groups are diminished. The results of research by Brewer (1999, 2000) also suggest that the extent to which ingroup boundaries and intergroup distinctions engender feelings of identity and loyalty to one's group, co-operation with an outgroup can threaten an individual's social identification. Thus, contrary to the contact hypothesis, members of the Aryan Nations may resist attempts by Aryan Nations leaders to form an alliance with followers of Islamic Jihad.

Concluding Comments

The present chapter examined Aryan Nations members' prejudice toward Jews. Consistent with Blumer's theory of prejudice, Aryan Nations members not only view themselves as inherently different from Jews but as superior to them due to their religious differences. According to Christian Identity, white Anglo-Saxons, not the Jewish people, are God's chosen people. The tenets of the Serpent Seed further suggest that Jewish people are Satan's offspring. Additionally, it is evident that members of the Aryan Nations see themselves as having certain proprietary claims to the United States or things that are

American and believe that Jews are not only encroaching on but usurping these rights and resources. For example, members of the Aryan Nations believe that the government of the United States as well as the media are controlled by Jews and that Jews are using the media to shape and control America's views, presenting themselves in a positive light and Muslims in a negative light. Thus Aryan Nations members, through their attitudes and orientation toward Jews, clearly exemplify the four key features of Blumer's relational model of prejudice.

The present chapter also examined the growing alliance between the Aryan Nations and followers of Islamic Jihad as expressed through interviews with members of the Aryan Nations. According to the contact hypothesis for prejudice to be reduced between two groups, one necessary component is a superordinate goal. The Aryan Nations and Islamic Jihadists share two common enemies and therefore two common goals. As stated previously, the media or perceived media persecution provides one common threat to both groups. Members of the Aryan Nations and Islamic Jihadists each believe the media presents their group in a biased and unfair light. The second and stronger shared threat is the Jew. Defeating the Jew provides the two groups with a strong superordinate goal and basis for an alliance.

However, as is evident from the contrasting viewpoints expressed by interviewees as to whether the Aryan Nations should remain a solely Christian organization, there is a growing difference among members of the movement with regard to an alliance with Islamic Jihadists and the role of Christian Identity in their organization. Some members of the Aryan Nations believe that their organization and its members should remain tied solely to Christian Identity. Others believe that people from other faiths, specifically Muslims, who share the Aryan Nations' goal of defeating Jews, should be allowed to join the movement. Leaders in the Aryan Nations have tried to satisfy people on both sides of the argument by dividing the Aryan Nations into two distinct entities, a political entity, Aryan Nations Proper, and a religious identity, the Tabernacles of the Phinehas Priesthood, and also by expressing respect for the followers of Islamic Jihad.

Given that not all members of the Aryan Nations are in agreement about the centrality of Christian Identity to the organization or about allowing Muslims to join the Aryan Nations, it is predicted that consistent with previous research (Blake, Shepard, & Mouton, 1964; Brewer, 1999, 2000; Brown & Wade, 1987; Deschamps & Brown, 1983; White & Langer, 1999) infighting within the Aryan Nations will increase leading to factionalism or horizontal hostility. As mentioned previously, group members do not always respond positively when boundaries between groups are diminished especially if the new members would devalue the ingroup identity (White & Langer, 1999). Consequently group members may resist working toward a superordinate goal in an attempt to preserve their ingroup distinctiveness.

The contact hypothesis suggests that working toward a superordinate goal will only serve to reduce prejudice between two groups if they are successful at achieving that goal (Blanchard, Weigel, & Cook, 1975; Worchel, Andreoli, & Folger, 1977; Worchel & Norvell, 1980). The results of research by Worchel and colleagues (Worchel et al., 1977; Worchel & Norvell, 1980) suggest that when co-operation between two previously competitive groups is unsuccessful the outgroup will be blamed for the failure unless there is an obvious and alternative cause for the failure. Given that it is highly unlikely that the Aryan Nations and Islamic Jihadists will be successful at accomplishing their shared goal of defeating the Jewish people, the alliance between these two groups is likely to be unstable and short-lived. As Brewer (1999, 2000) points out, two groups working together to achieve a shared goal requires trust. Especially when there is contempt or fear of the outgroup, in the face of failure, blaming and scapegoating are likely to occur.

Lastly, the present chapter examined how some members of the Aryan Nations are able to reconcile their definition of race with their recent alliance with Islamic Jihadists. The interviews and ethnographic data support the hypothesis that participation with Islamic Jihadists does not change the racial views of Aryan Nations members. The available literature on white supremacists has a tendency to focus on "collective social-psychological factors" (Blee, 1996), suggesting that individuals keep the same rigid beliefs throughout a lifetime (cf. Adorno, Frenkel-Brunswik, Levinson, & Sanford, 1950). While this data is consistent with that supposition, it also shows the complexity of beliefs that members share, and how exception to the racist rules can be made. The field of cultural studies (cf. Grossberg, Nelson, & Treichler, 1991; Turner, 2002) extends the first proposition. Cultural studies go further than the social-psychological exploration of discrimination and prejudice by suggesting that the culture of the Aryan Nations and the orientation and behaviour of its members are less overtly structured and consequently allow for changes in ideology to fit 'their mission'. Behaviour among individuals is not homogeneous, and such ideological differences cause friction among the members. The present research suggests that the Aryan Nations' ideology is more fluid than previously thought, and is changing. Part of the change is due to in-fighting within current white supremacist movements; juxtaposed with lack of action by 'white kindred'. The recent alliance with Islamic Jihadists has led to the development of a new social movement ideology that allows the white supremacist movement to remain alive in the United States. While an alliance with Islamic Jihadists is consistent with the Aryan Nations' anti-Semitic views, practices of selective adoption (Blee, 1996) are necessary for Aryan Nations members to remain consistent with their racist views.

In conclusion the Aryan Nations' prejudicial views toward Jews are consistent with Blumer's model of prejudice. While there is a growing alliance between certain members of the Aryan Nations and Islamic Jihadists, it is predicted that this alliance will continue to cause in-fighting within the Aryan Nations and may lead to the creation of splinter groups within the movement. Thus it is predicted that an alliance between the Aryan Nations and Islamic Jihadists will be an unstable one.

References

Adorno, T. W., Frenkel-Brunswik, E., Levinson, D. J., & Sanford, R. N. (1950). *The authoritarian personality.* New York: Harper.

Allport, G. W. (1954). *The nature of prejudice.* Cambridge, MA: Addison-Wesley.

Barkum, M. (1997). *Religion and the radical right.* Chapel Hill, NC: North Carolina Press.

Blake, R. R., Shepard, H. A., & Mouton, J. S. (1964). *Managing intergroup conflict in industry.* Texas: Gulf Publishing Company.

Blanchard, F. A., Weigel, R. H., & Cook, S. W. (1975). The effect of relative competence of group members upon interpersonal attraction in cooperating interracial groups. *Journal of Personality and Social Psychology, 32,* 519–530.

Blee, K. (1996). Becoming a racist. *Gender and Society, 10,* 680–703.

Blee, K. (2002). *Inside organized racism: Women in the hate movement.* Berkeley: University of California Press.

Blejwas, A., Griggs, A., & Potok, M. (2005). Terror from the right. *Intelligence Report, 118,* 33–46.

Blumer, H. (1958). Race prejudice as a sense of group position. *Pacific Sociological Review, 1,* 3–7.

Brewer, M. B. (1999). The psychology of prejudice: Ingroup love or outgroup hate? *Journal of Social Issues, 55,* 429–444.

Brewer, M. B. (2000). Superordinate goals versus superordinate identity as bases of intergroup cooperation. In D. Capozza, & R. Brown (Eds), *Social identity processes: Trends in theory and research* (pp. 117–132). London: Sage.

Brown, R. J., & Wade, G. S. (1987). Superordinate goals and intergroup behavior: The effects of role ambiguity and status on intergroup attitudes and task performance. *European Journal of Social Psychology, 17,* 131–142.

Butler, R. (Producer and Director) (2001). *My side of the story.* [Documentary video] (Available from www.aryan-nations.org)

Deschamps, J. C., & Brown, R. J. (1983). Superordinate goals and intergroup conflict. *British Journal of Social Psychology, 22,* 189–95.

Flynn, K., & Gerhardt, G. (1989). *The silent brotherhood.* New York: The Free Press.

Grossberg, L., Nelson, C., & Treichler, P. (1991). *Cultural studies.* New York: Routledge.

Sherif, M., Harvey, O. J., White, B. J., Hood, W. R., & Sherif, C. W. (1961). *The robbers cave experiment: Intergroup conflict and cooperation.* Middletown, CT: Wesleyan University Press.

Sternberg, R. (2003). A duplex theory of hate: Development and application to terrorism, massacres, and genocide. *Review of General Psychology, 7,* 299–328.

Sternberg, R. (2005). Understanding and combating hate. In R. J. Sternberg (Ed.), *The psychology of hate* (pp. 37–50). Washington, DC: American Psychological Association.

Struch, N., & Schwartz, S. H. (1989). Intergoup aggression: Its predictors and distinctions from ingroup bias. *Journal of Personality and Social Psychology, 56*, 364–373.

Tajfel, H. (1978). Social categorization, social identity and social comparison. In H. Tajfel (Ed.), *Differentiation between social groups* (pp. 61–76). London: Academic Press.

Tajfel, H., & Turner, J. C. (1979). An integrative theory of intergroup conflict. In W. G. Austin, & S. Worchel (Eds), *The social psychology of intergroup relations* (pp. 33–47). Monterey, CA: Brooks/Cole.

Tajfel, H., & Turner, J. C. (1986). The social identity theory of intergroup behavior. In S. Worchel, & G. Austin (Eds), *Psychology of intergroup relations* (pp. 7–24). Chicago: Nelson-Hall.

Taylor, D. M. (1997). The quest for collective identity: The plight of disadvantaged ethnic minorities. *Canadian Psychology, 38*, 174–190.

Taylor, D. M. (2002). *The quest for identity: From minority groups to generation Xers.* Westport, CT: Praeger.

Taylor, D. M., & Louis, W. (2005). Terrorism and the quest for identity. In F. M. Moghaddam, & A. J. Marsella (Eds), *Understanding terrorism* (pp. 169–186). Washington, DC: American Psychological Association.

Timeline: The Aryan Nations through the years Series. Retrieved December 12, 2007, from www.rickross.com/reference/aryan/aryan16.html

Turner, G. (2002). *British cultural studies: An introduction.* London: Routledge.

Aryan Nations. *Aryan Nations website.* Retrieved April 8, 2002, from www.twelvearyannations.com

Walters, J. (2001). *One Aryan Nation under God.* Naperville, IL: Sourcebooks, Inc.

White, J. B., & Langer, E. J. (1999). Horizontal hostility: Relations between similar minority groups. *Journal of Social Issues, 55*, 537–560.

Worchel, S., Andreoli, V. A., & Folger, R. (1977). Intergroup cooperation and intergroup attraction: The effect of previous interaction and outcome of combined effort. *Journal of Experimental Social Psychology, 13*, 131–140.

Worchel, S., & Norvell, N. (1980). Effect of perceived environmental conditions during cooperation on intergroup attraction. *Journal of Personality and Social Psychology, 38*, 764–772.

11

The Business of Kidnap
for Ransom

Everard Phillips

> Each hostage fears two things: if they come for him during the night, they
> will probably kill him; if they bring a video camera, that means beating,
> maiming, or raping.
>
> Dmitrii Balburov cited in Tishkov, 2004, p. 107

Synopsis: Kidnapping for ransom is examined as a business. This perspective
draws attention to the need for an organization to exist to perpetrate the crime
on a repetitive basis, whilst maintaining the ability to launder the money over
a long period of time. The distinction is drawn between independent operators
that kidnap for money and small groups that have access to a kidnapping
network (or syndicate). Independent operators are rarely likely to kidnap
for ransom, choosing only to ransom for small amounts of cash. These offenders are often petty criminals, although the motive behind the kidnapping is
monetary gain, the intention is not to build a business empire. In contrast,
small groups that kidnap with the intention of selling the hostage to a larger
group or simply ransoming the hostage themselves are in effect developing a
business.

Introduction

Post-war Iraq was dominated by reports of children, doctors, businessmen
and foreign contractors who had been kidnapped for ransom. Kidnapping
in Iraq had reached such epidemic proportions that it resembled a virtual

The Faces of Terrorism: Multidisciplinary Perspectives Edited by David Canter
© 2009 John Wiley & Sons Ltd.

industry in its own right. As many as 10 people a day were kidnapped by various groups in order to make a financial profit from the sale of life (Looney, 2005). Even submitting to a ransom payment did not guarantee the release of a loved one, it was common to find the bodies of women who had been tortured, raped and murdered by militia groups despite receiving payment (UNAMI, 2006). This pattern of criminal behaviour has been long established in Latin American countries since the 1970s (Clutterbuck, 1978), and is now an institutionalized problem at a societal level within this region.[1] Although there is a geographical concentration of kidnapping for ransom within certain Latin American countries, it is a global phenomenon that is not restricted by location or by type of offenders (UN, 2003, 2004a,b). The reality of contemporary kidnap for ransom behaviour is the vast spectrum of perpetrators that indulge in this offence, a spectrum that includes criminal, terrorist, insurgent and even tribal groups. This observation was highlighted in a report commissioned by the United Nations that outlined the involvement of both organized criminal and/or terror groups in over 54 of its Member States.[2]

The existence of prolific kidnapping for ransom activity in certain exclusive regions of the world suggests a range of environmental and social factors that may facilitate the development of this crime into a profit-making business. However, this thriving trade has been perceived by some authors as simply a method for monetary gain, in order to fund acts of terrorism or insurgency (Hagedorn-Auerbach, 1998; Hunter, 1996; Kiser, 2005; Looney, 2005). Kidnapping for ransom is part of a portfolio of predatory crimes that is reflective of an early stage of developmental behaviour for a radical group (Naylor, 1993). Emerging radical groups are vulnerable to detection from a host state; hence this behaviour allows a group the ability to acquire large sums of cash with a relatively low risk of response from the state. Terrorist groups that include the 'Red Brigades', Basque Fatherland and Liberty (ETA), and Abu Sayyaf Group (ASG) have used ransom money to establish their terrorist campaigns.

The clandestine nature of kidnapping for ransom makes it extremely difficult to garner reliable statistics on the actual level of kidnapping activity

---

[1] Many countries within Latin America were plagued by civil wars that involved communist insurgencies. During this period political kidnapping for ransom became a feature. Presently kidnapping is endemic of Mexico, Colombia, Brazil and remains a persistent problem within these countries, although kidnapping for ransom does exist in other Latin American countries such as Ecuador, Venezuela and Argentina.

[2] The report titled: 'International cooperation in the prevention, combating and elimination of kidnapping and the providing assistance to victims'. The report was compiled from the results of a survey sent out to the Member States of the United Nations. Replies were received from 54 Member States, the African Institute for the Prevention of Crime and the Treatment of Offenders, United Nations Development Programme, International Atomic Energy Agency, and the Department of Peacekeeping Operations of the Secretariat.

worldwide.[3] The central problem when attempting to examine the prevalence of the crime is that many victims do not report this offence to the relevant authorities, and therefore the statistics reported by a given state are unreliable for a detailed reflection. Lechner (2007) noted that in many instances 10% of kidnappings are reported to the authorities, highlighting a major problem in obtaining reliable information or statistics worldwide.[4] However, the issue of under-reporting kidnappings is a common problem in the failed state.[5] It facilitates a level of impunity that allows many criminal and terrorist elements to operate freely within various countries (Restrepo, Sanchez, & Cuellar, 2006). For instance, in the Philippines, kidnappers have been known to accept personal cheques in settlement of a ransom payment without risk of being apprehended by the authorities (Merkling & Davis, 2001). Detection, prosecution and conviction of offenders that kidnap for ransom accounted for approximately 1% of the Colombian experience during the 1990s; according to Merkling and Davis (2001) 99% of kidnappers in Colombia were never caught. Indeed, both Hunter (1996) and Hagedorn-Auerbach (1998) reported that only 2% of kidnappers in Colombia were ever prosecuted. Under such circumstances the futility of reporting the crime becomes apparent.

According to recent Colombian National Police statistics published for 2006, 1,468 people were victims of some form of extortion including kidnap for ransom. During this period, 364 victims were released by their abductors, 146 were rescued by police, 58 remain captive, 30 were released as a result of police pressure, and 28 died in captivity.[6] Although, the Colombian National Police reported that there were just over 200 kidnappings for ransom during this period of time, the Colombian Security and Democracy Foundation actu-

---

[3] Secrecy is an essential aspect of kidnapping for ransom that has a profound effect on not only eliciting the crime but also how the offence is studied and reported. Post-hoc to the event secrecy serves to protect the various parties involved while inadvertently masking the problem. The details of ransom payments are often held with a high level of secrecy for fear of other groups imitating the crime.

[4] It is generally accepted within the security and crisis management community that 10% of kidnappings are actually reported; however, Merkling and Davis (2001) suggested a conservative self-report figure of 50% of kidnap for ransoms.

[5] The under-reporting of kidnapping for ransom is a serious problem within many states. The predominant reason why families and employers fail to report kidnapping for ransom is fear of reprisal. In Colombia payment of a ransom may often be followed by a regular extortion fee from the kidnappers, a payment that insures that the hostage will not be kidnapped again. Hence, victims are locked into a prolonged business relationship that involves regular contact with the group. Under these conditions, a large number of Colombians prefer to settle the ransom in confidence without reporting the crime (Heeb, 2002).

[6] Note, statistics taken from *K&R and Extortion Monitor*, January 2007, a publication dedicated to reporting kidnappings and extortion cases around the world. The data for this publication is drawn from the Internet and therefore reflective of popular regional websites that report local news. Caution is advised when considering this form of information, since local and regional bias in media reporting are common.

ally reported that there were in fact 265 kidnappings for ransom during 2006.[7] From this, 111 kidnappings were directly attributed to the Revolutionary Armed Forces of Colombia (FARC) and the National Liberation Army (ELN). These statistics suggest that FARC rebels kidnapped an individual on average every five days, compared to ELN who perpetrated this crime on average every eight days. Despite the observation that the kidnapping activity of FARC has dropped by 45% over the last year, the report suggests that FARC continues to be responsible for a large proportion of the cases reported. Current figures indicate that FARC were responsible for 26% of the national total (68 kidnappings), compared to ELN who were responsible for 16% (43 kidnappings).

Of course, there are other groups responsible for kidnapping for ransom within Colombia; these include right-wing paramilitary groups such as the United Self-Defense Forces/Group of Colombia (AUC) who committed 1% of the total, and new emerging political groups responsible for over 5% of this margin. The remaining 52% of kidnappings for ransom within Colombia are attributed to criminal groups, who are thought to be responsible for 10% more kidnappings than in the previous year, and unknown elements within Colombian society. Kidnapping for ransom in Colombia earned US$ 322,725 million between 1991 and 1996; most recent figures have reported that kidnapping for ransom in Colombia nets groups an average of US$ 220 million a year (Riascos & Vargas, 2006, p. 5). Hunter (1996) estimated that since 1963 Colombian guerrillas may have acquired US$ 51 billion from illegal operations that include kidnapping for ransom.

Given that the methods of funding terrorism are diverse, and often reliant upon a range of criminal activities that include kidnapping for ransom, extortion, bank robbery, smuggling and financial fraud, many analysts argue that terrorist and insurgent groups operate simultaneously as a business whilst presenting the veneer of a radicalized movement (Dishman, 2001; McFarlane, 2003; Mincheva & Gurr, 2006; Schbley, 2000). Some have extended this debate further by defining a terror-crime nexus in which terrorist and criminal groups co-operate in order to increase profit and operational ability (Bibes, 2001; Makarenko, 2004; Mincheva & Gurr, 2006; Picarelli, 2006; Shelly & Picarelli, 2002; Williams, 1994). The terror-crime nexus is a characteristic of the failed or transitional state, in which insurgency is a key feature of the political and social landscape (Sung, 2004). States that include Colombia, the Philippines, Afghanistan and Iraq are affected by insurgencies that are self-maintained by criminal activity within those given countries. According to Looney (2005), Iraq is subject to an insurgency that has the characteristics of a business, where insurgents are able to garner huge profits from illicit activities, such as drug smuggling, kidnapping for ransom and trading gasoline on the black market – crimes that Looney distinguishes as the top three money earners for the

---

[7] Ibid.

various insurgent and criminal groups operating within Iraq. However, the industrious profiteering from crime is not only a feature of the failed state, but a consequence of the decentralization of many terror and criminal organizations that has encouraged the prevalence of kidnapping for ransom as a profit-driven crime within certain regions of the world (Dishman, 2005; Ortiz, 2002).

The premise that kidnap for ransom is defined as a business simply because money is the primary motive behind the crime, is weak and subject to anecdotal observation. It is argued here, that clear organizational structures are necessary for the continuity of this business (Williams, 2001) and therefore this characteristic should be comparable to other established criminal enterprises (Edwards & Gill, 2002). Moreover, it is important to define what determines a kidnapping as a profit-making business, in order to distinguish this behaviour from other forms of kidnapping behaviour (e.g. political or parental kidnapping). The objective of this chapter is to define the characteristics of a profit-based crime by drawing attention to key variables that are necessary for the permanence of a criminal business.

Defining Kidnap for Ransom a Profit-driven Crime

Kidnapping for ransom is part of the portfolio of criminal activities used by many groups to fund terrorism, insurgency and other crimes (McFarlane, 2003; Naylor, 1993). A conservative estimate of the annual global income derived from kidnapping for ransom is in excess of US$ 500 million (Briggs 2001, 2002).[8] Indeed, there is much consideration that kidnapping for ransom is a profit-making business (Briggs, 2001, 2002; Hagedorn-Auerbach, 1998; Hunter, 1996; Lechner, 2007; Mateo, 2004; Moor & Zumpolle, 2001). Central to this premise is the observation that the vast majority of kidnappings involve a monetary ransom demand; kidnappings within countries such as Mexico, Iraq, the Philippines, Trinidad and Tobago are elicited purely for profit rather than a preconceived political or social agenda.[9] Considering that in any one of the identified countries or kidnapping hot spots, an average of 10 people a day are kidnapped, and that the proliferation of this crime appears to be confined to failed or transitional states plagued by instability (Sung, 2004), the sheer

---

[8] Caution must be advised when considering this figure, since the kidnapping economy in Colombia alone is thought to value in excess of US$ 100 million. Consideration must be also given to the many other kidnapping hot spots in the world.

[9] There are additional countries that suffer from high levels of kidnap for ransom. Briggs (2002) reported the top 10 countries with the highest rates of kidnapping for ransom as: Colombia, Mexico, Brazil, the Philippines, Venezuela, Ecuador, the former Soviet Union, Nigeria, India and South Africa.

volume of financially motivated kidnappings, combined with its geographical concentration, adds some credence to the argument that kidnapping for ransom is profit driven. However, these observations remain anecdotal and therefore subject to a number of inherent weaknesses.

In order to clearly define kidnapping for ransom as a business, it is necessary to deconstruct kidnapping into its inherent characteristics, in comparison to other acts of terrorism or crime. In essence, it is the methods and not the motives of the radical group that should be examined if kidnapping is to be considered a business. If kidnapping is a profit-driven crime, then clearly identifiable organizational structures and market conditions are necessary for this business to flourish. Key characteristics would include the frequency with which the group engages in this crime and its sustainability over a long period of time. This suggests that the group must have an organization to manage multiple hostages at the same or different locations, whilst continuously laundering the money earned. There must be an existing social network available to sustain the complex infrastructure needed in order to kidnap for ransom on a repetitive basis (Arquilla & Ronfeldt, 2001; Milward & Raab, 2002; Schmid, 1996; Williams, 2001). Under these circumstances the kidnapping business should resemble a market-based criminal activity, and hence will have a structure similar to groups that traffic in people and illegal goods.

The relationship between market-based criminal activities and kidnap for ransom

Profit-driven crimes involve the transference of property (and money) from one party to another, whether by force, deception, or free market exchange (Naylor, 2003). This may require the provision of illicit products and services (e.g. narcotics or prostitution), or manipulating legal goods and services in illegal ways (e.g. bankruptcy fraud). Nevertheless, the method of transfer enables criminal offences to be categorized according to the manner in which cash or commodities are transferred. Naylor (2003) defined profit-driven crime as: predatory, crimes that involve the involuntary transference of cash or physical goods between two parties, one of which is an unwilling victim; market-based, the supply and demand of contraband products and services, characterized by voluntary transfers of cash (or property) within a multilateral platform that includes producers, distributors and retailers; commercial, the domain of legitimate corporations, involving the production and distribution of legal goods (or services), characterized by the illegal methods of transferring property between these parties (see Table 11.1 for a review of characteristics). Whether the crime involves bank robbery or telemarketing fraud, the motive for money is the shared characteristic of a profit-driven crime. Contemporary profit-driven criminal behaviour can be highly sophisticated, organized, and

Table 11.1. Representation of some of the key characteristics reported by Naylor (2003) that define predatory and market-based profit-driven crimes (data from Naylor, 2003, pp. 84–88).

The Characteristics of Predatory and Market-based Crimes	
Predatory Offences	*Market-based Offences*
Predatory crimes involve:	Market-based crimes involve:
• Redistribution of existing legally owned wealth from one party to another;	• The production and/or distribution of new goods and services that are inherently illegal;
• Bilateral relations between victim and perpetrator(s);	• Multilateral exchanges involving producers, distributors, retailers, and money managers on the supply side and willing consumers on the demand side;
• Involuntary transfers which generally use force (or its threat), though guile and deception may suffice;	
• Readily identifiable victims (individuals, institutions or corporations);	• An underground network;
	• Voluntary transfers;
	• Income earned by suppliers;
• Transfers which take place in cash or kind (physical goods, securities, even information);	• Transfers which take place mostly in cash or bank instruments;
	• An implicit notion of fair market value;
• Losses that are simple to determine, the robbed or defrauded person, institution, corporation can point to specific money and property.	• A need to find a means to treat 'proceeds' in the absence of individual victims.

driven by global demands for products and services (Schmid, 1996; Shelly & Picarelli, 2002).

According to Naylor's model, kidnapping is defined as a predatory crime, since the transference of cash is bilateral and dependent on force and coercion. However, there are manifestations of this crime that do suggest a multilateral format similar to that of market-based offences, and therefore may better define kidnapping as a business. These variables include frequency of kidnapping,[10] the valuation,[11] and subsequent distribution network for the trade in hostages, as well the management of income earned from this crime.

[10] The sheer scale of kidnappings for ransom within isolated regions of the world does offer some resemblance to the characteristics of a market-based offence. According to Root (2007), kidnappings for ransom in Mexico currently number an average of 4,500 individuals a year. Note, between four and ten people are kidnapped for ransom every day in countries that include Iraq, Mexico, Colombia, Ecuador, the Philippines, Nigeria and India.

[11] According to Naylor (2003), market-based offences are characterized by multilateral relationships and the implicit notion of fair market value for a given commodity, observations that parallel specific characteristics of kidnapping for ransom activity.

Contemporary kidnap for ransom behaviour involves an immense level of organization and networking;[12] however, these networks also facilitate the distribution of hostages from one group to another for eventual ransom. The distribution process is not necessarily within a criminal organization but between other criminal and radical groups. Kidnapping on this scale attracts a range of opportunists motivated by profit only; such actors include ransom brokers who act as intermediaries between the actual kidnappers and negotiators on a commission basis (Hagedorn-Auerbach, 1998, p. 33). Under this guise, even the method of capturing hostages resembles a market-based criminal activity. In Colombia guerrilla groups erect illegal roadblocks in order to randomly kidnap individuals for ransom (Heeb, 2002; Moor & Zumpolle, 2001),[13] a practice that demonstrates a commercialization of a market-based crime.

When individuals are kidnapped for ransom there is often a fair market value for the hostage. Certain conditions will affect this, these include the occupation, health, nationality, religion, gender, and age of the hostage, all of which are influential and provide an implicit notion of value. Briggs (2001, p. 18) observed that there are unique market conditions that also affect the value of a hostage, these include the current economy, public fear of the kidnapping, and the relative social value of individuals within that country. Even murdering captured hostages raises the price of an individual already held or that of a specific hostage type, an observation made by Looney (2005) who reported that the value of foreign nationals in Iraq positively correlated to the beheading of hostages by the insurgents.

The repercussion of the public beheading of hostages drove the street value of foreigners to a new high. Foreigners were often kidnapped by ordinary Iraqi criminal gangs and sold to insurgents for a higher price. The value of the hostage was based on the influence the insurgent group would wield, as a result of the previous beheadings of foreign hostages. Hence, insurgents could demand an even larger ransom than their original financial outlay for the hostage. The thriving trade of selling and re-selling hostages to rival gangs and radical groups itself creates a market value, whilst maintaining a supply chain with willing consumers that creates a demand for the commodity. These

[12] Hagedorn-Auerbach (1998, p. 32) describes the complexity of kidnapping within Latin America. Here one group may focus on researching a potential victim, another on surveillance of the target. A further group may devise the strategy for the kidnapping operation, while another group will implement the crime. Yet a further group will have responsibility for finding a location in which to hold and guard the hostage. Lastly a different group would be responsible for negotiating the ransom demand.

[13] Referred to by the guerrillas as 'Pesca Milagrosa' (translates as Miraculous Catches), individuals are forced out of their vehicles and then assessed as to their eligibility to raise a ransom. According to Moor and Zumpolle (2001) guerrillas may often compare the identity of the hostage so as to cross-reference the assets of the individual. This behaviour has also been observed in Chechnya (Tishkov, 2004) and Iraq.

factors once combined with the ability to continuously launder the funds achieved, suggest a market-based phenomenon as described by Naylor (2003).

Asset management is an important consideration for any group that engages in a wide portfolio of crime. Moreover, criminal and insurgent groups that draw an income from predatory crimes such as extortion (e.g. 'revolutionary taxation'), bank robbery, and kidnap for ransom, are consistently faced with the problem of managing the money achieved from these endeavours. In many cases, concealing the proceeds is simply a matter of course for the well-organized insurgent or criminal group. However, for groups that lack the sufficient network or organizational ability, disposing of a large ransom would pose great difficulty, as illustrated when the Argentinean group Ejercito de Revolucion Popular (ERP) extorted $3 million worth of 500 peso notes as a ransom for the release of a captive Firestone executive. In this instance, the actual ransom was physically large enough to fill an armoured vehicle (Naylor, 1993). Thus the reality of disposing of such large amounts of cash proves to be difficult. Not simply as a result of the quantity of cash, but because the serial numbers of the bills would invariably be recorded and therefore traceable. The ERP kidnapping illustrates the practical difficulties that groups must overcome if large cash ransoms have been accumulated over a period of time.

The Colombian insurgency serves as an example of the industrialized nature that defines profit-driven crime. Kidnapping for ransom netted Colombian guerrilla groups, the Revolutionary Armed Forces of Colombia (FARC) and the National Liberation Army (ELN), US$ 1.5 billion between 1991 and 1999 (Moor & Zumpolle, 2001, p. 33), and a further US$ 1.8 billion from extortion and theft.[14] In addition, Colombian insurgents derived an estimated US$ 3.2 billion from drug trafficking during the same period (Moor & Zumpolle, 2001). The organization's ability to manage large financial sums demonstrates a business model that is distinguishable from simple forms of criminal behaviour.

Kidnapping for ransom can only be considered a business if the group also has the ability to sustain this activity over a period of time whilst safely disposing of the profit from the crime. In order for the group to operate on a grand scale it must have the structure of a market-based criminal organization typical of smugglers or traffickers (Williams, 2001). Although Naylor (2003) suggests that the contrast between market-based and predatory crime is not always clearly distinguishable. He argues that some forms of predatory offences require market-based solutions to dispose of the proceeds. Kidnapping for ransom is an offence that is easily absorbed into the repertoire of an organized

[14]Although this figure has been reported by Moor and Zumpolle (2001) as representative of the income earned by both FARC and the ELN, kidnap for ransom is a major source of income for the ELN, representing 70% of the group's turnover, compared to a 40% turnover for FARC. The difference is attributed to the observation that FARC controls a greater amount of Colombian territory, which enables the group to earn additional income from drug trafficking and extortion.

group that is already engaged in market-based criminal activities. For a group to indulge in kidnapping on a scale tantamount to a business of industrial significance, the group must have the ability to safely dispose of the income without detection from local law enforcement agencies (Ping, 2006).

The overlap between trafficking, smuggling and kidnap for ransom

To sustain a successful kidnap for ransom business, groups must have an organized structure to support this activity over a period of time. Many criminal enterprises already display such prepared systems and are able to manage a portfolio of crimes that range from providing illicit services such as gambling and prostitution, to the production, distribution and supply of narcotics (McFarlane, 2003). These groups can build upon these foundations by diversifying from their existing criminal activities into other crimes such as kidnap for ransom. For instance, smuggling and trafficking, crimes reported to be worth over US$ 2 billion a year,[15] have an established successful network. The sheer scale of money earned would require a large supply of human resources and a prearranged organized structure to dispose of the profits necessary to run a well-managed business. However, diversification into kidnapping also occurs as a result of opportunism combined with direct experience of managing human commodities, combined with a criminal mindset.

There are a number of conceptual and physical similarities between trafficking/smuggling and kidnapping.[16] The businesses share parallels in that they require separate cells to complete different tasks that facilitate the successful completion of the crime (Miro & Curtis, 2003). These types of crimes require drivers, guards, surveillance teams, money handlers, and safe houses, although the emphasis on each role may differ depending on whether it is a kidnapping or a trafficking/smuggling operation. Nevertheless, the physicality of the crime combined with the fact that it primarily involves handling and hiding people suggests that the physical structure of the operation would be similar in practice. Traffickers/smugglers are more successful at kidnapping for ransom because they already have the structure in place and the organization to extort money from a third party. However, their success can also be attributed to their ability to operate in a clandestine manner (Arquilla & Ronfeldt, 2001;

[15] Figure taken from Wagner, D. (2006), Human trafficking's profits spur horrors. Retrieved August 24, 2006, from www.azcentral.com
[16] Trafficking relies on the abduction of women (and children), who are sold between gangs, and subsequently transported to a foreign country where they invariably become prostitutes or slave labour (Shelly, 2003). In contrast, smuggling does not involve forced migration, but instead individuals voluntarily migrate to a country of choice albeit with the assistance of an organized criminal network.

Milward & Raab, 2002; Williams, 2001), avoiding detection from local and state law enforcement, and corrupting local officials (Shelly, 2001).

Criminal diversification into kidnap for ransom also occurs because of an organizational mindset in which the group will exploit every opportunity in order to make a profit. Trafficking/smuggling people is a lucrative and easily replenished source of income for radical groups. It is a preferential form of criminal behaviour, since this crime boasts a constant renewable source and is easily exploited for an additional income, unlike the one-off profit from drug smuggling (Shelly, 2003). People smuggling offers an opportunity to earn a secondary income from 'debt slavery' and extortion (Schauer & Wheaton, 2006).[17] An additional practice by smugglers involves ransoming their human cargo back to the families of the illegal migrants in their country of origin (UN, 2003). Threats also arise from other criminal groups who will kidnap the illegal immigrants from the smugglers in order to collect a ransom payment for themselves. Exploitation is a key feature in people trafficking (or smuggling), it robs the individual of the right to self-determination on arrival at the country of destination, and allows the group to garner an additional income from kidnap for ransom activities.

The business manifestation of kidnap for ransom differs somewhat from the common criminals who although still kidnap for monetary reasons, lack the organization to industrialize this behaviour. Here groups band together on the basis of friendship to commit a one-off kidnapping, whilst choosing their victim carefully. In contrast to the business model of kidnapping, victimization for small groups is not random, but highly selective based on assumed wealth or ability to pay. Yang, Wu and Huang (2007) interviewed a sample of incarcerated Taiwanese kidnappers and found that the commonality for committing this crime lay in the need to obtain money quickly as a result of drug addiction, or because the offenders had absconded and required money. Ringleaders enlisted the help of friends or relatives, and formed groups comprising two to three members to carry out a one-off kidnapping. Hence, the structure and approach of common criminal elements differ significantly to that of the organized groups that kidnap for ransom on a grand scale.

It is possible for small groups to enter into the kidnapping market, but success will be indicative of the social and political landscape of the host country. In regions that suffer a complete breakdown of civil control, organized crimes that include smuggling and kidnapping thrive. Following the complete collapse of the Iraqi regime in 2003, coupled with the removal of the state's apparatus, Iraq descended into a chaos that resulted in the new

[17] Trafficked (and smuggled) individuals are forced into working as virtual slaves or prostitutes in order to repay the financial debt to the smugglers, hence providing a second source of revenue for the group. Schauer and Wheaton (2006) argued that trafficking could be defined as slavery because it initially involves extortion, coercion, restraint, gang rape and the real threat of physical harm and loss of liberty.

phenomenon of kidnap for ransom throughout the country. These conditions allowed smaller, less organized groups of common criminals to band together and operate alongside the existing organized criminal networks and subsequent insurgent groups within Iraq (Looney, 2005). Human smuggling and kidnapping share the same operational environment, i.e. both types of offences thrive in chaotic unstable countries that lack state control. Indeed, civil collapse allows small groups to network with larger organizations in order to engage in criminal activities.

There are certain conditions that create an opportunity for groups to build economies that parallel a state's ability to create wealth. The primary factor is whether a state is able to control effectively its borders and territories. Without sufficient control of its territories and state apparatus, groups with a subversive agenda will easily exploit the state. Albanese (2000) argued that there were three conditions that predicated the development of organized criminal activity: opportunity factors, the immediate environment, and the group's access to the skills required to commit the crime. The opportunity to develop an illicit economic enterprise could only result from exploiting the economic conditions of a failed state, its subsequent government regulations, and the effectiveness of law enforcement (Sung, 2004). Of course, opportunities are also created by local demands for illicit products and services, or by technological changes within that environment. Indeed, special language skills, technical or bureaucratic knowledge are often needed to accomplish certain types of organized crime (Picarelli, 2004).

A case in point is that of Chechnya. In the absence of a formal economy, ravaged by war that resulted in the destruction of the fledgling republic's infrastructure, agriculture and industries, Chechens thrived from the development of an informal black economy (Galeotti, 2002; Mukhina, 2005). Unemployment levels rose to 85%, which combined with the forced migration of the Chechen population created an even direr economic situation for the country. This presented an opportunity that was exploited by various actors, including Chechen rebels, criminal gangs and the Russian federal forces. According to Peimani (2004), there were no reliable statistics on the amount of gross revenue generated, but most common activities within the parallel black market included trafficking of illicit products (mostly drugs), kidnap for ransom, and the illegal production of oil; activities in which rebel groups could engage so as to raise funds for their armies. Even the Russian forces and non-militant Chechens were involved in the proliferation of the parallel black economy.

The Chechen business model

The kidnap for ransom industry within Chechnya is possibly the most extreme of all the kidnapping business models of modern time (Lentini & Bakashmar,

2007). Only Iraq has come close to this level of insidious violence and barbarity; even Colombia and Mexico both with well-established models, pale in comparison with Chechnya. The hostage taking developed into an important component that partly funded Chechnya's struggle for independence from the Russian Federation (Dishman, 2001; Galeotti, 2002; Lentini & Bakashmar, 2007; Moor & Zumpolle, 2001; Mukhina, 2005; Peimani, 2004,). Whilst the number of reported hostage takings ran into the hundreds, the turnover for the business resulted in a multimillion dollar market. Mukhina (2005) reported that between January 1997 and August 1999, 1,094 civilians were kidnapped for ransom, the average settlement ranged from $ 5,000 to $ 145,000 per hostage. This income was used for purchasing weapons and modern armaments during the conflict, and was also reinvested to fund further kidnappings so as to maintain the business. Kidnapping in Chechnya was perpetrated by all segments of Chechen society (Galeotti, 2002): criminal gangs, clans, bandits and rebel groups, even top-level government officials were suspected of involvement. The kidnap for ransom industry was such that there were dedicated 'hostage markets/prisons' and franchising rights (Galeotti, 2002; Tishkov, 2004).

Tishkov (2004) observed that the practice of hostage taking was a centuries-old tradition within Chechnya. It was common practice to hold prisoners of war in order to trade them for captives held by enemy forces or as slave labour. However, this tradition mutated into a new phenomenon during the first Chechen war of independence in 1996, as a result of the Russian Federation's practice of detaining civilians for questioning (Tishkov, 2004). Described as 'arbitrary detention and extortion', detainees could be bought back by paying a ransom to the Russian authorities (Moor & Zumpolle, 2001). The practice of buying civilian detainees was counterbalanced by exchanging captured federal soldiers. Often, Russian soldiers who were captured in battle were killed immediately only sparing a minority in order to sell for exchange. Hence, the relatives of a detainee could buy a federal soldier from a rebel group and then ransom him for their family member. Tishkov (2004) explained the process in which a family could visit a 'hostage market' and place an order to buy a captive. The families had the ability to choose in advance the category of hostage they required, whether it was a businessman, an officer, or a civil servant. Hostages were not the only commodities sold at the markets of Grozny and Urus-Martan; it was also possible to buy a kidnapping trademark or franchise in the business.

Buying a kidnapping franchise allowed smaller operators to demand a larger ransom for their efforts. Ordinarily, it was common for small-scale operators to kidnap and then sell their hostages to a larger organization (Galeotti, 2002). In fact, a hostage could be sold on a number of times before landing in the hands of a criminal group. Nevertheless, the practice of buying a 'trademark' enabled smaller groups to claim a larger ransom, whilst claiming to belong to a notorious kidnapping group (Tishkov, 2004). Fearing for the safety of the hostage, the families of captives would react by settling the ransom quickly. It seemed the more violent the reputation of the trademark, the more effective the ransom campaign would become. One of the most familiar trademarks used was that of Arabi Barayev, a Chechen rebel warlord known for his barbaric methods of executing captured federal soldiers and hostages (Lentini & Bakashmar, 2007). Groups would pay Barayev a percentage of the ransom achieved from a given kidnapping simply for using his name.

Extreme violence was a common feature in the Chechen negotiation process; kidnappers tortured or maimed hostages on video, by using various cruel methods of torture.[18] By using an emotive strategy, negotiations with the family were influenced by deliberately making them aware that the hostage was suffering. Pain alone induced a quick payment; Chechen kidnappers were often more sophisticated when inducing a ransom. Tishkov (2004) describes how five construction workers were captured in October 1997, one of whom was beheaded. Evidence of this execution was sent to the relatives of the remaining hostages accompanied by a ransom demand. The hostage in question had no relatives and was therefore of no value to the kidnappers; however, by executing him on video, the value of the remaining hostages increased as a result of the implied risk of death for the remaining hostages. Indeed, on this occasion reputation alone was enough to elicit a ransom, illustrating that the valuation of a hostage during Chechen kidnapping was also reliant upon the willingness to use violence.

Kidnapping for ransom in Chechnya was a highly sophisticated business model, which involved the valuation and distribution of hostages within a platform that holds the features of a market-based crime. The Chechen hostage trade involved a range of operators that served as an informal distribution network. Typically, hostages were abducted by smaller criminal groups, valued and then sold along the supply chain to larger criminal or rebel organizations. Once the hostage reached the end of the supply chain, the commodities were then stored in purpose-built prisons equipped with torture chambers.[19] The torture chambers themselves were incremental in increasing the value of the hostage, and also served as an effective method of controlling multiple hostages over the period of detention. The Chechen business model provides an effective example of the market nature of kidnapping for ransom behaviour.

---

[18] Cruel methods of torture included severing the ears, fingers and even the tips of tongues, and filing the teeth of the hostage. Hostages were also forced to watch the beheadings of other hostages or captured Russian soldiers (Tishkov, 2004).

[19] These prisons are known as 'Zindans'. Zindans were hidden in secret locations such as converted garages, underground pits and even cellars of private houses. According to Tishkov (2004) the Ministry of Sharia Security kept around 50 hostages, regularly replenished from Grozny's hostage market, within its own prison.

Conclusion

Kidnapping requires immense planning and organization in order to sustain the activity successfully over a long period of time. The analytical process that a radical group goes through is comparable to a corporate business plan. Kidnappers have to identify the risks to their business, variables that include: detection from law enforcement, the individual skills set of the group, and even the current political and social climate. This must be examined relative to the market value of the hostage, the turnaround of the crime, and the supply of hostages. The ability to store the hostage and shield them from detection is also an additional consideration. Decisions must be made on the preferred method of kidnapping, whether targeted or random; what form of ransom payment is required to escape detection from the authorities, whether payment is cash, commodity or by exchange. Moreover, the ability to resell the commodity is also paramount during this analytical process. These factors must be balanced successfully for kidnapping to be considered as a sustainable business.

If kidnapping for ransom is to become a viable business enterprise, it should be perceived as being profitable from the outset. The cost of running the operation must be balanced against the potential financial rewards of the venture. Acquiring weapons, salaries for the kidnappers, the expense of hiding and feeding the hostage, are all variable costs which must be taken into account in order for the crime to be beneficial. Inevitably these factors do lead to logical trends in the treatment of the hostage. In order to reduce the costs of captivity, kidnappers may often hide the hostage in their home, or bury them in purpose-built underground prisons. More organized groups or those operating within a conflict zone will often cut costs by holding a hostage in a makeshift prison (sometimes referred to as a 'hostage hotel', see Hagedorn-Auerbach, 1998, p. 33) with other hostages captured at different intervals. This was a common observation reported by hostages who survived kidnappings in post-war Iraq. For small-time operators that engage in kidnapping for ransom, time may be a predominate factor in resolving the hostage event. The longer the kidnapping event continues, the higher the cost incurred by the group.

Given that radical groups commit crime in order to maintain operational objectives, then it follows that specific high yielding crime such as kidnapping for ransom could be considered a business, on the basis that many groups engage in this behaviour for self-funding. However, kidnapping for ransom is also a complex social interaction; on one occasion it may be carried out for financial gain, and on another, for a political or social objective (Best, 1982; Turner, 1998; Tzanelli, 2006). It is a rare form of criminal behaviour that can be dual purpose, allowing a group to achieve multiple objectives in a single instance (Lentini & Bakashmar, 2007). Kidnapping can raise finance to fund other operations, whilst simultaneously demonstrating the state's inability to protect its citizens from harm, thereby de-legitimizing the governance of the state and increasing fear of crime (Heeb, 2002). This was an effect observed in Iraq, where prolific kidnapping for ransom combined with the insurgency undermined the fledgling government and its subsequent reconstruction of the country. Kidnapping may also garner publicity, or serve as a strategic opportunity to secure a prisoner release, or even to remove key protagonists from the immediate social or political arena (Kramer, 1998). The combination of the above observations challenges the notion that kidnapping for ransom is simply a profit-making business and offers alternatives to defining this behaviour.

For kidnapping to be considered a business, one must not disregard the additional characteristics that define it as such. These would include the capability of the organization to perpetrate the crime on a repetitive basis whilst maintaining the ability to launder the money over a long period of time. There is a distinction between independent operators that kidnap for money and small groups that have access to a kidnapping network (or syndicate); this may be the defining factor of what constitutes a kidnapping business. Independent operators, if successful, are more likely to kidnap for ransom on rare occasions, choosing only to ransom for small amounts of cash (Yang, Wu, & Huang, 2007). These offenders are often petty criminals; although the motive behind the kidnapping is monetary gain, the intention is not to build a business empire. In contrast, small groups that kidnap with the intention of selling the hostage to a larger group or simply ransoming the hostage themselves are in effect developing a business. Hence, money alone can not be the distinguishing variable that defines kidnapping as a business, organization and repetition must also be present.

References

Albanese, J. S. (2000). Do criminals organise around opportunities or do criminal opportunities create new offenders. *Journal of Contemporary Criminology, 16,* 409–423.

Arquilla, J., & Ronfeldt, D. (2001). *Networks and netwars* (pp. 61–97). Santa Monica: RAND Corporation.

Best, J. (1982). Crime as strategic interaction: The social organization of extortion. *Journal of Contemporary Ethnography, 11,* 107–128.

Bibes, P. (2001). Transnational organized crime and terrorism: Colombia, a case study. *Journal of Contemporary Criminal Justice, 17,* 243–258.

Briggs, R. (2001). *The kidnapping business.* London: The Foreign Policy Centre.

Briggs, R. (2002). Hostage Inc. *Foreign Policy, 131,* 28–29.

Clutterbuck, R. (1978). *Kidnap and ransom: The response.* London: Faber & Faber.

Dishman, C. (2001). Terrorism, crime, and transformation. *Studies in Conflict & Terrorism*, 24, 43–58.

Dishman, C. (2005). The leaderless nexus: When crime and terror converge. *Studies in Conflict & Terrorism*, 28, 237–252.

Edwards, A., & Gill, P. (2002). Crime as enterprise? The case of transnational organised crime. *Crime, Law & Social Change*, 37, 203–223.

Galeotti, M. (2002). Brotherhoods and Associates: Chechen networks of crime and resistance. *Low Intensity Conflict & Law Enforcement*, 11, 340–352.

Hagedorn-Auerbach, A. (1998). *Ransom: The untold story of international kidnapping.* New York: Henry Holt Company.

Heeb, A. (2002). *Violent crime, public perceptions and citizen security strategies in Colombia during the 1990s.* Unpublished doctoral thesis, Oxford University.

Hunter, T. (1996). Colombia's Kidnapping Incorporated. *Jane's Intelligence Review*, 8, 565.

Kiser, S. (2005). *Financing terror: An analysis and simulation for affecting Al Qaeda's financial infrastructure.* Santa Monica: RAND Corporation.

Kramer, M. (1998). The moral logic of Hizballah. In W. Reich (Ed.), *Origins of terrorism: Psychologies, ideologies, theologies, states of mind* (pp. 131–157). Washington, DC: The Woodrow Wilson Centre Press.

Lechner, A. (2007). Cosh or carry. *Intersec*, 17, July/August, 26–28.

Lentini, P., & Bakashmar, M. (2007). Jihadist beheading: A convergence of technology, theology, and teleology? *Studies in Conflict & Terrorism*, 30, 303–325.

Looney, R. (2005). The business of insurgency: The expansion of Iraq's shadow economy. *The National Interest*, 81, 1–6.

Makarenko, T. (2004). The crime-terror continuum: Tracing the interplay between transnational organised crime and terrorism. *Global Crime*, 6, 129–145.

Mateo, N. J. (2004). This business of kidnapping: Making sense of kidnapping within a business transaction perspective. *Philippine Journal of Psychology*, 37, 141–159.

McFarlane, J. (2003). Organised crime and terrorism in the Asia-Pacific region: The reality and response. *Transnational Organised Crime, Terrorism and Transnational Relations*, European Consortium for Political Research, 2nd General Conference, 18–12 September.

Merkling, S., & Davis, E. (2001). Kidnap and ransom insurance: A rapidly growing benefit. *Compensation & Benefits Review*, November/December, 40–45.

Milward, H. B., & Raab, J. (2002, October). *Dark networks: The structure, operation, and performance of international drugs, terror, and arms trafficking networks.* Paper presented at the International Conference on the Empirical Study of Governance, Management, and Performance, Barcelona, Spain.

Mincheva, L., & Gurr, T. R. (2006, March). *Unholy alliances? How trans-state terrorism and international crime make common cause.* Paper presented at the Annual Meeting of the International Studies Association, Panel on Comparative Perspectives on States, Terrorism and Crime, San Diego.

Miro, J. M., & Curtis, G. E. (2003). Organized crime and terrorist activity in Mexico, 1999–2002. The Library of Congress. Retrieved January 14, 2004 from www.loc.gov/rr/frd/

Moor, M., & Zumpolle, L. (2001). *The kidnap industry in Colombia – our business?* The Hague: Pax Christi Netherlands.

Mukhina, I. (2005). Islamic terrorism and the question of national liberation, or problems of contemporary Chechen terrorism. *Studies in Conflict & Terrorism, 28,* 515–532.

Naylor, R. T. (1993). The insurgent economy: Black market operations of guerrilla organisations. *Crime, Law and Social Change, 20,* 13–51.

Naylor, R. T. (2003). Towards a general model of profit-driven crimes. *British Journal of Criminology, 43,* 81–101.

Ortiz, R. D. (2002). Insurgent strategies in post-Cold War: The case of the revolutionary armed forces of Colombia. *Studies in Conflict & Terrorism, 25,* 127–143.

Peimani, P. (2004). *Armed violence and poverty in Chechnya.* A mini case study for the Armed Violence and Poverty Initiative. Centre for International Cooperation and Security of the Department of Peace Studies, University of Bradford, UK.

Picarelli, J. T. (2006). Transnational organised crime and terrorism: A theory of malevolent international relations. *Global Crime, 7,* 1–24.

Ping, H. (2006). Is money laundering a true problem in China? *International Journal of Offender Therapy and Comparative Criminology, 50,* 101–116.

Riascos, A. J., & Vargas, J. F. (2006, January). Violence and growth in Colombia: A brief review of the literature. Retrieved June 27, 2007, from: www.webpondo.org

Restrepo, E. M., Sanchez, F., & Cuellar, M. (2006). Impunity or punishment? An analysis of criminal investigation into kidnapping, terrorism and embezzlement in Colombia. *Global Crime, 7,* 176–199.

Root, J. (2007). In Mexico, crime continues its surge. *Yahoo News,* 22 September. Retrieved September 29, 2007, from www.yahoo.com

Schauer, E. J., & Wheaton, E. M. (2006). Sex trafficking into the United States: A literature review. *Criminal Justice Review, 31,* 146–169.

Schbley, A. H. (2000). Torn between God, family, and money: The changing profile of Lebanon's religious terrorists. *Studies in Conflict & Terrorism, 23,* 175–196.

Schmid, A. P. (1996). The links between transnational organized crime and terrorist crimes. *Transnational Organized Crime, 2,* 40–82.

Shelly, L. (2001). Corruption and organized crime in Mexico in the post-PRI transition. *Journal of Criminal Justice, 17,* 213–231.

Shelly, L. (2003). The trade in people in and from the former Soviet Union. *Crime, Law & Social Change, 40,* 231–249.

Shelly, L. I., & Picarelli, J. T. (2002). Methods not motives: Implications of the convergence of international organized crime and terrorism. *Police Practice and Research, 3,* 305–318.

Sung, H. E. (2004). State failure, economic failure, and predatory organised crime: A comparative analysis. *Journal of Research in Crime and Delinquency, 41,* 111–129.

Tishkov, V. (2004). *Chechnya: Life in a war-torn society.* Berkeley, CA: University of California Press.

Turner, M. (1998). Kidnapping and politics. *International Journal of the Sociology of Law, 26,* 145–160.

Tzanelli, R. (2006). Capitalizing on value: Towards a sociological understanding of kidnapping. *Sociology, 40,* 929–947.

United Nations (UN) Commission on Crime Prevention and Criminal Justice (2003, April). *International cooperation in the prevention, combating and elimination of kidnapping and in providing assistance to victims.* Retrieved July 23, 2007, from www.unodc.org/pdf/crime/commissions/12_commission/7add1.pdf

United Nations (UN) Commission on Crime Prevention and Criminal Justice (2004a, March). *International cooperation in the prevention, combating and elimination of kidnapping and in providing assistance to victims.* Retrieved March 30, 2007, from http://daccessdds.un.org/doc/UNDOC/GEN/V04/516/63/PDF/V0451663. pdf?OpenElement

United Nations (UN) Commission on Crime Prevention and Criminal Justice (2004b, April). *International cooperation in the prevention, combating and elimination of kidnapping and in providing assistance to victims.* Retrieved March 30, 2007, from http://daccessdds.un.org/doc/UNDOC/GEN/V04/529/58/PDF/V0452958. pdf?OpenElement

United Nations Assistance Mission for Iraq (UNAMI) (2006). Human Rights Report 1st November – 31st December. Retrieved March 3, 2007, from www.uniraq.org/FileLib/misc/HR%20Report%20Nov%20Dec%202006%20EN.pdf

Williams, P. (1994). Transnational criminal organisations and international security. *Survival, 36*, 96–113.

Williams, P. (2001). Transnational criminal networks. In J. Arquilla, & D. Ronfeldt (Eds), *Networks and netwars* (pp. 61–97). Santa Monica: RAND Corporation.

Yang, S. L., Wu, B., & Huang, S. L. (2007). Kidnapping in Taiwan: The significance of geographic proximity, improvisation, and fluidity. *International Journal of Offender Therapy and Comparative Criminology, 51*, 324–339.

12

Case Study – Ramzan Kadyrov in Chechnya: Authoritarian Leadership in the Caucasus

John Russell

Synopsis: Ramzan Kadyrov, the leader of Chechnya, has succeeded where many others have failed by merging the 'needs' of his countrymen with his and others 'greed'. His personal power is the only source of state power in Chechnya, filling the vacuum existing hitherto. Similarly, his control over personal profit means that he can not only exclude outsiders (i.e. Russians) from fleecing Chechen civilians on a grand scale, but can ensure at least some trickle-down effect to the benefit of all. Chechen society is now relatively secure, if only insofar as all who support Kadyrov are safe. Those that oppose him, needless to say, are not. Thus, there is an element of order in Chechen society but a notable absence of law-governed democracy. It seems likely therefore that Ramzan is to be the first and last 'King of Chechnya', and is likely to be remembered as an example of authoritarian rule that was judged, by Chechens, Russians and the international community alike, to be unworthy of imitation.

Strong Men in High Places

A dramatic shift has occurred recently in the conflict in Chechnya, the rebellious republic in the North Caucasus, which for well over a decade (some would say centuries) has been fighting to escape the stifling grip of Russia. In the first 10 years of the current confrontation, the disproportionate and

The Faces of Terrorism: Multidisciplinary Perspectives Edited by David Canter
© 2009 John Wiley & Sons Ltd.

indiscriminate violence visited by Russian armed forces on the civilian population resulted in up to 300,000 being killed, badly injured or displaced.[1]

The conflict attracted the world's attention in the first Russo-Chechen war (1994–96) largely because of the surprise victory by the Chechen insurgents (Gall & de Waal, 1997; German, 2003; Lieven, 1999) but, in the inter-war period, a series of gruesome beheadings and hostage takings by local warlords lost the Chechens much international sympathy (Lanskoy, 2003). This almost totally evaporated in the second conflict (1999–2006), due primarily to the bloody outcome of 'terrorist spectacular' sieges launched by the Chechens at the Dubrovka theatre in Moscow in October 2002 and the Beslan school in September 2004 (Dunlop, 2006).

This improvement in the situation in Chechnya, which is by no means acknowledged by all,[2] appears to be linked to the widely diverging fates of two charismatic Chechen leaders: Shamil Basayev, the leader of the 'irreconcilable' Chechen resistance and mastermind of the Budennovsk, Dubrovka and Beslan hostage-taking raids, who on 10 July 2006 was killed in mysterious circumstances in neighbouring Ingushetia (on the eve of the opening of the G8 meeting in St Petersburg, Russian President Vladimir Putin's home town); and Ramzan Kadyrov, who came to prominence in the aftermath of the assassination (by Basayev's forces in May 2004) of his father Akhmad – the first pro-Russian president of Chechnya – and who, on 2 March 2007, was confirmed as Chechen president, having been nominated for the post by Putin just two weeks previously.

Since then, it would seem, not only has all been relatively quiet on Europe's most south-easterly front, but a semblance of order, reconstruction and recovery appears to have been instituted by Chechnya's flamboyant new leader, significantly known locally as the 'Energizer' (Borisov, 2007). Indeed, the 32-year-old Kadyrov has apparently managed not only to effectively halt the war in Chechnya and install a Russian-style *vertikal'* of power in a land that for centuries has resisted resolutely such a form of autocratic rule, traditionally preferring instead a polycentric, clan-based model, but also in the process has become a leader of almost mythical status amongst many ordinary Chechens. Moreover, he is perceived as a future president (*Regnum.ru*, 2007), even a

---

[1] Even rough estimates of numbers killed during this conflict are extremely hard to verify. The figure of 300,000 dead comes not, as one might anticipate, from a rebel Chechen source, but from a deputy prime minister in the pro-Russian administration. Of course, he might have been inflating the figures to attract higher compensation payments. See '300,000 killed in Chechen wars – pro-Moscow official', *Moscow News*, 19 November 2004.

[2] See the letter signed by more than 100 members of Britain's political and cultural elite, 'Putin must act to end reign of fear and oppression in Chechnya', *The Independent*, 7 May 2007, which states "For the vast majority of the Chechen people, Kadyrov's presidency is little more than a regime of fear and oppression, with no way out and no avenues to seek justice for the daily crimes against civilians".

'second' Stalin (RFE/RL, 2006), by some Russians and is treated as an Idi Amin-like figure of fun, intimidation and awe by sections of the Western media.[3]

One detected an element of wishful thinking when Ramzan Kadyrov 'officially declared' on 5 January 2007, in an interview with *Russian Newsweek*, that peace had been achieved in the Chechen Republic,[4] and when, on 11 February 2007, the then Russian Defense Minister, Sergei Ivanov, referring to the conflict in Chechnya, confirmed that "the problem has been solved" (Chivers, 2007). Certainly, the Russian public was more sceptical; for, at approximately the same time as the above announcements, the opinion pollsters at *Levada-Centre* were conducting a poll which found that 50% of Russians thought the war in Chechnya was continuing and only 38% thought peace was being established.[5] Moreover, responding to a further claim by Kadyrov on 9 July 2007 that the conflict was over, a Chechen political analyst warned (Dudayev, 2007):

> The armed resistance in Chechnya and neighbouring regions is still alive and is still a fairly serious force. It's just that the military and political leadership in Russia has become hostage to its own claims that the fighting is over and that the fighters no longer present a real threat ... I think that sooner or later the separatists will make their presence felt. And quite loudly.

So, in examining just how 'King Ramzan' – as he is referred to by the Russian military in Chechnya (Osborn, 2006) – has been so successful in winning the battle for Chechen hearts and minds, while retaining the support of Putin's Russia (the source of so much of the misery that had befallen the Chechen people in the current phase of this long-running conflict), it is necessary also to determine the likely durability of Kadyrov's rule.

A range of theories drawn mainly from the disciplines of conflict resolution, terrorism and counterterrorism studies will be employed in order to determine whether the emergence of Kadyrov represents a short-term 'one-off' phenomenon in this remote mountainous republic – i.e. a throwback to pre-modern times – or whether wider conclusions may be drawn from his apparent success that might perhaps be applicable elsewhere in the Caucasus region or even as far afield as Iraq or Afghanistan, from the utility of authoritarian rule in post-conflict situations.

---

[3] Influenced, no doubt, by the success of the movie about Amin, *The Last King of Scotland*, a Russia Profile Weekly Review Panel, held in Moscow in March 2007, was entitled 'The Last King of Chechnya'; see *Johnson's Russia List*, 35, 9 March 2007. Retrieved August 14, 2007, from www.cdi.org/russia/johnson/2007-57-35.cfm

[4] Retrieved March 4, 2007, from http://chechnya.gov.ru/press/interview/4529.html

[5] Retrieved March 11, 2007, from www.levada.ru/press/2007030702.html

The Need, Greed (and Creed) Matrix

Of the many of theories regarding stimuli causing civil conflict, I find that advanced by I. William Zartman (Zartman, 2005) the most applicable to Chechnya (see Table 12.1).

Based upon his formula, one may identify the four basic 'needs' of a given society to be political power, economic opportunity, a secure society and a measure of law and order. I would argue that Ramzan Kadyrov has been the first person in the current conflict to be in a position to address these four basic needs in Chechnya in any coherent fashion and with any prospect of success. It is this fact, rather than the degree of success or failure with which his attempts have been met, that goes a long way to explaining his current popularity with both the Russian president and the Chechen people.

Prior to Kadyrov, there existed in Chechnya a vacuum of political power, which nurtured the rise of local warlords, military chiefs and gangsters who used their personal power to achieve their ends. Similarly, the almost complete absence of legitimate economic activity in the war zone led to these same local chiefs enriching themselves and their followers. Unsurprisingly both political and economic power was won and defended through the barrel of a gun, this being the surest form of security in a manifestly insecure society. By the same token, the virtual absence of any semblance of law and order consolidated the sphere of operation of these selfsame leaders. In other words, the absence of any legitimate mechanism to fulfil the basic needs of Chechen society led to the takeover of these functions by what I have termed 'entrepreneurs of violence' (Russell, 2007, pp. 110–130) motivated by a combination of greed and elements of creed (see Table 12.2).

Whereas each component of 'need' had its almost direct equivalent in 'greed', elements of 'creed' tended to be employed interchangeably or even cumulatively. Each had a particular potency in the truly appalling conditions of the Russo-Chechen conflict. For example, the Chechen cultural narrative (Russell, 2007, pp. 17–18) was nourished by three centuries of resistance to Russian rule, which in its turn had perpetrated a series of major atrocities against the Chechens, culminating in the wholesale deportation of the entire

Table 12.1. The intersection of need and greed in Chechnya

Need	Greed
POLITICAL POWER	PERSONAL POWER
ECONOMIC OPPORTUNITY	PERSONAL PROFIT
SECURE SOCIETY	MIGHT NOT RIGHT
RECHSSTAAT (LAW-GOVERNED STATE)	ENTREPRENEURS OF VIOLENCE

Table 12.2. Elements of creed exploited by Kadyrov in Chechnya

Creed
CHECHEN CULTURAL NARRATIVE
CHECHEN NATIONALISM
CHECHEN ETHNICITY
SUFISM

Chechen nation to Siberia and Kazakhstan in 1944. Insofar as Russian behaviour in the current conflict approached the brutality *of* these shameful precedents, it was not difficult to stir up massive Chechen resistance. On the other hand, the Russian cultural narrative was one of a *mission civilatrice*, by which the 'great Russian nation' brought the fruits of civilization to mountain tribes, whose resistance was taken as further proof of their backwardness. By countering the latter impression, and seeking generous compensation for past wrongs, Kadyrov has defused one of the major sources of resentment to Russian rule over Chechnya.

The at times seemingly genocidal tactics of the Russian armed forces inevitably increased the potency amongst Chechens of their distinct ethnicity, weakening at the same time the inter-ethnic bonds with the considerable number of non-Chechens (including Russians) hitherto resident in Chechnya. Paradoxically, the notion of the Chechen 'nation', demanding rights of 'nationhood' is a relatively modern concept that derives as much from comparison with similar anti-colonial movements as it does from Chechen history. On the other hand, the concept of a Russian 'nation' is ambiguous, meaning, for some, an ethnically pure Russian state or, for others, Russia as a great power maintaining its imperial hold over the non-Russian citizens (like the Chechens) of the Russian Federation. Although Kadyrov's manifest ability to stop Russians killing Chechens would appear to have moderated the Chechen emphasis of ethnicity over nation, and his acceptance of Chechnya's place within the Russian Federation to have endorsed Russia's great power ambitions at the expense of Chechen independence, his political, economic and social policies can be seen by most Chechens to be based on maximum freedom of action within Chechnya for himself and his ethnic supporters. In anything but the short term, this is not necessarily a recipe for stability, for as Svante Cornell (Cornell, 2002) has warned in writing about this region:

> The advocacy of resolving or preventing ethnic conflict through solutions based on the devolution of power along ethnic lines is at best a questionable and at worst a disastrous enterprise. The little publicized pitfalls of ethnofederalism hence need to be kept in mind while formulating policies in and toward multi-ethnic societies. (p. 276)

Finally, religion has traditionally been employed to justify or explain all manner of excesses in conflict situations and Chechnya is by no means an exception. What Kadyrov has succeeded in doing is to redirect the Chechen brand of Islam back towards traditional Sufi practices (Vachagaev, 2005) and away from the Wahhabi-led extremism that characterized the irreconcilable Chechen resistance movement under Basayev (Souleimanov, 2005). Although Sufism proved itself to be remarkably adept at withstanding the all-intrusive nature of the Soviet regime, it turned out to be incapable of countering effectively the scale of war unleashed by the Russian federal forces. Wahhabism, on the other hand, which justified the use of suicide bombing and the jihad against 'unbelievers', could at least claim to have hit back effectively at Russian brutality. It was only by reducing Russian military involvement in the conflict to a minimum that Kadyrov was able to allow Chechens to return to the form of Islam to which they were more accustomed.

Within the parameters of an asymmetric conflict, Chechen suicide bombing sought to punish the Russians for the indiscriminate aerial and heavy artillery bombardment with which they had punished the Chechens (see Table 12.3). By the same token the brutality of the Russian occupation was countered by an indomitable Chechen resolve to be free that was manifestly more potent than their occupiers' desire to remain. By reducing significantly the negative impact on Chechens of both Russian strategies, Kadyrov removed the need for and utility of the more extreme Chechen counter-measures.

In summary, what Kadyrov has successfully achieved is a merging of 'need' and 'greed', in that, while his personal power is, in effect, the only source of state power in Chechnya, it has filled the vacuum existing hitherto. Similarly, his control over personal profit means that he can not only exclude outsiders (i.e. Russians) from fleecing Chechen civilians on a grand scale, but can ensure at least some trickle-down effect to the benefit of all. Chechen society is now relatively secure, if only insofar as all who support Kadyrov are safe; those that oppose him, needless to say, are not. In other words, might still rules over right, unless, of course, one accepts, as many of his supporters apparently do, that Kadyrov is the embodiment of right. Thus, there is an element of order in Chechen society but a notable absence of law-governed democracy.

The salient point, however, is that after more than a decade of the most horrendous civil warfare, even the incomplete way in which the needs of the Chechen people are being addressed under Kadyrov appears to be far more preferable to the ordinary Chechen than the brutality, lawlessness and insecu-

Table 12.3. Punishment and denial in asymmetric warfare

	Punishment	Denial
Russians (stronger side)	Aerial and artillery bombardment, sweeps	Occupation
Chechens (weaker side)	Suicide bombing	Freedom

rity of the preceding decade. Lacking a definitive negotiated political solution like that brokered, for example, in Northern Ireland (Blank 2001; Bogoran & Soldatov, 2007), it is surely just a matter of time before a form of rule more 'Chechen' than Kadyrov's one-man authoritarianism will be sought.

A War of Four Conflicts

Whereas the Putin administration euphemistically termed the entire second Russo-Chechen war a 'counterterrorist operation', implying that it was no less than Russia's front in the global war on terror, it is generally agreed that this was an disingenuously opportunistic simplification of the true situation in Chechnya. Particularly after 9/11, this characterization diverted Western and Russian public opinion alike from the real causes of the confrontation. In a previous work (Russell, 2005) I have identified four distinct conflicts ongoing simultaneously within the Russo-Chechen war (see Table 12.4).

The remarkable impact that Ramzan Kadyrov has had in his brief period in charge has changed dramatically the nature of all four conflicts within the Russo-Chechen war. Thus, although manifestly proud of his ethnic heritage – he demonstratively wears the traditional Chechen skullcap in public (something his predecessor, Alu Alkhanov, rarely did)[6] – Kadyrov has adopted the

Table 12.4. Four Russo-Chechen conflicts

Name	Substance of conflict	Comparisons
1. CULTURAL	'Modernizing' Russia versus 'traditional' Chechnya	Aboriginees, Scottish Highlanders, Inuit, Native American Indians, Roma.
2. COLONIAL	Russian imperialism versus Chechen self-determination	Algeria, East Timor, Estonia, Kosovo, Tibet.
3. 'BLACK HOLE' OF LAWLESSNESS	'Might' over 'right', crime, corruption, clientelism	Afghanistan, Iraq, Lebanon, Sudan.
4. GLOBALIZATION	War on terror, North versus South, McWorld versus Jihad	Afghanistan, Iraq, Pakistan, Palestine.

[6] For a photograph of Kadyrov in skullcap alongside a bare-headed Alkhanov, see *Kommersant*, 23 September 2005. Kadyrov sported similar headgear when celebrating the winning of the Russian Cup by his soccer club, *Terek Grozny*, in May 2004. Retrieved August 13, 2007, from www. themoscowtimes.com/ind bar mitzvah exes/2004/05/31/01.html. And again when shown on national TV beside his father's grave, standing alongside Putin (and Alkhanov, bare-headed once more), *NTV*, 23 August 2004. Retrieved August 13, 2007, from www.moscowtimes.ru/ indexes/2004/08/23/01.html

trappings of modernity with gusto. From his menagerie of exotic pets – Ramzan is often pictured with his tiger (Franchetti, 2006), lion (Liss, 2006), or fighting dog (Politkovskaya, 2007) – to his fleet of high performance sports cars to his sumptuous palaces in Tsentrovoi and Gudermes; from the beauty competitions that he has personally sponsored [7] to the succession of such high-profile guests as former world heavyweight boxing champion, Mike Tyson,[8] Ramzan's style is distinctively glitzy. For example, *The Economist* (31 May 2007) described his inauguration as being: "Like a high-end bar mitzvah, only with more weapons". At the same time, however, he has been careful to court Chechen and Muslim traditions, including the banning of slot machines, the advocacy of polygamy and the wearing of the scarf and, most demonstrably, by constructing 'Europe's largest mosque' in Grozny (Walsh, 2005).

By accepting that Chechnya should remain part of the Russian Federation, Kadyrov has ensured that, in the short term at least, the colonial conflict has been put on ice. That, in return for this undertaking, the Russian president has granted his Chechen counterpart a degree of autonomy that previous generations of Chechen leaders could only dream of, has led to an apparent win-win situation between the two sides. This deal, however, is deeply unpopular with sections of the Russian political and military leadership which resent Kadyrov, who had fought against them in the first war, taking power in Chechnya. Characterized by sceptical Russian journalists as 'Chechen separatism under the Russian flag' (Markedonov, 2006) or 'separatism-lite' (Sukhov, 2005), there is genuine concern about the sustainability of this arrangement post-Putin (who stepped down as president in May 2008) or (given the attrition rate of past presidents in Chechnya), post-Kadyrov.

The essence of the criminal conflict (or 'black hole of lawlessness') was that Russian military and political leaders in Chechnya, often in collaboration with Chechens of all shades of opposition, would advocate policies that ensured the continuation of the war, to the obvious detriment of the civilian population. Kadyrov, by effectively monopolizing all illegitimate (and legitimate) operations on Chechen territory, has ended the need for this conflict to continue. His only fear must be that, insofar as the threat to Russia of Chechen terrorism recedes, the federal authorities might renege on its generous compensation payments for the havoc wrought by more than a decade of war. By the same token, insofar as those in Chechnya continuing the struggle against Russia are cut out of any benefits accruing from the Putin-Kadyrov deal, there is little prospect of their giving up the fight and thus little likelihood of genuine peace and security returning to this region any time soon.

---

[7] First beauty queen named in Chechnya, *Moscow News*, 28 May 2006.
[8] 'Boxer Tyson welcomed in Chechnya, *BBC*, 15 September 2005. Retrieved September 30, 2006, from http://news.bbc.co.uk/1/hi/world/europe/4250126.stm

The most significant shift, however, has occurred in the central struggle around globalization. Whereas, prior to Kadyrov, in three critical areas: US-led globalization; the war on terror; and the post-9/11 discourse of 'them' and 'us', Russia was broadly on the side of the West while Chechnya was unambiguously in the opposition camp, Putin's Russia and Kadyrov's Chechnya are now clearly on the same side, albeit neither are as pro-Western as anticipated. Indeed, rather than seeing their country as belonging primarily to the Western tradition, approximately three-quarters of Russians polled in August 2007 favoured a distinct 'Eurasian' path of development.[9]

Taken together, the Putin administration's use of the 'energy' card, the blatant manipulation of the electoral process and, in particular, the high-profile assassinations of journalists, such as Anna Politkovskaya, and opposition figures like Aleksandr Litvinenko appear to have reversed decisively Russia's trajectory towards European-style democracy. Meanwhile, in Chechnya, the ever-growing personality cult (Markedonov, 2007), menace, and power exuded by Ramzan Kadyrov is more reminiscent of Stalin or Saddam Hussein than that of the leader of a 21st-century European state.

However, although Kadyrov's authoritarian style of rule might cause some diplomatic embarrassment in democratic countries, the West has long since found ways to accommodate dictators one hundred times more deadly than Kadyrov. Moreover, judging by the fact that Putin's approval rating among Russians remained stratospherically high at 85% in July 2007,[10] it is clear that authoritarian rule is unlikely to generate similar discomfort in Russia. Even Stalin's rule is perceived there as being relatively benign; in March 2003, on the 50th anniversary of the Soviet dictator's death, 53% of Russians polled assessed his role in the country's development positively.[11] As for Kadyrov's realm itself, one Russian journalist (Allenova, 2007) simply admits: "In Chechnya they love Ramzan Kadyrov".

The Battle for Minds and Hearts

Of course, Ramzan Kadyrov cannot expect such levels of support from ordinary Russians: thus in January 2007 the *Levada-Centre* suggested that 35% of Russians polled considered that Kadyrov could not be trusted against just 33% who thought he could (32% expressed no view). In the same poll, 70% favoured the commencement of peace negotiations, with just 16% for continuing the war.[12]

[9] Retrieved August 14, 2007, from www.levada.ru/press/2007081001.html
[10] Retrieved August 14, 2007, from www.levada.ru/prezident.html
[11] Retrieved August 14, 2007, from www.levada.ru/press/2003030400.html
[12] Retrieved March 11, 2007, from www.levada.ru/press/2007030702.html

Table 12.5. Counterterrorist strategies and messages employed in Chechnya

Strategy	Message
(a) 'Hard'– counterterrorism	
ERADICATION	'We will waste them even in the shithouse'
COMBATING	'We will terrorize them onto the back foot'
(b) 'Soft'– anti-terrorism	
CONTAINMENT	'We shall win minds by isolating extremists'
ROOT CAUSES	'We shall win hearts by addressing your underlying grievances'

Unsurprisingly, many Russians feel uncomfortable with the fact that Chechnya appears to have been handed over to the very rebels against whom their armed forces had fought two bloody wars.

In Chechnya, however, perceptions are different. As Russian political commentator Yulia Latynina noted on his 31st birthday (Latynina, 2007), Kadyrov knows the local rules of the game better than any of his Chechen predecessors, let alone those Russians entrusted with Chechnya's recovery. His Chechen troops – the *kadyrovtsy* – are unlikely to repeat in scale or barbarity the crude mistakes of the federal forces in sledge-hammering the Chechen population, purportedly in order to crack the 'terrorist' nut.

As is illustrated above (see Table 12.5), prior to Kadyrov's elevation Russia had relied almost exclusively on 'hard' counterterrorist measures to the virtual exclusion of 'soft' anti-terrorist measures (Stepanova, 2003, p. 8) designed to win the minds and hearts of ordinary Chechens.

Russia is by no means the only modern state to emphasize the use of 'hard' military strategies in an asymmetric battle with those they label 'terrorists' (Russell, 2007, pp. 101–2). The utility to one's own side is that something decisive is seen to be done in countering a perceived threat. The downside of such emphasis is that civilians killed, injured or made homeless as 'collateral damage' in such 'counterterrorist' operations are, for protection, flung into the arms of the very insurgents against whom the battle is being waged.

Russia's manifest failure to make any attempt to isolate legitimate 'insurgents' from extremist 'terrorists' or even to discriminate between ordinary Chechen civilians and those that had taken up arms against federal forces, rekindled the widespread traditional hatred of the Russian occupiers. The apparent impunity with which suspected Russian war criminals were treated by the federal authorities led even such loyal pro-Kremlin Chechens as former president Alu Alkhanov to complain (Russell, 2007, p. 104).

Kadyrov, of course, was not shy of using strong-arm 'hard' strategies to consolidate himself in power, but he did so selectively and in combination with 'soft' strategies aimed at winning Chechen minds and hearts. Chechens might be eradicated or terrorized for opposing Ramzan, but not simply for being

Chechens. At the same time, such moves as having all Chechen prisoners returned to serve out their sentences in Chechnya and the curbing of the brutal activities of federally-run ORB-2 (Operative and Search Bureau) have predictably won widespread support among ordinary citizens (Leahy, 2006).

The most dramatic impact that Kadyrov has had in Chechnya, however, is to attract into his *kadyrovtsy* large numbers of armed Chechens who had previously fought, as did Ramzan himself, on the rebel side. Given the virtually total absence of the rule of law, these gunmen remain the prime arbiters of the daily fate of ordinary individuals in Chechnya. Ramzan appears to have been particularly successful in demonstrating to many of the former Chechen rebels that earning $500 a month (Voronov, 2006) within his forces provides them with a degree of both material and physical security that the opposition forces cannot match. The reliability of such former opponents, who now make up almost half of Kadyrov's forces (*NEWSru.com*, 2005), and the utility of an oath of loyalty sworn to Ramzan personally, rather than to Putin, have been questioned by Russian commentators (Krutikov, 2006).

Moreover, Kadyrov appears in danger of diluting his Chechen-wide appeal by adopting policies based on political favouritism and economic monopoly. For example, he appears already to have shown a distinct preference, even within his own clan, for Chechens from east of the Argun River, which splits the foothills and mountains of Chechnya from north to south, rather than the 'smart arses' from the West (*Agentsvo natsional'nykh novostei*, 2006), and is a proponent of the 'populist' *Qadiriya* rather than the more 'intellectual' *Naqshbandiya* brand of Sufism.

At the same time as receiving enormous compensation payments and subsidies from Russia, Ramzan has attracted generous investments from wealthy families in the Chechen diaspora and directed these, together with significant sums from the Akhmad Kadyrov Fund, towards the rebuilding of Chechnya's shattered infrastructure (Fuller, 2006). This fund he jealously controls, and all those working in the public sector or who seek Ramzan's favour are obliged to contribute. How long those Chechens exploited or shut out from Kadyrov's monopoly of political and economic power will continue to tolerate this situation is by no means clear.

Aims and Strategies

As is illustrated below (see Table 12.6), Kadyrov's coming to power appears to have endorsed the choice of fundamental strategies in Chechnya of not only the Russians and Chechens, but also of the international community.

Although the policy of 'Chechenization' (see Russell, 2007, pp. 82–88), i.e. handing over the responsibility for fighting Chechen separatists to pro-

Table 12.6. Aims and strategies in Chechnya

Aims	Strategies
Russian MAINTAIN TERRITORIAL INTEGRITY	CHECHENIZATION
Chechen RUSSIAN INFLUENCE OUT FROM CHECHNYA	SEPARATISM-LITE
International Community STABILITY IN REGION	POLITICAL SOLUTION

Moscow Chechen leaders, had been advocated as far back as 1995 (Fuller, 2004), it was not until mid-2000 when the newly-elected president Putin had identified Ramzan's father, Akhmad Kadyrov, as the Chechen most likely to implement his plan successfully, that the process really got under way.

Of course, in a democratic society with a strong independent media, questions would have been aired on behalf of a public concerned over the costs and wisdom of Putin's policy, which after more than a decade of brutal war and significant Russian losses has handed over power in Chechnya, effectively to his erstwhile enemies. Under Putin's authoritarian system, however, the Russian public is not consulted and it seems quite content for Putin to act in its name if this means reducing the likelihood of further Chechen terrorist attacks.

Nonetheless, a few brave voices of protest have been heard in Russia, criticizing Putin's Chechen policy and asking (Sukhov, 2005):

> What does Chechen power in the guise of Ramzan Kadyrov have in common with the Russian juridical space and for what, in any case, did we conduct a year-long counterterrorist operation that cost many thousands of lives?

Another influential Russian political commentator (Remizov, 2006) has categorized the system operating in Chechnya under Kadyrov's rule as 'developed feudalism', warning that this is an essentially expansionist phenomenon which could manifest itself both in the concentration of all levers of power in Chechnya in the hands of its leader, as well as in the attempt by the Putin administration to use Kadyrov and his methods to 'pacify' the Islamist opposition throughout the North Caucasus.

At the same time, Chechenization promises to deliver the Chechens (or at least those that side with Kadyrov) their key strategic goal, i.e. ridding their territory of Russian 'occupation'. For not only has the once considerable ethnic Russian community almost in its entirety left Chechnya, but the antagonism between Russian and Chechens, not least 'Caucasophobia' (Sikevich, 1999) –

that quintessentially Russian form of racism – the fear of violence and the general unattractiveness of Chechnya under Kadyrov virtually ensures that they will not return in any great numbers.

If the sole cost of achieving this is an undertaking to keep Chechnya in the Russian Federation and thus maintain Russia's territorial integrity, then Kadyrov's strategy of 'separatism-lite' appears a small price to pay for a virtual political *carte blanche* and economic blank cheque with which to control his realm. Moreover, insofar as this represents a 'political solution', it also meets the international community's main concern in the Russo-Chechen conflict. It is hardly surprising, however, that those elements, particularly in Western civic society, that understand the conflict in Chechnya do not find it difficult to expose the obvious dangers inherent in Putin's Chechen policy and are not afraid to ask the obvious question: could not such an unsatisfactory conclusion have been reached more than a decade ago thus sparing hundreds of thousands of casualties, refugees and the spread of instability throughout the region? In the circumstances, it is difficult not to agree with the conclusions drawn by *The Economist* (24 February – 2 March 2007) in response to Kadyrov's elevation:

> Under Mr Kadyrov in Chechnya, as under Mr Putin in all Russia, economic improvements have come at a cost of corruption, opacity and lawlessness. Both regimes rest on highly personalized rule that looks secure but may yet prove unstable.

Kadyrov's Violent Politics

Employing Alex Schmid's celebrated 'spectrum of political action' (see Table 12.7), the situation in Chechnya, prior to Ramzan Kadyrov's assumption of power, would appear to fall clearly within the sphere of 'violent politics' and at times (e.g. the bombardment of Grozny in 1995 and 1999), a state of war.

Applying Schmid's analysis to Chechnya, it was to be anticipated that the Russians' wholesale employment of state terrorism, ethnocide, internal war and political justice would be answered by Chechen terrorism, assassination, material destruction and guerrilla warfare.

As has been demonstrated, by taking over responsibility for fighting the Chechen insurgency from the Russian federal forces, much of the wanton brutality and indiscriminate violence has been replaced by a more selective form of violence that is more sensitive to Chechen custom and practice.

In this sense, one may no longer talk of a state of war in Chechnya. However, under Kadyrov, certain forms of state terrorism, assassination and violent repression clearly persist. The opposition, too, since the death of Basayev, has moved from suicide bombing and 'terrorist spectaculars', while retaining in

Table 12.7. Schmid's Spectrum of Political Action. Reproduced with permission from Taylor & Francis: Schmid, 2004, p. 199

State of Peace	
State Actor	*Non-state Actor*

Conventional Politics

I. Rule of Law (Routinized rule, legitimated by tradition, customs, constitutional procedures)	I. Opposition politics (Lobbying among power holders, formation of opposition press and parties, rallies, electoral contest, litigation [use of courts for political struggle])

Unconventional Politics

II. Oppression (Manipulation of competitive electoral process, censorship, surveillance, harassment, discrimination, infiltration of opposition, misuse of emergency legislation)	II. Non-violent action (Social protest for political persuasion of rulers and masses; demonstrations to show strength of public support; non-cooperation, civil disobedience, and other forms of non-violent action)

Violent Politics

III. Violent repression for control of state power	III. Use of violence for contestation challenging state power
III.1. (Political justice. Political imprisonment)	III. 1. Material destruction
III. 2. Assassination	III. 2. Assassination (Individuated political murder)
III. 3. State-terrorism (torture, death squads, disappearances, concentration camps)	III. 3. Terrorism (De-individuated political murder)
III. 4. Massacres	III. 4. Massacres
III. 5. Internal war	III. 5. Guerrilla warfare
III. 6. Ethnocide/Politicide/Genocide	III. 6. Insurgency, Revolution (if successful).

State of War

their insurgent arsenal assassination, more selective forms of terrorism, and elements of guerrilla warfare.

However, although Kadyrov has had some success in moving Chechen society into the sphere of unconventional politics, his ready resort to violence in order to maintain his position means that Chechnya currently experiences a potentially volatile mixture of both unconventional and violent politics.

In the meantime, Russia has slipped from a position prior to the first war in 1994 in which it seemed to be edging slowly towards elements of conventional politics, to a situation today in which non-violent reactions (demonstrations, civil disobedience) of non-state actors to their perceived oppression under the Putin administration, are met by the state with violent politics (assassination, political imprisonment, death squads). Paradoxically, therefore, just as Chechnya searches for a degree of relative normality after more than a decade of violent politics, Russia is becoming more and more like Chechnya. In both countries, the level of systemic corruption is likely to remain high and observance of the rule of law low, with the administrations in Russia and Chechnya each trusting more in violence than in legitimacy to maintain power.

Conclusion

Whereas some Western commentators (see note 2; Franchetti, 2007) support steadfastly the line of outspoken Russian journalists and human rights activists, epitomized by Anna Politkovskaya until her murder in October 2006, in refusing to recognize any positive benefits whatsoever in Kadyrov's rule, other observers, both in Russia and the West, while highly critical of both Kadyrov and Putin, have come to the uncomfortable conclusion that Chechenization represents the only achievable outcome available (Allenova, 2007; Latynina 2007). Whatever one thinks of his crude modus operandi, Ramzan Kadyrov to some extent represents, for Chechens, Russians and Western governments alike, that cliché from the world of *realpolitik* that: 'he may be a sonofabitch, but he's our sonofabitch'.

In the short term, Kadyrov's rule undoubtedly represents an improvement for large swathes of the Chechen population over the relentless misery and brutality of war. On a psychological level at least, the replacement on the Grozny skyline of bombed-out ruins, reminiscent of Stalingrad, by an imposing new mosque and modern administrative buildings allows the Chechens to focus on the future not the past. By the same token, the removal of the threat of disproportionate and indiscriminate brutality by Russian forces against Chechen civilians logically should mean that there will be no repeat in Russia of terror attacks on the scale of Budennovsk, Dubrovka or Beslan.

The danger is that 'Chechenization' is not really a political solution at all. Its critics point out that the reliance on the power and personal charisma of Putin in Moscow and Kadyrov in Grozny exemplifies the weakness inherent in the policy, resting as it does not on any firm legislative basis but on a private 'understanding' between two presidents whose tenure in office is strictly limited: Putin by the Russian Constitution and Kadyrov by the number of enemies he has made in the all-too-often violent politics of Russia and Chechnya.

Kadyrov's Chechen roots, the self-confidence born of being the son of a president and his ability to use force to coerce others to do his bidding are both strengths and weaknesses. Many in Russia fear that his very success in Chechnya could lead to a 'Kadyrovization' not just of the tinder box that is the North Caucasus, but of Russia itself. However, it is because the prospects in the medium to long term for a satisfactory resolution of the centuries-old Russo-Chechen conflict under Kadyrov remain as elusive as ever, that Ramzan is likely to be the first and last 'King of Chechnya', and is likely to be remembered as an example of authoritarian rule that was judged, by Chechens, Russians and the international community alike, to be unworthy of imitation.

References

Agentsvo natsional'nykh novostei (2006). Report, Svet i teni sem'i Kadyrovykh [Light and shadows of the Kadyrov family], 27 June. Retrieved February 7, 2007, from www.compromat.ru/main/chechnya/a.htm

Allenova, O. (2007). Pravoverny putinets [A faithful Putinite]. *Kommersant Vlast, 23*, 18 June.

Blank, S. (2001). Russia's Ulster: The Chechen war and its consequences. *Demokratizatsiya, 9*, 1.

Bogoran, I., & Soldatov, A. (2007). Kavkazskii front: novaya taktika chuzhikh oshibok [The Caucasian Front: the new tactic of others' mistakes]. *Novaya gazeta, 60*, 9 August.

Borisov, T. (2007). Ramzan Kadyrov: s voinoi pokoncheno navsegda [Ramzan Kadyrov: the war is over forever]. *Rossiiskaya gazeta*, 10 July.

Chivers, C. J. (2007). Russian official says insurgency in Chechnya has been tamed. *New York Times*, 12 February.

Cornell, S. (2002). Autonomy as a source of conflict: Caucasian conflicts in theoretical perspective. *World Politics, 54*, 245–276.

Dudayev, U. (2007). Upsurge of fighting in Chechnya. IWPR's *Caucasus Reporting Service, 400*, 12 July.

Dunlop, J. B. (2006). *The 2002 Dubrovka and 2004 Beslan hostage crises: A critique of Russian counter-terrorism*. Stuttgart: ibidem-Verlag.

Franchetti, M. (2006). In the torture cell of Chechnya's tyrant. *The Sunday Times*, 30 April.

Franchetti, M. (2007). Chechnya: video evidence of torture. *The Sunday Times*, 3 June.

Fuller, L. (2004). Look back in anger – ten years of war in Chechnya. *RFE/RL Features*, 11 December.

Fuller, L. (2006). Chechnya: Premier seeks to change his image. *RFE/RL Features*, 19 May.

Gall, C., & de Waal, T. (1997). *Chechnya: A small, victorious war*. London: Pan.

German, T. (2003). *Russia's Chechen war*. London: RoutledgeCurzon.

Krutikov, Y. (2006). Chechnyu sdast preemnik Putina [Chechnya will be surrendered by Putin's successor]. *Prognosis.ru*, 17 March. Retrieved January 10, 2007, from www.prognosis.ru.html?id=382

Lanskoy, M. (2003). Chechnya's internal fragmentation. *The Fletcher Forum of World Affairs, 27*, Summer/Fall, 185–205.

Latynina, Y. (2007). Fugasnoe samoderzhaviye [High-explosive autocracy]. *Kommersant*, 5 October.

Leahy, K. D. (2006). Kadyrov's bluff: Why Chechnya's strongman continues to test his political boundaries. *Central Asia-Caucasus Analyst*, 17 May.

Lieven, A. (1999). *Chechnya: Tombstone of Russian power*. New Haven: Yale University Press.

Liss, A. (2006). *Chechnya's gun-toting strongman, 26 November*. Retrieved September 17, 2006, from http://news.bbc.co.uk/1/hi/world/europe/4470784.stm

Markedonov, S. (2006). Terror zakonchil'sya. Zabud'te [The terror is over. Forget it]. *APN Mneniya*, 1 February. Retrieved September 25, 2006, from www.apn.ru/opinions/article9559.htm

Markedonov, S. (2007). Ramzan solntselikii [Ramzan – Radiant sun]. *APN Publikatsii*, 9 April. Retrieved April 10, 2007, from www.apn.ru/publications/article16854.htm

NEWSru.com, (2005). *Pochti polovina sotrudnikov militsii Chechnyi byvshiye boyeviki: 7 tysyach chelovek [Almost half of those serving in Chechnya's police force are former fighters: seven thousand persons]*, 21 October. Retrieved September 25, 2006, from www.newsru.com/russia/21oct2005/chechnya.html

Osborn, A. (2006). Ramzan Kadyrov: the Warrior King of Chechnya. *The Independent*, 4 January.

Politkovskaya, A. (2007). Inside the Dragon's Lair. *The Guardian*, 20 March.

Regnum.ru, (2007). Ramzan Kadyrov – budushchy president Rossii? Obzor chechen-skikh SMI s 15 po 31 marta 2007 goda [Ramzan Kadyrov – future president of Russia? Review of Chechen media from 15 to 31 March 2007]. Retrieved July 16, 2007, from www.regnum.ru/news/806101.html

Remizov, M. (2006). Chechenskuyu vitrinu 'razvitogo feodalizma' pora zakryvat [It is time to close the Chechen shop window of 'developed feudalism']. *APN Kommentarii*, *51*, 15 September. Retrieved September 17, 2006, from www.apn.ru/news/article10390.htm

RFE/RL (Radio Free Europe/Radio Liberty) (2006, 9 October). *Anna Politkovskaya's last interview*. Retrieved March 11, 2007, from www.rferl.org/featuresarticle/2006/10/fc088b08-0cbd-4800-b2ff-f00f5494fa5e.html

Russell, J, (2005). A war by any other name: Chechnya, 11 September and the war on terrorism. In R. Sakwa (Ed.), *Chechnya: from the past to the future* (pp. 239–264). London: Anthem.

Russell, J. (2007). *Chechnya: Russia's 'war on terror'*. Abingdon: Routledge.

Schmid, A. (2004). Frameworks for conceptualising terrorism. *Terrorism and Political Violence, 16*, 197–221.

Sikevich, Z. (1999). Etnichesaya nepriyazn' v massovoi sosnanii rossiyan (Ethnic hostility in the mass consciousness of Russians). In G. Vitkovskaya, & A. Malashenko (Eds), *Neterpimost' v Rossii: stariye i noviye fobii* [Intolerance in Russia: old and new phobias] (pp. 99–12). Moscow: Carnegie.

Souleimanov, E. (2005). Chechnya, Wahhabism and the invasion of Dagestan. *Middle East Review of International Affairs, 9*, 48–71.

Stepanova, E. (2003). *Anti-terrorism and peace-building during and after conflict*. Stockholm: SIPRI.

Sukhov, I. (2005). Chechensky ochag [Chechen home fire]. *APN Proyekt*, 16 August. Retrieved September 17, 2006, from www.apn.ru/publications/article1519.htm

Vachagaev, M. (2005). The role of Sufism in the Chechen resistance. Jamestown Foundation's *Chechnya Weekly*, 6.

Voronov, V. (2006). Chtoby tol'ko v spinu ne strelyali [So long as they don't shoot you in the back]. *Sovershenno Sekretno* [Top Secret], January. Retrieved February 7, 2007, from www.compromat.ru/main/chechnya/kadyrovramnach.htm

Walsh, N. P. (2005). Biggest mosque for Grozny. *The Guardian*, 4 August.

Zartman, I. W. (2005). Need, creed and greed in interstate conflict. In C. J. Arnson, & I. W. Zartman (Eds), *Rethinking the economics of war: The intersection of need, creed, and greed*. Baltimore: Johns Hopkins.

13

From 7/7 to 8/10: Media Framing of Terrorist Incidents in the United States and United Kingdom

Mary Brinson and Michael Stohl

Synopsis: Communication and media are as important to the terrorist and the government as the actual act of violence itself. Therefore analysis of news coverage and its implications are crucial for counterterrorism efforts. This paper consequently explores media framing of terrorist incidents and patterns of indexing in both the United States and United Kingdom. The study looks at several newspapers within these countries from the years of 2005 and 2006. Specifically, it investigates coverage during this time period concerning both the 7/7/05 London bombings and the 08/10/06 transatlantic terror plot. The study employs CRA (Centering Resonance Analysis) to evaluate the frames chosen to present the incidents in British and American media. The content analysis findings are extended to actual political elite statements and opinions in an effort to support Bennett's indexing theory and further it to a context of framing and terrorism.

On 7 July 2005 a series of three co-ordinated blasts hit London subways during morning rush hour, and less than an hour later a fourth bomb exploded on a bus. Fifty-two commuters were killed along with four suicide bombers, and around 700 people were injured. A year later on 9 August 2006 officials began arresting individuals in conjunction with an alleged transatlantic airline plot. The authorities charged that the suspects were planning to detonate liquid explosives on several flights from the United Kingdom to the United States. They reported that several airlines and up to 12 flights were targeted in the plot.

In this study we examine the continuing United Kingdom and United States press reporting on these two widely covered terror incidents. We explore how the events were framed and the implications for building public support for

---

The Faces of Terrorism: Multidisciplinary Perspectives Edited by David Canter
© 2009 John Wiley & Sons Ltd.

counterterrorist strategies that underlay the response of the authorities in the two countries to the attacks. We uncover the framing of these incidents in both mainstream British and American print outlets by using a unique semantic analysis program (CRA) which examines word influences to uncover latent clusterings of frames and themes. Whereas other content analysis methods equate word frequency with word importance, CRA employs linguistic theory concerning how people create coherence in their communication.[1]

Acts of terrorism are not only behaviours with devastating violent effects, but are also behaviours whose distinction from other acts of violence is that they are communicatively constituted. That is, the actions are intended to send an audience a message of fear and often to indicate that if policy and behaviours towards the terrorist (or those they purport to represent) do not change, more such terrorist actions will follow. The modern media, by covering the actions of the terrorist and the reactions of the authorities and the public, transmits both terrorist and government messages to the audience. Thus, the media and its reporting are central to terrorism and counterterrorism as political action.

Indeed, much of the early focus by both policy makers and scholars centred on the charge that the media, by covering acts of terrorism through its reporting, provides a boost to the terrorist by spreading both their message of fear and their political demands (see, for example, Miller, 1982; Picard, 1981; Picard, 1986). Perhaps the best-known explication of this charge was that of former UK Prime Minister Thatcher who argued that media reports provided the publicity, which were "the oxygen of terrorism". Similar charges that "journalists are the terrorist's best friend" have been levelled by scholars such as Laqueur (1999, p. 42). Such charges have focused attention on the question of whether coverage of terrorist incidents and of terrorists and their organizations should be restricted and by implication appear to assume that the coverage, simply by providing the terrorist the opportunity to 'communicate' with the public, favours the terrorist over the government. The prime minister followed her charge with restrictions on press coverage of terrorists and forbade the BBC from allowing the voice of IRA members to be aired.

Media

Framing and information flow – the sender

While Goffman (1974) was the first to specifically discuss framing, defining it as the "principles of organization which govern events – at least social ones –

---

[1] CRA program explained extensively in methods section.

and our subjective involvement in them" (p. 10), Lippmann (1922) had outlined its essentials capturing the idea in the phrase "pictures in their heads". He wrote: "the only feeling that anyone can have about an event he does not experience is the feeling aroused by his mental image of that event". Most individuals in countries of minimal historic terrorist activity do not have first-hand experience of such events and thus rely on the media (both news and entertainment) to provide the "pictures in their heads" about terrorism, and therefore the mental images that they rely on are those that have been created or in Goffman's language "framed" for them.

The study of framing, and the processes and context in which it operates, including the individual cognitive processing and the collective and structural processes which underlie and produce it have been at the heart of much media study over the past three decades. The concept of framing has metamorphosed into an integrated, complex media theory that many scholars have attempted to understand, apply, expand, and control (Entman, 1993; Gamson & Modigliani, 1971; Scheufele, 1999; Shah, Kwak, Schmierbach, & Zubric, 2004). In building upon Goffman's original concept of framing, while many different approaches and definitions have been established, perhaps none have dominated the literature as much as those of Robert Entman. Framing, according to Entman is an organizational tool, used by both framers and individuals to select, make salient, and highlight a piece of text to better understand it. Frames diagnose, evaluate, and prescribe. More specifically, "frames, then *define problems* – determine what a causal agent is doing with what costs and benefits, usually measured in terms of common cultural values; *diagnose causes* – identify the forces creating the problem; *make more judgments* – evaluate causal agents and their effects; and *suggest remedies* – offer and justify treatments for the problems and predict their likely effects" (Entman, 1993, p. 52).

Entman also discusses issues of frame dominance and frame origination. He suggests that frames can range from total dominance to total frame parity. Dominance represents one-sidedness in framing of a particular issue, and frame parity represents the existence of counter-frames (1991, 2003). In order to achieve parity, news must offer a "complete alternative narrative, a tale of problem, cause, remedy, and moral judgment" (2003, p. 418), unfortunately, "frame parity is the exception, not the rule" (p. 418). If media framing of terrorism is one-sided and without debate regarding sources, connections, implications, policies, and prescription – then individuals will be left with nothing to evaluate. The only viewpoints or symbolic images in their heads used in judgment making, are those of the dominant media frame. If the political elites succeed in filtering only their storyline through the media gatekeepers, then the news functions "ultimately to reinforce support for political leaders and the security policies they implement" (Norris, Kern, & Just, 2003, p. 1). In this situation, journalism would appear to err on the side of the government due to over-reliance on interpretations from political elites. Norris also argues that one-sided messages of terrorism will influence public opinion, how people evaluate terrorism and its actors, and perceptions of future risks and threats. "The news frame is also predicted to shape the public policy agenda, including the response to events by government officials and the security services, both directly, and also indirectly via public opinion" (Norris et al., 2003, p. 8). This argument challenges the assumption discussed above that conventional journalism errs on the side of the terrorist reinforcing the fear they intend to cause and lending them legitimacy and credibility, as well as unintentionally encouraging further incidents through a contagion effect. And as we have seen in the context of the Bush administration in the aftermath of September 11 the government frame may also serve to constitute the very definition of the problem as the media overwhelmingly adopted the language of the "global war on terror" when reporting on terrorism.

Significant previous research has demonstrated that news coverage regarding the majority of post-World War II foreign policy crises in the United States consistently presents the agendas of the political elite (Bennett, 1990). These patterns highlight journalistic gatekeeping practices in coverage of government policy (Alexseev & Bennett, 1995; Zaller & Chiu, 1996) and support what Bennett identified as indexing (1990). Bennett argues that American journalists 'index' the range of voices and viewpoints in both news and editorials according to the range of views expressed in mainstream government debate about a given topic. In reviewing media theories of framing, indexing, priming, and agenda setting, this study will explore Bennett's indexing argument that news coverage of terrorism generally indexes the range of elite opinion and combined with what Bennett has also referred to as the authority-disorder bias in news gathering (pp. 48–53).

This bias originates from the misplaced assumption that authority figures, experts, and well-placed informants know enough to offer a complete story so that reporters need not delve deeper or need not be sceptical of their informants' expertise or motives. News stories built in this way are thus likely to reflect the dominant frame of the political elites or authorities (Bennett, Lawrence, & Livingston, 2006). The result Bennett and colleagues argue with respect to the United States is that "the press has grown too close to the sources of power in this nation, making it largely the communication mechanism of the government, not the people … this is an odd situation in what may well be the freest press system in the world" (Bennett, Lawrence, & Livingston, 2007, p. 1).

Indexing can often be even more prevalent when dealing with international news and foreign policy, because journalists are more reluctant to probe further than their government sources. This leads to reluctance to criticize government foreign policies (Althaus, 2003; Bennett et al., 2006). This is the result of many influences such as economic factors, lack of access, and lack of knowledge.

Entman's cascading network activation model identifies the challenge of providing a frame parity that contrasts the elite message. This model highlights the reinforcement of agendas set, decisions made, and news stories made salient by the public's opinion toward them. The top of the model shows the government (both administrators and elites) as being the initiator of ideas, decisions, news frames. This is effectively passed down to media sources; the media takes the information, and possibly adds organizational biases, personal opinions to the information or possibly does this by omission or overemphasis of certain topics/ideas. These are put into frames (news stories, words) in which the public engages.

Thematic vs. Episodic Framing and Generic vs. Issue Specific – The Message

This study analyses the news coverage of terrorist events in terms of both thematic and episodic coverage. These categorizations help understand the reasoning behind changes in frames of a particular incident. Episodic framing is generally more concrete, descriptive coverage of a specific event or individual circumstance, whereas thematic framing is more abstract and generally requires interpretive analysis (Iyengar, 1991). Iyengar and Simon discuss patterns of framing in foreign policy and the research supports the idea that thematic reporting tends to influence individuals to hold societal conditions and public policies responsible as opposed to episodic coverage which tends to influence them to think in terms of individuals. Thematic coverage tends to be broader in scope, often including policy debate, background info, trends, consequences (Iyengar & Simon, 1993). Episodic coverage is more prevalent immediately following an event being covered, while thematic coverage generally becomes more evident after some time has passed. Although this study analyses both episodic and thematic time periods, it is the thematic frames that become more dominant in the period between the two major events that anchor the study.

Looking at the combinations of Entman's cascading model and Bennett's indexing theory, it is easy to see how news coverage of terrorism would 'err' on the side of governments, "due to over-reliance upon the framework of interpretation offered by public officials, security experts and military commentators, with news functioning ultimately to reinforce support for political leaders and the security policies they implement" (Norris et al., 2003, p. 1).

This leads to the following hypotheses:

H1: If political elites frame terrorism primarily as an international threat, the media reporting will produce a higher number of semantic network clusters connecting terrorist activity with words of more international scope as well as higher influence values on words of international scope, than the media reporting in countries where the political elites frame terrorism as having domestic roots.

H2: If political elites frame terrorism primarily as having domestic roots, media reporting will produce a higher number of semantic network clusters connecting terrorist activity with words of more domestic scope as well as higher influence values on words of domestic scope, than the media reporting in countries where the political elites frame terrorism as an international threat.

We will explore these hypotheses across distinct time periods in the immediate aftermath of the events and in the 'quiet' period between them, and through the filters of both conservative and liberal newspapers in both the United Kingdom and the United States.

Methods

Sample

News articles from mainstream newsprint press were included from both countries. Both conservative and liberal papers are utilized in each market. In the US market, *The New York Times*, the *Los Angeles Times* and *The Wall Street Journal* are included and in the UK market, *The Times* of London, *The Guardian* and *The Independent*.

Articles were searched through online university access, and were qualified by including the search terms of 'London', 'terror', and either 'Muslim' or 'Islam' in the headline or first paragraph of the article. In the London Times articles we allowed for London to appear anywhere in the article, in order to include relevant texts that were not responding to previous qualifiers. All texts were converted into text files and run through the CRA file generator with a processing rules sheet eliminating the inclusion of meaningless words such as: Mr, photographer, illustration, photo and caption. The program automatically ignores words such as 'the', 'it', and 'a'. Duplicate files were deleted from the study as well as any unrelated stories and short, inconsequential blurbs that contained too few words to be effectively run through the CRA system.

Articles were drawn from the years 2005 and 2006 in their entirety. These dates were chosen in order to cover both episodic and thematic news coverage surrounding the terrorism incidents including the London subway bombing in July 2005 and the British airline plot of August 2006.

In order to review both active periods (periods of time directly following a major terror incident) and quiet periods (down time between major terror incidents), we break down the two-year period into several increments. The first period from 1 January 2005 – 6 July 2005 is included as the quiet period leading up to the first incident. The second period included is the week following the London subway bombings (7 July 2005 – 14 July 2005). We also included the month following (7 July 2005 – 7 August 2005) as a separate analysis. The next quiet period included is 7 August 2005 – 10 August 2006. Then the week and month following the London terror plot (11 August 2006 – 18 August 2006 and 11 August 2006 – 11 September 2006). Finally, the final quiet period of 11 September 2006 – 31 December 2006 is included.

There are 241 texts included in the American papers and 392 texts within the British articles.

Procedures, CRA

Centering Resonance Analysis (CRA) was performed on newspaper articles in both the United States and London from 1 January 2005 through 31 December 2006. Whereas other content analysis methods equate word frequency with word importance, CRA is based on linguistic theory concerning how people create coherence in their communication. Crawdad Text Analysis System (Crawdad) is software that performs this qualitative analysis and text mining. CRA visualizes a text as a network of interconnected words, and generates a CRA network, which contains information, influence, and coherence about the contents of the text. Crawdad then provides a variety of analytical and text mining functions so that the information and themes in the texts can be explored (Corman, Kuhn, McPhee, & Dooley, 2002).

Three applications of CRA are utilized in this study: The first is *Visualizer*, which creates the CRA network and a tabular summary of influential words for one or more files. Word influence is calculated based on the structural position of the word within the CRA network. Influence scores (I) of a word (i) are a function of between-centredness, represented by the following equation: $I_i^T = \dfrac{\sum_{j<k} g_{jk}(i)/g_{jk}}{[(N-1)(N-2)/2]}$; where $g(jk)$ is the number of shortest paths connecting the j and k words, $g(jk)(i)$ is the number of those paths containing the word i, and N is the number of words in the network. This equation calculates pairs of words, searching every time another given word appears between them (Corman et al., 2002).

The second application administered is *Comparator*, which uses this information to find common and unique words and clusters between two sets of texts and assesses their importance in the overall structure. Finally, the third technique utilized is the *Classifier*, which automatically sorts texts into clusters based on similarity of content. Classifier provides a versatile interactive modelling window so you can search the entire solution space, and generate concept maps of each cluster (Corman & Dooley, 2006).

Results

Our results show support for indexing theory, and also highlight different aspects of framing that appear throughout the texts. In reviewing the CRA analysis results we found news clusters or frames that support President Bush and Prime Minister Blair's opinions on those responsible for terrorist incidents. We discovered that these frames are also more evident and have higher word influence values in specific situations such as ideology of source (liberal vs. conservative), and time period of media coverage (episodic vs. thematic). The following discussion analizes the different frames found in the CRA maps, comparing the different countries, time periods and political ideologies of the source.[2] These findings are extended to actual statements from the administration reflecting these frames and thus supporting Bennett's indexing theory.

US vs. British press coverage

While Mr Blair and Mr Bush have co-operated most closely on Iraq and the war on terrorism, their communication of messages regarding these issues and policies can be quite different in the immediate aftermath of a terror attack. These differences are reflected both in direct statements from the two administrations as well as in the news coverage during these time periods. President Bush was in the UK at the time of the 7/7 attacks awaiting the opening of the G8 summit. This provides President Bush with a convenient platform to further his "war on terror frame". In Mr Bush's view, the bombings in London illustrate themes he has been pushing hard recently: that the struggle against radical Islamist terrorists has not abated and that the violence in Iraq merely illustrates the many forms it can take. "The war on terror goes on", Mr Bush said in brief comments at the opening session of the G8 summit, which was taking place at the time of the attacks. His words echoed a speech he gave recently in Fort Bragg, NC, when he sought to rekindle domestic support for the US engagement in Iraq, which he called "the central front in the war on terror" (Block, 2005). This information highlights how framing terrorist events

[2]Number of articles included per breakdown: US Episodic 1 – 100; US Episodic 2 – 50; US Thematic – 82; UK Episodic 1 – 99; UK Episodic 2 – 63; UK Thematic – 144. More detail in methods sections.

as international in origin would benefit the Bush administration. The international, external frame would help create support for the 'war on terror', often connected to involvement in the Iraq war, as exemplified above. He is quick to let the public know that al-Qaeda is the root cause. On 11 July, Bush's homeland security advisor, Fran Townsend, said that British and American authorities were looking for a key al-Qaeda operative in Europe tied to past international terror attacks (Wilkinson, 2005). Perhaps because the attacks occurred on British rather than American soil, Mr Bush did not appear concerned with considering whether the attack was a response to British participation in the war in Iraq.

Prime Minister Blair, on the other hand, was in a defensive position after the July 7th attacks. The incident took place on his 'soil' therefore leaving him much more vulnerable to critique. During this time period, many were already questioning his Iraq policy and this policy was soon blamed for the attacks and with the previous 3/11/05 attack in Madrid linked to Spanish participation in Iraq a parallel existed for discussion. Former foreign secretary, Sir Malcolm Rifkind stated "I have no doubt that the Iraq war has created a political vacuum in that country that al-Qaeda and other terrorists are seeking to exploit" (Grice, 2005). In a statement to the United Nations Security Council on terrorism on 14 July, Blair argued that "the root cause therefore is not a decision on foreign policy … it is a doctrine of fanaticism, and we must unite to uproot it … by taking action against those who incite, preach or teach this extremism, wherever they are, in whichever country, and also by eliminating our own ambivalence …" (Blair, 2005). In this statement he disconnects the act from Iraq, but also does not make specific allegations against al-Qaeda as President Bush does in his statements.

These contrasting viewpoints voiced during the immediate, episodic periods are maintained throughout the thematic periods as well. Bush continues to hold al-Qaeda responsible while the Blair administration is extremely cautious about this connection in its announcements. By making connections to al-Qaeda and larger, international networks, Blair would increase accusations that he caused Britain to become more susceptible to terrorism by his involvement in the Iraq war. Instead he frames the attacks as random, domestic terror incidents.

The House of Commons Intelligence Report argues that "this was an attack by a cell of four home-grown terrorists. There is no evidence that they were connected to a wider network, no firm evidence that they were radicalized by anybody else, no evidence of any al-Qaeda connection. These people were, we are told, most probably self-radicalized. The attacks were planned in isolation and the method of the attacks was relatively unsophisticated" (British Government, 2006).

If indexing theory were supported, we would expect to see these viewpoints reflected in our CRA influential word maps. The maps should show the US press clusters including words of international scope, words relating to al-Qaeda and the war on terror. On the other hand, we would expect this to be less prevalent in the majority of the British press clusters. And, in fact, this is the case. The most significant indicator of indexing found in the US and UK press is that al-Qaeda remains a constant influential term in all of the US maps. However, in the British maps it is non-existent. In each breakdown analysis of US media, whether it is thematic coverage, episodic coverage, liberal sources, or conservative sources, or all US press combined – al-Qaeda remains influential. In one episodic time period of UK coverage (7 July 2005–7 August 2005), al-Qaeda appears, but it is not influential enough to appear in the mapping structure, and it makes no other appearances. This is reflective of our previous discussions of the differing viewpoints. In general the US maps include words of much more international scope, while the British press seems to focus more on local issues relating to laws and community. (Maps 1 and 2 here)

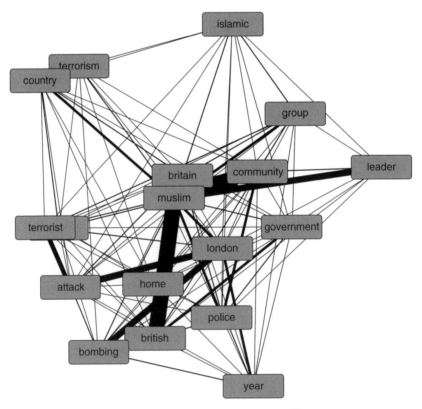

Map1 UK thematic period (August 7, 2005–August 10, 2006)

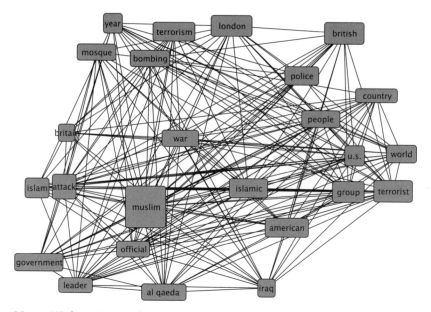

Map 2 US thematic period (August 7, 2005–August 10, 2006)

Some of the more influential words found in the US press maps are: *Islam – country – terrorism – officials – US security – Pakistan – Bali – bombing*, clearly indicators that the US press often discusses international issues surrounding the incidents. We also see these international thematic clusters in the summary below such as *al-Qaeda – US – security – Italian – Pakistan*, and *Bali – bombing*, connecting the event to other terrorist events and larger terror networks and attacks.

In contrast to this, in the British press, during the thematic period between incidents, local, event-driven episodic themes appear. Some of the more influential words found are: *Muslim – police – British – Britain – London – people – community*. There are specific references to the *Forest Gate* raid, and one specific cluster continues to appear throughout, that of *community – police – minority*. Sometimes *London, neighbourhood* or *people* are significant, but generally this theme of local, domestic origins remains constant. It is very rare to see *Iraq* appearing as influential in any of the British time segments.

There are some interesting differences when the articles are filtered according to source ideology. The newspapers categorized as more 'conservative' seem to more strongly reflect President Bush and Prime Minister Blair's frames than the liberal papers. In the United States, we categorize the liberal papers as the *Los Angeles Times* and *The New York Times* and the conservative source as *The Wall Street Journal*. In the British papers, the London Times is categorized as more conservative while *The Independent* and *The Guardian* are more

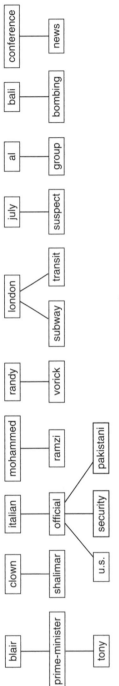

Chart 13.1. Thematic period (8 August 2005–9 August 2006) – US press clusters[4]

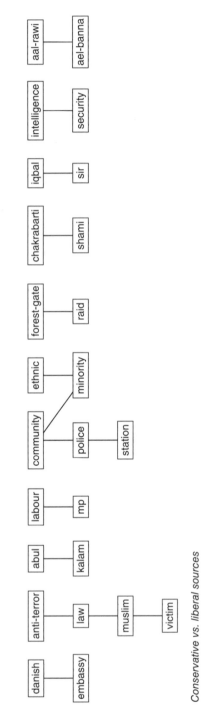

Conservative vs. liberal sources

Chart 13.2. Thematic Period (8 August 2005–9 August 2006) – British press clusters

liberal. Significant differences were found between the liberal and conservative papers. Neither British nor US conservative maps include any mention of *Iraq*. In the US conservative, thematic coverage, the term *US* is central connected to *terrorist attack, Islamic group, al-Qaeda, Islamic world*, and *war – terrorism*. This is a direct reflection of Bush statements made throughout the episodic and thematic time periods. However, in the UK conservative thematic coverage, *government* is central, connected to *Pakistan, Islamic* and *community*. Where the word Pakistan appears in these reports it appears most often as a modifier for the origins of the suspects rather than in the context of a discussion on the nation of Pakistan.

In the liberal papers, the US thematic coverage is significantly different from the conservative coverage. *Leader* is the central term, surrounded by *UK* and *US*, connected to *terrorism, Islam, Iraq war*, and *al-Qaeda*. This may represent a dissenting position to Bush coming from the liberal papers, possibly reflecting the beginnings of elite dissensus in which questions arose as to the responsibility of Blair and Bush because they had chosen to go to war in Iraq. *Britain, war,* and *Iraq* also appear in the British liberal papers. The thematic coverage of the liberal UK papers focuses on the community theme with no international mentions.

Thematic vs. Episodic time periods

As stated previously, thematic framing consists of abstract themes, often broader in scope, and generally requires interpretive analysis. Episodic framing is more concrete, descriptive coverage of a specific event (Bennett, 1990). The one-year time period after the London subway bombings and before the British airline plot, represents a thematic time period where we can see thematic implications of the influential words and clusters. The month immediately following both the July 7th attack and the August 10th transatlantic airline plot represent episodic time period. However, episodic and thematic type coverage are not limited to their subsequent time periods. For example, in thematic US maps, we see these international thematic clusters such as *al-Qaeda – US – security – Italian – Pakistan*, and *Bali – bombing*, but there also exist lingering episodic influential words such as *London – subway – transit*, and *July – suspect*.[3] These types of descriptive event words are common in episodic coverage.

The British episodic chart during this period is very localized with two main clusters. The first focuses on the Muslim community (possibly reflecting the local discontent in Muslim British neighbourhoods). Words with high influence include: *Muslim – British – Islamic – community – people – leader – government*. The second cluster contains episodic information, focusing on

[3] For more detailed mapping structures, see figure captions section.

THEMATIC DATES (08/07/05–08/10/06)

	US Articles	UK Articles	US + UK Articles
Conservative	No mention of *Iraq*. *US* is central, connected to *terrorist attack*, *Islamic group*, *al-Qaeda*, *Islamic world* and *war – terrorism*.	No mention of *Iraq*. No *al-Qaeda*. *Government* is central connected to *Pakistan*, *Islamic*, and *community*.	No mention of *Iraq*. *Terrorist* is top/centre connected to *attack*, *Pakistan*, *Britain*, *American government*, and *war – terror*.
Liberal	*Leader* in centre of map. Connected to *US* and *UK*. *Terrorism*, *Iraq war*, *Islam*, and *al-Qaeda* stem from *leader*.	*Community* a strong theme, i.e. *people* and *home*. No mention of *Iraq*. No international terms.	*Britain – government* are central. Connected to *leader, terrorist, country,* and *American*.
Conservative + Liberal	*Al-Qaeda* highly influential	Local issues focus, i.e. *Anti-terror law, Muslim – victim, community – ethnic – minority*. No mention of *al-Qaeda*	Same as thematic maps except *government* is central influential term. *Community* a central theme. *Iraq war* somewhat central, connected to *terrorism, government* and *US*.

Chart 13.3.

more specific details of the attack, influential words including: *attack – London – bombing – bomber – terrorist – bomb – suicide – Thursday.*

Iyengar also argues that episodic coverage is more likely to produce a sense of individual responsibility versus a larger societal responsibility generally found in thematic coverage. His study on poverty showed that episodic coverage resulted in people holding the individual responsible while the thematic coverage resulted in people holding society or the government responsible (1991). When we combined all US and UK coverage during the given episodic and thematic time periods, an interesting pattern was discovered. As the number of words in this extensive file is so large, the influential words are relatively generic including the most common words we have seen throughout the analysis such as *community, terrorism, government, attack*, etc. However, the central influential word connecting all others in the first episodic period is *people*. The thematic period remains nearly identical except *people* disappears and is replaced by the word *government*. Finally when we return to the second episodic period, the word *people* emerges again as the central term. This assumption would require further investigation, but could possibly represent this framing concept of individual versus a larger responsibility as proposed by Iyengar.

Conclusions

The most significant indicator of indexing found in the US and UK press is that al-Qaeda remains a constant influential term in all of the US maps. However, in the British maps it is non-existent. In each breakdown analysis of US media, whether it is thematic coverage, episodic coverage, liberal sources, or conservative sources, or all US press combined – al-Qaeda remains influential. In contrast to this, in the British press, during the thematic period between incidents, local, event-driven episodic themes appear. In general the US maps include words of much more international scope, while the British press seems to focus more on local issues relating to laws and community.

There are some interesting differences when the articles are filtered according to source ideology. The newspapers categorized as more 'conservative' seem to more strongly reflect President Bush and Prime Minister Blair's frames than the liberal papers but these differences are most clearly found in the period between the two events when more 'reflective' articles are presented.

Thus, in general, the findings of this study support Bennett's indexing theory, and extend the analysis to the frames presented. Previously, Alexseev and Bennett have found that the UK and US elite press, when concerning issues of national security, generally voice the opinions of the political elite (1995). In this study we find that when covering incidents and the issue of terrorism, not only are the elite press providing significant voice for government

EPISODIC DATES (07/07/05–08/07/05; 08/10/06–09/10/06)

	US Articles	UK Articles	US + UK Articles
Conservative	High influence words include *al-Qaeda*, and *Pakistan*, and *Islamic group* all connected.	*Group* is central term connected to *al-Qaeda, Pakistan, Islamic, bombing,* and *British.*	*Al-Qaeda, Pakistan,* and *Islamic* all appear influential.
Liberal	Humanistic terms, i.e. *Human rights, American Muslims, Islamic community.* No mention of *Pakistan* or *al-Qaeda. Britain – war* is influential. *Iraq* influential but at bottom of map.	No mention of *al-Qaeda* or *Pakistan.*	No mention of *al-Qaeda, Pakistan* or *Islamic.*
Conservative + Liberal	*Al-Qaeda* highly influential. No mention of *Iraq. Madrid* and *September 11* connection.	*Iraq* somewhat central. *Al-Qaeda* not influential to show on maps.	Same as thematic maps except *people* is the central influential word. *Community* a central theme.

Chart 13.4.

positions, they are also presenting that voice within the particular frames that their respective governments provide for both the events as they occur and how the issue is considered during the quiet periods. In regard to our original question, this study suggests that the media coverage in these particular situations, seems to 'err' on the side of the government, by creating frames in the news supportive of the government position, as opposed to providing the terrorists with the 'oxygen' they seek to have their message prevail. Because communication and media are as important to the terrorist and the government as the actual act of violence itself, analysis of news coverage and its implications are crucial for counterterrorism efforts.

In the light of this analysis, and support for our hypotheses, further investigation regarding public response would increase the importance of these findings. Implications for counterterrorism efforts should be further studied by evaluating the measures that individuals are willing to tolerate depending on how terrorism is framed. We would expect, for example, a frame which characterized the threat of terrorism as originating within the country but from 'outgroup' immigrant communities to produce different tolerances for invasions of civil liberties than frames which did not identify particular 'outgroups' or those that identify foreigners (al-Qaeda or the Global Network of Terror). We would also expect that the frames presented by the two governments represented in this study would lead to different approaches to counterterrorism policy within their societies in general. Having identified the source of the problem as coming from within the Pakistani community in London, UK counterterrorism efforts have emphasized building ties between the immigrant community and the local police while US efforts seek the external causes.

This study focused on the elite print press. Analysing national televised news in both countries would provide an interesting addition to this study. In general television news provides much less depth than in the stories presented by the newspapers but in our current period is used more frequently as a news source than newspapers. A comparison of the frames and the indexing between the two media on this issue would be useful and the differences in impact explored in terms of its influence on approval for counterterrorism policies should be pursued. In addition, as the numbers of individuals who receive their news via podcast is expanded the depth of coverage is likely to diminish even further and the impact of the frames established should increase even more.

References

Alexseev, M. A., & Bennett, W. L. (1995). For whom the gates open: News reporting and government source patterns in the United States, Great Britain, and Russia. *Political Communication, 12*, 395–412.

Althaus, S. L. (2003). When news norms collide, follow the lead: New evidence for press independence. *Political Communication, 20*, 381–414.

Bennett, W. L. (1990). Toward a theory of press-state relations in the United States. *Journal of Communications, 40*, 103–125.

Bennett, W. L., Lawrence, R. G., & Livingston, S. (2006). None dare call it torture: Indexing and the limits of press independence in the Abu Ghraib scandal. *Journal of Communication, 56*, 467–485.

Bennett, W. L., Lawrence, R. G., & Livingston, S. (2007). *When the press fails: Political power and the news media from Iraq to Katrina.* Chicago: University of Chicago Press.

Blair, T. (2005, 14 September). *Statement to United Nations Security Council on terrorism.* Retrieved October 31, 2007, from www.number10.gov.uk/Page8191.

Block, R. (2005). US raises terror alert for transit. *The Wall Street Journal*, 8 July.

British Government (2006, May). *House of Commons Intelligence Report.*

Corman, S., & Dooley, K. (2006). Crawdad Desktop 2.0.

Corman, S. R., Kuhn, T., McPhee, R. D., & Dooley, K. (2002). Studying complex discursive systems: Centering resonance analysis of communication. *Human Communication Research, 28*, 157–206.

Entman, R. M. (1991). Framing U.S. coverage of international news: Contrasts in narratives of the KAL and Iran air incidents. *Journal of Communication, 41*, 6–27.

Entman, R. M. (1993). Framing: Toward clarification of a fractured paradigm. *Journal of Communication, 43*, 51–58.

Entman, R. M. (2003). Cascading activation: Contesting the White House's frame after 9/11. *Political Communication, 20*, 415–432.

Gamson, W. A., & Modigliani, A. (1971). *Untangling the cold war.* Boston: Little Brown.

Goffman, E. 1974. *Frame Analysis.* Boston: New England University Press.

Grice, A. (2005). Bomber's video: Reaction: 'No excuse' for speaking in the name of Islam, says Straw. *The Independent*, 3 September.

Iyengar, S. (1991). *Is anyone responsible? How television frames political issues.* Chicago: University of Chicago Press.

Iyengar, S. & Simon, A. News coverage of the Golf crisis and public opinion: A study of agenda-setting, priming, and framing. *Communication Research, 20*, 365–383.

Laqueur, W. (1999). *The new terrorism.* Oxford: Oxford University Press.

Lippmann, W. (1922). *Public Opinion.* New York: Free Press.

Miller, A. (Ed.) (1982). *Terrorism, the media, and the law.* Dobbs Ferry, NY: Transnational.

Norris, P., Kern, M., & Just, M. (2003). Framing terrorism. In P. Norris, M. Kern, & M. Just (Eds), *Framing terrorism.* New York: Routledge Press.

Picard, R. G. (1981). The journalist's role in coverage of terrorist events. In O. A. Alali, & K. K. Eke (Eds), *Media coverage of terrorism: Methods of diffusion* (pp. 40–62). Newbury Park, CA: Sage Publications.

Picard, R. G. (1986). News coverage as the contagion of terrorism: Dangerous charges backed by dubious science. *Political Communication and Persuasion, 3*, 385–400.

Scheufele, D. A. (1999). Framing as a theory of media effects. *Journal of Communication, 49*, 103–122.

Shah, D. V., Kwak, N., Schmierbach, M., & Zubric, J. (2004). The interplay of news frames on cognitive complexity. *Human Communication Research, 30*, 102–120.

Wilkinson, T. (2005). The bombings in London. *The Los Angeles Times*, 11 July.

Zaller, J., & Chiu, D. (1996). Government's little helper: U.S. press coverage of foreign policy crises, 1945–1991. *Political Communication, 13*, 385–405.

14

Cyberterrorism: The Emerging Worldwide Threat

Amanda M. Sharp Parker

Synopsis: The possibilities for cyberterrorism and its distinctions from cyber crime are examined. The particular threats posed by the emerging technical possibilities are discussed and the need for these to be taken seriously emphasized. Concerted international co-operation is necessary to combat this threat because the special quality of this form of terrorism is that it is not housed in any one country.

Introduction

Cyberterrorism: the convergence of cyberspace and terrorism (Denning, 2000). As terrorists continue to look for new ways to target the population, it is necessary to recognize that every aspect of our society is vulnerable to a cyberterrorism attack. This includes our critical infrastructures, some of which the United States Government has warned may be increasingly vulnerable to cyberterrorism (United States Department of State (USDOS), 2003).

It is evident that there is no one universal definition of terrorism. Governments, researchers and practitioners have argued and proposed multiple definitions of terrorism. Many of these have similar criteria for an event to be labelled as terrorism, but there is no one agreed definition. The same is true for cyberterrorism. Cyberterrorism is a fairly recent phenomenon so there are far fewer definitions; however, there is no one agreed conceptualization. Based on the research by Denning (2000), Vatis (2001), Conway (2002), Pollitt (2004) and definitions by the United States Government, cyberterrorism will

The Faces of Terrorism: Multidisciplinary Perspectives Edited by David Canter
© 2009 John Wiley & Sons Ltd.

be conceptualized as 'a premeditated criminal act or actions; political, social or religious in nature, against information, computer systems, computer programs, and/or data which results in violence against or severe harm caused to civilians, by sub-national groups or clandestine agents'.

Prior to the 11 September 2001 terror attacks in New York, Virginia and Pennsylvania (9/11 attacks from here on), the United States Government had acknowledged America's vulnerability to cyberterrorism. In the document *Cyberterror, Prospects and Implications*, the government outlined three levels of cyberterror threats: simple-unstructured, advanced-structured, and complex co-ordinated (Center for the Study of Terrorism and Irregular Warfare, 1999). It is also imperative to mention that the government failed to recognize the severity of the damage that could result from a cyberterror attack. In this report, it is documented "cyberterror does not have the potential to produce mass casualities" (Center for the Study of Terrorism and Irregular Warfare, 1999). This is a gross underestimation of the damage that cyberterrorism could produce.

Although governments around the world have become increasingly aware of the potential threat of cyberterrorism, the fact that a cyberterror event has yet to occur makes prevention against such an attack difficult. It is known that many terrorist groups have increased their use of technology and the Internet for recruitment, fund-raising and training, but it is not known how they will use this ever-increasing technology for attacks. Problems associated with assessing the threat of cyberterrorism or preparing to defend against cyberterrorism include: a lack of knowledge regarding potential damage or extent of damage caused by such attacks, a deficient knowledge of terrorist groups' technological capabilities, and a lack of assurance as to which targets are most vulnerable to a cyberterror attack.

Terrorists' Use of Technology

Although terrorists have not yet resorted to cyberterrorism, terrorist groups are not unfamiliar with the concept of cyber attacks. Already terrorist groups such as the Tamil Tigers of Sri Lanka and Aum Shinrikyo, based in Japan, have used simulated cyber attacks against their own governments. Al-Qaeda, responsible for the 9/11 terror attacks, uses the Internet and high-tech computer systems in their organization. The United States Government believes that al-Qaeda is training its members in cyberterrorism tactics. It has seized computers from this Afghanistan-based group, and has found information about major American infrastructures contained in the computers' databases. Other terrorist groups, including Hezbollah, Hamas, Revolutionary Armed Forces of Columbia (FARC), Tamil Tigers (LTTE), the Irish Republican Army (IRA) (prior to their ceasefire), and Abu Nidal are incorporating the use of cyber tactics into their organizations for recruitment, fund-raising, training and planning future terror attacks (Cilluffo & Pattak, 2006; Kramarenko, 2004).

Omar Bakri Muhammad, a supporter of Osama bin Laden, claims that al-Qaeda has the technology to launch a cyber attack and supports this by stating "Islam authorizes the use of all technologies for offensive purposes when Islam is under attack" (Verton, 2003). His view of bin Laden supporters is that the majority of these supporters have degrees in computer science, computer programming, or information technology (IT). Furthermore, US investigators have evidence that al-Qaeda members have frequented Internet sites that provide instruction on how power, water, transportation systems and other grid systems run (Gellman, 2002). Bin Laden has publicly announced his goal of destroying the economy of capitalist states and Muhammad views the stock markets in New York, London, and Tokyo as ideal potential targets. Muhammad has been quoted, "I would not be surprised if tomorrow I hear of a big economic collapse because of somebody attacking the main technical systems in big companies" (Verton, 2003).

In June 2001, Frank Cilluffo, Special Adviser to the US President and Adviser for the External Affairs Office of US Homeland Security, was quoted as saying; "While bin Laden may have his finger on the trigger, his grandchildren may have their finger on the computer mouse" (Verton, 2003). This quote paints a chilling picture of the severity of the future of cyberterrorism.

There are many opponents of the concept of cyberterrorism who side with the idea that cyberterrorism is not a valid threat and that it cannot produce casualities. It has been stated that cyberterrorism cannot exist because "there is no terror in cyberspace" (Berinato, 2002). The director of operations for the Massachusetts Water Resource Authority (MWRA) claims that cyberterrorists would have to break through "ridiculous barriers" to carry out such an attack (Berinato, 2002).

The severity of cyberterrorism is often downplayed and tainted by the media's manipulation of the word. Often the media will use the term cyberterrorism deliberately to attract attention. For example, a Canadian headline read "Canadian boy admits cyber terrorism of his family" (Krasavin, 2002). In actuality, the police reported that the boy was responsible for emails and pranks sent to his family that reportedly "terrorized" them (Krasavin, 2002). In July 2007, an Internet report acknowledged a trial in London as the "world's first real cyberterrorism trial" (Sullivan, 2007). Three individuals were charged with using the Internet to raise funds for al-Qaeda and to help plan attacks. The trial went on for two months until the three changed their plea to guilty (Sullivan, 2007). These preceding examples are both cases of cyber crime not cyberterrorism. Moreover, only one of the two actually supported a terrorist group. Furthermore, the casual use of the term 'cyberterrorism' has painted a false picture that cyberterrorism is not a serious threat.

Table 14.1. Goals and potential targets of cyberterrorists

Country's Status	Goal	Potential Targets
Peacetime	Espionage	US Government, university research centres, private companies
Confrontation	Preparation for cyber attacks by identifying vulnerable targets	US information systems, identifying key targets, lace US infrastructure with 'back door' and other means of access
Wartime/Crisis	Attack	Critical infrastructure and economic functions. Erode the public's confidence in the county's information system

Source: (USDOS, 2003).

Richard Clarke, former special adviser to President Bush on cyber security, could not agree more. He is quoted as saying "People downplay the importance of cyber security, claiming that no one will ever die in a cyber attack, but they're wrong. This is a serious threat" (Hoopes, 2005).

After the 9/11 attacks, the United States Government re-evaluated the threat of cyberterrorism. The government published *The National Strategy to Secure Cyberspace* in 2003. This document outlined the possible goal and targets of cyberterrorists during peace, confrontation and while at war (USDOS, 2003) (Table 14.1). Although a step in the right direction towards prevention, cyber-terrorism is not occurring in the 'goal' and 'target' sections during peacetime or during confrontation. These actions illustrate cases of merely hacking or perhaps cyber crime. Only during wartime or crisis is there a potential for cyberterrorism, but the attack must cause public fear and harm as outlined by the definition of cyberterrorism to be classified as such. Simply attacking a website is not cyberterrorism.

Cyberterrorism and Cyber Crime

It is important not to confuse the two very different concepts of cyber crime and cyberterrorism, as the intent, perpetrators, and harm of each are vastly dissimilar. A terrorist who hacks into a personal bank account to steal credit card information is not a cyberterrorist, even if the funds gained are used to support terrorism. This is simply a case of hacking, or cyber crime committed by a terrorist. Although these actions could be devastating to an individual or a family, cyberterrorists aim for destruction on a higher and more fatal level.

Although cyberterrorism has yet to occur; it is a very realistic possibility in a world where technology is expanding at an astounding rate. Imagine the following scenario: a protected water plant in San Francisco; security personnel monitoring the surrounding ground and all visitors. Entrance to the classified areas requires specific documentation that is strictly enforced. Now, imagine across the ocean, a lone individual, a cyberterrorist, sitting at home, at work, or at a cyber café. This individual has managed to breach the secure computerized network of the water treatment plant and is able to modify the filtration system. The cyberterrorist has raised the level of chlorine in the water to an extremely dangerous concentration. The result of this cyberterrorism attack would be widespread including agricultural contamination, environmental

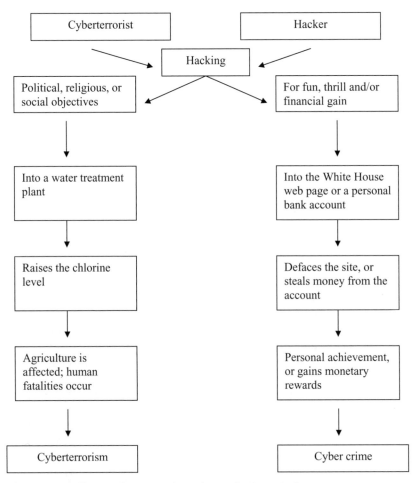

Chart 14.1. Differences between cyber crime and cyberterrorism

pollution, and most importantly, fatality for those people who consumed the water, unaware of the danger. All of this would occur, and the terrorist would never have to set foot inside the facility.

Vatis outlines other possibilities of cyber attacks (2001). Some of the forms of attacks he discusses include: web defacement, semantic attacks, domain name service attacks, distributed denial of service attacks, and worms (Vatis, pp. 14–16). Although terrorists may utilize one or all of these attacks, they do not fit the criteria of cyberterrorism; they are all forms of cyber crime. Vatis also elaborates on other forms of attack, including the manipulation of electrical infrastructures and water management, which do fit the criteria of cyberterrorism if the manipulation is conducted online and causes harm to the public. These elements need to be recognized immediately as vulnerable sections of the infrastructure (Vatis, 2001).

The main differences between cyberterrorism and cyber crime are the motivation of the perpetrators, the targets, the perpetrators' goals and the level of destruction caused. Individuals who commit cyber crimes are personally motivated, but cyberterrorists have a much deeper motivation, be it political, religious or social. Furthermore, the goal of cyberterrorists is to cause harm, death, and/or excessive damage to as much of the public as possible. The goal of cyber criminals is again personal; their goals may include monetary rewards or the personal achievement of breaking into a specific computer system (Chart 14.1).

Potential Targets of Cyberterrorism

Cyberterrorists' sole focus is not on computer systems as is inferred by the name, but on a myriad of information technologies. Cyberterrorists could attack medical systems, affecting hospital procedures and equipment, including pacemakers and life-support machines. Cyberterrorists could focus their attacks on transportation. They could affect computer chips in cars, traffic control systems, or air traffic controls. Cyberterrorists might attack electric plants, public communications systems, or banking/economic infrastructures. They could also focus the attacks on our military, including equipment and communications (Collin, 2004.). Even more vulnerable are the systems that run everyday life. Computers keep facilities we take for granted open 24 hours a day, 7 days a week. These computer systems are constantly "reading and adjusting data, opening a valve here, closing a tank there" (Hoopes, 2005; Verton, 2003). Finally, the emergency system associated with public telephone lines (e.g. the 911 emergency systems) could possibly be subjected to a cyberterror attack (Lewis, 2002). This could be detrimental for the American public, who have come to depend on the services provided by this emergency system.

The list of possible targets seems to be endless. Any infrastructure that utilizes technology is vulnerable to a cyberterror attack. In *The President's Commission on Critical Infrastructure Protection*, the United States Government has outlined a list of potential targets that may be vulnerable to a cyberterrorism attack. The targets include:

1. Information and communications
2. Electrical power systems
3. Gas and oil (production, transportation and storage)
4. Banking and finance
5. Transportation
6. Water supply systems
7. Emergency services
8. Governmental services (Embar-Seddon, 2002)

These are very general areas, but they all rely on computer systems to function at full capacity. For example, oil industries rely on both Supervisory Control and Data Acquisition (SCADA) and Energy Management Systems (EMS) to ensure their business is running at full strength. A terror attack against this industry would subsequently affect other industries (i.e. transportation). This could be devastating to a society that has come to rely on such advances (Vatis, 2001).

Many modern infrastructures rely on SCADA systems to run their industry (Giacomello, 2004). Hydroelectric dams and electronic grids (including air traffic controls) are two vulnerable industries that have the potential for being targets of cyberterror attacks. According to Michael Chertoff, former Assistant United States Attorney General, tons of explosives would be necessary to physically destroy a dam (Gellman, 2002). Trying to plant such explosives close to a dam would put authorities on high alert. However, it is possible to access the dam's controls via cyberspace. Opening the dam's floodgates could result in massive destruction and death.

As improbable as this scenario may seem, it is a very real possibility. One al-Qaeda computer, which is now in US custody, contained detailed information about a non-specified dam. The sophisticated software programs on the computer allowed for the simulated destruction of the dam (Gellman, 2002).

Furthermore, although the details of the following example have been deliberated over by the media, it is evident that cyberterrorism is not that far of a stretch. According to *The Washington Post*, in 1998, a 12-year-old hacker was playing on the computer and found himself on Arizona's Roosevelt dam's control page. Unknown to him at the time, but according to federal authorities, he had complete access to the dam's SCADA system. This included complete control of the dam's floodgates (Gellman, 2002). The child had no malicious intent in his actions, and did not realize the access he had. However, a cyberterrorist does have malicious intent. If cyberterrorists found themselves in the same position, they could easily open the floodgates, releasing the 489 trillion gallons of water held in the dam onto Arizona. It has been speculated that this would create a "flood plain encompassing the cities of Mesa and Tempe – with a combined population of nearly a million" (Gellman, p. 4).

The Maroochy Shire Case
(Maroochy Shire Council, 2006)

There are many who are still sceptical about the feasibility of a cyberterror attack or the damage that could be caused by such an attack; however, for validation they need only look back to the year 2000. Along the Sunshine Coast in Queensland, Australia, a cyber attack occurred. The only factor that differentiated this attack from cyberterrorism was the motivation behind the attack. In this case, the motivation was personal, not political, social or religious. More importantly, this was the first time in history that an individual was easily able to attack a country's infrastructure as well as the general public, using only a digital control system (Barker, 2002).

Vitek Boden, an engineer and computer expert, was able to hack into the Pacific Paradise sewage pumping station, just north of Maroochydore, Queensland in Maroochy Shire, Australia (Barker, 2002). Boden was able break into the station's mainframe and take over the controls. He did this using only a laptop computer and a two-way radio (Hughes, 2003). Over a period of two to three months Boden attempted to hack into the system 46 times (Barker, 2002). He was able to modify the sewage system's operations so that communication between computers would shut down and alarms were not being triggered. During this time, he also released millions of litres of raw sewage into the Sunshine Coast's waterways (Hughes, 2003). Boden was arrested after three months of attacks, but not before major damage had been done (Hughes, 2003). Janelle Bryant, an investigator for the Queensland Environmental Protection Agency (EPA), summed up the damage caused: "marine life died, the creek water turned black and the stench was unbearable" (Barker, p. 1).

Boden was found guilty on 30 counts of computer hacking and sentenced to 2 years of incarceration (Barker, 2002). Although Boden's actions were premeditated, they were motivated by his personal vendetta against a company who would not hire him. Had his actions been politically, socially or religiously motivated, then this case would have been the first real occurrence of cyberterrorism. This example illustrates that cyberterrorism is feasible and can cause massive physical damage, without the physical presence of a perpetrator.

The Future

Based on the preceding example, it is clearly accurate that cyberterrorism is more than just hype. It is necessary for governments to take preventative actions before terrorist organizations can use the example in Australia as a training mechanism for their own cyberterror attacks. Governments should assume that all infrastructures that rely on technology to run their operations are at risk for cyberterrorism. Once these infrastructures have been acknowledged, the vulnerabilities of the technological operations must be analysed. Specifically, governments must question: What would terrorist groups gain by attacking each infrastructure? Which infrastructure allows for the greatest amount of damage to the public? Where are the weaknesses in the infrastructures' technology? Once specific problems and/or vulnerabilities have been identified, then the government and the individual infrastructures can begin improving the security of the facility. This is especially important when the breaks in security involve the technological components of the infrastructure.

Similar to the systematic emergency response system that is in place in the event of natural disasters, a comparable system is needed for cyberterrorism. Co-operation is necessary at all levels of government. Managing disasters entails a partnership between federal, state, and local governments, the private sector, and community leadership to enact a national strategy of preparation (Gilmore, 2006). Gilmore states that "There needs to be an actual military-style response plan for the first 72 hours after an attack ... It must be a complete plan that includes everyone, where everybody knows their role and what their role is in the entire community of preparedness and response" (2006).

There are problems associated with this high level of preparedness. One of the main concerns is the cost associated with such sophisticated prevention. Just as terrorism knows no boundaries, neither does cyberterrorism. This is a major concern for countries that cannot financially afford the high-tech devices necessary to protect all critical infrastructures. Golubev identifies cyberterrorism as a two-part problem for Ukraine. On the one side, Ukraine cannot afford the technology necessary to protect all infrastructures from cyberterrorism. On the other side, these infrastructures are strategic resources, and need constant supervision (Golubev, 2005). Moreover, there is a problem with the longevity of high-tech protection. Once a hacker is able to break into the system, security upgrades are necessary, or the protection will be rendered useless.

Summary

Cyberterrorism is a growing concern in today's high technological world. The targets are vulnerable and careful measures must be taken to reduce this vulnerability. Although there are critics of the feasibility of cyberterrorism, those who do not believe that cyberterrorism is a 'real' form of terrorism, many more academics, practitioners and governments have begun to realize that major destruction and human fatalities are not only possible, but probable, via cyberterrorism. Governments need to work together to strengthen the electronic security of their critical infrastructures in order to prevent cyberterrorism. Furthermore, governments should have a systematic plan of response in the event of cyberterrorism. Finally, communication between countries is a necessity, as cyberterrorism is not limited to just one corner of the world.

References

Barker, G. (2002). Cyber terrorism a mouse-click away. Retrieved June 24, 2007, from www.theage.com.au/articles/2002/07/07/1025667089019.html

Berinato, S. (2002). The truth about cyberterrorism. *CIO Magazine*, 15 March.

Center for the Study of Terrorism and Irregular Warfare (1999). *Cyberterror: Prospects and implications.*

Cilluffo, F., & Pattak, P. B. (2006). Cyber threats: Ten issues to consider. In R. Howard, J. Forest, & J. Moore (Eds), *Homeland security and terrorism* (pp. 167–181). New York: McGraw-Hill.

Collin, B. C. (2004). *The future of cyberterrorism: Where political and virtual worlds converge.* Retrieved December 13, 2004, from http://afgen.com/terrorism1.html

Conway, M. (2002). What is cyberterrorism? *Current History*, *101*, 436–442.

Denning, D. (2000). *Cyberterrorism.* Testimony before the Special Oversight Committee on Armed Services, US House of Representatives, 23 May. Retrieved May 1, 2005, from www.cs.georgetown.edu/~denning/infosec/cyberterror.html

Embar-Seddon, A. (2002). Cyberterrorism. Are we under siege? *American Behavioral Scientist*, *45*, 1033–1043.

Gellman, B. (2002). *Cyber-attacks by Al-Qaeda feared.* Retrieved May 4, 2007, from www.washingtonpost.com/wp-dyn/content/article/2006/06/12/AR2006061200711.html

Giacomello, G. (2004). Bangs for the buck: A cost–benefit analysis of cyberterrorism. *Studies in Conflict & Terrorism*, *27*, 387–408.

Gilmore, J. (2006). *Grassroots response: Citizens taking care of citizens during disasters.* Heritage Lecture Series. Washington, DC: Heritage Foundation.

Golubev, V. (2005). *Cyberterrorism as a new form of terrorism.* Retrieved May 4, 2007, from www.crime-research.org/library/Golubev_august1.html

Hoopes, N. (2005). New focus on cyber-terrorism. *The Christian Science Monitor*, 16 August. Retrieved December 12, 2005, from www.csmonitor.com/2005/0816/p01s02-stct.html

Hughes, G. (2003). *The cyberspace invaders.* Retrieved June 24, 2007, from www.theage.com.au/cgi-bin/common/popupPrintArticle.pl?path=/articles/2003/06/21/1056119529509.html

Kramarenko, D. (2004, April 14). *Terrorism and high technologies*. Computer Crime Research Center. Retrieved March 24, 2005, from www.crime-research.org/news/ 14.04.2004/211/

Krasavin, S. (2002). *What is cyberterrorism?* Retrieved April 13, 2007, from www.crime-research.org/library/Cyber-terrorism.htm

Lewis, J. A. (2002). *Assessing the risk of cyberterrorism, cyber war and other cyber threats.* Washington, DC: Center for Strategic and International Studies.

Maroochy Shire Council (2006). *Maroochy Shire division map.* Retrieved August 15, 2007, from www.maroochy.qld.gov.au/sitePage.cfm?code=shire_map

Pollitt, M. M. (2004). *Cyberterrorism, fact or fancy?* Retrieved December 13, 2004, from www.cs.georgetown.edu/~denning/infosec/pollitt.html

Sullivan, B. (2007). Cyberterror and ID theft coverage in London. Retrieved July 7, 2007, from http://redtape.msnbc.com/2007/07/cyber-terror-an.html

United States Department of State (USDOS) (2003). *The National Strategy to Secure Cyberspace.* Retrieved April 1, 2005, from www.dhs.gov/xlibrary/assets/National_ Cyberspace_Strategy.pdf

Vatis, M. A. (2001). *Cyber attacks during the war on terrorism: A predictive analysis.* Institute for Security Technological Studies, Dartmouth College, NH.

Verton, D. (2003). *Black ice: The invisible threat of cyber-terrorism.* Emeryville, CA: McGraw-Hill Company.

15

Disengaging from Terrorism[1]

John Horgan[2]

Synopsis: Analyses of the behaviour of individual terrorists have for too long been associated with narrow and restrictive views of the potential offered by psychological perspectives. Fortunately, traditional approaches are finally giving way to fresh, exciting frameworks through which developmental analyses of the terrorist are emerging. Despite this, however, questions of how and why individuals disengage from terrorism have thus far received little systematic attention. This chapter seeks to redress this deficiency by presenting some preliminary assertions and assumptions about the nature of individual disengagement from terrorism. Despite an absence of empirically-validated information with which some of these assertions may presently be tested, this should not dissuade us from exploring a host of relevant issues. Some of the principal conclusions to emerge from this analysis are that not only is the disengagement phase of involvement as potentially complex as that which typifies 'becoming involved' in the first place, but that, ironically, it is in understanding why people leave terrorism behind that we may be able to work towards constructing more meaningful preventative measures to deter initial involvement. Furthermore, such analysis will ultimately, I argue, lead to

[1]This paper is developed from some earlier work, specifically arguments presented in J. Horgan, 'Leaving Terrorism Behind', in A. Silke (Ed.), *Terrorists, victims, society* (London: John Wiley & Sons, Ltd., 2003), and J. Horgan, *The psychology of terrorism* (London: Routledge, 2005a). This chapter also serves as a preliminary discussion point for a Research Fellowship project on disengagement, sponsored by the Airey Neave Trust in mid-2006, which the author has recently begun in order to test the hypotheses developed in these discussions. The results of this research will be published in J. Horgan (2009), *Walking Away from Terrorism: Accounts of Disengagement from Radical and Extremist Movements*, London: Routledge.
[2]I am grateful for comments from Max Taylor on an earlier draft of this paper.

The Faces of Terrorism: Multidisciplinary Perspectives Edited by David Canter
© 2009 John Wiley & Sons Ltd.

a more meaningful inclusion of analyses of individual terrorists in the development of counterterrorism initiatives.

Introduction

For the most part, strategies for responding to terrorism can be broadly categorized into those with a military focus, and those with a law enforcement focus. These categories are not necessarily mutually exclusive but have the utility of characterizing one of the main points of difference between American and European approaches to terrorism. In this regard, American approaches to terrorism typically tend to emphasize 'quasi militaristic [and] overtly proactive' stances, whereas European approaches tend to primarily emphasize policing responses (see Thachuk, 2006). Whatever the value of one approach or the other (or one *over* the other), there is gradual recognition that neither derive from any particularly clear conceptual base, nor in framing responses do either necessarily draw on empirical evidence to shape or structure intervention. Given doubts that seem to be arising out of the experience of fighting the 'war on terrorism',[3] perhaps it is time to explore alternative kinds of counterterrorism initiatives, particularly those that draw on sound conceptual bases.

One area that might be explored further relates to initiatives that address issues of psychological process in the development of the terrorist (Horgan, 2005a; Taylor & Horgan, 2006). Relatively poor progress in bridging theoretical and practical issues in counterterrorism may account for some continuing major obstacles to conceptual development in the area (the lack of empirical data with which to test our hypotheses being the second). Given this, however, we are sometimes too quick to presume a lack of relevance of existing conceptual anchor points, perhaps especially when they emerge from disciplines other than our own. The consequent danger of being without intellectual starting points when studying terrorism is that we can quickly find ourselves with other problems, becoming so absorbed by the complexity of conflicting explanations that we fail to see common themes, and more importantly, fail to focus on more practical objectives for countering involvement in terrorism.

Related to this, it ought to be pointed out that currently there is not merely confusion about what a 'psychology of terrorism' implies, but that even in some of the simplest critical analyses of the concept of the terrorist or of terrorism, a multiplicity of inconsistent and confusing uses of psychological findings emerge. Because of this confusion, some may conclude that an attempt to develop a psychology of terrorism (let alone a psychology of 'disengagement' from terrorism) is an unattainable objective. The current state of knowledge

[3] For example, see http://news.bbc.co.uk/1/hi/world/americas/5383614.stm

and debate on this issue suggests that we should attempt to develop a more sophisticated way of understanding involvement in terrorism. This may include an exploration of ways in which our understanding of psychological processes can inform and improve our understanding of terrorism (and all that that implies). We may also find that 'description' represents a more realistic objective than 'explanation', given our current conceptual and theoretical limitations.

With this in mind, the arguments based in this chapter as they relate to understanding 'disengagement' from terrorism remain tentative hypotheses, and until the relevant data are identified and these hypotheses tested, we ought to treat them as limited. However, despite these necessary limitations, the views expressed in this paper represent a different approach to understanding the terrorist to those that have traditionally characterized psychological approaches to understanding the development of the terrorist. As argued in an earlier article (Horgan, 2005a; Taylor & Horgan, 2006), acknowledging that involvement and engagement in terrorism is best thought of as a *process* brings fresh perspectives through emphasizing critical distinctions that enable us to understand the reality of involvement in terrorism as well as provide a conceptual base from which we might develop beneficial analyses. By considering involvement in terrorism in terms of *process*, Horgan, and Taylor and Horgan suggest that a number of benefits may become apparent, not least that we may begin to help to move aspects of these debates away from complex but essentially sterile discussions that postulate terrorism as some sort of abstract event. This allows us instead to focus on identifiable behaviours and their antecedents, and on expected consequences and outcomes that are associated with terrorism. Furthermore, this way of thinking attempts to capture a meaning for psychological approaches that do not depend upon narrow definitions derived from elsewhere, or from definitions that have to be so general as to be meaningless and of no real utility to anyone.

The perspective developed in Taylor and Horgan and in earlier work (Horgan, 2005a; Taylor, 1988) represents a different approach to traditional analyses of the terrorist in that there is an explicit effort made to consider the broader issue of involvement in terrorism as a process comprised of discrete phases: 'becoming' a terrorist,[4] 'being' a terrorist (understood as both (a) remaining involved and (b) engaging in terrorist offences) and 'disengaging' from terrorism (Horgan, 2005a). A critical conceptual point that is important for informing response strategies (at whatever stage they may be focused) is that the factors that impinge upon the individual at each of these phases may (a) not be necessarily related to each other, and (b) may not necessarily reflect upon each other. In other words, answering the call of one of these phases of

---

[4]The term 'becoming a terrorist' might be more usefully reinterpreted as 'initially becoming engaged and/or involved in doing terrorism'.

the process may not reveal anything useful or insightful about the other. This logic is consistent with Rational Choice perspectives in criminology, and the implications of thinking about terrorism in such a way are essentially a recognition that answering questions about why people may wish to become involved in terrorism then may have little bearing on the answers that explain what they do (or are allowed to do) as terrorists (or something else), or how they actually become and remain involved in specific terrorist operations (Taylor, 1992). Similarly, answering questions about what keeps people involved with a terrorist movement may have surprisingly little if any bearing on what subsequently sees them disengaging from terrorist operations or from the organization (and/or broader movement) altogether.

Becoming Involved in Terrorism

In attempting to make practical progress here, identifying issues relating to 'how' people become involved may be more valuable than attempting to arrive at answers on 'why' people become involved (Horgan, 2005b). Essentially then we need to shift our expectations away from the goal of arriving at a simple, and probably naïve, answer about terrorist motivation. This complexity is captured well by Taylor and Quayle (1994) who describe involvement in terrorism as:

> … in this respect no different from any of the other things that people do. In one sense, embarking on a life of terrorism is like any other life choice … To ask why an individual occupies a particular social, career or even family role is probably a deceptively easy but essentially unanswerable question. What we can do, however, is to identify factors in any particular situation that help us understand why particular life choices have been made. This same analysis applies to the development of the terrorist. (pp. 34–35)

The common personal, situational, and cultural factors across accounts that reveal why and how people become involved are usually quite broad and seem unrelated in a practical sense, in that rarely is there a clear, singular, involvement catalyst that is identifiable in that decision. Even when an individual him or herself suggests the perceived presence of such a catalyst, we ought to interpret its significance with great caution since personal accounts often obscure acknowledgement of the expected positive features of involvement. We might run the risk therefore of forming quite an incomplete and biased interpretation of an already biased account. When we are in a position to consider accounts from activists around the world, different qualities are certain to emerge, with different emphases on particular 'push' and 'pull' factors, reflecting different roles held by different people under different degrees of ideological content, social, ideological and organizational control, commitment, etc. Sometimes the extent to which evidence of the presence of these issues emerging in interviews can simply reflect the degree to which an individual activist is articulate or not, and whether he or she has verbalized openly the rationale or morality of his or her activities and other such co-incidentals. Frequently the terrorists providing the accounts will have acquired the ability to couch an explanation for their behaviour (at whatever stage of the process) into such an elaborate, spiritually or ideologically dogmatic framework that we receive very little (if any) notion of the specific limiting factors that may have impinged upon individual thinking and personal decision making that led the individual either into the movement in the first place, or further into a sense of 'increased' involvement and engagement.

Roots vs. *Routes*

When we try to develop a picture of the individual pathways and associated relevant experiences of individuals who progress into, and through terrorism, two broad trends tend to typify 'route' qualities, and these would seem to apply to all terrorists: a sense of gradual socialization into terrorism appears to be a common theme, with an initial sense of involvement seemingly characterized by gradual increases in commitment. Group factors are also centrally important in attempting to identify supportive qualities of initial engagement. Overall, we get a sense that the boundaries between apparent *degrees* of involvement are often more psychological than physical (although engaging in actual terrorist operations can bring with them a sense of ritual aimed at unambiguously solidifying commitment to the group and its activities), with a sense of premium attached not only to membership, but moreover to certain, specific roles.

There are frequently overlooked and misinterpreted positive features of increased engagement for the individual terrorist. These include the rapid acquisition of some sort of skill or skills (be they physical or psychological); an increased sense of empowerment, purpose and self-importance; an increased sense of control which appears to reflect the common effects of ideological control and self-propaganda, as well as the use of particular involvement steps as currency, which mirrors the point above about the necessary distinctions between degrees of involvement. Additionally, the individual terrorist gains a tangible sense of acceptance within the group, and in combination with this, the acquisition of real status within the broader community, which is often expressed subsequently via identification with the broader supportive community. A perceived sense of reward quite possibly represents the only common denominator across *all* potential terrorists in terms of understanding the common factors that impinge upon the wide variety of different people who engage in terrorist movements in very diverse ways.

Although it is not difficult to identify the broad socio-political preconditions for a climate that is conducive to the emergence of terrorism (Bjorgo, 2005), it remains the case that few people will be led by that climate to engage in terrorism, let alone in specific violent terrorist activity. It may be possible to identify predisposing risk factors, as Horgan (2005a, see especially ch. 4) has done, that may help us understand why this sense of *openness to engagement* is more readily found in some people than in others – even within the same group of people, all of whom may have been clearly exposed to the same assumed generating conditions to terrorism. For all terrorists in all movements, involvement is perhaps best characterized by development based on initial supportive qualities that vary in their significance for the individual, the individual group, and the relationship which both of these have with each other and with their surrounding environment (environment here refers to a broad array of competing influences, be they physical, ideological, social, etc.). The reality is that there are many risk factors for involvement (often so complex in their combination that it can be difficult to delineate them, particularly when considering practical counterterrorism initiatives) that can come to bear on an individual's intentional or unintentional socialization into involvement with terrorism.

There is one critical factor, however, that may be relevant to thinking about how disengagement initiatives might be developed: again, it relates to the initial sense of 'reward' that the recruit has about what 'being in this movement' represents. That is a very powerful motivating factor not only as far as initial recruitment is concerned but in terms of sustaining that person's commitment to the movement once a member. In practical terms, this might result in heightened status, respect, authority, both within the immediate peer group, the broader radical movement, and of course, at least as imagined by the recruit, the broader 'represented' community. The point here is that the recruit comes to feel important in what he/she do. In recognizing the group dimension to involvement in terrorism (at whatever stage the individual may be), the consequences of what that recognition implies are obvious: psychological qualities of group membership quickly become apparent for the extreme potential both to attract members as well as to bind them together via sustained commitment and engagement. Extreme conformity and strict obedience are organizational cornerstones that leaders will put in place through various mechanisms to enhance the effective maintenance of what is already a difficult, secret, and above all *illegal* movement. It follows then, that maintaining such conformity is paramount, and having a shared purpose or sense of unity and direction, which in itself is catalysed by having a clearly identifiable enemy (and its activities), facilitates this. We have also seen that the distinction between where one lies with respect to the 'initially becoming involved' and 'being involved' is in one sense as much a psychological issue as anything else, but thinking of participation in terrorist events as a possible delineation point is useful: any remaining hurdles of finally having one's identity reaffirmed within the terrorist group often comes through engagement in activity considered centrally valuable to the organization.

It is worth making one final comment on these issues. It follows from the above discussion that explanations in terms of 'root causes' (so popular in everyday political commentary on terrorism) are clearly called into question. Explanations of terrorism that seek to privilege one *kind* of explanation over another miss the essential point about conceptualizing terrorism as a process, and tend to commit the logical error of confusing causation with correlation. Although it might appear obvious, in the study of abnormal behaviour, psychologists have long recognized that some behaviours do not necessarily have a single, or even an *identifiable* cause – perhaps we need to do likewise when thinking about terrorism.

Disengaging from Terrorism

I will not discuss the phase of 'being a terrorist' as it has been examined elsewhere (Horgan, 2005a, see ch. 5), but will move directly to the final phase – disengagement. At the outset, it seems important to acknowledge that we know very little about what happens for the individual terrorist to leave terrorism behind. On behavioural issues, the research community has for far too long focused on issues to do with becoming involved, leaving a significant gap in our knowledge. A disheartening reason for this is an ambivalent perception by researchers towards issues concerning and arising from, disengagement. Many researchers assume that terrorists and their movements are somehow no longer 'relevant', or deserving of serious, urgent study, once their involvement in terrorism has ceased (or the movement has entered a ceasefire or peace process). Yet it is precisely at this phase that former terrorists are most likely to be willing to speak to researchers and grant interviews (it has never been easier than now, from a practical perspective, to speak with major figures involved in all of the Northern Irish and Colombian terrorist movements, for example, yet only a paltry handful of researchers have decided to engage these actors in this way). From a policy perspective, it is clear that understanding and encouraging disengagement could have a crucial role to play in countering extremist violence.

Before we can move towards trying to ascertain the nature of this relationship, however, and in thinking about disengagement from terrorism in general terms, there are some questions we need to answer in relation to what happens to people who leave terrorism, issues relating to what influences them to leave (either voluntarily or involuntarily), as well as the implications of such movement. Indeed, a broader issue here, and one that is especially relevant given the complexity of what 'becoming involved' seems to now suggest, concerns what we mean by 'disengaging' or 'leaving' at all. Leaving terrorism behind, either from an individual or collective perspective, might on the one hand suggest critical cognitive and social changes, in terms of abandoning the shared social norms, values, attitudes and aspirations so carefully forged while the individual was still an active member of a terrorist group – this is what is usually meant by the term 'de-radicalization'. On the other hand it might indicate some continued adherence to these values and attitudes, and engaging in some other socially relevant behaviour but no longer engaging in actual terrorist operations.

Obviously, disengagement cannot be studied in isolation. To gain a fuller understanding of how and why people leave terrorism behind we do need to consider the varied and complex reasons as to why and how people join a terrorist group in the first place, and also how and why they remain in an organization (Figure 15.1). Also, we will need to consider reasons that can inhibit or block the exit (be it *psychological* – e.g. through disillusionment with some aspect of the group – or *physical* – e.g. through apprehension by the security services, or the decision to call a ceasefire). To further complicate matters, we might think of each of these as either *voluntary* in origin (e.g. the decision that continued membership of the group is no longer as important as some overriding personal issue) or *involuntary* (e.g. an individual is forced to leave in the face of some external issue such as the reality of arms decommissioning, or some new legislative initiative, and the implications this has for organizational dissipation), or a combination, for instance in the form of an outright rejection of the group's ideals as a result of a political shift in the group's stance. And to even further complicate matters, the 'disengaged' individual may consequently (after having experienced a disengagement process) be considered as, broadly speaking, either *repentant* or *unrepentant*. Significantly, in this respect,

		Voluntary		Involuntary	
		Repentant	Unrepentant	Repentant	Unrepentant
Individual	Physical				
	Psychological				
Collective	Physical				
	Psychological				

Figure 15.1. A matrix of potential disengagement dimensions

we must also acknowledge that being 'disengaged' (in whatever expression that might emerge or be characterized) does not by any means necessarily result in de-radicalization (Horgan, in press, ch. 1).

We already then have some broad potential categories with which we can consider the influences 'pushing or 'pulling' a person to leave terrorism behind: voluntary and involuntary disengagement, through psychological and physical 'routes', that may be associated with repenting or not.

The Seeds of Psychological Disengagement

A successful terrorist movement will attract new members by creating and fostering positive perceptions about involvement. If effective, this means that people will actively seek out involvement in a terrorist movement rather than remain a passive actor in some kind of 'grooming' process. It is often the case that in earning trust, respect and a place in the terrorist movement, members (or potential recruits) will encounter psychological barriers that they must overcome or to which they must adapt. If not, the seeds of what we might term 'psychological' disengagement will already begin to set, and a variety of influences appear to directly or indirectly facilitate (or even encourage) the prospect of leaving.

The perceived or actual rewards involved in terrorist groups can include an enormous amount of excitement, status, purpose, admiration, coupled with what McCauley and Segal (1989) refer to as "mutual solidarity and feelings of comradeship", and these supportive qualities of involvement are exceptionally important, especially given the kinds of new demands facing the terrorist recruit. Indeed, given illegal underground life more generally, these features can become quite potent. The reality of balancing out the negative features of increased, sustained and focused involvement with the positive supportive qualities is rarely straightforward, however, and the negative intensity of the group is demonstrated by many accounts of members who have left the organization and have written memoirs or autobiographies. For instance, Michael Baumann (cited in Alexander & Myers, 1982), a former member of the German *2nd June Movement*, reflects on the negative influence exercised by the power of the group:

> … the group becomes increasingly closed. The greater the pressure from the outside, the more you stick together, the more mistakes you make, the more pressure is turned inward … this crazy concentration all day long, those are all the things that come together horribly at the end, when there's no more sensibility in the group: only rigid concentration, total pressure to achieve, and it keeps going, always gets worse. (p. 174)

Increased security often brings greater pressure arising from attempts to safeguard against infiltration or internal disputes. In February of 1969, Japanese police discovered 14 bodies in the snowy mountains outside Tokyo. It transpired that they had all been members of the Japanese Red Army, and had been tortured and killed by their fellow members as a result of internal squabbling over ideological issues.

While some recruits will adjust to the pressure, others do not. Again, there is little reliable data on this issue, but we do know that individual terrorists make requests to 'leave', having decided that the lifestyle is not for them. Anecdotal evidence suggests that sometimes this is not a problem, given the implicit assumption that the member will 'not talk'. Indeed the Italian Red Brigades (on which Jamieson (1989) gives a detailed examination of the factors affecting disengagement) appeared to have realized the importance of identifying probable 'drop-outs' from the outset: "when a firing group went into action, one, or at the most two, 'novices' were taken along to provide cover and to test their nerve and reliability under pressure". The Red Brigades adopted what was tantamount to a crude psychometric screening tool via assessment under extraordinary pressure.

For many facing self-doubt, however, leaving may not be so easy. After all, regardless of what stage along the 'becoming involved' and 'being involved' continuum a person lies, the organization will seek a return on their investment and a promise to keep one's mouth shut may not be enough. The leadership of the Baader-Meinhof group never hesitated to clarify this: "Whoever is in the group simply has to hold out, has to be tough" (Post, 1987, p. 310). In later stages they threatened that the only way out for any doubters would be "feet first". Similarly, Spire, a former member of the French Communist Party, describes the fear of ostracism and marginalization if one "challenges the ideology ... or the fashionable beliefs" (Spire, 1988). Spire described in detail his own attempts to rationalize "breaches of faith, oppression, and political crimes" because he felt "terrified at the thought of being marginalized by beloved fellow comrades and colleagues". Adriana Faranda of the Italian Red Brigades also reflects on the pressures associated with membership and the negative social and psychological consequences of sustained membership:

> ... choosing to enter the Red Brigades – to become clandestine and therefore to break off relations with your family, with the world in which you'd lived until the day before – is a choice so total that it involves your entire life, your daily existence. It means choosing to occupy yourself from morning till night with problems of politics, or organization, and fighting; and no longer with normal life – culture, cinema, babies, the education of your children, with all the things that fill other people's lives. These things get put to one side, ignored, because they simply do not exist anymore. And when you remove yourself from society, even from the most ordinary things, ordinary ways of

relaxing, you no longer share even the most basic emotions. You become abstracted, removed. In the long run you actually begin to feel different. Why? Because you are different. You become closed off, become sad, because a whole area of life is missing, because you are aware that life is more than politics and political work. (Jamieson, 1989, pp. 267–268)

Another significant pressure that may later catalyse the move (psychological or physical) to leave is the uncomfortable realization that the initial aspirations and personal hopes associated with membership are quite removed from the day-to-day reality of what the duties and responsibilities of this new role involve. Brockner and Rubin (1985) developed the notion of *psychological traps*, which refer to situations where an individual, having decided upon some course of action that he or she expects will return a reward (in the broadest possible sense), for example, joining a terrorist group or remaining in such a group, finds that the actual process of goal attainment requires a continuing and repeated 'investment'. This 'repeated investment', in a psychological sense, will probably be required of that individual to sustain his or her involvement, but still the achievement of the eventual goal may continue to be a very distant realization. Brockner and Rubin note that somewhere in this process will be an inevitable stage when people find themselves in a 'decisional no-man's land', facing the realization that they have made quite a substantial investment but have still not yet achieved their expected goal.

At this point, the individual is at a crossroads, and experiences a decisional crisis. The investment of time, energy and hope may seem too large (especially when combined with the intense social, group, and ideological pressures one must bear per se as a result of membership). On the other hand, withdrawal means the abandonment of what has gone before, and the individual may feel a commitment if only to personally justify the investment already made. The ensuing entrapment, Max Taylor describes, encompasses "the spiraling of commitment, so frequently seen in members of terrorist groups" (Taylor, 1988, p. 168).

Other Psychological Influences

Post (1987) highlights the fact that the group pressures can have a variety of implications for decision making within that group. Individual judgment in most decision-making groups tends to be "suspended and subordinated to the group process" (Post, 1987, p. 310). Post describes Janis' work on groupthink, the phenomenon that occurs in situations where group cohesiveness is high and the ability of the group to engage in critical decision-making processes is interfered with. In such cases, the desire of group members to portray unanimity in the context of their decision making appears to take precedence over their motivation to 'realistically appraise' alternative decisions. The group becomes blind to the possibility that its decision might not be the most effective, and ultimately this may prevent the group from attaining its goal. Post notes that there is an overwhelming sense of 'wishful thinking' in such groups, but emphasizes that the processes by which such faulty decision making can occur are quite simple: when one joins a group, the group's views become evident from discussion, and new members may seek approval by sharing those views in an attempt to display commitment to the group's ideal and thereby demonstrate loyalty.

At the same time, however, the terrorist may find that some of his or her most deeply held political ideals – the ones that played a role in influencing them to become involved in the movement in the first place – are being compromised as a result of the stifling 'climate' within the group or through the role of certain individuals within it. This can give rise to enormous dissent, whether expressed overtly or not. A good example comes from an interview conducted by the author in Northern Ireland. The following interview segment illustrates how several factors can come into play and how conformity, obedience, groupthink and the influence exerted by a minority can – eventually – lead to a change in direction for the group, and can contribute to one member's gradual disillusionment with the movement:

> The meeting was called, and we all knew there was going to be trouble. We were all told we had to be there and I'd say a lot of fellas were told they were going to be told off in front of everyone. [The leader] came in and called things to order. He went around to each of us and wanted reports. When he came to me I was last, but I had to speak up. I told him that our arms situation was in dire straits and unless we were going to do something about it quick, let alone about the lack of funds, that we were just shooting ourselves in the foot. I had the greatest faith in that man, but he had this way of not wanting to see the reality of things as they were. So I said, we need to elect a Quartermaster, and that person would have complete responsibility for the procuring of the stuff as well as managing it, you know? He wasn't pleased at that because like I said, his ideas about the organization was that it was 'grand', 'no problem' like. When the meeting ended, one of the lads caught up with me on the steps, and I never liked the [man] anyway, but he actually shook my hand! He said 'congratulations, that needed to be said'. No one else would have said it if I didn't open up my mouth.

The organization this person belonged to was the Official IRA, a movement that became defunct in the early 1970s primarily because it was unable to develop an effective political presence. This interviewee, one of the founding members of the group, left the movement and eventually emigrated:

I went to [country] for several years I was just so pissed off with the whole thing. We were originally established to espouse socialism. And I know we offended a lot of people [laughs] especially since we were simply spouting every party line that came from Moscow, but [the leader] brought the trouble on himself by not being in touch with the mood on the ground and I never really patched things up with him after that … It's miserable when you … believe in it, believe in the movement and the, ah, initial socialist ideals I suppose. I gave up my house, my car … you had people give up their farms, and for what in the end? Arguing about guns all the time because we'd no money.

This man's disillusionment developed over some time. Comparison with Alison Jamieson's interviews with Faranda reveals unmistakable similarities. Faranda described her 'dissociation' from the Red Brigades as:

… a process which matured very gradually … it's not a traumatic leap, it's more a matter of a thousand little stages. It encompasses everything though; reasoning, valuations, questions which involve not just one action, not one way of conducting the armed struggle, not one revolutionary project – everything. It involves the revolution itself; Marxism, violence, the logic of enmity, of conflict, of one's relationship with authority, a way of working out problems, of confronting reality and of facing the future … I haven't taken one huge traumatic leap. It's not as if I was one person one day and a different one the next (Jamieson, 1989, p.283).

What is significant here is that both of these accounts point to a gradual process of disengaging that appears similar to the process that characterizes involvement in terrorism in the first place. For others, however, singular cata-lytic events appear to spur a more abrupt psychological disengagement. An example of 'things having gone too far' comes from the case of Nasir bin Abbas, until recently a leading member of the Jemaah Islamiyah movement in Indonesia. Abbas' role in the movement extended to organizing and providing training for terrorists at the movement's Camp Hudabiya (which Abbas described as a "fully fledged military academy" (see Taylor, 2006), built in an area cleared out of dense jungle). While Abbas was never in doubt about his own philosophy of killing "foreign forces occupying Muslim countries like the Soviets in Afghanistan, the Americans in Iraq or the Philippine army occupy-ing ancestral lands in Mindinao", his conversion was catalysed by his decision that "killing innocent civilians – men, women and children – is forbidden". The seeds of Abbas' disengagement, he himself traced back to the Bali bomb-ings in 2002 when 202 civilians were killed. Abbas subsequently discovered that it was his former students who had participated in the attack: "I feel sorry, I feel sin … because they used the knowledge to kill civilians, to kill innocent people". Given Abbas' experiences, there are interesting parallels to draw with the work of Judge Hamoud al-Hitar in Yemen in his strategies of 're-educating' terrorists through the 'Committee for Dialogue' Programme.[5]

In summary, we can tentatively identify factors that appear to contribute to a move towards psychological disengagement:

- Negative sentiments as a result of experiencing the qualities associated with sustained, focused membership (e.g. the influence of unbearable group and organizational psychological pressures); and as a result,
- A sense of changing priorities (e.g. the longing for a social/psychological state which (real or imaginary) the member feels is lacking, or existed before membership, often a result of self-questioning but mostly following prolonged social/psychological investment as a member from which little return appears evident);
- A sense of growing disillusionment with the avenues being pursued (e.g. with the political aims (as illustrated in the Official IRA interviewee example); or with the operational tactics and the attitudes underpinning them (as illustrated by the statements of Nasir bin Abbas).

Physical Disengagement

In many ways, the reasons for what might be called 'physical' disengagement may be easier to identify. Relevant disengagement behaviours and their antecedents might be thought of as 'physical' where there is a change in the role of an individual terrorist away from opportunities to engage in violent behaviour, whether or not this move results in a lessening of commitment to the group. Often there can be physical disengagement from terrorist activity per se, but no change or reduction in ideological support (or indeed, the social and psychological control that the particular ideology exerts on the individual). Indeed, in some cases physical disengagement from terrorism (in terms of being removed from the activity of committing terrorist violence) might involve any of the following, none of which should be considered exclusive:

- Apprehension by the security services, perhaps with subsequent imprisonment (or if not, forced movement by the leadership of the member into a role whereby he or she is less likely to risk arrest);
- Forced movement into another role, for example, as a result of disobeying orders: at the very least ostracism may occur, if not outright execution, but if there is some mitigating circumstance the member may instead be pushed into another functional role;

[5] See for example of details http://www.csmonitor.com/2005/0204/p01s04-wome.html

- An increase in 'other role' activity whereby the original role becomes displaced (e.g. an area of specialization that relates directly to the commission of terrorist offences such as exploiting one's technical acumen by assisting in the preparation of equipment), or increased involvement in political activity (often as a result of imprisonment, which, ironically for some represents a final consolidation of communal identity);
- Being ejected from the movement (e.g. for improper use of arms, money, etc. or some disrespectful behaviour that warrants dismissal but not execution);
- As with psychological disengagement, a change in priorities.

The crucial difference between physical and psychological disengagement is that the terrorist may continue playing a part in the movement but may move into another role/function in order to facilitate new personal circumstances (e.g. getting married or having children, and moving into a support or ancillary role as a result); they may still continue to engage in 'terrorism'-related behaviours, but not in a direct way with respect to 'terrorist events' or operations per se. The other direction from which this role change might emerge is from the leadership, who may place a heavier emphasis on political activity in the months approaching an election. In simple practical terms, this might involve an active terrorist engaging in distributing posters or helping to organize political rallies.

A vital source from which one can formulate hypotheses relating to disengagement processes is analysis of organizational issues, as far as the terrorist leadership is concerned, both with respect to promoting engagement and inhibiting any form of (but especially psychological) disengagement. In any case, a clear priority for research will be in understanding role migration between and within members. This kind of detail can only emerge through detailed case histories, and particularly through interviews with former terrorists themselves.[6]

Implications of Leaving

The focus of this chapter so far has been on tentative attempts to identify some of the influences that might contribute to disengagement. However, a further illustration of just how complex the issue is can be found when we consider the actual implications of leaving. Terrorists who leave a movement (for

---

[6]The author, in mid-2006, began a major research project on disengagement, with the support of the Airey Neave Trust, in which members of 13 terrorist movements are being directly interviewed about their experiences of disengagement. For the results of these interviews, see Horgan (2009).

whatever reason) might not necessarily have appreciated the extent to which certain aspects of their lives will be limited thereafter. The psychological pressures that follow the former terrorist wherever he or she goes sometimes become so intense as to convince him or her into surrendering. For instance, Kuldip Singh, a former member of the Khalistan Liberation Force, surrendered to the police in 2000 for crimes committed in 1991 (Horgan, 2005a). Police reports stated that Singh's confession was spurred by his wish to start a new life following his trial. That same year, Hans Joachin Klein, a former colleague-in-arms of Carlos the Jackal, was tried before a court, 25 years after his role in the infamous Carlos-led attack on the Organization of Petroleum-Exporting Countries (OPEC) oil ministers' meeting in 1974 and after a lifetime on the run from the authorities. And in the same year, the founding member of the Japanese Red Army terror group, Fusako Shigenobu was arrested in western Japan after more than 25 years underground. While protection from the enemy may not be enough to keep the members part of the group at the initial phase(s), there may be little to protect them from relentless law-enforcement and intelligence efforts to bring them to justice.

Security services will often attempt to recruit ex-terrorists in an effort to persuade them to provide evidence against a terrorist movement. This may even become a factor in facilitating a way out of the group for an individual in the first place. Sean O'Callaghan (1998) has long occupied a valuable educational role in raising awareness about the Provisional IRA and their activities, so much so that he is still very much a wanted figure by his former comrades. Eamon Collins, another PIRA informer, gave evidence (as did O'Callaghan) at the trial of an alleged PIRA leader, and was subsequently murdered. Government credibility is crucial if disengagement is to be promoted as a possible counterterrorism strategy (indeed this has been a major issue in some early fledgling efforts to promote disengagement in different countries), but the tactics used by many governments have been less than tasteful in attempting to procure 'supergrasses' in Northern Ireland or the more imaginative 'pentiti' programme in Italy where former terrorists (and members of the Mafia) received reduced sentences or other concessions for their assistance in police investigations.

The Irish and British Governments attempted to facilitate organizational disengagement by Irish Republicans by reiterating their view that they did not view the PIRA's engagement in arms decommissioning as an act of 'surrender'. This in effect was part of a 'face-saving' strategy via which the PIRA leadership could attempt to gradually de-escalate its campaign (on all levels bar political). However, the reintegration of terrorists into society poses significant challenges in ways perhaps not considered at the time of the formulation of these policies. In Northern Ireland, despite the monumental progress made in the region, forgiveness does not come cheap, and while high-level terrorist violence may currently remain a thing of the past, the civil violence and naked sectarianism slowly destroying community-based peace efforts have not been encouraging signs of expected progress. The failure to conduct risk assessments, and implement appropriate strategies where appropriate, on prisoners released as a result of the Good Friday Agreement may, we suspect, have contributed significantly to this.

Even when the entire terrorist movement begins to dissipate, the route individual members may take can vary enormously. Some might drift towards other illegal activity (such as organized crime), an option made easier if the individual was involved in similar activity whilst a member of the terrorist network (e.g. in the context of fundraising). In such circumstances, the individual may still attempt to employ the nom de guerre of the movement in the face of threats from rival groupings. Others might drift into social isolation and the psychological problems this can create (depression, substance abuse, etc.), while others might find employment and a healthy life with new relationships. Gaining employment in itself may not imply a loss of commitment and engagement, especially when such employment involves community activism or youth work.

Often the perceived availability of viable avenues might reflect such issues as: (a) the extent of the person's involvement in the group (e.g. very part-time, part-time, or full-time), (b) the extent to which psychological support and identity comes solely from the terrorist group itself, and (c) whether or not the terrorist feels that his or her (perhaps lifetime) commitment to the group has actually been worth it. Following the decommissioning announcement, many Irish Republicans have continued their soul-searching, and some security analysts believe that it is possibly only because the other dissident groups in Ireland are perceived as either in complete disarray (i.e. the Real IRA) or too 'ideologically motivated' (i.e. the Continuity IRA) that there was not a mass shifting of allegiance.

Understanding Disengagement

As acknowledged at the beginning, it is too ambitious to provide a detailed discussion of disengagement from terrorism from the kinds of individual and group psychological perspectives offered here. In the absence of data, the assertions in this paper can only be considered preliminary; we are still only at the beginning stages of uncovering the 'story' of disengagement. Still, we do now have some potential starting points. If anything concrete has emerged from the preceding examples it is surely that our notion of 'leaving terrorism' needs to be considered in a more sophisticated way, with the same levels of complexity as the complex combination of factors that push and pull individuals into terrorism in the first place. This does not devalue any present or future process-based model of terrorism, but we do need to recognize the disengagement phase as the least informed.

In the preceding discussion, we might well have considered disengagement from a variety of levels of analysis. In many cases, the 'ending' of terrorism is a process that for a terrorist organization begins and progresses over a significant period of time and that often starts with the realization that terrorist violence on its own rarely, if ever, manages to achieve its aims. In the case of the Provisional IRA, the joint development of what senior Republican Danny Morrison once famously described as the "ballot box and armalite strategy" – the pursuit of the movement's political aspirations along with an increasingly discriminating and tactical use of its 'armed struggle' – probably signalled the beginning of the process that recently culminated in decommissioning.

It might be too obvious at this point to suggest that more research is needed, but given the lack of basic data (from which we might in the future move from the merely speculative more easily), at least the call for more research in this particular area should be forgiven; most of the examples in this paper derive from European accounts, perhaps unsurprisingly given that it has been home to the most commonly studied terrorist movements. There is practically no data on these issues regarding movements like al-Qaeda. Apart from direct interviewing of former terrorists, a strategy which I have long advocated and described, the most readily available data from which we might construct a model of disengagement comes from dated autobiographical sources, and while more basic research using such sources ought to be encouraged, caution must be exercised in assessing the value of the data from such sources. Rather than attempting to seek some 'truth' in such sources, a more promising avenue would be to explore the nature of the accounts presented in such texts, perhaps in an effort to identify common themes and processes. This would be one clear way of moving towards a different kind of terrorist 'profiling' that would offer important benefits over vague attempts at constructing personality-based profiles for unclear purposes.

Reliance on autobiographical sources tends to bring with it a variety of problems, perhaps the most obvious being that there is little autobiographic material available. First-hand research, primarily via interview, is necessarily limited for some by a number of different practical issues. Such research is clearly possible, and the experiences of a small number of researchers have demonstrated that terrorist organizations generally tend to co-operate and are facilitative of researchers' approaches.

A further implication of the discussion presented here relates to the supportive services that might be made available to terrorists and activists who have for whatever reason sought psychological 'disengagement', and the more general issue of the development of strategies to encourage or support disengagement. At a personal level, locating intervention strategies within the context of 'therapy' is clearly inappropriate, even after conviction. On the other hand, there is little empirical evidence available on which to base initiatives. A promising area to develop, however, both in terms of prison-based and self-help strategies, might lie in recent work developing from recent development in Cognitive Behaviour Therapy (CBT), termed Acceptance and Commitment Therapy.[7] Hayes, Reville, Akihiko and Rye (2002) offer one promising way of conceptualizing this.

In conclusion then, it is important to state that attempts to answer questions about why people leave terrorism should not obscure the complexity of the question and the possible assumptions that underpin it. It is for this reason that the question 'Why do people leave terrorism?' is as conceptually and pragmatically difficult to answer as 'Why do people become terrorists?' Leaving terrorism may be the result of circumstances outside of one's control, it may be the culmination of chance events, and just like joining a terrorist group it may even resemble the culmination of a consideration of factors set against an array of personal, social or occupational issues that in hindsight are no longer accessible in any reliable way. How these factors, available and expressed at and from different levels, relate to one another remains poorly understood. If, as has been frequently argued, terrorism is a product of its own time and place, this thinking can also be extended to terrorist decision making and to the processes influencing how terrorists see themselves. Disengagement from terrorism from an individual perspective ought to be viewed with the same complexity as issues relating to the phase of initially becoming involved in the first place. If at some future point there are calls for a taxonomy of factors contributing to disengagement (some have been suggested here), researchers will first and foremost have to acknowledge the dynamic processes influencing individual behaviour regarding any stage, role or function of the terrorist group for the individual involved.

References

Alexander, Y., & Myers, K. A. (Eds) (1982). *Terrorism in Europe*. London: Croom Helm.

Bjorgo, T. (Ed.) (2005). *Root causes of terrorism*. London: Routledge.

Brockner, J., & Rubin, J. Z. (1985). *Entrapment in escalating conflicts*. New York: Springer-Verlag.

[7] Acceptance and Commitment Therapy (ACT) is an empirically based psychological intervention that uses acceptance and mindfulness strategies, together with commitment and behaviour change strategies, to increase psychological flexibility. It is derived from recent radical behaviourist work in the area of relational frame theory and belongs firmly within the context of Cognitive Behaviour Therapy. The core conception of ACT is that psychological suffering is usually caused by the interface between human language and cognition, and the control of human behaviour by direct experience.

Hayes, S. C., Reville, N., Akihiko, M., & Rye, A. K. (2002). Prejudice, terrorism and behavior therapy. *Cognitive and Behavioral Practice, 9*, 296–301.

Horgan, J. (2005a). *The psychology of terrorism*. London: Routledge.

Horgan, J. (2005b). The social and psychological characteristics of terrorism and terrorists. In T. Bjorgo (Ed.), *Root causes of terrorism*. London: Routledge.

Horgan, J. (2009). *Walking away from terrorism: Accounts of disengagement from radical and extremist movements*. London: Routledge.

Jamieson, A. (1989). *The heart attacked: Terrorism and conflict in the Italian State*. London: Marian Boyars.

McCauley, C. R., & Segal, M. E. (1989). Terrorist individuals and terrorist groups: The normal psychology of extreme behaviour. In J. Groebel, & J. H. Markstein (Eds), *Terrorism: Psychological perspectives* (pp. 41–64). Seville: University of Seville Publications.

O'Callaghan, S. (1998). *The informer*. London: Granta.

Post, J. M. (1987). Group and organisational dynamics of political terrorism. In P. Wilkinson, & A. M. Stewart (Eds), *Contemporary research on terrorism* (p. 310). Aberdeen: Aberdeen University Press.

Spire, A. (1988). Le Terrorisme Intellectuel. *Patio, 11*, 150–158.

Taylor, M. (1988). *The terrorist*. London: Brassey's.

Taylor, M. (1992). Rational choice, behaviour analysis and political violence. In R. V. Clarke, & M. Felson (Eds), *Routine activity and rational choice – Advances in criminological theory*. Rutgers, NJ: Transaction Press.

Taylor, M., & J. Horgan J. (2006). A conceptual framework for addressing psychological process in the development of the terrorist. *Terrorism and Political Violence. 18*:4, 585–601.

Taylor, M., & Quayle, E. (1994). *Terrorist lives. (pp.34–35)*. London: Brassey's.

Taylor, P. (2006). The Jihadi who turned 'Supergrass'. *BBC News*. Retrieved June 22, 2009 from: http://newsvote.bbc.co.uk/mpapps/pagetools/print/news.bbc.co.uk/1/hi/programmes/5334594.stm

Thachuk, K. L. (2006). Countering terrorism across the Atlantic. *Defense Horizons*, July, *53*, 1–8.

16

De-radicalization and the Staircase from Terrorism

Fathali M. Moghaddam[1]

Synopsis: Drawing on the metaphor of a narrowing staircase leading step-by-step to the final terrorist act on the top floor of a building, proposals are made for de-radicalization programmes targeted at individuals who have reached different floors of the staircase to terrorism. Thought and action on each floor of the staircase is characterized by particular psychological processes so that different strategies are needed to move people down to lower floors and out of the building. The overall conclusion is a proposal for the main long-term goal of de-radicalization, the transformation of the *psychological citizen*; the psychological characteristics that citizens need to have in order to effectively participate in and sustain a particular political system.

De-radicalization and the Staircase from Terrorism

Terrorism, "politically motivated violence, perpetrated by individuals, groups, or state-sponsored agents, intended to instill fear and helplessness in a population in order to influence decision making and to change behavior" (Moghaddam, 2005a, p. 161) continues to be a major national and international challenge. Although 'home grown' Western terrorists have been active in Northern Ireland (Coogan, 2002), Spain (Balfour, 2005), the United States (Linenthal, 2001) and other democratic societies, the greater challenge since

[1] Address for correspondence: Fathali M. Moghaddam, Department of Psychology, White Gravenor Building (3rd floor), Georgetown University, Washington, DC, USA. 20057.
Email: moghaddf@georgetown.edu

The Faces of Terrorism: Multidisciplinary Perspectives Edited by David Canter
© 2009 John Wiley & Sons Ltd.

the 1980s has been a sharp rise in terrorist activity emanating from Islamic communities in the Middle East and elsewhere, particularly in the form of suicide terrorism incited by violent Salafists and other extremist groups (Bloom, 2005; Khosrokhavar, 2005; McDermott, 2005; Oliver & Steinberg, 2005; Pape, 2005; Pedahzur, 2005).

Psychologists have made important contributions to a better understanding of both the roots of terrorism and the consequences of terrorist acts for victims (Bongar, Brown, Beutler, Breckenridge, & Zimbardo, 2006; Danieli, Brom, & Waizer, 2005; Horgan, 2005; Moghaddam & Marsella, 2004; Sageman, 2004; Stout, 2002). However, more attention needs to be given to the increased radicalization of Islamic communities and the terrorism emanating from these communities in both non-Western and Western societies. This is not because other types of terrorism have ended (e.g. since 2005 terrorism is once again on the rise in Spain), but because the most serious global threat at present and in the foreseeable future is from Islamic terrorism (including in Europe, see Perlez, 2007; von Hippel, 2007).

A salient feature of many Islamic communities around the world, including in some Western societies now home to millions of Muslim immigrants (e.g. South Asians in the UK, North Africans in France, Turks in Germany), is that they express strong support for extreme positions and groups (Pew Research Center, 2006). For example, the percentages of Muslims who *deny* that Arabs carried out the 9/11 attacks are: British Muslims 56%, French Muslims 46%, German Muslims 44%, in Indonesia 65%, in Egypt 59%, in Turkey 59%, and in Jordan 53%. Moreover, tens of millions of Muslims in both Western and non-Western societies report that violence against civilian targets is sometimes justified in order to defend Islam (British Muslims 15%, French Muslims 16%, German Muslims 7%, in Indonesia 10%, in Egypt 28%, in Turkey 17%, and in Jordan 29%). Of course radicalization does not always have negative consequences; but it can be problematic when it leads to moral or practical support for violent actions, and terrorism in particular.

In order to better understand the process of radicalization associated with terrorism, I introduced the metaphor of a narrowing staircase leading step-by-step to the final terrorist act on the top floor of a building (Moghaddam, 2005a). Imagine a staircase in a building, where everyone lives on the ground floor, but a few people eventually move up the staircase to higher floors. Thought and action on each floor of the staircase is characterized by particular psychological processes. For example, on the ground floor, where well over a billion Muslims live, thought and action is characterized by identity ('What kind of a person am I?' 'What kind of group do I belong to?'), by perceptions of fairness ('Am I being treated fairly?') and by psychological interpretation of material conditions (particularly related to the question of whether one's material needs are being met adequately). Some individuals become so dissatisfied with their life conditions that they move up to the first floor in changing their situation.

On the first floor, individuals are particularly concerned with opportunities for social mobility and for being included in the procedures that lead to decision making. Those who find their individual mobility paths blocked, their voice silenced, and a lack of opportunity to participate in decision making, move up to the second floor, where they are directed toward external targets for displacement of aggression. In the current political and cultural context of Islamic communities, the United States and Israel are the most common external targets.

A number of factors have enhanced the importance of the mosque as a political centre in Islamic communities, and increased the influence of fundamentalists in mosques in both Western and non-Western societies. Within a number of major Islamic countries, such as Saudi Arabia, Egypt and Pakistan, despotism, corruption, and the severe repression of secular opposition groups has meant that political activism is driven into mosques, where religious fundamentalists have more opportunities to exert influence. Within Western societies, the continued isolation of Muslims has meant that it is mosques rather than the offices of mainstream political parties of their adopted countries that serve as their political meeting centres. In turn, the isolation of Muslims and feelings of collective alienation have prepared the ground for fundamentalists to gain influence in some mosques.

Those individuals who continue to the third floor of the staircase to terrorism now become more disengaged from mainstream morality, that condemns terrorism, and engage with a morality that justifies terrorism. On this floor, individuals come to endorse the view that 'We must fight the evil enemy in any way we can'. Some of these individuals move up the steps to the fourth floor where the legitimacy of terrorist organizations is accepted more strongly, and an 'us versus them' categorical thinking becomes the norm. This mirrors the 'you are either with us or against us' rhetoric adopted by some Western leaders. Finally, from among the individuals who reach the fourth floor and are psychologically prepared to become terrorists, some individuals are recruited and commit terrorist acts on the fifth floor.

The power of this incremental radicalization process is demonstrated by psychological research on conformity and obedience (Moghaddam, 2005b, ch. 15 & 16; Zimbardo, 2007). An example is the step-by-step procedure used in Milgram's (1974) studies on obedience to authority, where naïve participants in the role of 'teacher' were induced to increase the punishment (apparently) inflicted on a 'learner' (actually a confederate of the experimenter) in 15 volt increments. Just as Milgram (1974) found that individual characteristics (in his studies, 'authoritarianism') were related to which particular individuals moved to the next level of obedience, individual differences are probably also related to movement up and down the staircase to terrorism. The identification of these individual differences is one aspect of the staircase that requires closer attention in future research, as is movement down the staircase.

There is an urgent need to give particular attention to psychological processes underlying de-radicalization in the post 9/11 era. First, because the main focus of discussions on de-radicalization prior to 9/11 was left-wing radical groups (e.g. see the classic discussion of Tucker, 1967, on the de-radicalization of Marxist movements, and the more recent discussion of Sprinzak, 1998, on the Weathermen, an extremist, violent left-wing American group). Second, although some criticisms of the distinction between 'old' versus 'new' terrorism are valid and 21st century terrorism does have features in common with 'old' terrorism, it is clearly the case that the 'new' terrorism has some completely new characteristics, such as its reliance on web technology (Takeyh & Gvosdev, 2002). Phenomena such as al-Qaeda now exert their influence as global 'cultural carriers' (Moghaddam, 2002) that convey ideology, morality and values, in large part through electronic communications (witness the video of Osama bin Laden distributed via the Internet in September 2007).

The goal of the present discussion is to use the metaphor of a staircase from terrorism to explore the psychology of de-radicalization. This paper provides a general framework to guide and stimulate further exploration. In the next two parts of the paper, I first discuss radicalization and de-radicalization processes, then consider de-radicalization programmes targeted at individuals who have reached different floors of the staircase to terrorism. In the final section, my focus is on what I propose should be the main long-term goal of de-radicalization, the transformation of the *psychological citizen*, the psychological characteristics that citizens need to have in order to effectively participate in and sustain a particular political system.

Radicalization and De-radicalization

Almost eight decades of psychological research on attitudes, from the pioneering research of LaPiere (1934) to 21st century studies (Haddock, 2004), suggest that radicalization of attitudes need not result in radicalization of behaviour. It is useful to distinguish between cognitive, affective and behavioural components of radicalization. At the cognitive level, radicalization in Islamic communities involves two features: first, knowledge about alternative moral systems that support terrorism; second, the incorporation of an alternative morality as integral to one's identity (i.e. coming to perceive oneself as a person who legitimately condones terrorism). At the affective level, radicalization involves undergoing social learning that prepares an individual to take terrorist action. Such learning processes focus on sidestepping the inhibitory mechanisms described by Lorenz (1966) that prevent humans from injuring or killing others, and also have to be sidestepped in military training (Grossman, 1995). Given that such radicalization has taken place and some individuals have reached the final floor of the staircase to terrorism, how should we approach the challenge of de-radicalization?

De-radicalization

We already have some clear signposts as to how de-radicalization can best take place. First, the literature on de-radicalization (e.g. Alexander, 2002; Art & Richardson, 2007; Bernard, 2005; Crenshaw, 1991, 1995; Cronin, 2006; Ross & Gurr, 1989; United States Institute of Peace, 1999) suggests that for any given individual or group, the path to de-radicalization is not necessarily the reverse of the path to radicalization. For example, an individual who has been influenced by a separatist goal and a charismatic leader to become radicalized may become de-radicalized by a different set of factors, such as a changed political climate and a sharp drop in popular support for his group among the local population (as has been the case in Ireland particularly since the mid-1990s).

A second point is that the de-radicalization programme that would be most successful depends in part on the particular floor of the staircase to terrorism reached by the individual, and the psychological processes that characterize that particular floor. For example, a de-radicalization programme that targets individuals on the first floor should be tailored to the psychological processes of procedural justice and individual mobility. A programme targeting individuals on the final floor should focus on de-radicalization after capture in cases where the individual is to be reintroduced into society at a later time. In this regard, particularly useful lessons can be learned from the experiences of Italian authorities with the reintegration of Red Brigades members (Catanzaro, 1991) into Italian society. The relationship between de-radicalization and the different floors is elaborated in the main section of this paper.

Third, de-radicalization programmes should also be tailored as far as possible to match the particular role an individual fulfils in a terrorist network. Too little attention has been given to the specialization that takes place as individuals move up the staircase to terrorism. Through an in-depth study of different terrorist movements, I identified nine main specialized roles (Moghaddam, 2006a): source of inspiration (serves as a symbolic figurehead to terrorist movements), strategist (makes planning and management more effective); networker (acts as the glue that holds different terrorist cells and individuals together, to create a terrorist movement); expert (applies expert knowledge, in areas such as electronic communications and explosives, to help carry out specific terrorist operations); cell manager (works to ensure the security, 'effective functioning', and continuation of the terrorist cell); local agitator and guide (networks between potential terrorists recruits and recruiters); cell member (serves in a small group to carry out and support terrorist attacks); fodder (functions as a tool for terrorist attack); fund-raiser (gathers resources to support terrorist operations). These roles were distinguished on the basis of different criteria, such as asset (that an individual brings to the network), function, service length, level and type of expertise, and motivation (in a more micro-level differentiation, Nesser (2005) identified four different cell member types: 'the entrepreneur', 'the impressionist whizz kid', 'the misfit', and 'the drifter'). These nine specialized roles suggest that practitioners should develop a different type of intervention for each type of specialized role, in relation to each level of the staircase. However, because of space limitations, in this discussion I give primacy to the characteristics of the levels on the staircase, and only give secondary attention to the specialized roles in terrorist networks. Again, this is a gap that future research can rectify.

Programmes for de-radicalization should take into account that individuals in the different specialized roles are not randomly or evenly distributed on the different floors of the staircase to terrorism. For example, individuals in the role of 'fodder' are located on the final floor where the terrorist act takes place, but fund-raisers can remain on the third or fourth floor, where they have adopted a morality supportive of terrorism but are not directly involved in, or even knowledgeable about or witnesses to, specific terrorist attacks.

The Staircase from Terrorism

The staircase metaphor helps to identify more specific goals for de-radicalization programmes directed at individuals on each floor of the staircase from terrorism, starting from the final floor where individuals have received full preparation to function as terrorists.

Fifth floor

Individuals who have reached this 'top' floor have been trained to carry out terrorist attacks (mainly in the role of 'cell member' or 'fodder'). Typically the terrorist attacker is situated within a tightly knit, secretive group, and is induced to incrementally move toward the final attack. As the time of attack approaches, the potential terrorist is persuaded to write out his (the individual is typically male) will and testament, and also to make a video recording for distribution after his death. Cognitive dissonance theory and self-perception theory (see Moghaddam, 1998, pp. 114–123) both suggest that such acts will make it far more difficult for the potential suicide bomber to change his mind: because he is motivated to match his behaviour to his expressed beliefs and vows (cognitive dissonance theory) and because having behaved like a terrorist he now sees himself to be a terrorist (self-perception theory).

The number of individuals who reach the fifth floor, and consequently the size of the de-radicalization programmes needed, will be influenced by macro socio-economic-political cycles (Enders & Sandler, 2000). These cycles tend to vary in length and many terrorist groups have short lives of less than a year, but there is evidence from historical trends that religious terrorism is the longest lasting (Rapoport, 1984).

One of the macro factors that can influence the number of individuals who reach the final floor of the staircase to terrorism is the size and age of the population. In societies with large youth populations, as is the case in the Near and Middle East where approximately 60% of the population is below 21 years old, terrorist recruiters have a larger pool of young men to draw from. Young men are characterized by higher risk taking and aggression in most societies.

How might de-radicalization take place among those who have reached the final floor? First, a terrorist could be captured and de-radicalized through special educational programmes. For example, since the late 1990s the government of Yemen has conducted a state-sponsored de-radicalization programme that targets captured Islamic radicals (Taarnby, 2005). The programme involves senior clerics who debate captured radicals on central issues in Islam (such as the meaning of jihad), under conditions of mutual respect and within accepted dialogue rules. This programme has had reasonable success, although it is possible that some radicals have reported changes in their beliefs, without experiencing a genuine change, simply to win freedom.

Second, government attacks that weaken the terrorist network could eventually lead to de-radicalization. Such attacks might lead to the capture or killing of a charismatic terrorist leader. Unfortunately, this scenario is less applicable to the 'new' Islamic terrorism, because it is decentralized, more reliant on the World Wide Web and less reliant on any single leader.

Third, the number of terrorists reaching the final floor might decrease because of transformation of the terrorist network. For example, this could be because a particular goal has been achieved, or because the terrorist movement has become incorporated into mainstream political process, or because the terrorists have transformed into an organization with purely monetary criminal goals.

Fourth floor

Individuals who reach the fourth floor have already adopted attitudes supportive of a morality condoning terrorism. Now they become ensnared (by networkers or local agitators and guides) in terrorist networks, to serve, for example, as cell members or managers, or experts. Those who are recruited typically find themselves the focus of intense indoctrination, as they take on the cultural norms of their small (4–7 member) secretive cells. Two psychological processes are central to their experiences as cell members: solidification of categorical 'us vs. them' thinking, and legitimization of the terrorist cause.

One of the most important reasons for the decline of terrorist movements in the past has been a failure to continue recruitment and to pass on the 'terrorist cause' to a next generation. Given that the fourth floor is where recruitment takes place, de-radicalization programmes should give particular priority to individuals who have reached this floor. Such programmes should focus on two goals, related to the psychological processes dominant on this floor.

A first goal is to defeat the push to justify a categorical 'us vs. them', 'good vs. evil' view of the world. This can best be achieved by avoiding categorical language in messages sent to both non-Western and Western communities. Also, stronger bridges should be constructed across major groups in society by highlighting cross-cutting categories (Urban & Miller, 1998) that help people recognize continuities and overlaps in their group memberships, as well as superordinate goals that all groups want to achieve but no group can achieve without co-operation from others (such as environmental challenges facing all humankind, Taylor & Moghaddam, 1994, ch. 3).

Second, programmes should attack the legitimacy of the terrorist cause. Too little has been done to unravel the premise, underlying terrorist movements, that it is legitimate to attack and kill civilians. Despite the radicalization that has taken place in Islamic societies, the majority of Muslims believe it is never justified to attack civilians (Pew Research Center, 2006). This is akin to the findings of studies of obedience and conformity, from Sherif in the 1930s to contemporary research (Moghaddam, 2005b, chs. 15 & 16), where some participants refuse to obey to harm others and refuse to conform to incorrect norms. These 'disobedient' and 'non-conformist' individuals provide a springboard from which to launch a more open society, and the same function can be served by the Muslims who believe it is never justified to attack civilians.

Third floor

Engagement with a morality supportive of terrorism moves ahead on the third floor, at the same time that disengagement from a moderate morality becomes realized. In many cases individuals are lured into a terrorist supportive morality through social affiliations (Sageman, 2004). De-radicalization programmes aimed at individuals who have reached this floor need to focus on strategies to engage young people in activities and goals associated with mainstream society. This is a considerable challenge, given the enormous size of the young population in most Islamic societies.

Despite the lack of educational and employment opportunities in Islamic societies such as Egypt, Pakistan, and Jordan, a great deal can be done to influence both the practice and perception of social mobility. Experimental research suggests that the perception that individual mobility is possible, even when the probability of success is low, is a powerful factor in increasing trust in the fairness of a system (following Lalonde & Silverman, 1994). Western countries can in practice improve individual mobility options in a highly cost-effective manner by increasing scholarships and fellowships in education, and helping to expand the education and training sector generally.

Psychologists need to give more attention to formulate and help implement appropriate training opportunities for developing world psychologists (Moghaddam & Taylor, 1986; Zebian, Alamuddin, Maalouf, & Chatila, 2007). Many of the educational opportunities currently available for developing world students are designed to educate specialists for research and practice in Western societies and are not appropriate for non-Western and particularly Islamic societies (see Moghaddam, 1997, ch. 5). The outcome is inappropriately trained non-Western specialists who fail to contribute constructively to national development in their countries of origin.

Second floor

Individuals who arrive on the second floor are experiencing increasing frustration. They have already tried and found blocked various avenues to social mobility, and to gaining a voice in procedures leading to decisions that impact their everyday lives. Most importantly, they are frustrated by their strong sense of inadequate identity (Moghaddam, 2006a). Who is to blame for these inadequacies? A long line of research suggests that how this question is answered is vitally important, because the assumed 'causes' can become targets of displaced aggression (Miller, Pederson, Earlywine, & Pollock, 2003).

In the context of Islamic societies particularly, the United States is being targeted as the most serious source of problems. This is reflected in international surveys showing a sharp decline in favourable opinions of the United States (Pew Research Center, 2006). Between 2000 and 2006, the percentage of respondents who expressed favourable opinions of the United States went down from 75 to 30 in Indonesia, 52 to 12 in Turkey, and 25 (in 2002) to 15 in Jordan. There was a slight upward shift in favourable opinions in Pakistan, but this still only resulted in a 27% favourable rating in 2006 (the decline in favourable opinions of the United States extended to the EU. For example, in the UK the percentage favourable went down from 83 in 2000 to 56 in 2006).

This same anti-US trend is reflected in the percentage of respondents who perceive the United States in Iraq as the greatest danger to world peace, an even greater danger than Iran: Indonesia, US a danger 31, Iran a danger 7; Egypt, US a danger 56, Iran a danger 14; Jordan, US a danger 58, Iran a danger 19; Turkey, US a danger 60, Iran a danger 16; Pakistan, US a danger 28, Iran a danger 4 (the picture is more mixed in the EU, with some countries seeing Iran as a greater danger to world peace than the US).

More broadly, the US is being identified as the sole source of local and international problems, particularly in the Near and Middle East. Corruption and despotism, economic and health inadequacies, and just about every other problem is described as having only one major root cause: the US and its allies. This attributional style serves to support local despots and corruption, by displacing negative sentiments onto the US. Of course the US must take responsibility for the consequences of its policies in the region, but de-radicalization programmes should aim to shift attitudes so that local regimes also take greater responsibility for inefficiencies and corruption in local governments.

First floor

The search for upward mobility options and opportunities to have a voice in matters that impact on their own lives leads individuals to the first floor of the staircase to terrorism. These are the first concrete steps associated with radicalization of attitudes, but individuals on this floor are still far away from supporting terrorism either in expressed attitudes or overt behaviour. They are only searching for avenues for improvement and voice, trying different doors and spaces on the first floor. Individuals on this floor do not perceive themselves as radicals.

De-radicalization programmes targeting individuals on the first floor need to be broad cultural, educational, and political programmes. In the cultural arena, programmes should expand in local cultural organizations and activities that can absorb particularly young people. These should include traditional artistic and cultural arenas, such as those reflecting indigenous arts and crafts, architecture, tapestry and carpets, and poetry. In education, far greater efforts are needed to strengthen indigenous educational resources and institutions, which could provide appropriate training for local youth and decrease dependence on imported expertise. In the political arena, indigenous traditions, such as those already available in Islamic societies (e.g. see the discussion on democratic traditions in Shia Islam in Moghaddam, 2006a, ch. 10) can be used to expand participation and voice to individuals on the first floor.

The Ground Floor and the Psychological Citizen

De-radicalization will be most effective when it is directed toward a particular goal. My proposal is that on the ground floor where the vast majority of people are situated, the goal of such programmes should be to transform the psychological citizen, through programmes that seek both 'top-down' and 'bottom-up' solutions to change (Moghaddam, 2002). It is not enough to focus on top-down, macro-level economic and political solutions as a way of bringing about social change, because the everyday styles of thinking and doing, and the normative systems that regulate social relations at the micro level can act to thwart top-down policies. This in part explains the so-called 'paradox of revolution', where even revolutionary changes at the top do not necessarily bring about desired changes at the micro level of everyday life (Moghaddam, 2002, particularly ch. 2).

The inadequacy of just relying on 'top-down' policies has led to greater attention to social and psychological processes in social change, justice, and democracy (Finkel & Moghaddam, 2004; Sniderman, Fletcher, Russell, & Tetlock, 1996; Sullivan & Transue, 1999; Tetlock, 1998). There is also a wider discussion of the relationship between Islam and democracy (e.g. Hunter & Malik, 2005; Ro'i, 2004; Sadiki, 2004). But there is need for more focused and careful examination of the psychological citizen on the ground floor in Islamic societies, and the key psychological changes required of individuals in interaction in order for a political system to become more open and fair.

In order to function and continue, each type of political system requires psychological citizens with particular styles of thought and action. For example, the nature of obedience, conformity, and relationship with leadership required of psychological citizens in order to sustain a dictatorship is very different from that required of citizens in order to sustain a democracy. Dictatorships require more unquestioning obedience, higher conformity, and subservience to centralized, often life-long leadership. In order to sustain democracy, on the other hand, psychological citizens must critically examine leadership choices, participate in decision-making procedures, and be prepared to be non-conformists and to act as whistle-blowers in the interest of an open society. Also, psychological citizens in democracies must come to support a norm of circulation of leadership, as opposed to life-long leadership, and minimal government secrecy, as opposed to government monopoly of information.

Psychological research suggests that involvement with the procedures of decision making can serve a foundational role in transforming the psychological citizen (Tyler & Huo, 2002), particularly in increasing trust that serves as an essential building block of democracy (Warren, 1999). In the context of the Near and Middle East, individual citizens need a minimal 'scaffolding' (following Vygotsky, see Moghaddam, 2005b, ch. 10) to support a basic level of involvement in decision-making procedures. Psychologists have already developed expertise in building this kind of scaffolding, for example, as evident in community psychology in Latin America where democratic processes have gained strength (Sanchez, 1996).

Universals and the Psychological Citizen: The Example of Identity Needs

Despite differences in the characteristics of the psychological citizen required to sustain dictatorships, democracies, and other political systems, psychological research also suggests certain universals. An example that is particularly important for this discussion is the identity needs of the psychological citizen across cultures. Psychological research suggests that the need for a positive and distinct identity is present across cultures and in important ways influences individuals, particularly in intergroup contexts (Moghaddam, 2006b).

The universality of identity needs arises out of the function served by identity in human social evolution (Moghaddam, 2008). By training the young to seek social approval and to try to achieve positiveness and distinctiveness (according to local norms and rules), human societies achieve an effective means of ensuring a minimal level of conformity and obedience, and thus more efficient group performance and utilization of resources. As adults, individuals will seek to meet (socially constructed and socially instilled) identity needs, and in this way become better integrated in the larger society.

Although certain identity needs are universal, there are cultural differences in the criteria used to evaluate the adequacy of identity. For example, in the tightly knit, highly radicalized small cells that operate on the fourth and fifth levels of the terrorism staircase, it is actions in support of terrorism that are evaluated most favourably. The normative system of these cells, and the influence of the (typically charismatic) cell leader, lead recruits to 'become ready' to commit suicide terrorism as a way of satisfying identity needs. In addition to focusing on the capture, destruction or transformation of such cells, long-term programmes are needed to influence the criteria used to assess identity on the ground floor where the vast majority of people exist.

Concluding Comment

The staircase metaphor suggests the need for a multi-method approach to de-radicalization, with different short-term and long-term programmes needed to target people in different specialized roles on each of the different floors. In the longer term, priority should be given to the hundreds of millions of people on the ground floor. Although international surveys suggest that radicalization has taken place among Muslims on the ground floor in the first decade of the 21st century, there is good reason to believe that de-radicalization can also take place rapidly. De-radicalization programmes will be more effective through a combination of top-down and bottom-up policies, and psychological science can help design better policies of both types.

Finally, future research should focus on a number of gaps that are implicit in this discussion. First, different types of intervention need to be developed, aimed at people in the nine specialized roles in terrorist organizations. Second, research is needed on the individual difference characteristics related to movement up and down the staircase to terrorism, to address questions such as: 'what are the individual characteristics of persons who are more likely to move up from the ground floor to the first floor, from the first floor to the second floor – and move down from the fourth floor to the third floor, from the third floor to the second floor' and so on. Third, research is needed to further clarify different processes associated with radicalization and de-radicalization of individuals as opposed to the radicalization and de-radicalization of groups.

References

Alexander, Y. (2002). *Combating terrorism: Strategies of ten countries*. Ann Arbor, MI: University of Michigan Press.

Art, R. J., & Richardson, L. (2007). *Democracy and counterterrorism*. Washington, DC: United States Institute of Peace.

Balfour, S. (Ed.) (2005). *The politics of contemporary Spain*. London: Routledge.

Bernard, C. (Ed.) (2005). *A future for the young: Options for helping Middle Eastern youth escape the trap of radicalization*. Santa Monica, CA: RAND Corporation.

Bloom, M. (2005). *Dying to kill: The allure of suicide terror*. New York: Columbia University Press.

Bongar, B., Brown, L. M., Beutler, L. E., Breckenridge, J. N., & Zimbardo, P. (Eds) (2006). *Psychology of terrorism*. New York: Oxford University Press.

Catanzaro, R. (Ed.) (1991). *The Red Brigades and left-wing terrorism in Italy*. London: Pinter.

Coogan, T. P. (2002). *The IRA*. New York: Palgrave.

Crenshaw, M. (1991). How terrorism declines. *Terrorism and Political Violence, 3*, 69–87.

Crenshaw, M. (Ed.) (1995). *Terrorism in context*. University Park: Pennsylvania University Press.

Cronin, A. K. (2006). How al-Qaida ends: The decline and demise of terrorist groups. *International Security, 31*, 7–48.

Danieli, Y., Brom, D., & Waizer, J. (Eds) (2005). *The trauma of terror: Sharing knowledge and sharing care*. New York: Haworth Press.

Enders, W., & Sandler, T. (2000). Is transnational terrorism becoming more threatening? A time-series investigation. *Journal of Conflict Resolution, 44*, 307–332.

Finkel, N., & Moghaddam, F. M. (Eds) (2004). *The psychology of rights and duties: Empirical contributions and normative commentaries*. Washington, DC: American Psychological Association Press.

Grossman, D. (1995). *On killing: The psychological cost of learning to kill in war and society*. New York: Little Brown.

Haddock, G. (Ed.) (2004). *Contemporary perspectives on the psychology of attitudes*. Hove, England: Psychology Press.

Horgan, J. (2005). *The psychology of terrorism*. London: Routledge.

Hunter, S. T., & Malik, H. (Eds) (2005). *Modernization, democracy, and Islam*. Westport, CT: Praeger.

Khosrokhavar, F. (2005). *Suicide bombers: Allah's new martyrs* (Trans. D. Macey). London: Pluto Press.

Lalonde, R. N., & Silverman, R. A. (1994). Behavioral preferences in response to social injustice: The effects of group permeability and social identity salience. *Journal of Personality and Social Psychology, 66*, 78–85.

LaPiere, R. T. (1934). Attitude and actions. *Social Forces, 13*, 230–237.

Linenthal, E. T. (2001). *The unfinished bombing: Oklahoma City in American memory*. New York: Oxford University Press.

Lorenz, K. (1966). *On aggression* (Trans. M. Wilson). New York: Harcourt, Brace & World.

McDermott, T. (2005). *Perfect soldiers: The hijackers – who they were, why they did it*. New York: HarperCollins.

Milgram, S. (1974). *Obedience to authority: An experimental view*. New York: Harper & Row.

Miller, N., Pederson, W. C., Earlywine, M., & Pollock, V. E. (2003). A theoretical model of triggered displaced aggression. *Personality and Social Psychology Review, 7*, 75–97.

Moghaddam, F. M. (1997). *The specialized society: The plight of the individual in an age of individualism*. Westport, CT: Praeger.

Moghaddam, F. M. (1998). *Social psychology: Exploring universals in social behavior*. New York: Freeman.

Moghaddam, F. M. (2002). *The individual and society: A cultural integration*. New York: Worth.

Moghaddam, F. M. (2005a). The staircase to terrorism: A psychological exploration. *American Psychologist, 60*, 161–169.

Moghaddam, F. M. (2005b). *Great ideas in psychology: A cultural and historical introduction*. Oxford: Oneworld.

Moghaddam, F. M. (2006a). *From the terrorists' point of view: What they experience and why they come to destroy*. Westport, CT: Praeger Security International.

Moghaddam, F. M. (2006b). Interobjectivity: The collective roots of individual consciousness and social identity. In T. Postmes, & J. Jetten (Eds), *Individuality and the group: Advances in social identity* (pp. 155–174). London: Sage.

Moghaddam, F. M. (2008). *Multiculturalism and intergroup relations: Psychological implications for democracy in global context*. Washington, DC: American Psychological Association Press.

Moghaddam, F. M., & Marsella, A. J. (Eds) (2004). *Understanding terrorism: Psychosocial roots, consequences, and interventions*. Washington, DC: American Psychological Association Press.

Moghaddam, F. M., & Taylor, D. M. (1986). What constitutes an 'appropriate psychology' for the developing world? *International Journal of Psychology, 21*, 253–267.

Nesser, P. (2005). Profiles of Jihadist terrorists in Europe. In C. Bernard (Ed.), *A future for the young: Options for helping Middle Eastern youth escape the trap of radicalization* (pp. 31–49). Santa Monica, CA: RAND Corporation.

Oliver, A. M., & Steinberg, P. F. (2005). *The road to Martyr's Square: A journey into the world of the suicide bomber.* New York: Oxford University Press.

Pape, R. A. (2005). *Dying to win: The strategic logic of suicide bombing.* New York: Random House.

Pedahzur, A. (2005). *Suicide terrorism.* London: Polity Press.

Perlez, J. (2007). Seeking terror's causes, Europe looks within. *The New York Times,* September 11, p. A6.

Pew Research Center (2006). *Conflicting views in a divided world: How global public views Muslim-Western relations, global issues, U.S. role in the world, Asian rivalries.* Washington, DC: Author.

Rapoport, D. C. (1984). Fear and trembling: Terrorism in three religious traditions. *American Political Science Review, 78,* 658–677.

Ro'i, Y. (Ed.) (2004). *Democracy and pluralism in Muslim Eurasia.* London: Frank Cass.

Ross, J. I., & Gurr, T. R. (1989). Why terrorism subsides: A comparative study of Canada and the United States. *Comparative Politics, 21,* 405–426.

Sadiki, L. (2004). *The search for Arab democracy: Discourses and counter-discourses.* London: Hurst.

Sageman, M. (2004). *Understanding terror networks.* Pennsylvania: University of Pennsylvania Press.

Sanchez, E. (1996). The Latin American experience in community social psychology. In S. C. Carr, & J. F. Schumaker (Eds), *Psychology and the developing world* (pp. 119–129). Westport, CT: Praeger.

Sniderman, P. M., Fletcher, J., Russell, P., & Tetlock, P. E. (1996). *The clash of rights: Liberty, equality, and legitimacy in liberal democracy.* New Haven: Yale University Press.

Sprinzak, E. (1998). The psychopolitical formation of extreme left terrorism in a democracy: The case of the Weathermen. In W. Reich (Ed.), *Origins of terrorism: Psychologies, ideologies, theologies, and states of mind* (pp. 65–85). Washington, DC: Woodrow Wilson Center Press.

Stout, C. E. (Ed.) (2002). *The psychology of terrorism* (4 vols). Westport, CT: Praeger.

Sullivan, J. L., & Transue, J. E. (1999). The psychological underpinnings of democracy: A selective review of research on political tolerance, interpersonal trust, and social capital. *Annual Review of Psychology, 50,* 625–650.

Taarnby, M. (2005). Yemen's committee for dialogue: The relativity of a counter terrorism success. In C. Bernard (Ed.), *A future for the young: Options for helping Middle Eastern youth escape the trap of radicalization* (pp. 129–139). Santa Monica, CA: RAND Corporation.

Takeyh, R., & Gvosdev, N. (2002). Do terrorist networks need a home? *Washington Quarterly, 25,* 97–108.

Taylor, D. M., & Moghaddam, F. M. (1994). *Theories of intergroup relations: International social psychological perspectives* (2nd ed.) Westport, CT: Praeger.

Tetlock, P. E. (1998). The ever-shifting psychological foundations of democratic theory: Do citizens have the right stuff? *Critical Review, 12,* 545–561.

Tucker, R. C. (1967). The de-radicalization of Marxist movements. *The American Political Science Review, 61*, 343–358.

Tyler, T. R., & Huo, Y. J. (2002). *Trust in the law*. New York: Russell Sage Foundation.

United States Institute of Peace (1999). *How terrorism ends*. Special Report No. 48. Washington, DC: Author.

Urban, L. M., & Miller, N. (1998). A theoretical analysis of crossed categorization effects: A meta analysis. *Journal of Personality and Social Psychology, 74*, 894–908.

Von Hippel, K. (Ed.) (2007). *Europe confronts terrorism*. New York: Palgrave Macmillan.

Warren, M. E. (Ed.) (1999). *Democracy and trust*. Cambridge, UK: Cambridge University Press.

Zebian, S., Alamuddin, R., Maalouf, M., & Chatila, Y. (2007). Developing an appropriate psychology through culturally sensitive research practices in the Arab-speaking world: A content analysis of psychological research published between 1950 and 2004. *Journal of Cross-Cultural Psychology, 38*, 91–122.

Zimbardo, P. (2007). *The Lucifer effect: Understanding how good people turn evil*. New York: Random House.

Index